Croatian

PHRASEBOOK & DICTIONARY

D0089390

Acknowledgments
Publisher Mina Patria
Product Editor Elizabeth Jones
Series Designer James Hardy
Language Writers Gordana & Ivan Ivetac
Cover Image Researcher Naomi Parker

Thanks
Sasha Baskett, Elin Berglund, Larissa Frost, Chris Love, Kate Mathews, Wayne Murphy, John Taufa, Angela Tinson, Tony Wheeler, Branislava Vladisavljevic

Published by Lonely Planet Publications Pty Ltd
ABN 36 005 607 983

3rd Edition – March 2015
ISBN 978 1 74321 437 4
Text © Lonely Planet 2015
Cover Image Porec, Istria, Croatia, Alan Copson/AWL ©
Printed in China   10 9 8 7 6 5 4 3 2

Contact lonelyplanet.com/contact

All rights reserved. No part of this publication may be reproduced, stored in a retrieval system or transmitted in any form by any means, electronic, mechanical, photocopying, recording or otherwise, except brief extracts for the purpose of review, without the written permission of the publisher. Lonely Planet and the Lonely Planet logo are trade marks of Lonely Planet and are registered in the U.S. Patent and Trademark Office and in other countries. Lonely Planet does not allow its name or logo to be appropriated by commercial establishments, such as retailers, restaurants or hotels. Please let us know of any misuses: www.lonelyplanet.com/ip

Although the authors and Lonely Planet try to make the information as accurate as possible, we accept no responsibility for any loss, injury or inconvenience sustained by anyone using this book.

Paper in this book is certified against the Forest Stewardship Council™ standards. FSC™ promotes environmentally responsible, socially beneficial and economically viable management of the world's forests.

MIX
Paper from
responsible sources
FSC™ C021741

The editor would like to acknowledge the following for their contributions to this phrasebook:

Gordana and Ivan Ivetac for their polished translations and linguistic and cultural expertise. Both Gordana and Ivan are NAATI-accredited Croatian-to-English translators and interpreters with extensive experience in the field.

Zeljko Basic and Jack Gavran for help with the transliteration system and general queries.

make the most of this phrasebook ...

Anyone can speak another language! It's all about confidence. Don't worry if you can't remember your school language lessons or if you've never learnt a language before. Even if you learn the very basics (on the inside covers of this book), your travel experience will be the better for it. You have nothing to lose and everything to gain when the locals hear you making an effort.

finding things in this book

For easy navigation, this book is in sections. The Tools chapters are the ones you'll thumb through time and again. The Practical section covers basic travel situations like catching transport and finding a bed. The Social section gives you conversational phrases, pick-up lines, the ability to express opinions – so you can get to know people. Food has a section all of its own: gourmets and vegetarians are covered and local dishes feature. Safe Travel equips you with health and police phrases, just in case. Remember the colours of each section and you'll find everything easily; or use the comprehensive Index. Otherwise, check the two-way traveller's Dictionary for the word you need.

being understood

Throughout this book you'll see coloured phrases on each page. They're phonetic guides to help you pronounce the language. You don't even need to look at the language itself, but you'll get used to the way we've represented particular sounds. The pronunciation chapter in Tools will explain more, but you can feel confident that if you read the coloured phrase slowly, you'll be understood.

communication tips

Body language, ways of doing things, sense of humour – all have a role to play in every culture. 'Local talk' boxes show you common ways of saying things, or everyday language to drop into conversation. 'Listen for ...' boxes supply the phrases you may hear. They start with the phonetic guide (because you'll hear it before you know what's being said) and then lead in to the language and the English translation.

CONTENTS

5

CONTENTS

7

croatian

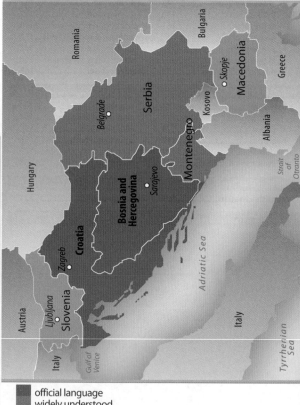

official language
widely understood
generally understood

For more details, see the **introduction.**

Croatian is the language of one of the world's newer countries. Like the country itself, Croatian has an intriguing, cosmopolitan, and at times fraught, history.

Croatian's linguistic ancestor was brought to the region in the sixth and seventh centuries AD by the South Slavs who may have crossed the Danube from the region now known as Poland. This ancestral language split off into two branches: East South Slavic, which later evolved into Bulgarian and Macedonian, and West South Slavic, of which Slovene, Serbian and Croatian are all descendants.

Croatia may be a peaceful country today but the Balkan region to which it belongs has a long history of invasion and conflict. These upheavals have enriched and politicised the language. The invasion by Charlemagne's armies and forced conversion to the Roman Church in AD 803 left its mark on Croatian in the form of words borrowed from Latin and the adoption of the Latin alphabet rather than the Cyrillic alphabet (with which Serbian is written). Subsequent invasions by the Hapsburg, Ottoman and Venetian empires added vibrancy to the language through the influx of German, Turkish and Venetian dialect loan words. Many words from the standard Italian of Croatia's neighbour Italy have also added colour.

Linguists commonly refer to the languages spoken in

at a glance ...

language name:
Croatian

name in language:
hrvatski jezik
hr·vat·skee *je*·zeek

language family: Slavic

approximate number of speakers: 5 million

close relatives:
Bosnian, Macedonian, Serbian and Slovenian

donations to English:
cravat, dalmatian

Croatia, Serbia, Bosnia-Hercegovina and Montenegro as members of the macro-language Serbo-Croatian while acknowledging differences between the individual languages. Croats, Serbs, Bosnians and Montenegrins themselves also generally maintain that they speak different languages. This polarisation of language identities reflects the desire to retain separate ethnic identities.

The good news is that if you venture into Serbia, Bosnia or Montenegro you'll be able to enrich your travel experience there by using this chapter -- Croatian, Serbian and Montenegrin are all mutually comprehensible, and it's an official language in Bosnia-Herzegovina. In case of the most common differences between Croatian and Serbian, both translations are given and indicated with c/s. The Cyrillic alphabet (used in Serbia, Bosnia and often in Montenegro) is also included on the page opposite. People in Macedonia and Slovenia, who speak closely related languages, generally understand Croatian.

Croatian has plenty of appeal. As well as its rich vocabulary, it has a lovely repertoire of soft lisping sounds such as *sh*, *zh* and *ch* and a lilting musical rhythm due to its use of high and low pitches. It also has an intriguing grammar, quite different from English. It is, however, readily understandable.

Take this phrasebook with you to help make your trip hassle free. It's packed with all the practical language information you'll need and it will also open up a world of possibilities for social interaction and cultural exchange with the locals. Need more encouragement? Remember, the contact you make through using Croatian will make your travel experience unique. Local knowledge, new relationships and a sense of satisfaction are on the tip of your tongue, so don't just stand there – say something!

abbreviations used in this book

m	masculine	pol	polite
f	feminine	inf	informal
n	neuter	imp	imperfective
sg	singular	perf	perfective
pl	plural	lit	literally

Croatian pronunciation is quite straightforward for English speakers as many of the sounds are similar to English sounds. Some claim, in fact, that for English speakers, Croatian pronunciation is the easiest to master among the European languages.

vowel sounds

There are seven vowel sounds in Croatian. In the written language, vowels that appear next to each other don't run together to form diphthongs (vowel sound combinations) as in English. When you see two or more vowels written next to each other in a Croatian word, pronounce each vowel separately.

symbol	english equivalent	croatian example	transliteration
a	father	*zdravo*	*zdra*·vaw
ai	aisle	*ajvar*	*ai*·var
aw	raw	*brod*	brawd
e	let	*pet*	pet
ee	bee	*sidro*	*see*·draw
oo	book	*skupo*	*skoo*·paw
oy	boy	*tvoj*	tvoy

consonant sounds

Croatian consonant sounds all have equivalents, or close equivalents, in English. The rolled r sound can be pronounced in combination with another consonant (or more than one consonant) as a separate syllable, as in the word *Hrvat* hr·vat 'Croatian'. If these syllables without vowels look a bit intimidating, try inserting a slight 'uh' sound before the r to help them run off your tongue more easily. The sound s can appear as a syllable on its own.

symbol	english equivalent	croatian example	transliteration
b	big	glaz**b**a	glaz·ba
ch	chilli	**č**etiri, **ć**uk	che·tee·ree, chuk
d	din	**d**oru**č**ak	daw·roo·chak
f	fun	**f**otogra**f**	faw·taw·graf
g	go	**j**agoda	ya·gaw·da
h	hit	**h**odnik	hawd·neek
j	jam	**dž**ep, **đ**ak	jep, jak
k	kick	**k**rov	krawv
l	loud	**l**utka	loot·ka
l'	million	kaša**lj**	kash·al'
m	man	**m**ozak	maw·zak
n	no	**n**afta	naf·ta
n'	canyon	sije**čanj**	see·ye·chan'
r	rag (but 'rolled')	**r**adnik	rad·neek
s	salt	**s**astanak	sas·ta·nak
sh	show	ko**š**ta	kawsh·ta
t	tin	sa**t**	sat
ts	hits	prosina**c**	pro·see·nats
v	very	**v**iza	vee·za
y	yes	s**vj**etlost	svyet·lawst
z	zoo	**z**ec	zets
zh	pleasure	ko**ž**a	kaw·zha

When y comes after another consonant and before a vowel (as in the word *djeca* dye·tsa) it runs together with the preceding consonant and vowel. The preceding consonant is then pronounced with the tongue rising up towards the roof of the mouth. Something similar happens in English when you say 'and you' quickly. You don't need to be too conscious of this feature as it should happen more or less automatically as you follow the pronunciation guides.

stress & pitch accent

Certain syllables in Croatian have stress, which means you emphasise one syllable over another. As a general rule, in two-syllable words stress usually falls on the first syllable. In words of three or more syllables, stress may fall on any syllable except the last. In our pronunciation guides, the stressed syllable is italicised.

Croatian also has what's known as pitch accent. A stressed vowel may have either a rising or a falling pitch and be long or short. The combination of stress, pitch and vowel length in a given syllable can affect the meaning of a word. The word *sam* pronounced with a short vowel and falling pitch means 'alone' and sounds like 'sum'. When it's pronounced with a long vowel with falling pitch however, it means 'I am' and sounds like 'sarm'.

You don't need to worry about reproducing this feature of Croatian and we haven't indicated it in this book, as it only distinguishes meaning in a very few cases. In such cases it should be clear from the context what is meant. You may notice though that the speech of native speakers has an appealing musical lilt to it. You may also notice marks over the vowels in some dictionaries and grammar books to indicate vowel length and pitch.

reading & writing

Croatian is so closely related to Serbian that many people describe them as two dialects of the same language. However, religion and historical circumstances dictated that Croatian be written in the Latin alphabet, like English, rather than the Cyrillic alphabet, like Serbian. The Croatian alphabet has 30 letters, of which three are digraphs (single sounds made up of a combination of two letters). The accents above letters change the pronunciation of letters. The letter *c* for example is pronounced like the 'ts' in 'cats', while the letter *č* is pronounced like the 'ch' in 'cheese'.

Croatian spelling is absolutely phonetic – there's a fixed regular correspondence between letters and the way they're pronounced even when they're combined into words. What you see is what you say!

letter for letter

The table below shows the correspondences between the Croatian alphabet and the Serbian Cyrillic alphabet. This could come in handy if you venture beyond the confines of Croatia and want to try to read and understand written Serbian.

croatian		serbian		croatian		serbian	
A a	a	А а	a	*L l*	el	Л л	el
B b	be	Б б	be	*Lj lj*	l'	Љ љ	l'
C c	tse	Ц ц	tse	*M m*	em	М м	em
Č č	tch	Ч ч	tch	*N n*	en	Н н	en
Ć ć	ch	Ћ ћ	ch	*Nj nj*	n'	Њ њ	n'
D d	de	Д д	de	*O o*	aw	О о	aw
Dž dž	dzh	Џ џ	dzh	*P p*	pe	П п	pe
Đ đ	j	ђ ђ	j	*R r*	er	Р р	er
E e	e	Е е	e	*S s*	es	С с	es
F f	ef	Ф ф	ef	*Š š*	sh	Ш ш	sh
G g	ge	Г г	ge	*T t*	te	Т т	te
H h	ha	Х х	ha	*U u*	oo	У у	oo
I i	ee	И и	ee	*V v*	ve	В в	ve
J j	y	Ј ј	y	*Z z*	zed	З з	zed
K k	ka	К к	ka	*Ž ž*	zh	Ж ж	zh

This chapter is arranged alphabetically for ease of navigation and is designed to help you go beyond the phrases in this book to create your own sentences. Don't worry too much about the rules of grammar. A couple of well-chosen words and gestures and a desire to communicate will generally help you get your message across.

All illustrations of points shown in the tables (other than examples of verbs) are given in the nominative case unless otherwise stated (for an explanation of case see **me, myself & I**). We haven't given you all the different case forms and endings, but if you want to delve into them there are many good basic textbook grammars of Croatian available, a useful one being *Colloquial Croatian and Serbian* by Celia Hawkesworth (Routledge, 1998).

a/an & the

There are no equivalents of the English articles 'a/an' and 'the'. In Croatian the context indicates whether something is meant to be indefinite (corresponding to 'a/an') or definite (corresponding to 'the').

adjectives see describing things

articles see a/an & the

be

Below are the present tense forms of the verb *biti* 'be'. The pronouns are in brackets because they're mostly not used in Croatian as the verb endings tell you who's doing the action of the verb, ie who's the subject.

I am	*(ja) sam*	(ya) sam
you are sg inf	*(ti) si*	(tee) see
you are sg pol	*(vi) ste*	(vee) ste
he/she/it is	*(on/ona/ono) je* m/f/n	(awn/*aw*·na/ *aw*·naw) ye
we are	*(mi) smo*	(mee) smaw
you are pl	*(vi) ste*	(vee) ste
they are m/f/n	*(oni/one/ona) su*	(*aw*·nee/*aw*·ne/ *aw*·na) soo

I'm Australian.
  Ja sam Australac/   ya sam a·oo·*stra*·lats/
  Australka. m/f   a·oo·*stral*·ka
  (lit: I am Australian)

If you want to form a negative sentence with 'be' to express 'I'm/You're not' etc, just add the prefix *ni-* to the forms of *biti* above, eg *nisam, nisi,* etc.

I'm not Croatian.
  Ja nisam Hrvat/Hrvatica. m/f   ya *nee*·sam *hr*·vat/hr·*va*·tee·tsa
  (lit: I not-am Croat)

case see me, myself & I

describing things

Adjectives take different endings depending on the gender of the noun described, whether it's singular or plural and according to case (see **me, myself & I**).

gender/number	adjective ending
masculine singular	ends in a consonant or -*i*
masculine plural	ends in -*i*
feminine singular	ends in -*a*
feminine plural	ends in -*e*
neuter singular	ends in -*o*
neuter plural	ends in -*a*

He's a good man. (masculine noun and adjective)
On je dobar čovjek.   awn ye *daw*·bar *chaw*·vyek
(lit: he is good man)

She's a good woman. (feminine noun and adjective)
Ona je dobra žena.   *aw*·na ye *daw*·bra *zhe*·na
(lit: she is good woman)

doing things

In Croatian each verb has two forms. This is because Croatian makes the distinction between 'action as process' and 'action as completion' and calls the former the imperfective aspect and the latter the perfective aspect.

The imperfective aspect is used for actions that are thought of as continuing, habitual, ongoing or incomplete, while the perfective aspect is for actions that are thought of as complete or limited. Note that verbs in the perfective aspect can't refer to present events because actions in the present are, by nature, unfinished. Both forms of the verb are provided in the dictionary.

past

Talking about the past in Croatian isn't hard. You just take the present tense of the verb *biti* (see **be**) and follow it with a verb form known as the active past participle. Forming the active past participle of most verbs is quite straightforward. The majority of verbs in Croatian end in -*ti* and to turn these verbs into the active past participle you just remove the -*ti* ending and add the endings shown in the table on the next page. The endings agree in gender and number with the subject of a sentence.

gender/number of subject	active past participle ending
masculine singular	-o
masculine plural	-li
feminine singular	-la
feminine plural	-le
neuter singular	-lo
neuter plural	-la

Here's an example with the verb *imati* 'have':

I had a ticket.

Ja sam imao/imala   ya sam ee·*ma*·aw/ee·*ma*·la
kartu. m/f   *kar*·too
(lit: I am had ticket)

present

There are a few intricacies to forming the present tense of verbs in Croatian, more than is possible to outline here. A rule of thumb though, which works for many verbs, is to remove the *-ti* from the infinitive (dictionary form) of a verb and to add the following endings as shown here for the verb *čitati* 'read':

person		ending	present tense form	
I	*ja*	-m	*čitam*	*chee*·tam
you sg inf	*ti*	-š	*čitaš*	*chee*·tash
he/she/it	*on/ona/ ono* m/f/n	no ending	*čita*	*chee*·ta
we	*mi*	-mo	*čitamo*	chee·*ta*·maw
you sg pol & pl	*vi*	-te	*čitate*	chee·*ta*·te
they m/f/n	*oni/one/ ona*	-ju	*čitaju*	chee·*ta*·yoo

You'll find the present tense forms of the useful verbs 'be' and 'have' under those headings in this phrasebuilder.

future

To talk about future events you use a form of the verb *htjeti* (lit: 'want' but equivalent to 'will' in English) followed by the infinitive (dictionary) form of a verb.

I will	*(ja) ću*	(ja) choo
you will sg inf	*(ti) ćeš*	(tee) *chesh*
you will sg pol	*(vi) ćete*	(vee) *che*·te
he/she/it will	*(on/ona/ono) će*	(awn/aw·na/aw·ne) che
we will	*(mi) ćemo*	(mee) *che*·maw
you will pl	*(vi) ćete*	(vee) *che*·te
they will m/f/n	*(oni/one/ona) će*	(aw·nee/aw·ne/aw·na) che

I will read.
  Ja ću čitati.   ya choo *chee*·ta·tee
  (lit: I will read)

gender

In Croatian, all nouns – words that denote a person, thing or idea – have one of three genders: masculine, feminine or neuter. Gender is assigned to words more or less arbitrarily, though masculine and feminine persons and animals mostly carry masculine and feminine gender, respectively.

The gender of nouns is indicated where relevant in this phrasebook and for all nouns in the dictionary. Here are some handy generalisations to help you identify what gender a noun in the singular might be:

· masculine nouns mostly end in a consonant, eg, *muž* 'husband'
· feminine nouns often end in -*a*, eg *žena* 'woman'
· neuter nouns end in -*o* or -*e*, eg *vino* 'wine' and *dijete* 'child'

Verbs can take different endings according to gender too. They reflect the gender of the subject (the doer of the action). One expression that you'll come across frequently in this phrasebook is 'I'd like …' which translates as *Želio/Željela bih …* m/f. The gender markers indicate that if you're a man you select the first option, while if you're a woman you select the second.

I'd like to withdraw money. (man speaking)

| *Želio bih* | zhe·lee·aw beeh |
| *podignuti novac.* | paw·deeg·noo·tee *naw*·vats |

(lit: I-want-m would change money)

I'd like to withdraw money. (woman speaking)

| *Željela bih* | zhe·lye·la beeh |
| *podignuti novac.* | paw·deeg·noo·tee *naw*·vats |

(lit: I-want-f would change money)

---

gender in this book

Throughout this book we've used the abbreviations m, f and n to indicate gender. The order of presentation is masculine, feminine and then neuter.

If a letter or letters have been added to a masculine form to denote a feminine or neuter form these will appear in parentheses, eg *Židov(ka)* 'Jew' which has the masculine form *Žid* and the feminine form *Židovka*. Where the change involves more than the addition of a letter, different words are given separated by a slash. Sometimes, it's just a case of substituting the final letter of a word to make feminine or neuter forms as in this example: *mladi/a* mla·dee/a 'young' which has the masculine form *mladi* and the feminine form *mlada*.

---

have

To say that you have something you just use a form of the verb *imati* 'have' followed by the noun. As the direct object of the sentence, the nouns possessed should be in the accusative case, but you're sure to be understood if you just use the nominative case (dictionary form) of a noun (see **me, myself & I** for an explanation of the word case).

I have	*(ja) imam*	(ja) *ee*·mam
you have sg inf	*(ti) imaš*	(tee) *ee*·mash
you have sg pol	*(vi) imate*	(vee) ee·*ma*·te
he/she/it has	*(on/ona/ono) ima* m/f/n	(awn/*aw*·na/ *aw*·naw) *ee*·ma
we have	*(mi) imamo*	(mee) ee·*ma*·maw
you have pl	*(vi) imate*	(vee) ee·*ma*·te
they have m/f/n	*(oni/one/ona) imaju*	(*aw*·nee/*aw*·ne/ *aw*·na) ee·*ma*·yoo

I have a car.
> *Imam auto.*   ee·mam *a*·oo·taw
> (lit: I-have car)

me, myself & I

In Croatian, the endings of nouns, adjectives and pronouns may change depending on their 'case'. The case of a word conveys grammatical information. Case can indicate whether a word is the subject (doer of the action), object (undergoer of the action) or indirect object (recipient of an action) of a sentence. These roles are signified by the nominative, accusative and dative cases respectively. It can also indicate possession, location, motion or the means with which something is done. There are seven cases in Croatian. Most of these have equivalents in English prepositions such as 'with', 'into', 'in', 'of' and so on. Other cases have no equivalents in English because English uses a fixed word order to signify basic grammatical relations. Croatian case endings are too numerous to list here but if you really want to learn the language, try to get hold of a comprehensive grammar guide to get you started.

All the nouns, pronouns and adjectives in the phrases in this book are, of course, in the appropriate case so you don't need to worry about this feature of Croatian. It does explain though, why you may see one word in several different guises. The town *Pula* can become *Pulu* or *Puli* when used with prepositions, for example. It also explains why word order in Croatian might sometimes seem muddled up (see **word order**).

more than one

There are a few tricks to forming the plural of nouns in Croatian. In the case of masculine nouns there's a distinction between animate nouns (those referring to living beings, animals etc) and inanimate nouns (those referring to objects).

animate masculine nouns of one syllable	*-ovi* or *-evi*
animate masculine nouns of more than one syllable	*-i*
inanimate masculine nouns	*-ovi* or *-evi*
feminine nouns ending in –a	*-e*
feminine nouns ending in a consonant	*-i*
neuter nouns	*-a*

my & your

A common way of indicating possession is to use what are known as possessive pronouns ('my, your, his, her' etc in English). These agree in gender (masculine or feminine), number (singular or plural) and case (see **me, myself & I**) with the person or thing possessed.

	masculine singular		feminine singular	
my	*moj*	moy	*moja*	moy·a
your	*tvoj*	tvoy	*tvoja*	tvoy·a
his	*njegov*	nye·gawv	*njegova*	nye·gaw·va
her	*njen*	nyen	*njena*	nye·na
our	*naš*	nash	*naša*	na·sha
your	*vaš*	vash	*vaša*	va·sha
their	*njihov*	nyee·hawv	*njihova*	nyee·haw·va

	neuter singular		plural (all genders)	
my	*moje*	*moy·e*	*moji*	*moy·ee*
your	*tvoje*	*tvoy·e*	*tvoji*	*tvoy·ee*
his	*njegovo*	*nye·gaw·vaw*	*njegovi*	*nye·gaw·vee*
her	*njeno*	*nye·naw*	*njeni*	*nye·nee*
our	*naše*	*na·she*	*naši*	*na·shee*
your	*vaše*	*va·she*	*vaši*	*va·shee*
their	*njihovo*	*nye·haw·vaw*	*njihovi*	*nyee·haw·vee*

That's my brother and that's my sister.
> *To je moj brat a to je*   taw ye moy brat a taw ye
> *moja sestra.*   *moy·*a *ses·*tra
> (lit: that is my brother and that is my sister)

negative

Croatian negatives are easy. Just add the word *ne* 'not' before the verb.

I (don't) speak Croatian.
> *Ja (ne) govorim hrvatski.*   ya (ne) *gaw·*vaw·reem *hr·*vat·skee
> (lit: I (not) speak Croatian)

Ne is used with all negative forms like *nikada* 'never' and *nitko* 'nobody' etc.

I never drink spirits.
> *Ja nikada ne pijem*   ya *nee·*ka·da ne *pee·*yem
> *žestoka alkoholna pića.*   zhe·*staw·*ka *al·*kaw·hawl·na *pee·*cha
> (lit: I never not drink strong alcoholic drinks)

personal pronouns

Personal pronouns are not usually necessary in the subject position (for the doer, eg 'I'), unless you want to emphasise who the doer is. This is because the doer is indicated with a verb ending. As for the direct object (undergoer of the action) pronouns, they have long and short forms indicated by the brackets. The short forms are neutral while the long forms are for emphasis. The short forms are generally much more common.

subject (nominative case) pronouns					
I	*ja*	ya	we	*mi*	mee
you sg inf	*ti*	tee	you pl	*vi*	vee
you sg pol	*vi*	vee			
he	*on*	awn	they m/f/n	*oni/ one/ ona*	*aw*·nee/ *aw*·ne/ *aw*·na
she	*ona*	*aw*·na			
it	*ono*	*aw*·naw			

direct object (accusative case) pronouns					
me	*me(ne)*	me(·ne)	us	*nas*	nas
you sg inf	*te(be)*	te(·be)	you pl	*vas*	vas
you sg pol	*vas*	vas			
him	*(nje)ga*	(nye·)ga	them m/f/n	*(nj)ih*	(ny)eeh
her	*nju/je**	nyoo/ye			
it	*(nje)ga*	(nye·)ga			

* long form *nju* and short form *je*.

The polite form of 'you', *vi*, can be used when addressing strangers, older people or people in positions of authority. When talking to family, friends or peers you can use the informal form *ti*.

In this phrasebook we've generally given phrases in the polite form but where you see the abbrevation **inf** you have an informal option to use where appropriate.

plural see more than one

pointing things out

To point things out in Croatian you use the words *evo/eno* 'here/there is' or 'here/there are' before the thing that you're drawing attention to.

There's my sister.
Eno moje sestre.   *e·naw moy·e se·stre*
(lit: there-is my sister)

If you want to indicate that there's an absence of something, you use the word *nema* 'there is not'.

There's no-one home.
Nema nikoga doma.   *ne·ma nee·kaw·ga daw·ma*
(lit: there-is-not nobody home)

Another way to or point out a person or object is to use one of the following words for 'this/these' or 'that/those' and 'that over there' (ie, referring to a thing further away) before the noun.

this		that		that over there	
ovaj m	*aw·vai*	*taj* m	tai	*onaj* m	*aw·nai*
ova f	*aw·va*	*ta* f	ta	*ona* f	*aw·na*
ovo n	*aw·vaw*	*to* n	taw	*ono* n	*aw·naw*

This island is beautiful.
Ovaj otok je predivan.   *aw·vai aw·tawk ye pre·dee·van*
(lit: this island is beautiful)

polite & informal see personal pronouns

possession see my & your and have

questions

Questions may be introduced by the use of question words as in English. These are the most common ones:

what	*što*	shtaw
What are you doing?	*Što radite?*	shtaw *ra*·dee·te
who	*tko*	tkaw
Who are you?	*Tko ste vi?*	tkaw ste vee
where	*gdje*	gdye
Where do you live?	*Gdje živite?*	gdye *zhee*·vee·te
where to	*kamo*	*ka*·maw
Where are you going to?	*Kamo idete?*	*ka*·maw ee·de·te
why	*zašto*	*za*·shtaw
Why are you visiting Croatia?	*Zašto posjećujete Hrvatsku?*	*za*·shtaw paw·*sye*·choo·ye·te hr·vat·skoo
how	*kako*	*ka*·kaw
How are you?	*Kako ste?*	*ka*·kaw ste
when/ at what time	*kada*	*ka*·da
When do you leave?	*Kada krećete?*	*ka*·da *kre*·che·te
how much	*koliko*	kaw·*lee*·kaw
How much is a ticket?	*Koliko je jedna karta?*	kaw·*lee*·kaw ye *yed*·na *kar*·ta

To form a yes-no type question you insert the word *li* (a question particle) immediately after the main verb in the question. The verb must always come first in the question sentence.

Have you been to Croatia before?
   Jesi li bio/bila ikada   *ye*·see lee *bee*·aw/*bee*·la ee·ka·da
   u Hrvatskoj? m/f   oo *hr*·vat·skoy
   (lit: are-you *li* been ever in Croatia)

The simplest way to form questions is to keep the structure of a statement but raise your intonation (making your voice rise in pitch) towards the end of the sentence.

   You can also form questions by adding the expression *zar ne* 'isn't it' to the end of a statement, which usually implies that you'll get a positive response.

Beautiful day, isn't it?
   Predivan dan, zar ne?   *pre*·dee·van dan zar ne
   (lit: beautiful day isn't it)

You can just use *zar* on its own at the start of a question but this gives a tone of surprise to the question.

You're studying Croatian?
   Zar učiš Hrvatski?   zar oo·cheesh *hr*·vat·skee
   (lit: really you-are-studying Croatian)

talking about location

You can specify the location of something by using a preposition (like 'in') in front of the place, just as you do in English. In Croatian, prepositions change the case (see **me, myself & I**) of the nouns that they come before. You don't need to worry about this as people will understand you if you just pick nouns referring to a place out of a dictionary. English and Croatian prepositions don't necessarily translate one-for-one so that, for example, you may see 'at' translated as *kod*, *pri*, *na* or *u* in different contexts.

I'd like to get off at Pula.
   Želim izaći u Puli.   *zhe*·leem ee·*za*·chee oo *poo*·lee
   (lit: I-want get-off at Pula)

verbs see doing things

word order

Generally, basic sentences in Croatian follow the same word order as in English (subject first, followed by the verb, followed by the object). However, because Croatian has case (see **me, myself & I**) to indicate who did what to whom, sentences do not have to be limited to this fixed order for their meaning to be clear.

People describe Croatian as having 'free word order' but this doesn't mean that it's totally random. Word order in Croatian can vary to emphasise different elements in a sentence, for example to highlight information that's new or particularly informative. So remember if you're trying to decipher or form a Croatian sentence, that word order in Croatian can be quite flexible.

say what?

Croatian is not uniform all over the country but has many dialectical variations. It's typically divided into three major dialects: Cakavian, Kajkavian and Stokavian.

The three major dialects draw their names from the different ways that each dialect has of saying the word 'what': *ča*, *kaj* and *što*. *Čakavski* cha·kav·skee is spoken on the Adriatic Coast. *Kajkavski* kai·kav·skee is spoken in the Zagreb and Zagorje regions. *Štokavski* shtaw·kav·skee is centred around Hercegovina and Slavonia. *Štokavski* has three subdialects, Ekavian (the basis of Serbian), Ikavian and Iekavian. The Iekavian dialect has special status as the literary standard and is the form of Croatian used in the mass media. This phrasebook also uses the *Štokavski* standard.

language difficulties

Do you speak (English)?
Govorite/
Govoriš li
(engleski)? pol/inf

gaw·vaw·ree·te/
gaw·vaw·reesh lee
(*en*·gle·skee)

Does anyone speak (English)?
Da li itko govori
(engleski)?

da lee *eet*·kaw *gaw*·vaw·ree
(*en*·gle·skee)

Do you understand?
Da li razumijete/
razumiješ? pol/inf

da lee ra·*zoo*·mee·ye·te/
ra·*zoo*·mee·yesh

Yes, I understand.
Da, razumijem.

da, ra·*zoo*·mee·yem

No, I don't understand.
Ne, ja ne razumijem.

ne, ya ne ra·*zoo*·mee·yem

I (don't) understand.
Ja (ne) razumijem.

ya (ne) ra·*zoo*·mee·yem

I speak (English).
Ja govorim
(engleski).

ya *gaw*·vaw·reem
(*en*·gle·skee)

I don't speak (Croatian).
Ja ne govorim
(hrvatski).

ya ne *gaw*·vaw·reem
(*hr*·vat·skee)

I speak a little.
Ja govorim malo.

ya *gaw*·vaw·reem *ma*·law

What does 'dobro' mean?
Što znači 'dobro'?

shtaw *zna*·chee *daw*·braw

How do you ...?	*Kako se ...?*	*ka·kaw se ...*
pronounce this	*izgovara*	*eez·gaw·va·ra*
write 'dobro'	*piše 'dobro'*	*pee·she daw·braw*
Could you	*Možete li*	*maw·zhe·te lee*
please ...?	*molim vas ...?* pol	*maw·leem vas ...*
	Možeš li	*maw·zhesh lee*
	molim te ...? inf	*maw·leem te ...*
repeat that	*to*	taw
	ponoviti	paw·*naw*·vee·tee
speak more	*govoriti*	gaw·*vaw*·ree·tee
slowly	*sporije*	*spaw*·ree·ye
write it down	*to napisati*	taw na·*pee*·sa·tee

---

tongue torture

Tongue twisters are called *jezikolomke* ye·zee·*kaw*·lawm·ke (lit: tongue breakers) in Croatian. You should have fun exercising your tongue with these little numbers, particularly as they're laced with 'r's between and before consonants. If you're having trouble negotiating these tricky syllables, refer to **pronunciation**, page 11.

Na vrh brda vrba mrda.
na vrh *br*·da *vr*·ba *mr*·da
(High on the hilltop, the willow sways.)

Cvrči cvrči cvrčak na čvoru crne smrče.
tsvr·chee tsvr·chee tsvr·chak na *chvaw*·roo tsr·ne smr·che
(A cricket chirps and chirps on the knotted branch of a black spruce.)

Crni jarac crnom trnu crn vrh grize.
Ne grizi mi crni jarče, crnom trnu crn vrh!
tsr·nee ya·rats tsr·nawm tr·noo tsrn vrh gree·ze.
ne gree·zee mee tsr·nee yar·che, tsr·nawm trn vrh
(A black billy goat is chewing the black tip of a black thorny shrub. Don't you chew the top of my black thorny shrub off, you black billy goat!)

cardinal numbers

osnovni brojevi

0	*nula*	*noo*·la
1	*jedan/jedna/*	*ye*·dan/*yed*·na/
	jedno m/f/n	*yed*·naw
2	*dva/dvije* m&n/f	dva/*dvee*·ye
3	*tri*	tree
4	*četiri*	*che*·tee·ree
5	*pet*	pet
6	*šest*	shest
7	*sedam*	*se*·dam
8	*osam*	*aw*·sam
9	*devet*	*de*·vet
10	*deset*	*de*·set
11	*jedanaest*	ye·*da*·na·est
12	*dvanaest*	*dva*·na·est
13	*trinaest*	*tree*·na·est
14	*četrnaest*	che·*tr*·na·est
15	*petnaest*	*pet*·na·est
16	*šesnaest*	*shes*·na·est
17	*sedamnaest*	se·*dam*·na·est
18	*osamnaest*	aw·*sam*·na·est
19	*devetnaest*	de·*vet*·na·est
20	*dvadeset*	*dva*·de·set
21	*dvadesetjedan/*	*dva*·de·set·*ye*·dan/
	dvadesetjedna/	*dva*·de·set·*yed*·na/
	dvadesetjedno m/f/n	*dva*·de·set·*yed*·naw
30	*trideset*	*tree*·de·set
40	*četrdeset*	che·tr·*de*·set
50	*pedeset*	pe·*de*·set
60	*šezdeset*	shez·*de*·set
70	*sedamdeset*	se·dam·*de*·set
80	*osamdeset*	aw·sam·*de*·set
90	*devedeset*	de·ve·*de*·set
100	*sto*	staw
1,000	*tisuću*	*tee*·soo·choo
1,000,000	*jedan milijun*	*ye*·dan mee·*lee*·yoon

ordinal numbers

1st	prvi/a/o m/f/n	pr·vee/a/aw
2nd	drugi/a/o m/f/n	droo·gee/a/aw
3rd	treći/a/e m/f/n	tre·chee/a/e
4th	četvrti/a/o m/f/n	chet·vr·tee/a/aw
5th	peti/a/o m/f/n	pe·tee/a/aw

fractions

a quarter	četvrtina	chet·vr·tee·na
a third	trećina	tre·chee·na
a half	polovina	paw·law·vee·na
three-quarters	tri četvrtine	tree chet·vr·tee·ne
all	sve	sve
none	ništa	neesh·ta

useful amounts

How much/many?	Koliko?	kaw·lee·kaw
Please give me ...	Molim dajte mi ...	maw·leem dai·te mee ...
a few	nekoliko	ne·kaw·lee·kaw
less	manje	ma·nye
(just) a little	(samo) malo	(sa·maw) ma·law
a lot	puno	poo·naw
many	mnogo	mnaw·gaw
more	više	vee·she
some	malo	ma·law

For more amounts, see **self-catering**, page 158.

time & dates

telling the time

Official times are given according to the 24-hour clock. In conversation, though, Croatians mainly use the 12-hour clock.

What time is it?	*Koliko je sati?*	kaw·*lee*·kaw ye *sa*·tee
It's one o'clock.	*Jedan je sat.*	ye·dan ye sat
It's (ten) o'clock.	*(Deset) je sati.*	(*de*·set) ye *sa*·tee
Five past (ten).	*(Deset) i pet.*	(*de*·set) ee pet
Quarter past (ten).	*(Deset) i petnaest.*	(*de*·set) ee *pet*·na·est
Half-past (ten).	*(Deset) i po.*	(*de*·set) ee paw
Quarter to (ten).	*Petnaest do (deset).*	*pet*·na·est daw (*de*·set)
Twenty to (ten).	*Dvadeset do (deset).*	dva·de·set daw (*de*·set)
At what time?	*U koliko sati?*	oo kaw·*lee*·kaw *sa*·tee
am	*prijepodne*	pree·ye·*pawd*·ne
pm	*popodne*	paw·*pawd*·ne

the calendar

days

Monday	*ponedjeljak*	paw·*ne*·dye·lyak
Tuesday	*utorak*	oo·*taw*·rak
Wednesday	*srijeda*	sree·*ye*·da
Thursday	*četvrtak*	chet·*vr*·tak
Friday	*petak*	*pe*·tak
Saturday	*subota*	soo·*baw*·ta
Sunday	*nedjelja*	*ne*·dye·lya

months

January	siječanj	see·ye·chan'
February	veljača	ve·lya·cha
March	ožujak	aw·zhoo·yak
April	travanj	tra·van'
May	svibanj	svee·ban'
June	lipanj	lee·pan'
July	srpanj	sr·pan'
August	kolovoz	kaw·law·vawz
September	rujan	roo·yan
October	listopad	lee·staw·pad
November	studeni	stoo·de·nee
December	prosinac	praw·see·nats

nature's seasons

The names of the months look unrecognisable because, unlike the English months, they're not based on the Roman calendar. Instead they draw their meanings from ancient Slavic roots depicting the evolution of the seasons in the natural world. Some of these meanings are now obscure to Croatian speakers themselves but others retain delightfully poetic meanings. Here are a few of them:

January	siječanj	timber-cutting time
April	travanj	the season of growing grass
June	lipanj	linden-blossom time
July	srpanj	the time of the sickle (harvest time)
October	listopad	literally: leaf-fall

dates

What date is it today?
Koji je danas datum? — kaw·yee ye da·nas da·toom

It's (18 October).
(Osamnaesti listopad). — (aw·sam·na·e·stee lee·staw·pad)

seasons

spring	*proljeće* n	*praw*·lye·che
summer	*ljeto* n	*lye*·taw
autumn/fall	*jesen* f	*ye*·sen
winter	*zima* f	*zee*·ma

present

now	*sada*	*sa*·da
this ...		
afternoon	*ovog*	*aw*·vawg
	popodneva	paw·*pawd*·ne·va
month	*ovog mjeseca*	*aw*·vawg *mye*·se·tsa
morning	*ovog jutra*	*aw*·vawg *yoo*·tra
week	*ovog tjedna*	*aw*·vawg *tyed*·na
year	*ove godine*	*aw*·ve *gaw*·dee·ne
today	*danas*	*da*·nas
tonight	*večeras*	ve·*che*·ras

past

(three days) ago	*prije (tri dana)*	*pree*·ye (tree *da*·na)
day before yesterday	*prekjučer*	*prek*·yoo·cher
last ...		
month	*prošlog mjeseca*	*prawsh*·lawg *mye*·se·tsa
week	*prošlog tjedna*	*prawsh*·lawg *tyed*·na
year	*prošle godine*	*prawsh*·le *gaw*·dee·ne
last night	*sinoć*	*see*·nawch
since (May)	*od (svibnja)*	awd (*sveeb*·nya)

yesterday ...	jučer ...	yoo·cher ...
afternoon	popodne	paw·pawd·ne
evening	uvečer	oo·ve·cher
morning	ujutro	oo·yoo·traw

future

day after tomorrow	prekosutra	pre·kaw·soo·tra
in (six days)	za (šest dana)	za (shest da·na)
next ...		
month	idućeg mjeseca	ee·doo·cheg mye·se·tsa
week	idućeg tjedna	ee·doo·cheg tyed·na
year	iduće godine	ee·doo·che gaw·dee·ne
tomorrow ...	sutra ...	soo·tra ...
afternoon	popodne	paw·pawd·ne
evening	uvečer	oo·ve·cher
morning	ujutro	oo·yoo·traw
until (June)	do (lipnja)	daw (leep·nya)

during the day

afternoon	poslijepodne n	paw·slee·ye·pawd·ne
dawn	zora f	zaw·ra
day	dan m	dan
evening	večer f	ve·cher
midday	podne n	pawd·ne
midnight	ponoć f	paw·nawch
morning	jutro n	yoo·traw
night	noć f	nawch
sunrise	izlazak sunca m	eez·la·zak soon·tsa
sunset	zalazak sunca m	za·la·zak soon·tsa

How much is it?
Koliko stoji?   kaw·*lee*·kaw *stoy*·ee

Can you write down the price?
Možete li napisati   *maw*·zhe·te lee na·*pee*·sa·tee
cijenu?   tsee·*ye*·noo

Do you accept ...?	*Da li*	da lee
	prihvaćate ...?	*pree*·hva·cha·te ...
credit cards	*kreditne*	*kre*·deet·ne
	kartice	*kar*·tee·tse
debit cards	*debitne*	*de*·beet·ne
	kartice	*kar*·tee·tse
travellers	*putničke*	*poot*·neech·ke
cheques	*čekove*	*che*·kaw·ve
Where can I ...?	*Gdje mogu ...?*	gdye *maw*·goo ...
I'd like to ...	*Želio/Željela*	zhe·lee·aw/*zhe*·lye·la
	bih ... m/f	beeh ...
cash a cheque	*unovčiti*	oo·*nawv*·chee·tee
	ček	chek
change a	*zamijeniti*	za·mee·*ye*·nee·tee
travellers cheque	*putnički ček*	*poot*·neech·kee chek
change money	*zamijeniti*	za·mee·*ye*·nee·tee
	novac	*naw*·vats
get a cash	*uzeti*	oo·ze·tee
advance	*predujam u*	*pre*·doo·yam oo
	gotovini	gaw·taw·*vee*·nee
withdraw money	*podignuti*	*paw*·deeg·noo·tee
	novac	*naw*·vats

What's the charge for that?

Kolika je pristojba za to?	kaw·lee·ka ye pree·stoy·ba za taw

What's the exchange rate?

Koji je tečaj razmjene?	koy·ee ye te·chai raz·mye·ne

Could I have a receipt, please?

Mogu li dobiti račun, molim?	maw·goo lee daw·bee·tee ra·choon maw·leem

Where's ...?	Gdje se nalazi ...?	gdye se na·la·zee ...
an automated teller machine	bankovni automat	ban·kawv·nee a·oo·taw·mat
a foreign exchange office	mjenjačnica za strane valute	mye·nyach·nee·tsa za stra·ne va·loo·te

I'd like ..., please.	Želio/Željela bih ... m/f	zhe·lee·aw/zhe·lye·la beeh ...
my change	moj ostatak novca	moy aw·sta·tak nawv·tsa
a refund	povrat novca	pawv·rat nawv·tsa

---

the colour of money

The currency in Croatia is the *kuna* (*koo*·na), which is divided into 100 *lipa* (*lee*·pa). Interestingly, the currency takes its name from the marten, a ferret-like animal whose pelt was used as a means of exchange in the Middle Ages. The word *lipa* means 'linden tree'. Though it has no obvious association with trade, the linden tree has a sacred significance in Slavic mythology as, among other things, a symbol of good luck and prosperity.

getting around

snalaženje

Which ... goes	Koji ... ide	koy·ee ... ee·de
to (Dubrovnik)?	za (Dubrovnik)?	za (doo·brawv·neek)
boat	brod	brawd
bus	autobus	a·oo·taw·boos
plane	zrakoplov	zra·kaw·plawv
tram	tramvaj	tram·vai
train	vlak	vlak

When's the	Kada ide ...	ka·da ee·de ...
... (bus)?	(autobus)?	(a·oo·taw·boos)
first	prvi	pr·vee
last	zadnji	zad·nyee
next	slijedeći	slee·ye·de·chee

What time does it leave?
U koliko sati kreće? oo kaw·lee·kaw sa·tee kre·che

What time does it get to (Pula)?
U koliko sati stiže oo kaw·lee·kaw sa·tee stee·zhe
u (Pulu)? oo (poo·loo)

Is this seat free?
Da li je ovo sjedište da lee ye aw·vaw sye·deesh·te
slobodno? slaw·bawd·naw

That's my seat.
Ovo je moje sjedište. aw·vaw ye moy·e sye·deesh·te

Please tell me when we get to (Pula).
Molim vas recite mi maw·leem vas re·tsee·te mee
kada stignemo u (Pulu). ka·da steeg·ne·maw oo (poo·loo)

Please stop here.
Molim vas stanite maw·leem vas sta·nee·te
ovdje. awv·dye

transport

39

tickets

Where do I buy a ticket?
Gdje mogu kupiti kartu?
gdye *maw*·goo *koo*·pee·tee *kar*·too

Do I need to book?
Trebam li rezervirati?
tre·bam lee re·zer·vee·ra·tee

A ... ticket (to Split).	Jednu ... kartu (do Splita).	yed·noo ... kar·too (daw splee·ta)
1st-class	prvorazrednu	pr·vaw·raz·red·noo
2nd-class	drugorazrednu	droo·gaw·raz·red·noo
child's	dječju	dyech·yoo
one-way	jednosmjernu	yed·naw·smyer·noo
return	povratnu	paw·vrat·noo
student's	studentsku	stoo·dent·skoo

I'd like a ... seat.	Želio/Željela bih ... sjedište. m/f	zhe·lee·aw/zhe·lye·la beeh ... sye·deesh·te
nonsmoking	nepušačko	ne·poo·shach·kaw
smoking	pušačko	poo·shach·kaw

I'd like a/an ... seat.	Želio/Željela bih sjedište ... m/f	zhe·lee·aw/zhe·lye·la beeh sye·deesh·te ...
aisle	u sredini	oo sre·dee·nee
window	do prozora	daw praw·zaw·ra

I'd like to ... my ticket, please.	Želio/Željela bih ... svoju kartu, molim. m/f	zhe·lee·aw/zhe·lye·la beeh ... svoy·oo kar·too maw·leem
cancel	poništiti	paw·nee·shtee·tee
change	promijeniti	praw·mee·ye·nee·tee
confirm	potvrditi	pawt·vr·dee·tee

Is there (a) ...?	Imate li ...?	ee·ma·te lee ...
air-conditioning	klima-uređaj	klee·ma·oo·re·jai
blanket	deku	de·koo
toilet	zahod	za·hawd

PRACTICAL

40

How much is it?
Koliko stoji?   kaw·*lee*·kaw *stoy*·ee

How long does the trip take?
Koliko traje putovanje?   kaw·*lee*·kaw *trai*·e poo·taw·*va*·nye

Is it a direct route?
Je li to direktan pravac?   ye lee taw dee·*rek*·tan *pra*·vats

What time should I check in?
U koliko se sati   oo kaw·*lee*·kaw se *sa*·tee
trebam prijaviti?   *tre*·bam pree·*ya*·vee·tee

Can I get a sleeping berth?
Mogu li dobiti   maw·goo lee *daw*·bee·tee
kabinu s ležajem?   ka·*bee*·noo s *le*·zhai·em

listen for ...

aw·nai/*aw*·na/*aw*·naw	*Onaj/Ona/Ono.* m/f/n	**That one.**
aw·vai/*aw*·va/*aw*·vaw	*Ovaj/Ova/Ovo.* m/f/n	**This one.**
oo za·kash·*nye*·nyoo	*u zakašnjenju*	**delayed**
paw·neesh·te·naw	*poništeno*	**cancelled**
paw·poo·nye·naw	*popunjeno*	**full**

luggage

prtljaga

Where can I find ...?	*Gdje se nalazi ...?*	gdye se *na*·la·zee ...
the baggage claim	*šalter za podizanje prtljage*	*shal*·ter za paw·dee·za·nye prt·*lya*·ge
a luggage locker	*pretinac za odlaganje prtljage*	*pre*·tee·nats za awd·*la*·ga·nye prt·*lya*·ge

My luggage has been ...	Moja prtljaga je ...	moy·a prt·lya·ga ye ...
damaged	*oštećena*	awsh·te·che·na
lost	*izgubljena*	eez·goob·lye·na
stolen	*ukradena*	oo·kra·de·na

That is/isn't mine.
To je/nije moje. taw ye/*nee*·ye *moy*·e

Can I have some coins/tokens?
Mogu li dobiti *maw*·goo lee *daw*·bee·tee
nekoliko kovanica/ ne·*kaw*·lee·kaw kaw·*va*·nee·tsa/
žetona? zhe·*taw*·na

bus & coach

autobus

How often do buses come?
Koliko često kaw·*lee*·kaw *che*·staw
dolaze autobusi? *daw*·la·ze a·oo·*taw*·boo·see

Does it stop at (Split)?
Da li staje u (Splitu)? da lee *stai*·e oo (*splee*·too)

What's the next stop?
Koja je slijedeća stanica? *koy*·a ye slee·*ye*·de·cha *sta*·nee·tsa

I'd like to get off at (Split).
Želim izaći u (Splitu). zhe·leem ee·*za*·chee oo (*splee*·too)

How long do we stop here?
Koliko dugo kaw·*lee*·kaw *doo*·gaw
ostajemo ovdje? *aw*·stai·e·maw *awv*·dye

city	*gradski*	*grad*·skee
inter-city	*međugradski*	me·joo·*grad*·skee
local	*mjesni*	*mye*·snee

train

What station is this?
 Koja stanica je ovo?   koy·a *sta*·nee·tsa ye *aw*·vaw

What's the next station?
 Koja je slijedeća stanica?   koy·a ye slee·*ye*·de·cha *sta*·nee·tsa

Does it stop at (Pula)?
 Da li staje u (Puli)?   da lee *stai*·e oo (*poo*·lee)

Do I need to change?
 Trebam li presjedati?   *tre*·bam lee pre·*sye*·da·tee

Which carriage is (for) …?	*Koja kola su za …?*	koy·a *kaw*·la soo za …
(Dubrovnik)	*(Dubrovnik)*	(*doo*·brawv·neek)
1st class	*prvi razred*	prvee *raz*·red
dining	*ručavanje*	roo·*cha*·va·nye

Is it …?	*Da li je …?*	da lee ye …
direct	*direktan*	dee·*rek*·tan
express	*brzi*	*br*·zee

you might read …

brzi vlak	*br*·zee vlak	**fast train**
dolasci	*daw*·las·tsee	**arrivals**
lokalni vlak	law·*kal*·nee vlak	**local train**
ne vozi	*ne vaw*·zee	**no service Sundays**
nedjeljom	*ne*·dye·lyawm	**and public holidays**
i blagdanima	ee *blag*·da·nee·ma	
obvezatno	awb·ve·*zat*·naw	**compulsory seat**
rezerviranje	re·zer·*vee*·ra·nye	**reservation**
sjedišta	*sye*·deesh·ta	
odlasci	*awd*·las·tsee	**departures**
poslovni	*paw*·slawv·nee	**executive train**
vlak	vlak	**(1st class only)**
presjedanje	pre·*sye*·da·nye	**change of trains**
svakodnevno	*sva*·kawd·nev·naw	**daily**

tram

Is this the tram to (Arena)?
　Je li ovo tramvaj　　　　ye lee *aw*·vaw *tram*·vai
　koji ide do (Arene)?　　*koy*·ee ee·de daw (a·*re*·ne)

Could you tell me when we get to (Arena)?
　Možete li mi reći kada　*maw*·zhe·te lee mee re·chee *ka*·da
　stignemo kod (Arene)?　*steeg*·ne·maw kawd (a·*re*·ne)

boat

brod/čamac

The word *brod* (brawd) is generally used for a ship, whereas the word *čamac* (*cha*·mats) usually refers to a smaller private boat.

What's the sea like today?
　Kakvo je danas more?　*kak*·vaw ye *da*·nas *maw*·re

Are there life jackets?
　Postoje li prsluci　　　*paw*·stoy·e lee *pr*·sloo·tsee
　za spašavanje?　　　　za spa·*sha*·va·nye

What island is this?
　Koji otok je ovo?　　　*koy*·ee *aw*·tawk ye *aw*·vaw

What beach is this?
　Koja plaža je ovo?　　*koy*·a *pla*·zha ye *aw*·vaw

I feel seasick.
　Osjećam morsku bolest.　*aws*·ye·cham *mawr*·skoo *baw*·lest

anchor	*sidro* n	see·draw
anchorage	*sidrarina* f	see·*dra*·ree·na
cabin	*kabina* f	ka·*bee*·na
captain	*kapetan* m	ka·*pe*·tan
car deck	*platforma za*	plat·*fawr*·ma za
	vozila na brodu f	*vaw*·zee·la na *braw*·doo
car ferry	*trajekt za*	*trai*·ekt za
	prijevoz vozila m	pree·*ye*·vawz *vaw*·zee·la

charter yacht	zakupljena jahta f	za·koop·lye·na yah·ta
deck	paluba f	pa·loo·ba
ferry	trajekt m	trai·ekt
oar	veslo n	ve·slaw
port	luka f	loo·ka
sail	jedro n	ye·draw
speedboat	gliser m	glee·ser
yacht	jahta f	yah·ta

How much is the daily hire of your charter boats?

Koliki stoji dnevni	kaw·lee·kee stoy·ee dnev·nee
zakup vaših čamaca?	za·koop va·sheeh cha·ma·tsa

Is the skipper included?

Da li je u to uključen	da lee ye oo taw ook·lyoo·chen
i skipper?	ee skee·per

Where can I anchor a boat like this?

Gdje smijem usidriti	gdye smee·yem oo·seed·ree·tee
ovakav čamac?	aw·va·kav cha·mats

Which navigational devices is it equipped with?

Kojim navigacionim	koy·eem na·vee·ga·tsee·aw·neem
uređajima je opremljen?	oo·re·jai·ee·ma ye aw·prem·lyen

taxi

I'd like a taxi ...	Trebam taksi ...	tre·bam tak·see ...
at (9am)	u (devet	oo (de·vet
	prijepodne)	pree·ye·pawd·ne)
now	sada	sa·da
tomorrow	sutra	soo·tra

Where's the taxi rank?

Gdje je taksi stanica?	gdye ye tak·see sta·nee·tsa

Is this taxi free?

Da li je ovaj taksi	da lee ye aw·vai tak·see
slobodan?	slaw·baw·dan

Please put the meter on.
　Molim uključite　　　　　maw·leem ook·*lyoo*·chee·te
　taksimetar.　　　　　　　tak·see·*me*·tar

How much is it to …?
　Koliko stoji prijevoz　　kaw·*lee*·kaw *stoy*·ee pree·*ye*·vawz
　do …?　　　　　　　　daw …

Please take me to (this address).
　Molim da me odvezete　maw·leem da me *awd*·ve·ze·te
　na (ovu adresu).　　　na (*aw*·voo a·*dre*·soo)

How much is it?
　Koliko to stoji?　　　　kaw·*lee*·kaw taw *stoy*·ee

Please …	*Molim vas …*	maw·leem vas …
slow down	*usporite*	oo·*spaw*·ree·te
stop here	*stanite ovdje*	*sta*·nee·te *awv*·dye
wait here	*pričekajte ovdje*	*pree*·che·kai·te *awv*·dye

car & motorbike

car & motorbike hire

I'd like to hire a/an …	*Želio/Željela bih iznajmiti …* m/f	zhe·lee·aw/zhe·lye·la beeh eez·*nai*·mee·tee …
4WD	*automobil sa pogonom na sva četiri kotača*	a·oo·taw·*maw*·beel sa *paw*·gaw·nawm na sva che·tee·ree kaw·*ta*·cha
automatic	*automobil sa automatskim mjenjačem*	a·oo·taw·*maw*·beel sa a·oo·*taw*·mat·skeem mye·*nya*·chem
manual	*automobil sa ručnim mjenjačem*	a·oo·taw·*maw*·beel sa *rooch*·neem mye·*nya*·chem
motorbike	*motocikl*	maw·taw·*tsee*·kl

With …	*Sa …*	sa …
air-conditioning	*klima-uređajem*	*klee*·ma·oo·re·jai·em
a driver	*vozačem*	vaw·*za*·chem

How much for	*Koliko stoji*	kaw·*lee*·kaw *stoy*·ee
… hire?	*… najam?*	*… nai*·am
daily	*dnevni*	*dnev*·nee
weekly	*tjednl*	*tyed*·nee

Does that include insurance/mileage?
Da li to uključuje i   da lee taw ook·*lyoo*·choo·ye ee
osiguranje/   aw·see·goo·*ra*·nye/
kilometražu?   kee·law·me·*tra*·zhoo

on the road

What's the speed limit?
Koja je dozvoljena   *koy*·a ye *dawz*·vaw·lye·na
brzina?   br·zee·na

Is this the road to (Pazin)?
Je li ovo cesta za (Pazin)?   ye lee *aw*·vaw tse·sta za (*pa*·zeen)?

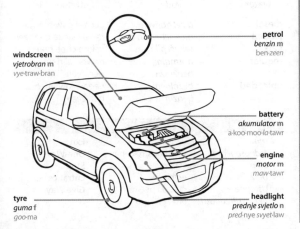

petrol
benzin m
ben·zeen

windscreen
vjetrobran m
vye·traw·bran

battery
akumulator m
a·koo·moo·*la*·tawr

engine
motor m
maw·tawr

tyre
guma f
goo·ma

headlight
prednje svjetlo n
pred·nye svyet·law

Is it a tollway?

Da li se na ovom
putu plaća cestarina?

da lee se na *aw*·vawm
poo·too *pla*·cha tse·*sta*·ree·na

(How long) Can I park here?

(Koliko dugo) Mogu
ovdje parkirati?

(kaw·*lee*·kaw *doo*·gaw) maw·goo
awv·dye par·*kee*·ra·tee

Where's a petrol station?

Gdje je benzinska
stanica?

gdye ye ben·zeen·ska
sta·nee·tsa

Can you check the ...?	Možete li provjeriti ...?	*maw*·zhe·te lee *praw*·vye·ree·tee ...
oil	ulje	*oo*·lye
tyre pressure	tlak zraka u gumama	tlak *zra*·ka oo *goo*·ma·ma
water	vodu	*vaw*·doo

diesel	dizel gorivo n	*dee*·zel *gaw*·ree·vaw
leaded	olovni benzin m	*aw*·lawv·nee ben·*zeen*
LPG	tekući plin m	te·*koo*·chee pleen
regular	normalni benzin m	*nawr*·mal·nee ben·*zeen*
unleaded	bezolovni benzin m	be·zaw·*lawv*·nee ben·*zeen*

road signs

Izlaz	*eez*·laz	**Exit**
Jednosmjerno	*yed*·naw·smyer·naw	**One-Way**
Stop	stawp	**Stop**
Ulaz	*oo*·laz	**Entrance**
Ustupite Pravo Prednosti	*oo*·*stoo*·pee·te *pra*·vaw *pred*·naw·stee	**Give Way**

problems

I need a mechanic.
Trebam tre·bam
automehaničara. a·oo·taw·me·ha·nee·cha·ra

The car/motorbike has broken down (at Pazin).
Automobil/Motocikl a·oo·taw·maw·beel/maw·taw·tsee·kl
se pokvario (u Pazinu). se pawk·va·ree·aw (oo pa·zee·noo)

I've had an accident.
Imao/Imala sam ee·ma·aw/ee·ma·la sam
prometnu nezgodu. m/f praw·met·noo nez·gaw·doo

The car/motorbike won't start.
Automobil/Motocikl a·oo·taw·maw·beel/maw·taw·tsee·kl
neće upaliti. ne·che oo·pa·lee·tee

I have a flat tyre.
Imam probušenu ee·mam praw·boo·she·noo
gumu. goo·moo

I've lost my car keys.
Izgubio/Izgubila eez-*goo*-bee-aw/eez-*goo*-bee-la
sam ključeve od sam *klyoo*-che-ve awd
automobila. m/f a-oo-taw-maw-*bee*-la

I've locked the keys inside.
Zaključao/Zaključala zak-lyoo-cha-aw/*zak*-lyoo-cha-la
sam ključeve unutra. m/f sam *klyoo*-che-ve oo-*noo*-tra

I've run out of petrol.
Nestalo mi je benzina. ne-sta-law mee ye ben-*zee*-na

Can you fix it (today)?
Možete li ga *maw*-zhe-te lee ga
popraviti (danas)? *paw*-pra-vee-tee (*da*-nas)

How long will it take?
Koliko dugo će trebati? kaw-*lee*-kaw *doo*-gaw che *tre*-ba-tee

bicycle

I'd like …	*Želio/Željela*	zhe-lee-aw/*zhe*-lye-la
	*bih … * m/f	beeh …
my bicycle	*popravak*	*paw*-pra-vak
repaired	*svoga bicikla*	*svaw*-ga bee-*tsee*-kla
to buy a bicycle	*kupiti bicikl*	*koo*-pee-tee bee-*tsee*-kl
to hire a	*iznajmiti*	eez-*nai*-mee-tee
bicycle	*bicikl*	bee-*tsee*-kl

I'd like a …	*Želio/Željela bih*	zhe-lee-aw/*zhe*-lye-la beeh
bike.	*… bicikl.* m/f	… bee-*tsee*-kl
mountain	*brdski*	*brd*-skee
racing	*trkaći*	*tr*-ka-chee
second-hand	*polovni*	*paw*-lawv-nee

Do I need a helmet?
Treba li mi kaciga? *tre*-ba lee mee *ka*-tsee-ga

Is there a bicycle-path map?
Da li postoji karta da lee *paw*-stoy-ee *kar*-ta
biciklističkih staza? bee-tsee-*klee*-steech-keeh *sta*-za

I'm ... | Ja sam ovdje ... | ya sam *awv*·dye ...
in transit | u prolazu | oo *praw*·la·zoo
on business | poslovno | *paw*·slawv·naw
on holiday | na odmoru | na *awd*·maw·roo

I'm here for | Ostajem ovdje | aw·sta·yem *awv*·dye
(three) ... | na (tri) ... | na (tree) ...
days | dana | *da*·na
months | mjeseca | *mye*·se·tsa
weeks | tjedna | *tyed*·na

I'm going to (Zagreb).
Ja idem u (Zagreb). — ya *ee*·dem oo (*za*·greb)

I'm staying at (the Intercontinental).
Odsjesti ću u — *awd*·sye·stee choo oo
(Interkontinentalu). — (*een*·ter·kawn·tee·nen·*ta*·loo)

The children are on this passport.
Djeca su na — *dye*·tsa soo na
ovoj putovnici. — *aw*·voy poo·*tawv*·nee·tsee

listen for ...		
groop·naw	grupno	group
s aw·*bee*·te·lyee	s obitelji	family
sa·mee	sami	alone
poo·*tawv*·nee·tsa	putovnica f	passport
vee·za	viza f	visa

I have nothing to declare.
    Nemam ništa za   ne·mam *neesh*·ta za
    prijaviti.   pree·*ya*·vee·tee

I have something to declare.
    Imam nešto za   ee·mam *nesh*·taw za
    prijaviti.   pree·*ya*·vee·tee

Do I have to declare this?
    Trebam li ovo   *tre*·bam lee *aw*·vaw
    prijaviti?   pree·*ya*·vee·tee

That's (not) mine.
    To (nije) moje.   taw (*nee*·ye) *moy*·e

I didn't know I had to declare it.
    Nisam znao/znala da   *nee*·sam *zna*·aw/*zna*·la da
    to treba prijaviti. **m/f**   taw *tre*·ba pree·*ya*·vee·tee

signs		
Carinarnica	tsa·ree·*nar*·nee·tsa	**Customs**
Karantena	ka·ran·*te*·na	**Quarantine**
Oslobođeno	aw·*slaw*·baw·je·naw	**Duty-Free**
od Carine	awd *tsa*·ree·ne	
Pregled	*pre*·gled	**Passport Control**
Putovnica	poo·*tawv*·nee·tsa	
Ulazak	oo·la·zak	**Immigration**
u Zemlju	oo zem·lyoo	

Where's (the market)?
Gdje je (tržnica)? gdye ye (*tr*·zhnee·tsa)

How do I get there?
Kako mogu tamo stići? ka·kaw *maw*·goo ta·maw *stee*·chee

How far is it?
Koliko je udaljeno? kaw·*lee*·kaw ye oo·da·lye·naw

Can you show me (on the map)?
Možete li mi to *maw*·zhe·te lee mee taw
pokazati (na karti)? paw·*ka*·za·tee (na *kar*·tee)

It's ...	*Nalazi se ...*	na·la·zee se ...
behind ...	*iza ...*	ee·za ...
close	*nedaleko*	ne·da·le·kaw
here	*ovdje*	awv·dye
in front of ...	*ispred ...*	ee·spred ...
near ...	*blizu ...*	*blee*·zoo ...
next to ...	*pored ...*	*paw*·red ...
on the corner	*na uglu*	na oo·gloo
opposite ...	*nasuprot ...*	na·soo·prawt ...
straight ahead	*ravno naprijed*	*rav*·naw na·pree·yed
there	*tamo*	ta·maw

Turn ...	*Skrenite ...*	skre·nee·te ...
at the corner	*na uglu*	na oo·gloo
at the traffic lights	*na semaforu*	na se·ma·faw·roo
left	*lijevo*	lee·*ye*·vaw
right	*desno*	de·snaw

listen for ...

... *kee*·law·me·ta·ra	... *kilometara*	... kilometres
... mee·*noo*·ta	... *minuta*	... minutes
... *me*·ta·ra	... *metara*	... metres

directions

north	sjever	sye·ver
south	jug	yoog
east	istok	ees·tawk
west	zapad	za·pad

By ...

bus	autobusom	a·oo·taw·boo·sawm
foot	pješke	pyesh·ke
taxi	taksijem	tak·see·yem
train	vlakom	vla·kawm
tram	tramvajem	tram·vai·em

typical addresses

What's the address?
Koja je adresa?   koy·a ye a·dre·sa

avenue	avenija f	a·ve·nee·ya
lane	prolaz m	praw·laz
street	ulica f	oo·lee·tsa

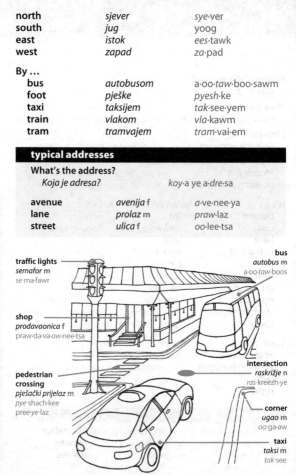

bus
autobus m
a·oo·taw·boos

traffic lights
semafor m
se·ma·fawr

shop
prodavaonica f
praw·da·va·aw·nee·tsa

pedestrian crossing
pješački prijelaz m
pye·shach·kee
pree·ye·laz

intersection
raskrižje n
ras·kreezh·ye

corner
ugao m
oo·ga·aw

taxi
taksi m
tak·see

finding accommodation

Where's a ...?	*Gdje se nalazi ...?*	gdye se *na*·la·zee ...
bed and	*konačište i*	*kaw*·na·cheesh·te ee
breakfast	*doručak*	*daw*·roo·chak
camping ground	*kamp*	kamp
guesthouse	*privatni*	*pree*·vat·nee
	smještaj	smyesh·tai
	za najam	za nai·am
hotel	*hotel*	*haw*·tel
nudist camping	*nudistički*	noo·*dee*·steech·kee
ground	*kamp*	kamp
pension	*pansion*	pan·*see*·awn
room for rent	*najmljena soba*	nai·mlye·na *saw*·ba
youth hostel	*prenoćište za*	pre·*naw*·cheesh·te za
	mladež	*mla*·dezh
Can you	*Možete li*	*maw*·zhe·te lee
recommend	*preporučiti*	pre·paw·*roo*·chee·tee
somewhere ...?	*negdje ...?*	*neg*·dye ...
cheap	*jeftino*	*yef*·tee·naw
good	*dobro*	*daw*·braw
luxurious	*luksuzno*	*look*·sooz·naw
nearby	*blizu*	*blee*·zoo
romantic	*romantično*	raw·*man*·teech·naw

What's the address?
Koja je adresa?   koy·a ye a·*dre*·sa

local talk		
dive	*ozloglašena*	aw·*zlaw*·gla·she·na
	gostionica f	gaw·stee·*aw*·nee·tsa
rat-infested	*ušljivo*	*oosh*·lyee·vaw
top spot	*odlično mjesto* n	*awd*·leech·naw *mye*·staw

booking ahead & checking in

I'd like to book a ..., please.	Želio/Željela bih rezervirati ..., molim. m/f	zhe·lee·aw/zhe·lye·la beeh re·zer·vee·ra·tee ... maw·leem
campsite	mjesto za kampiranje	mye·staw za kam·pee·ra·nye
room	sobu	saw·boo

I have a reservation.
Imam rezervaciju. ee·mam re·zer·va·tsee·yoo

My name's ...
Moje ime je ... moy·e ee·me ye ...

For (three) nights/weeks.
Na (tri) noći/tjedna. na (tree) naw·chee/tyed·na

From (2 July) to (6 July).
Od (2. srpnja) do (6. srpnja). awd (droo·gawg srp·nya) daw (she·stawg srp·nya)

Do I need to pay upfront?
Trebam li platiti unaprijed? tre·bam lee pla·tee·tee oo·na·pree·yed

Is breakfast included?
Da li je doručak uključen? da lee ye daw·roo·chak ook·lyoo·chen

Do you offer half-board?
Da li nudite polu-pansion? da lee noo·dee·te paw·loo·pan·see·awn

Do you have a swimming pool?
Imate li bazen za plivanje? ee·ma·te lee ba·zen za plee·va·nye

listen for ...

kaw·lee·kaw naw·chee	Koliko noći?	How many nights?
paw·poo·nye·naw	popunjeno	full
poo·tawv·nee·tsa	putovnica	passport

56

PRACTICAL

How much is it per …?	Koliko je po …?	kaw·lee·kaw ye paw …
night	noći	naw·chee
person	osobi	aw·saw·bee
week	tjednu	tyed·noo
Can I pay by …?	Mogu li platiti sa …?	maw·goo lee pla·tee·tee sa …
credit card	kreditnom karticom	kre·deet·nawm kar·tee·tsawm
debit card	debitnom karticom	de·beet·nawm kar·tee·tsawm
travellers cheque	putničkim čekom	poot·neech·keem che·kawm

For other methods of payment, see **money**, page 37.

room at the inn

These local room classifications will come in handy if you're booking a room in a private home. This is one of the best accommodation options in Croatia. Not only is it cheaper than a hotel but interacting with your hosts will give you an opportunity to experience local culture.

jedna zvjezdica   *yed·na zvye·zdee·tsa*
one-star (room with a bathroom shared between two rooms or with the owner)

dvije zvjezdice   *dvee·ye zvye·zdee·tse*
two-star (room with a bathroom shared with one other room)

tri zvjezdice   *tree zvye·zdee·tse*
three-star (room with a private bathroom)

Be sure to check when booking whether the price is per person or per room by asking:

Is this the price per …?	Da li je ovo cijena po …?	da lee ye aw·vaw tsee·ye·na paw …
person	osobi	aw·saw·bee
room	sobi	saw·bee

Do you have a ...	*Imate li ...*	ee·ma·te lee ...
room?	*sobu?*	saw·boo
double	*dvokrevetnu*	dvaw·kre·vet·noo
single	*jednokrevetnu*	yed·naw·kre·vet·noo

Do you have a twin room?
Imate li jednokrevetnu   ee·ma·te lee yed·naw·kre·vet·noo
sobu sa francuskim   saw·boo sa fran·tsoo·skeem
ležajem?   le·zhai·em

Can I see it?
Mogu li je vidjeti?   maw·goo lee ye vee·dye·tee

I'll take it.
Uzet ću ovu.   oo·zet choo aw·voo

requests & queries

When/Where is breakfast served?
Kada/Gdje služite   ka·da/gdye sloo·zhee·te
doručak?   daw·roo·chak

Please wake me at (seven).
Probudite me u   praw·boo·dee·te me oo
(sedam) molim.   (se·dam) maw·leem

Do you have a/an ...?	*Imate li ...?*	ee·ma·te lee ...
elevator/lift	*dizalo*	dee·za·law
laundry service	*usluge pranja*	oo·sloo·ge pra·nya
	rublja	roob·lya
safe	*sef*	sef
swimming pool	*bazen za*	ba·zen za
	plivanje	plee·va·nye

Can I use the ...?	*Mogu li*	maw·goo lee
	koristiti ...?	kaw·ree·stee·tee ...
kitchen	*kuhinju*	koo·hee·nyoo
laundry	*praonicu*	pra·aw·nee·tsoo
telephone	*telefon*	te·le·fawn

Do you ... here?	Da li ... ovdje?	da lee ... *awv*·dye
arrange tours	*organizirate*	awr·ga·*nee*·zee·ra·te
	turistička	too·*ree*·steech·ka
	putovanja	poo·taw·*va*·nya
change money	*mijenjate*	mee·*ye*·nya·te
	novac	*naw*·vats

Could I have ...,	*Mogu li dobiti*	*maw*·goo lee *daw*·bee·tee
please?	*... molim?*	... *maw*·leem
an extra	*jednu dodatnu*	*yed*·noo *daw*·dat·noo
blanket	*deku*	*de*·koo
a mosquito net	*mrežu za*	*mre*·zhoo za
	komarce	kaw·*mar*·tse
a receipt	*račun*	*ra*·choon
my key	*moj ključ*	moy klyooch

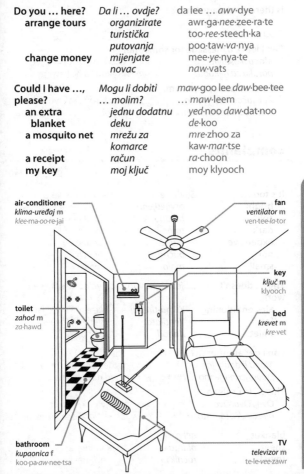

air-conditioner
klima-uređaj m
klee·ma·oo·re·jai

fan
ventilator m
ven·tee·*la*·tor

key
ključ m
klyooch

toilet
zahod m
za·hawd

bed
krevet m
kre·vet

bathroom
kupaonica f
koo·pa·*aw*·nee·tsa

TV
televizor m
te·le·*vee*·zawr

Is there a message for me?
   Ima li koja poruka   ee·ma lee *koy*·a *paw*·roo·ka
   za mene?   za *me*·ne

Can I leave a message for someone?
   Mogu li ostaviti   *maw*·goo lee *aw*·sta·vee·tee
   poruku za nekoga?   *paw*·roo·koo za *ne*·kaw·ga

I'm locked out of my room.
   Zaključao/Zaključala   zak·lyoo·cha·aw/*zak*·lyoo·cha·la
   sam svoju sobu iznutra. m/f   sam svoy·oo *saw*·boo eez·*noo*·tra

complaints

It's too …	*Suviše je …*	soo·vee·she ye …
bright	*osvijetljeno*	aw·svee·*yet*·lye·naw
cold	*hladno*	*hlad*·naw
dark	*tamno*	*tam*·naw
expensive	*skupo*	*skoo*·paw
noisy	*bučno*	*booch*·naw
small	*malo*	*ma*·law

The … doesn't work.	*… je neispravan.*	… ye *ne*·ee·spra·van
air-conditioning	*Klima-uređaj*	*klee*·ma·oo·re·jai
fan	*Ventilator*	ven·tee·*la*·tawr
toilet	*Zahod*	*za*·hawd

Can I get another …?
   Mogu li dobiti još   *maw*·goo lee *daw*·bee·tee yawsh
   jedan/jednu/jedno …? m/f/n   ye·dan/*yed*·noo/*yed*·naw …

This … isn't clean.
   Ovaj/Ova/Ovo …   aw·vai/*aw*·va/*aw*·vaw …
   nije čist/čista/čisto. m/f/n   *nee*·ye cheest/*chees*·ta/*chees*·taw

blanket	*deka* f	*de*·ka
sheet	*plahta* f	*plah*·ta
towel	*ručnik* m	*rooch*·neek

Who is it?	Tko je?	tkaw ye
Just a moment.	Samo trenutak.	sa·maw tre·noo·tak
Come in.	Uđite.	oo·jee·te
Come back later, please.	Molim vas, vratite se kasnije.	maw·leem vas vra·tee·te se ka·snee·ye

checking out

odlazak

What time is checkout?
U koliko sati
treba napustiti sobu?
oo kaw·lee·kaw sa·tee
tre·ba na·poo·stee·tee saw·boo

Can I have a late checkout?
Smijem li sobu
napustiti kasnije od
navedenog vremena?
smee·yem lee saw·boo
na·poo·stee·tee ka·snee·ye awd
na·ve·de·nawg vre·me·na

Can you call a taxi for me (for 11 o'clock)?
Možete li mi pozvati
taksi (za 11 sati)?
maw·zhe·te lee mee paw·zva·tee
tak·see (za ye·da·na·est sa·tee)

I'm leaving now.
Ja sada odlazim.
ya sa·da awd·la·zeem

Can I leave my bags here?
Mogu li ovdje
ostaviti svoje torbe?
maw·goo lee awv·dye
aw·sta·vee·tee svoy·e tawr·be

There's a mistake in the bill.
Ima jedna greška
na računu.
ee·ma yed·na gresh·ka
na ra·choo·noo

Could I have my ..., please?	Mogu li dobiti ..., molim?	maw·goo lee daw·bee·tee ... maw·leem
deposit	svoj depozit	svoy de·paw·zeet
passport	svoju putovnicu	svoy·oo poo·tawv·nee·tsoo
valuables	svoje dragocjenosti	svoy·e dra·gaw·tsye·naw·stee

accommodation

61

I had a great stay, thank you.
  Moj boravak je bio
  ugodan, hvala vam.
  moy *baw*·ra·vak ye *bee*·aw
  oo·gaw·dan *hva*·la vam

I'll recommend it to my friends.
  Preporučit ću vas
  svojim prijateljima.
  pre·paw·*roo*·cheet choo vas
  svoy·eem *pree*·ya·te·*lyee*·ma

I'll be back …	*Vraćam se*	*vra*·cham se
	natrag …	*na*·trag …
in (three) days	*za (tri) dana*	za (tree) *da*·na
on (Tuesday)	*u (utorak)*	oo (*oo*·taw·rak)

signs		
Slobodno	*slaw*·bawd·naw	**Vacancy**
Mjesto	*mye*·staw	
Bez Slobodnih	bez *slaw*·bawd·neeh	**No Vacancy**
Mjesta	*mye*·sta	

camping

kampiranje

Do you have …?	*Imate li …?*	*ee*·ma·te lee …
electricity	*struju*	*stroo*·yoo
a laundry	*praonicu*	pra·*aw*·nee·tsoo
shower	*tuševe*	*too*·she·ve
facilities		
a site	*mjesto za*	*mye*·staw za
	kampiranje	kam·*pee*·ra·nye
tents for hire	*šatore za*	*sha*·taw·re za
	najam	*nai*·am

How much	*Koliko stoji*	kaw·*lee*·kaw *stoy*·ee
is it per …?	*po …?*	paw …
caravan	*kamp kućici*	kamp *koo*·chee·tsee
person	*osobi*	*aw*·saw·bee
tent	*šatoru*	*sha*·taw·roo
vehicle	*vozilu*	*vaw*·zee·loo

PRACTICAL

Can I …?	Mogu li …?	maw·goo lee …
camp here	ovdje kampirati	awv·dye kam·pee·ra·tee
park next	parkirati pored	par·kee·ra·tee paw·red
to my tent	svoga šatora	svaw·ga sha·taw·ra

Is it coin-operated?
Treba li ubaciti kovanice?
tre·ba lee oo·ba·tsee·tee kaw·va·nee·tse

Is the water drinkable?
Da li je ova voda pitka? da lee ye aw·va vaw·da peet·ka

Who do I ask to stay here?
Koga trebam pitati kaw·ga tre·bam pee·ta·tee
da li mogu ostati ovdje? da lee maw·goo aw·sta·tee awv·dye

Could I borrow …?
Da li bih mogao/mogla da lee beeh maw·ga·aw/maw·gla
posuditi …? m/f paw·soo·dee·tee …

renting

I'm here to	Ja sam došao/	ya sam daw·sha·aw/
see the …	došla vidjeti	daw·shla vee·dye·tee
for rent.	… za najam. m/f	… za nai·am
Do you have	Imate li …	ee·ma·te lee …
a/an …	za najam?	za nai·am
for rent?		
apartment	stan	stan
cabin	kabinu	ka·bee·noo
house	kuću	koo·choo
room	sobu	saw·boo
villa	vilu	vee·loo
furnished	namješteno	nam·yesh·te·naw
partly	djelomično	dye·law·meech·naw
furnished	namješteno	nam·yesh·te·naw
unfurnished	nenamješteno	ne·nam·yesh·te·naw

staying with locals

Can I stay at your place?
Mogu li ostati kod vas?   maw·goo lee *aw*·sta·tee kawd vas

Is there anything I can do to help?
Mogu li vam pomoći   maw·goo lee vam *paw*·maw·chee
na bilo koji način?   na *bee*·law *koy*·ee *na*·cheen

Thanks for your hospitality.
Hvala vam na   *hva*·la vam na
gostoprimstvu.   gaw·staw·*preems*·tvoo

I have a (sleeping bag).
Ja imam (svoju vreću   ya *ee*·mam (*svoy*·oo vre·choo
za spavanje).   za *spa*·va·nye)

Can I …?	Mogu li …?	maw·goo lee …
bring anything	donijeti neku	daw·nee·*ye*·tee *ne*·koo
for the meal	hranu za naš	*hra*·noo za nash
	obrok	*awb*·rawk
do the dishes	oprati suđe	aw·pra·tee *soo*·je
set/clear	namjestiti/	na·mye·stee·tee/
the table	raščistiti stol	rash·*chee*·stee·tee stawl

the host with the most

Croatian hosts delight in regaling visitors with homemade delicacies and drinks. If you're fortunate enough to be invited to share a meal you can express your appreciation of your host's culinary prowess in the following manner:

Kako je ovo dobro i ukusno!
ka·kaw ye *aw*·vaw   This is so good and tasty!
daw·braw ee *oo*·koo·snaw

For their part, your hosts will implore you to eat to excess, possibly by saying:

Jedi sinko/kćeri, samo udri!
ye·dee seen·kaw/k·*che*·ree   Eat, my son/daughter. Let it rip!
sa·maw oo·dree

looking for ...

u potrazi za ...

Where's ...?	Gdje je ...?	gdye ye ...
a department store	robna kuća	rawb·na koo·cha
the market	tržnica	tr·zhnee·tsa
a supermarket	supermarket	soo·per·mar·ket

Where can I buy (a padlock)?
Gdje mogu kupiti (lokot)?
gdye maw·goo koo·pee·tee (law·kawt)

For phrases on directions, see **directions**, page 53, and for additional shops and services, see the **dictionary**.

making a purchase

kako nešto kupiti

I'm just looking.
Ja samo razgledam.
ya sa·maw raz·gle·dam

I'd like to buy (an adaptor plug).
Želim kupiti (utikač za konverter).
zhe·leem koo·pee·tee (oo·tee·kach za kawn·ver·ter)

How much is it?
Koliko stoji?
kaw·lee·kaw stoy·ee

Can you write down the price?
Možete li napisati cijenu?
maw·zhe·te lee na·pee·sa·tee tsee·ye·noo

Do you have any others?
Imate li bilo kakve druge?
ee·ma·te lee bee·law kak·ve droo·ge

Can I look at it?
Mogu li to pogledati?
maw·goo lee taw paw·gle·da·tee

Could I have it wrapped?
Možete li mi to
zamotati?
*maw·zhe·te lee mee taw
za·maw·ta·tee*

Does it have a guarantee?
Ima li ovo garanciju?
ee·ma lee aw·vaw ga·ran·tsee·yoo

Can I have it sent abroad?
Možete li mi to
poslati u inozemstvo?
*maw·zhe·te lee mee taw
paw·sla·tee oo ee·naw·zemst·vaw*

Can you order it for me?
Možete li to naručiti
za mene?
*maw·zhe·te lee taw na·roo·chee·tee
za me·ne*

Can I pick it up later?
Mogu li doći
po to kasnije?
*maw·goo lee daw·chee
paw taw ka·snee·ye*

It's faulty.
Neispravno je.
ne·ees·prav·naw ye

Do you accept …?	*Da li prihvaćate …?*	*da lee pree·hva·cha·te …*
credit cards	*kreditne kartice*	*kre·deet·ne kar·tee·tse*
debit cards	*debitne kartice*	*de·beet·ne kar·tee·tse*
travellers cheques	*putničke čekove*	*poot·neech·ke che·kaw·ve*
Could I have a …, please?	*Mogu li dobiti …, molim?*	*maw·goo lee daw·bee·tee … maw·leem*
bag	*vrećicu*	*vre·chee·tsoo*
receipt	*račun*	*ra·choon*
I'd like …, please.	*Želio/Željela bih …* m/f	*zhe·lee·aw/zhe·lye·la beeh …*
my change	*moj ostatak novca*	*moy aw·sta·tak nawv·tsa*
a refund	*povrat novca*	*pawv·rat nawv·tsa*
to return this	*ovo vratiti*	*aw·vaw vra·tee·tee*

bargaining

Prices in shops are generally fixed but you could try bargaining at a market, *tržnica* (*tr*·zhnee·tsa).

That's too expensive.
  To je preskupo. taw ye *pre*·skoo·paw

Do you have something cheaper?
  Imate li nešto jeftinije? ee·ma·te lee *nesh*·taw yef·*tee*·nee·ye

I'll give you (five kuna).
  Dati ću vam (pet kuna). *da*·tee choo vam (pet *koo*·na)

local talk		
bargain	*prigodna cijena* f	*pree*·gawd·na tsee·*ye*·na
rip-off	*prekomjerna*	*pre*·kaw·myer·na
	cijena f	tsee·*ye*·na
sale	*rasprodaja* f	*ra*·spraw·da·ya
specials	*posebne ponude* f pl	*paw*·seb·ne *paw*·noo·de

clothes

My size is ... *Moja veličina je ...* *moy*·a ve·lee·*chee*·na ye ...
  (40) (*četrdeset*) (che·tr·*de*·set)
  large *krupna* *kroop*·na
  medium *srednja* *sred*·nya
  small *sitna* *seet*·na

Can I try it on?
  Mogu li to probati? *maw*·goo lee taw *praw*·ba·tee

It doesn't fit.
  Ne odgovara mi to. ne awd·*gaw*·va·ra mee taw

For sizes, see **numbers & amounts,** page 31. For clothing items, see the **dictionary.**

Though it might relate to an outmoded item of apparel, the word 'cravat' has interesting origins. It's thought to stem from the word *Hrvat* (*hr*·vat) meaning 'a Croat'. These neck scarves were purportedly so named because they were worn by Croatian mercenaries serving in the French army during the Thirty Year's War of the early 17th century.

The black-and-white spotted dogs known as Dalmatians meanwhile, are thought not to have originated in the coastal province of Dalmatia but to have been brought there by Roma people for use as guard dogs.

repairs

popravci

Can I have my ... repaired here?

Mogu li popraviti		*maw*·goo lee *paw*·pra·vee·tee
svoj/svoju/svoje ...		svoy/svoy·oo/svoy·e ...
ovdje? m/f/n		*awv*·dye

When will my ... be ready?	*Kada će biti gotov/ gotove ...?* sg/pl	*ka*·da che *bee*·tee *gaw*·tawv/ *gaw*·taw·ve ...
backpack	*moj ranac* sg	moy *ra*·nats
camera	*moj foto-aparat* sg	moy *faw*·taw·a·*pa*·rat
(sun)glasses	*moje naočale (za sunce)* pl	*moy*·e *na*·aw·cha·le (za *soon*·tse)
shoes	*moje cipele* pl	*moy*·e *tsee*·pe·le
watch	*sat* sg	sat

hairdressing

I'd like (a) ...	Želio/Željela bih ... m/f	zhe·lee·aw/zhe·lye·la beeh ...
blow wave	feniranje	fe·nee·ra·nye
colour	bojenje kose	boy·e·nye kaw·se
haircut	šišanje	shee·sha·nye
my beard	podrezivanje	paw·dre·zee·va·nye
trimmed	brade	bra·de
shave	brijanje	bree·ya·nye
trim	skraćivanje	skra·chee·va·nye

Don't cut it too short.
Nemojte me ošišati   ne·moy·te me aw·shee·sha·tee
prekratko.   pre·krat·kaw

Please use a new blade.
Molim vas koristite   maw·leem vas kaw·ree·stee·te
novi žilet.   naw·vee zhee·let

Shave it all off!
Obrijte sve potpuno!   aw·breey·te sve pawt·poo·naw

I should never have let you near me!
Nisam vam nikada trebao   nee·sam vam nee·ka·da tre·ba·aw
ni dozvoliti blizu!   nee dawz·vaw·lee·tee blee·zoo

For colours, see the **dictionary**.

books & reading

Do you have ...?	Imate li ...?	ee·ma·te lee ...
a book by	knjigu	knyee·goo
(August Senoa)	(Augusta Šenoe)	(a·oo·goo·sta she·naw·e)
an entertain-	vodič o	vaw·deech aw
ment guide	zbivanjima u	zbee·va·nyee·ma oo
	svijetu	svee·ye·too
	razonode	ra·zaw·naw·de

Is there an English-	Postoji li ... za	paw·stoy·ee lee ... za
language ...?	engleski jezik?	en·gle·skee ye·zeek
bookshop	knjižara	knyee·zha·ra
section	odjel	awd·yel

I'd like (a) ...	Želio/Željela	zhe·lee·aw/zhe·lye·la
	bih ... m/f	beeh ...
dictionary	rječnik	ryech·neek
newspaper	novine (na	naw·vee·ne (na
(in English)	engleskom)	en·gles·kawm)
notepad	bilježnicu	bee·lyezh·nee·tsoo

Can you recommend a book for me?

Možete li mi	maw·zhe·te lee mee
preporučiti jednu	pre·paw·roo·chee·tee yed·noo
knjigu?	knyee·goo

Do you have Lonely Planet guidebooks?

Imate li Lonely Planet	ee·ma·te lee lawn·lee ple·net
priručnike?	pree·rooch·nee·ke

listen for ...

maw·goo lee vam paw·maw·chee	
Mogu li vam pomoći?	**Can I help you?**
nesh·taw droo·gaw	
Nešto drugo?	**Anything else?**
ne ne·ma·maw taw·ga	
Ne, nemamo toga.	**No, we don't have any.**

music

glazba

I'd like a ...	Želio/Željela	zhe·lee·aw/zhe·lye·la
	bih... m/f	beeh ...
blank tape	jednu praznu	yed·noo praz·noo
	kazetu	ka·ze·too
CD	jedan CD	ye·dan tse de
DVD	jedan DVD	ye·dan de·ve·de

PRACTICAL

I'm looking for something by (Oliver Dragojevic).

Tražim nešto od	tra·zheem nesh·taw awd	
(Olivera Dragojevića).	(aw·lee·ve·ra dra·goy·e·vee·cha)	

What's their best recording?

Koji je njegov	koy·ee ye nye·gawv	
najbolji album?	nai·baw·lyee al·boom	

Can I listen to this?

Mogu li ovo	maw·goo lee aw·vaw	
poslušati?	paw·sloo·sha·tee	

photography

I need ... film	Trebam ... film	tre·bam ... feelm
for this	za ovaj	za aw·vai
camera.	foto-aparat.	faw·taw·a·pa·rat
APS	APS	a pe es
B&W	crno-bijeli	tsr·naw·bee·ye·lee
colour	kolor	kaw·lawr

I need ... film	Trebam film ...	tre·bam feelm ...
for this	za ovaj	za aw·vai
camera.	foto-aparat.	faw·taw·a·pa·rat
slide	za dijapozitive	za dee·ya·paw·zee·tee·ve
(200) speed	brzine (dvijesto)	br·zee·ne (dvee·ye·staw)

Can you ...?	Možete li ...?	maw·zhe·te lee ...
develop this	razviti ovaj	raz·vee·tee aw·vai
film	film	feelm
load my film	staviti moj film	sta·vee·tee moy feelm
	u foto-aparat	oo faw·taw·a·pa·rat

When will it be ready?

Kada će to biti	ka·da che taw bee·tee	
gotovo?	gaw·taw·vaw	

How much is it?

Koliko to stoji?	kaw·lee·kaw taw stoy·ee	

I need a passport photo taken.

Trebam se slikati
za putovnicu.

tre·bam se *slee*·ka·tee
za poo·*tawv*·nee·tsoo

I'm not happy with these photos.

Nisam zadovoljan/
zadovoljna sa ovim
fotografijama. m/f

nee·sam za·daw·vaw·lyan/
za·daw·vawl'·na sa *aw*·veem
faw·taw·*gra*·fee·ya·ma

I don't want to pay the full price.

Ne želim platiti
punu cijenu.

ne *zhe*·leem *pla*·tee·tee
poo·noo tsee·*ye*·noo

---

souvenirs

embroidery	*vez* m	vez
folklore items	*folklorni*	*fawl*·klawr·nee
	predmeti m pl	*pred*·me·tee
handicrafts	*ručni rad* m	*rooch*·nee rad
lace	*čipka* f	*cheep*·ka
paintings	*slike* f pl	*slee*·ke
pottery	*grnčarija* f	grn·*cha*·ree·ya
silver jewellery	*srebrni nakit* m	*sre*·br·nee *na*·keet
sculptures	*skulpture* f pl	*skoolp*·too·re
stone carvings	*Bračanske*	*bra*·chan·ske
from Brač	*rezbarije*	rez·*ba*·ree·ye
	u kamenu f pl	oo *ka*·me·noo
woodcarvings	*drvorezi* m pl	*dr*·vaw·re·zee

books on historical and cultural heritage

knjige o povjesnoj
i kulturnoj baštini f pl

knyee·ge aw *paw*·vye·snoy
ee *kool*·toor·noy *bash*·tee·nee

jewellery and souvenirs made of shells, sea urchins etc

ukrasi iz mora m pl

oo·*kra*·see eez *maw*·ra

traditional folk costumes

tradicionalne narodne
nošnje f pl

tra·dee·tsee·aw·*nal*·ne *na*·rawd·ne
nawsh·nye

post office

poštanski ured

Postal services are catered for by HTP Hrvatska. If you just want to send a few postcards you can avoid going to the post office by buying stamps, *poštanske marke* (*pawsh*-tan-ske *mar*-ke), from any kiosk newsagent and dropping your mail into a yellow mailbox, *poštanski sandučić* (*pawsh*-tan-ske san-doo-cheech).

I want to send a ...	*Želim poslati ...*	zhe-leem paw-sla-tee ...
fax	*telefaks*	te-le-faks
letter	*pismo*	pee-smaw
parcel	*paket*	pa-ket
postcard	*dopisnicu*	daw-pee-snee-tsoo
I want to buy a/an ...	*Želim kupiti ...*	zhe-leem koo-pee-tee ...
aerogram	*avionski*	a-vee-awn-skee
	telegram	te-le-gram
envelope	*omotnicu*	aw-mawt-nee-tsoo
stamp	*jednu poštansku*	yed-noo pawsh-tan-skoo
	marku	mar-koo
customs declaration	*prijava robe na carini* f	pree-ya-va raw-be na tsa-ree-nee
domestic	*domaće*	daw-ma-che
fragile	*lomljivo*	lawm-lyee-vaw
international	*međunarodno*	me-joo-na-rawd-naw
mail	*pošta* f	pawsh-ta
mailbox	*poštanski sandučić* m	pawsh-tan-skee san-doo-cheech
postcode	*poštanski broj* m	pawsh-tan-skee broy
post office	*poštanski ured* m	pawsh-tan-skee oo-red

communications

73

snail mail

airmail	*zračna pošta* f	*zrach*·na *pawsh*·ta
express mail	*ekspres pošta* f	*eks*·pres *pawsh*·ta
registered mail	*preporučena pošta* f	pre·*paw*·roo·che·na *pawsh*·ta
sea mail	*prekomorska pošta* f	pre·kaw·mawr·ska *pawsh*·ta
surface mail	*obična pošta* f	aw·beech·na *pawsh*·ta

Please send it by air/surface mail to (Australia).
Molim da pošaljete to zračnom/običnom poštom u (Australiju). — maw·leem da *paw*·sha·lye·te taw zrach·nawm/aw·beech·nawm pawsh·tawm oo (a·oo·*stra*·lee·yoo)

It contains (souvenirs).
Ovo sadrži (suvenire). — aw·vaw sa·dr·zhee (soo·ve·*nee*·re)

Where's the poste restante section?
Gdje se nalazi post restant odjel? — gdye se *na*·la·zee pawst re·*stant* awd·yel

Is there any mail for me?
Ima li bilo kakve pošte za mene? — *ee*·ma lee *bee*·law kak·ve *pawsh*·te za *me*·ne

phone

What's your phone number?
Koji je vaš/tvoj broj telefona? pol/inf — *koy*·ee ye vash/tvoy broy te·le·*faw*·na

Where's the nearest public phone?
Gdje je najbliži javni telefon? — gdye ye *nai*·blee·zhee *yav*·nee te·*le*·fawn

I want to …	Želim …	zhe·leem …
buy a	kupiti	koo·pee·tee
phonecard	telefonsku	te·le·fawn·skoo
	karticu	kar·tee·tsoo
call (Singapore)	nazvati	naz·va·tee
	(Singapur)	(seen·ga·poor)
make a (local)	obaviti	aw·ba·vee·tee
call	(lokalni) poziv	(law·kal·nee) paw·zeev
reverse the	obaviti poziv	aw·ba·vee·tee paw·zeev
charges	na račun	na ra·choon
	pozvanog	pawz·va·nawg
speak for	govoriti (tri)	gaw·vaw·ree·tee (tree)
(three) minutes	minute	mee·noo·te

How much does … cost?	Koliko košta …?	kaw·lee·kaw kawsh·ta …
a (three)-minute	poziv od	paw·zeev awd
call	(tri) minute	(tree) mee·noo·te
each extra	svaka	sva·ka
minute	naknadna	nak·nad·na
	minuta	mee·noo·ta

Can I look at a phone book?

Mogu li pogledati	maw·goo lee paw·gle·da·tee
u imenik?	oo ee·me·neek

The number is …

Broj je …	broy ye …

What's the area/country code for (New Zealand)?

Koji je područni/	koy·ee ye paw·drooch·nee/
državni pozivni broj	dr·zhav·nee paw·zeev·nee broy
za (Novi Zeland)?	za (naw·vee ze·land)

Hello.	Halo.	ha·*law*
It's ...	Ovdje ...	*awv*·dye ...
Is ... there?	Da li je ... tamo?	da lee ye ... *ta*·maw
Can I speak to ...?	Mogu li dobiti ...?	*maw*·goo lee *daw*·bee·tee ...
It's engaged.	Zauzeto je.	za·oo·ze·taw ye
I've been cut off.	Prekinuli su me.	*pre*·kee·noo·lee soo me
The connection is bad.	Veza je loša.	*ve*·za ye *law*·sha

listen for ...

kree·vee broy	
Krivi broj.	**Wrong number.**
tkaw *zaw*·ve	
Tko zove?	**Who's calling?**
s keem *zhe*·lee·te *raz*·gaw·va·ra·tee	
S kim želite razgovarati?	**Who do you want to speak to?**
sa·maw tre·*noo*·tak	
Samo trenutak.	**One moment.**
awn/*aw*·na *nee*·ye *awv*·dye	
On/Ona nije ovdje.	**He/She is not here.**

Please tell (him/her) I called.

Molim da (mu/joj) kažete da sam zvao. m — *maw*·leem da moo/yoy *ka*·zhe·te da sam *zva*·aw

Molim da (mu/joj) kažete da sam zvala. f — *maw*·leem da moo/yoy *ka*·zhe·te da sam *zva*·la

Can I leave a message?

Mogu li ostaviti poruku? — *maw*·goo lee *aw*·sta·vee·tee *paw*·roo·koo

My number is ...

Moj broj je ... — moy broy ye ...

I don't have a contact number.

Nemam broj na koji me možete dobiti. — *ne*·mam broy na *koy*·ee me *maw*·zhe·te *daw*·bee·tee

I'll call back later.

Nazvati ću kasnije. — *naz*·va·tee choo *ka*·snee·ye

mobile phone/cellphone

mobilni telefon

I'd like a …	Trebao/Trebala bih … m/f	tre·ba·aw/tre·ba·la beeh …
charger for my phone	punjač za moj telefon	poo·nyach za moy te·le·fawn
mobile phone/ cellphone for hire	iznajmiti mobilni telefon	eez·nai·mee·tee maw·beel·nee te·le·fawn
prepaid mobile phone/ cellphone	unaprijed plaćeni mobilni telefon	oo·na·pree·yed pla·che·nee maw·beel·nee te·le·fawn
SIM card	SIM karticu	seem kar·tee·tsoo

What are the rates?
Koje su cijene telefoniranja?
koy·ee soo tsee·ye·ne te·le·faw·nee·ra·nya

(3 kuna) per (30) seconds.
(3 kune) po (30) sekundi.
(tree koo·ne) paw (tree·de·set) se·koon·dee

the internet

internet

Where's the local Internet café?
Gdje je mjesni internet kafić?
gdye ye mye·snee een·ter·net ka·feech

How do I log on?
Kako mogu pristupiti mreži?
ka·kaw maw·goo pree·stoo·pee·tee mre·zhee

Please change it to English-language setting.
Molim vas da promijenite jezičnu opciju na engleski jezik.
maw·leem vas da praw·mee·ye·nee·te ye·zeech·noo awp·tsee·yoo na en·gle·skee

I'd like to ...	Želio/Željela bih ... m/f	zhe·lee·aw/zhe·lye·la beeh ...
check my email	provjeriti svoj email	praw·vye·ree·tee svoy ee·ma·eel
get Internet access	pristup internetu	pree·stoop een·ter·ne·too
use a printer	koristiti pisač	kaw·ree·stee·tee pee·sach
use a scanner	koristiti skener	kaw·ree·stee·tee ske·ner

Do you have ...?	Imate li ...?	ee·ma·te lee ...
Macs	Macintosh	me·keen·tawsh
	računala	ra·choo·na·la
PCs	PC-e	pe tse e
a Zip drive	pogon za Zip diskete	paw·gawn za zeep dee·ske·te

How much per ...?	Koja je cijena po ...?	koy·a ye tsee·ye·na paw ...
hour	satu	sa·too
(five) minutes	(pet) minuta	(pet) mee·noo·ta
page	stranici	stra·nee·tsee

It's crashed.

Došlo je do prestanka rada računala. — dawsh·law ye daw pre·stan·ka ra·da ra·choo·na·la

I've finished.

Završio/Završila sam. m/f — za·vr·shee·aw/za·vr·shee·la sam

---

say I!

When you see a phrase containing the word 'I' in English, you'll notice that the Croatian translation often has two options to choose from. These are separated by a slash and are followed by the gender markers m/f, as in the phrase: Želio/Željela bih ... m/f 'I'd like ...'.

The two alternatives are masculine and feminine verb forms. Making the right selection is simple as it's based on the gender of the speaker – the person saying 'I'. If you're a man, you choose the first option and say Želio bih. If you're a woman, you say Željela bih. See the a–z phrasebuilder, page 19 for more on gender in Croatian.

Where can I …?	Gdje mogu …?	gdye *maw*·goo …
I'd like to …	Želio/Željela bih … m/f	*zhe*·lee·aw/*zhe*·lye·la beeh …
cash a cheque	unovčiti ček	oo·*nawv*·chee·tee chek
change a travellers cheque	zamijeniti putnički ček	za·mee·*ye*·nee·tee *poot*·neech·kee chek
change money	zamijeniti novac	za·mee·*ye*·nee·tee *naw*·vats
get a cash advance	uzeti predujam u gotovini	oo·ze·tee *pre*·doo·yam oo gaw·taw·*vee*·nee
withdraw money	podignuti novac	*paw*·deeg·noo·tee *naw*·vats

Where's …?	Gdje se nalazi …?	gdye se *na*·la·zee …
an ATM	bankovni automat	*ban*·kawv·nee a·oo·*taw*·mat
a foreign exchange office	mjenjačnica za strane valute	*mye*·nyach·nee·tsa za *stra*·ne va·*loo*·te

What time does the bank open?

U koliko sati se otvara banka? oo kaw·*lee*·kaw *sa*·tee se *awt*·va·ra *ban*·ka

The ATM took my card.

Bankovni automat mi je oduzeo karticu. *ban*·kawv·nee a·oo·*taw*·mat mee ye aw·doo·ze·aw *kar*·tee·tsoo

I've forgotten my PIN.

Zaboravio/Zaboravila sam svoj osobni tajni broj. m/f za·*baw*·ra·vee·aw/za·*baw*·ra·vee·la sam svoy *aw*·sawb·nee *tai*·nee broy

Can I use my credit card to withdraw money?

Mogu li koristiti svoju kreditnu karticu za podizanje novca? *maw*·goo lee kaw·ree·*stee*·tee *svoy*·oo *kre*·deet·noo *kar*·tee·tsoo za *paw*·dee·za·nye *nawv*·tsa

What's the ...?   *Koji/Kolika*   *koy·ee/kaw·lee·ka*
                       je ...? m/f   *ye ...*
    charge for that   *pristojba za to* f   *pree·stoy·ba za taw*
    exchange rate   *tečaj razmjene* m   *te·chai raz·mye·ne*

Has my money arrived yet?
    Da li je moj novac   da lee ye moy *naw*·vats
    stigao?   *stee*·ga·aw

How long will it take to arrive?
    Koliko će trebati   kaw·lee·kaw che tre·ba·tee
    da stigne?   da *steeg*·ne

For other useful phrases, see **money**, page 37.

---

listen for ...		
ee·den·tee·fee·*ka*·tsee·ya	*identifikacija*	**identification**
poo·*tawv*·nee·tsa	*putovnica*	**passport**

    ee·ma·maw ye·dan *praw*·blem
    Imamo jedan problem.   **There's a problem.**

    mee taw ne *maw*·zhe·maw oo·*ra*·dee·tee
    Mi to ne možemo uraditi.   **We can't do that.**

    nee·ye vam *aw*·sta·law *neesh*·ta *nawv*·tsa
    Nije vam ostalo ništa novca.   **You have no funds left.**

    pawt·*pee*·shee·te *awv*·dye
    Potpišite ovdje.   **Sign here.**

I'd like a/an ...	Želio/Željela bih ... m/f	zhe·lee·aw/zhe·lye·la beeh ...
audio set	set slušalica	set sloo·sha·lee·tsa
catalogue	katalog	ka·ta·log
guidebook	turistički	too·ree·steech·kee
in English	vodič na engleskom	vaw·deech na en·gles·kawm
(local) map	kartu (mjesta)	kar·too (mye·sta)

Do you have information on ... sights?	Da li imate informacije o ... znamenitostima?	da lee ee·ma·te een·fawr·ma·tsee·ye aw ... zna·me·nee·taw·stee·ma
cultural	kulturnim	kool·toor·neem
historical	povijesnim	paw·vee·ye·sneem
religious	vjerskim	vyer·skeem

I need a guide.
Trebam vodiča.
tre·bam vaw·dee·cha

I'd like to see ...
Želio/Željela bih vidjeti ... m/f
zhe·lee·aw/zhe·lye·la beeh vee·dye·tee ...

Could you take a photo of me?
Možete/Možeš li me slikati? pol/inf
maw·zhe·te/maw·zhesh lee me slee·ka·tee

Can I take a photo (of you)?
Mogu li ja slikati (vas/tebe)? pol/inf
maw·goo lee ya slee·ka·tee (vas/te·be)

I'll send you the photo.
Poslati ću vam/tebi tu fotografiju. pol/inf
paw·sla·tee choo vam/te·bee too faw·taw·gra·fee·yoo

Who made it?
 Tko je to napravio?   tkaw ye taw *na·*pra·vee·aw

How old is it?
 Koliko je to staro?   kaw·*lee·*kaw ye taw *sta·*raw

behold the grb!

On a sojourn in Croatia one thing that becomes imprinted upon your subconscious is the ubiquitous red-and-white checked emblem in the shape of a shield. It's known as the *Hrvatski grb* (hr·vat·skee grb) 'the Croatian coat of arms' or simply as *grb*. It's been around for hundreds of years and is about as potent a symbol of nationalism as you can find.

The origins of the *grb* are obscure but legend has it that a Croatian king defeated a Venetian prince at chess to maintain Croatia's freedom and so the chessboard was symbolically enshrined as a symbol of this freedom. Today, following the breakaway from the former Yugoslavia, the *grb* is proudly displayed everywhere to celebrate independence for which the Croats have yearned for over a millenium.

getting in

ulaz

What time does it open/close?
 U koliko sati se   oo kaw·*lee·*kaw *sa·*tee se
 otvara/zatvara?   *awt·*va·ra/*zat·*va·ra

What's the admission charge?
 Koliko stoji ulaznica? kaw·*lee·*kaw *stoy·*ee oo·laz·nee·tsa

Is there a	*Imate li*	ee·ma·te lee
discount for ...?	*popust za ...?*	*paw·*poost za ...
children	*djecu*	*dye·*tsoo
families	*obitelji*	aw·*bee·*te·lyee
groups	*grupe*	*groo·*pe
seniors	*starije ljude*	*sta·*ree·ye *lyoo·*de
pensioners	*umirovljenike*	oo·mee·rawv·lye·*nee·*ke
students	*studente*	*stoo·*den·te

tours

Can you recommend a ...?	*Možete li mi preporučiti ...?*	maw·zhe·te lee mee pre·paw·roo·chee·tee ...
When's the next ...?	*Kada je idući/ iduća ...?* m/f	ka·da ye ee·doo·chee/ ee·doo·cha ...
boat trip	*izlet brodom* m	eez·let braw·dawm
day trip	*dnevni izlet* m	dnev·nee eez·let
tour	*turistička ekskurzija* f	too·ree·steech·ka ek·skoor·zee·ya
Is ... included?	*Da li je ... uključen/ uključena?* m/f	da lee ye ... ook·lyoo·chen/ ook·lyoo·che·na
accommodation	*smještaj* m	smye·shtai
food	*hrana* f	hra·na
transport	*prijevoz* m	pree·ye·vawz

The guide will pay.
   Vodič će platiti.   *vaw*·deech che *pla*·tee·tee

The guide has paid.
   Vodič je platio/platila. m/f   *vaw*·deech ye *pla*·tee·aw/*pla*·tee·la

How long is the tour?
   Koliko traje ekskurzija?   kaw·*lee*·kaw *trai*·e ek·*skoor*·zee·ya

What time should we be back?
   U koje bi se vrijeme   oo *koy*·e bee se vree·*ye*·me
   trebali vratiti?   tre·ba·lee *vra*·tee·tee

I'm with them.
   Ja sam s njima.   ya sam s *nyee*·ma

signs

Besplatan Ulaz	be·spla·tan *oo*·laz	**Free Admission**
Informacije	een·fawr·*ma*·tsee·ye	**Information**
Izlaz	*eez*·laz	**Exit**
Misa u Toku	*mee*·sa oo *taw*·koo	**Service (Mass) in Progress**
Muški	*moosh*·kee	**Men**
Ne Diraj	ne *dee*·rai	**Do Not Touch**
Otvoren	*awt* vawr·en	**Open**
Ulaz	*oo*·laz	**Entrance**
WC	ve·*tse*	**Toilets**
Zabranjen Ulaz	za·bra·nyen *oo*·laz	**No Entry**
Zabranjene Blic Kameri	za·bra·nye·ne bleets *ka*·me·ree	**No Flash Photography**
Zabranjeno Fotografirati	za·bra·nye·naw faw·taw·gra·*fee*·ra·te	**No Photography**
Zabranjeno Pušenje	za·bra·nye·naw *poo*·she·nye	**No Smoking**
Zatvoren	zat vawr·en	**Closed**
Ženski	*zhen*·skee	**Women**

I'm attending a …	*Ja idem na …*	ya *ee*·dem na …
conference	*konferenciju*	kon·fe·*ren*·tsee·yoo
course	*tečaj*	te·chai
meeting	*sastanak*	sa·sta·nak
trade fair	*sajam*	sai·am
Where's the …?	*Gdje je …?*	gdye ye …
business centre	*poslovni*	paw·slawv·nee
(eg in hotel)	*centar*	tsen·tar
conference	*konferencija*	kon·fe·*ren*·tsee·ya
meeting	*sastanak*	sa·sta·nak
I'm with …	*Ovdje sam sa …*	awv·dye sam sa …
(Kras)	*(Krašem)*	(kra·shem)
my colleague(s)	*svojim kolegom/*	svoy·eem kaw·*le*·gawm/
	kolegama sg/pl	kaw·*le*·ga·ma
(two) others	*(dvoje) drugih*	(dvoy·e) droo·geeh

I'm alone.
  Ja sam sam/sama. m/f   ya sam sam/*sa*·ma

home alone

There's a little trick to the pronunciation of the above phrase *Ja sam sam*. It might look like simple repetition, but to be understood you'll need to say the first *sam* shorter than the second. You'll also need to pitch your voice a bit lower for the second *sam*. This aspect of Croatian is called pitch accent. See **pronunciation**, page 13, for an explanation of how it works if you're curious.

I have an appointment with …
  Ja imam sastanak sa …   ya *ee*·mam *sa*·sta·nak sa …

I'm staying at …, room …
  Ostajem u …, soba …   aw·stai·em oo … *saw*·ba …

I need ...	Treba mi ...	tre·ba mee ...
a computer	računalo	ra·choo·na·law
an Internet connection	priključak na internet	pree·klyoo·chak na een·ter·net
an interpreter	tumač	too·mach
more business cards	još posjetnica	yosh paw·syet·nee·tsa
to send a fax	da pošaljem telefaks	da paw·sha·lyem te·le·faks

Here's my business card.
Evo vam moja posjetnica.   e·vaw vam moy·a paw·syet·nee·tsa

That went very well.
To je odlično prošlo.   taw ye awd·leech·naw prawsh·law

Thank you for your time.
Zahvaljujem na vašem vremenu.   za·hva·lyoo·yem na va·shem vre·me·noo

Shall we go for a drink/meal?
Hoćemo li na piće/ večeru?   haw·che·maw lee na pee·che/ ve·che·roo

It's on me.
Ja častim.   ya cha·steem

---

down to business

Croatian business etiquette doesn't present any real peculiarities. One thing to be conscious of, though, is that Croatians in coastal areas have a more relaxed and flexible attitude to time than their Anglo-Saxon counterparts. Agitation about deadlines or punctuality might meet with the standard response:

Relax, we still have time.
Stani malo, imamo još vremena.   sta·nee ma·law ee·ma·maw yosh vre·me·na

Away from the coastal areas, Croatians see themselves as hard-working and efficient go-getters in the Central European mould. They tend to be more bureacratic and punctual in their business dealings than their Latin-influenced compatriots.

senior & disabled travellers
stariji i onesposobljeni putnici

Because of the number of wounded war veterans, more attention is being paid to the needs of disabled travellers. In Zagreb, ZET Electric Tram Company (*Zagrebački Električni Tramvaj*) offers a service for disabled people.

I have a disability.
Ja sam onesposobljen/   ya sam aw·ne·*spaw*·sawb·lyen/
onesposobljena. m/f   aw·ne·*spaw*·sawb·lye·na

I need assistance.
Ja trebam pomoć.   ya tre·bam *paw*·mawch

What services do you have for people with a disability?
Koje usluge nudite   koy·e oo·sloo·ge noo·dee·te
za onesposobljene?   za aw·ne·*spaw*·sawb·lye·ne

Are there disabled toilets?
Imate li zahod   ee·ma·te lee za·hawd
za onesposobljene?   za aw·ne·*spaw*·sawb·lye·ne

Are there disabled parking spaces?
Postoji li parkiralište   paw·stoy·ee lee par·*kee*·ra·leesh·te
za onesposobljene?   za aw·ne·*spaw*·sawb·lye·ne

Is there wheelchair access?
Imate li pristup za   ee·ma·te lee *pree*·stoop za
invalidska kolica?   een·*va*·leed·ska kaw·*lee*·tsa

How wide is the entrance?
Koje širine je ulaz?   koy·e shee·*ree*·ne ye oo·laz

I'm deaf.
Ja sam gluh/gluha. m/f   ya sam glooh/*gloo*·ha

I have a hearing aid.
Ja nosim slušni aparat.   ya *naw*·seem *sloosh*·nee a·*pa*·rat

Are guide dogs permitted?
Da li je dozvoljen   da lee ye *dawz*·vaw·lyen
pristup psima   *pree*·stoop *psee*·ma
vodičima?   vaw·*dee*·chee·ma

How many steps are there?
Koliko stepenica ima?   kaw·*lee*·kaw ste·pe·nee·tsa *ee*·ma

Is there a lift?
Da li postoji dizalo?   da lee *paw*·stoy·ee *dee*·za·law

Are there rails in the bathroom?
Imate li ručke za   ee·ma·te lee *rooch*·ke za
oslanjanje u kupaonici?   aw·sla·nya·nye oo koo·pa·*aw*·nee·tse

Could you call me a disabled taxi?
Da li biste mi mogli   da lee bee·ste mee *maw*·glee
pozvati taksi za   pawz·va·tee *tak*·see za
onesposobljene?   aw·ne·spaw·sawb·lye·ne

Could you help me cross the street safely?
Da li biste mi mogli   da lee *bee*·ste mee *maw*·glee
pomoći sigurno   paw·maw·chee see·goor·naw
prijeći ulicu?   pree·*ye*·chee oo·lee·tsoo

Is there somewhere I can sit down?
Ima li negdje gdje   ee·ma lee *ne*·gdye gdye
mogu sjesti?   *maw*·goo sye·stee

guide dog	*pas vodič* m	pas *vaw*·deech
older person	*starija osoba* f	sta·ree·ya aw·saw·ba
person with	*onesposobljena*	aw·ne·*spaw*·sawb·lye·na
a disability	*osoba* f	aw·saw·ba
ramp	*kosina za pristup*	kaw·*see*·na za *pree*·stoop
	kolicima f	kaw·*lee*·tsee·ma
walking frame	*metalno pomagalo*	me·tal·naw paw·*ma*·ga·law
	za hodanje n	za *haw*·da·nye
walking stick	*štap za hodanje* m	shtap za *haw*·da·nye
wheelchair	*invalidska*	een·*va*·leed·ska
	kolica f pl	kaw·*lee*·tsa

travelling with children

putovanje sa djecom

Is there a ...?	Imate li ...?	ee·ma·te lee ...
baby change room	sobu za previjanjebeba	saw·boo za pre·vee·ya·nye be·ba
child-minding service	usluge čuvanja djece	oo·sloo·ge choo·va·nya dye·tse
child-sized portion	dječju porciju	dyech·yoo pawr·tsee·yoo
children's menu	dječji jelovnik	dyech·yee ye·lawv·neek
crèche	jaslice	ya·slee·tse
discount for children	popust za djecu	paw·poost za dye·tsoo
family ticket	kartu za cijelu obitelj	kar·too za tsee·ye·loo aw·bee·tel'

I need a/an ...	Treba mi ...	tre·ba mee ...
baby seat	sjedalo za dijete	sye·da·law za dee·ye·te
(English-speaking) baby-sitter	dadilja (koja govori engleski)	da·dee·lya (koy·a gaw·vaw·ree en·gle·skee)
booster seat	potporno dječje sjedalo	pawt·pawr·naw dyech·ye sye·da·law
cot	dječji krevet	dyech·yee kre·vet
highchair	visoka stolica za bebe	vee·saw·ka staw·lee·tsa za be·be
plastic bag	plastična vrećica	pla·steech·na vre·chee·tsa
potty	tuta	too·ta
sick bag	vrećica za povraćanje	vre·chee·tsa za paw·vra·cha·nye
stroller	dječja hodalica	dyech·ya haw·da·lee·tsa

Where's the nearest …?	Gdje je najbliži/a/e …? m/f/n	gdye ye nai·blee·zhee/a/e …
drinking fountain	izvor pitke vode m	eez·vawr peet·ke vaw·de
park	park m	park
playground	igralište n	ee·gra·leesh·te
swimming pool	bazen za plivanje m	ba·zen za plee·va·nye
tap	slavina f	sla·vee·na
theme park	tematski luna-park m	te·mat·skee loo·na·park
toy shop	prodavaonica igračaka f	praw·da·va·aw·nee·tsa ee·gra·cha·ka

Do you sell …?	Da li prodajete …?	da lee praw·dai·e·te …
baby wipes	vlažne maramice za bebe	vlazh·ne ma·ra·mee·tse za be·be
painkillers for babies	dječje tablete protiv bolova	dyech·ye ta·ble·te praw·teev baw·law·va
disposable diapers/ nappies	pelene za jednokratnu upotrebu	pe·le·ne za yed·naw·krat·noo oo·paw·tre·boo
tissues	papirnate rupčiće	pa·peer·na·te roop·chee·che

Do you hire out …?	Da li iznajmljujete …?	da lee eez·naim·lyoo·ye·te …
prams	dječja kolica	dyech·ya kaw·lee·tsa
strollers	dječje hodalice	dyech·ye haw·da·lee·tse

I need a pram.
Trebaju mi dječja kolica.
tre·bai·oo mee dyech·ya kaw·lee·tsa

Is there space for a pram?
Ima li mjesta za kolica?
ee·ma lee mye·sta za kaw·lee·tsa

Are there any good places to take children around here?
Ima li u okolini dobrih mjesta za djecu?
ee·ma lee oo aw·kaw·lee·nee daw·breeh mye·sta za dye·tsoo

Are children allowed?
   Da li je dozvoljen   da lee ye *dawz*·vaw·lyen
   pristup djeci?   pree·stoop dye·tsee

Where can I change a nappy?
   Gdje mogu   gdye *maw*·goo
   promijeniti pelene?   praw·mee·ye·nee·tee *pe*·le·ne

Do you mind if I breast-feed here?
   Da li vam smeta   da lee vam *sme*·ta
   ako ovdje dojim?   a·kaw awv·dye *doy*·eem

Could I have some paper and pencils, please?
   Mogu li dobiti malo   *maw*·goo lee *daw*·bee·tee *ma*·law
   papira i olovku molim?   pa·*pee*·ra ee *aw*·lawv·koo *maw*·leem

Is this suitable for (three)-year old children?
   Da li je ovo pogodno   da lee ye *aw*·vaw *paw*·gawd·naw
   za (tri) godine   za (tree) *gaw*·dee·ne
   staru djecu?   *sta*·roo dye·tsoo

Do you know a dentist/doctor who is good with children?
   Da li znate zubara/   da lee *zna*·te zoo·*ba*·ra/
   liječnika koji je dobar   lee·*yech*·nee·ka *koy*·ee ye *daw*·bar
   sa djecom?   sa *dye*·tsawm

For health issues, see **health**, page 177.

talking with children

When's your birthday?
   Kada je tvoj rođendan?   *ka*·da ye tvoy *raw*·jen·dan

When's your name day?
   Kada je tvoj imendan?   *ka*·da ye tvoy *ee*·men·dan

Do you go to school/kindergarten?
   Ideš li u školu/   *ee*·desh lee oo *shkaw*·loo/
   vrtić?   vr·teech

What grade are you in?
   U kojem si razredu?   oo *koy*·em see *raz*·re·doo

Do you like …?   *Voliš li …?*   *vaw*·leesh lee …

   school   *školu*   *shkaw*·loo

   sport   *sport*   spawrt

   your teacher   *svog nastavnika*   svawg *na*·stav·nee·ka

What do you do after school?
> *Čime se baviš nakon*   *chee*·me se *ba*·veesh *na*·kawn
> *nastave?*   *na*·sta·ve

Do you learn English?
> *Učiš li engleski?*   *oo*·cheesh lee *en*·gle·skee

I come from very far away.
> *Ja dolazim iz*   ya *daw*·la·zeem eez
> *jako daleke zemlje.*   *ya*·kaw *da*·le·ke *zem*·lye

Are you lost?
> *Da li si se izgubio/*   da lee see se eez·*goo*·bee·aw/
> *izgubila?* m/f   eez·*goo*·bee·la

---

gender reminder

Throughout this book we've used the abbreviations m, f and n to indicate gender. The order of presentation is masculine, feminine and then neuter.

If a letter or letters have been added to a masculine form to denote a feminine or neuter form, these will appear in parentheses. Where the change involves more than the addition of a letter, different words are given separated by a slash. Sometimes, it's just a case of substituting the final letter of a word to make feminine or neuter forms as in this example: *mladi/a* (*mla*·dee/a) 'young' which has the masculine form *mladi* and the feminine form *mlada*.

Gender marking mostly applies to nouns and adjectives but it can apply to verb forms also. See gender in the **a–z phrasebuilder**, page 19 for more on gender in Croatian.

basics

Yes.	*Da.*	da
No.	*Ne.*	ne
Please.	*Molim.*	maw·leem
Thank you (very much).	*Hvala vam/ti (puno).* pol/inf	hva·la vam/tee (poo·no)
You're welcome.	*Nema na čemu.*	ne·ma na che·moo
Excuse me. (to get attention)	*Oprostite.*	aw·praw·stee·te
Excuse me. (to get past)	*Ispričavam se.*	ee·spree·cha·vam se
Sorry.	*Žao mi je.*	zha·aw mee ye

greetings & goodbyes

pozdravi dobrodošlice i oproštaja

It's usual for both men and women to shake hands when meeting for the first time and often on subsequent encounters too. Greeting someone with a kiss on each cheek is reserved for close friends.

Hello.	*Bog.*	bawg
Hi.	*Ćao.*	cha·aw
Good morning.	*Dobro jutro.*	daw·braw yoo·traw
Good afternoon/day.	*Dobar dan.*	daw·bar dan
Good evening.	*Dobra večer.*	daw·bra ve·cher

meeting people

How are you?
   Kako ste/si? pol/inf   *ka*·kaw ste/see

Fine. And you?
   Dobro. A vi/ti? pol/inf   *daw*·braw, a vee/tee

What's your name?
   Kako se zovete/zoveš? pol/inf   *ka*·kaw se *zaw*·ve·te/*zaw*·vesh

My name is …
   Zovem se …   *zaw*·vem se …

I'd like to introduce you to …
   Želim vas/te   *zhe*·leem vas/te
   upoznati sa … pol/inf   oo·*pawz*·na·tee sa …

I'm pleased to meet you.
   Drago mi je da   *dra*·gaw mee ye da
   smo se upoznali.   smaw se oo·*pawz*·na·lee

This is my …	*Ovo je moj/moja/*	*aw*·vaw ye moy/*moy*·a/
	moje … m/f/n	*moy*·e …
child	*dijete* n	dee·*ye*·te
colleague	*kolega/*	kaw·*le*·ga/
	kolegica m/f	kaw·*le*·gee·tsa
friend	*prijatelj/*	pree·ya·tel'/
	prijateljica m/f	pree·ya·*te*·lyee·tsa
husband	*muž* m	moozh
partner	*suprug/*	soo·proog/
(intimate)	*supruga* m/f	soo·*proo*·ga
wife	*žena* f	*zhe*·na

For other family members, see **family**, page 101.

Bye.	*Ćao.*	*cha*·aw
Goodbye.	*Zbogom.*	*zbaw*·gawm
Good night.	*Laku noć.*	*la*·koo nawch
See you later.	*Doviđenja.*	daw·vee·*je*·nya

getting friendly

Croatian has two forms for the singular 'you', *ti* (tee) and *vi* (vee) though the pronouns themselves are not often used because verbs carry endings that indicate whether *ti* or *vi* is being referred to. With family, friends, children or peers, use the informal *ti* forms of the verb. The polite *vi* forms should be used when addressing strangers or people you've just met. Also use the polite forms to address a person considerably older than you, as to use *ti* forms could be seen as very disrespectful.

Phrases in this book are mostly given in the polite form but where you see **inf** you have a casual option to use where appopriate. If you feel (or someone else feels) that you're on a familiar-enough footing to use *ti* forms, the following phrase can be used:

You don't have to address me politely – we can use *ti*.

Nemorate mi persirati,	ne·maw·ra·te mee per·*see*·ra·tee
možemo prijeći na ti.	maw·*zhe*·maw pree·*ye*·chee na tee

addressing people

obraćanje ljudima

Croatians use a person's proper title when addressing an older person, an unfamiliar person, a someone in a position of authority or in other more formal contexts. The proper use of titles is seen as reflecting an individual's good upbringing. The convention is to write titles with an exclamation mark following them.

Mr/Sir	*Gospodine!*	gaw·*spaw*·dee·ne
Mrs/Madam	*Gospođo!*	gaw·spaw·jaw
Ms	*G'đo!*	g·jaw
Miss	*Gospođice!*	gaw·spaw·jee·tse
Doctor	*Doktore!*	dawk·taw·re
Professor	*Profesore!*	praw·fe·saw·re

meeting people

95

In addition to these generic titles, you can address people by using one of the forms below, as appropriate. Some of these might seem a little odd or abrupt to English speakers but they're quite usual in Croatian. Again these titles are generally reserved for more formal contexts, including official situations or when a service is being rendered, such as in a shop or restaurant.

Boy	Dečko!	dech·kaw
Friend	Prijatelju!	pree·ya·te·lyoo
Girl	Djevojčice!	dye·voy·chee·tse
Young man	Momče!	mawm·che
Young woman	Djevojko!	dye·voy·kaw
An older female (lit: aunt)	Teta!	te·ta
An older male (lit: uncle)	Čiko!	chee·kaw

making conversation

Croatians are generally open and outgoing people so you shouldn't find it too hard to strike up a conversation. Good conversation topics to break the ice include football (soccer) and sports in general, food and wine and world events. Tread very lightly when discussing religion (in what is a profoundly Catholic country), politics and, most importantly, the war in the former Yugoslavia.

What a beautiful day!
Kakav predivan dan!   ka·kav pre·dee·van dan

It's so nice here.
Predivno je ovdje.   pre·deev·naw ye awv·dye

What are you up to?
Što se radi?   shtaw se ra·dee

What's up?
Što ima?   shtaw ee·ma

Nice/Awful weather, isn't it?
Lijepo/Užasno   lee·*ye*·paw/*oo*·zha·snaw ye
vrijeme, zar ne?   vree·*ye*·me zar ne

How are things?
Kako stoje stvari?   *ka*·kaw *stoy*·e *stva*·ree

Everything OK?
Sve u redu?   sve oo *re*·doo

Do you live here?
Vi živite ovdje? pol   vee *zhee*·vee·te *awv*·dye
Ti živiš ovdje? inf   tee *zhee*·veesh *awv*·dye

Where are you going?
Gdje idete/ideš? pol/inf   gdye *ee*·de·te/*ee*·desh

What are you doing?
Što radite/radiš? pol/inf   shtaw *ra*·dee·te/*ra*·deesh

Do you like it here?
Da li vam/ti se   da lee vam/tee se
sviđa ovdje? pol/inf   *svee*·ja *awv*·dye

I love it here.
Obožavam ovo mjesto.   aw·*baw*·zha·vam *aw*·vaw *mye*·staw

What's this called?
Kako se ovo zove?   *ka*·kaw se *aw*·vaw *zaw*·ve

Can I take a photo (of you)?
Mogu li (vas/te)   *maw*·goo lee (vas/te)
slikati? pol/inf   *slee*·ka·tee

That's (beautiful), isn't it?
To je (predivno), zar ne?   taw ye (*pre*·deev·naw) zar ne

Just joking.
Samo se šalim.   *sa*·maw se *sha*·leem

Are you here on holiday?
Jeste/Jesi li ovdje   *ye*·ste/*ye*·see lee *awv*·dye
na odmoru? pol/inf   na *awd*·maw·roo

I'm here …	*Ja sam ovdje …*	ya sam *awv*·dye …
for a holiday	*na odmoru*	na *awd*·maw·roo
on business	*poslovno*	*paw*·slawv·naw
to study	*kao student*	*ka*·aw *stoo*·dent

How long are you here for?

Koliko dugo	kaw·*lee*·kaw doo·gaw
ste/si ovdje? pol/inf	ste/see *awv*·dye

I'm here for (four) weeks/days.

Ja sam ovdje na	ya sam *awv*·dye na
(četiri) tjedna/dana.	(che·tee·ree) tyed·na/*da*·na

nationalities

Where are you from?

Odakle ste/si? pol/inf		aw·*da*·kle ste/see

I'm from ...	*Ja sam iz ...*	ya sam eez ...
Australia	*Australije*	a·oo·*stra*·lee·ye
England	*Engleske*	*en*·gles·ke
the USA	*Amerike*	a·*me*·ree·ke

For more nationalities, see the **dictionary**.

age

How old ...?	*Koliko ...*	kaw·*lee*·kaw ...
	godina?	*gaw*·dee·na
are you	*imate/imaš* pol/inf	ee·ma·te/*ee*·mash
is your son	*vaš/tvoj* pol/inf	vash/tvoy
	sin ima	seen *ee*·ma
is your daughter	*vaša/tvoja* pol/inf	*va*·sha/*tvoy*·a
	kći ima	k·*chee ee*·ma

I'm ... years old.
  Imam ... godina.   ee·mam ... gaw·dee·na
He/She is ... years old.
  On/Ona ima ... godina.   awn/aw·na ee·ma ... gaw·dee·na
Too old!
  Prestar/Prestara! m/f   pre·star/pre·sta·ra
I'm younger than I look.
  Mlađi/Mlađa sam nego   mla·jee/mla·ja sam ne·gaw
  što izgledam. m/f   shtaw eez·gle·dam

For your age, see **numbers & amounts**, page 31.

occupations & studies

What's your occupation?
  Čime se bavite/   chee·me se ba·vee·te/
  baviš? pol/inf   ba·veesh

I'm a ...	*Ja sam ...*	ya sam ...
chef	*šef kuhinje/*	shef koo·hee·nye/
	šefica kuhinje m/f	shef·ee·tsa koo·hee·nye
journalist	*novinar/*	naw·vee·nar/
	novinarka m/f	naw·vee·nar·ka
manual labourer	*fizički radnik/*	fee·zeech·kee rad·neek/
	fizička radnica m/f	fee·zeech·ka rad·nee·tsa
mechanical engineer	*inženjer strojarstva* m&f	een·zhe·nyer stroy·ar·stvaw
musician	*muzičar/*	moo·zee·char/
	muzičarka m/f	moo·zee·char·ka
public servant	*službenik/*	sloozh·be·neek/
	službenica m/f	sloozh·be·nee·tsa
teacher	*nastavnik/*	na·stav·neek/
	nastavnica m/f	na·stav·nee·tsa
trades person	*zanatlija/*	za·nat·lee·ya/
	obrtnica m/f	aw·brt·nee·tsa

meeting people

99

local talk

Come in/Sit down.	*Izvolite.*	eez·*vaw*·lee·te
Come on then!	*Daj ajde više!*	dai ai·de vee·she
Great!	*Super!*	*soo*·per
Hey!	*Hej!*	hey
It's OK.	*U redu je.*	oo *re*·doo ye
Just a minute.	*Trenutak.*	tre·*noo*·tak
Maybe.	*Možda*	*mawzh*·da
No problem.	*Nema problema.*	ne·ma praw·*ble*·ma
No way!	*Nema šanse!*	ne·ma *shan*·se
See you.	*Vidimo se.*	*vee*·dee·maw se
Sure.	*Svakako!*	*sva*·ka·kaw
Watch out!	*Pazite/Pazi!* pol/inf	pa·*zee*·te/*pa*·zee

I work in ...	*Ja sam zaposlen/*	ya sam za·*paw*·slen/
	zaposlena u ... m/f	za·*paw*·sle·na oo ...
administration	*upravi*	oo·*pra*·vee
health	*zdravstvu*	*zdrav*·stvoo
retail	*trgovini*	tr·*gaw*·vee·nee
	na malo	na *ma*·law

I'm ...	*Ja sam ...*	ya sam ...
retired	*umirovljen/*	oo·*mee*·rawv·lyen/
	umirovljena m/f	oo·*mee*·rawv·lye·na
self-employed	*samostalno*	sa·maw·*stal*·naw
	zaposlen/	za·*paw*·slen/
	zaposlena m/f	za·*paw*·sle·na
unemployed	*nezaposlen/*	ne·za·*paw*·slen/
	nezaposlena m/f	ne·za·*paw*·sle·na

I'm studying ...	*Ja studiram ...*	ya *stoo*·dee·ram ...
humanities	*društvene*	*droosht*·ve·ne
	znanosti	zna·*naw*·stee
Croatian	*hrvatski*	hr·vat·skee
science	*znanost*	zna·nawst

What are you studying?

Što vi studirate? pol	shtaw vee *stoo*·dee·ra·te
Što ti studiraš? inf	shtaw tee *stoo*·dee·rash

SOCIAL

family

In Croatia, family is sacred and people you meet may well ask you about yours. It'll be appreciated if you reciprocate. Take care not to offend, however, by expressing surprise about aspects of family life that may seem unusual by the standards of your own culture (such as adult children still living at home).

Do you have a …?	Imate/Imaš li …? pol/inf	ee·ma·te/ee·mash lee …
I have a …	Ja imam …	ya ee·mam …
I don't have a …	Ja nemam …	ya ne·mam …
brother	brata	bra·ta
daughter	ćerku	cher·koo
family	obitelj	aw·bee·tel'
father	oca	aw·tsa
granddaughter	unuku	oo·noo·koo
grandfather	djeda	dye·da
grandmother	baku	ba·koo
grandson	unuka	oo·noo·ka
husband	muža	moo·zha
mother	majku	mai·koo
partner (intimate)	supružnika	soo·proozh·nee·ka
sister	sestru	ses·troo
son	sina	see·na
wife	ženu	zhe·noo

I'm …	Ja sam …	ya sam …
married	u braku	oo bra·koo
separated	rastavljen/ rastavljena m/f	ra·stav·lyen/ ra·stav·lye·na
single	neoženjen/ neudata m/f	ne·aw·zhe·nyen/ ne·oo·da·ta

Are you married?

Jeste li vi vjenčani? pol	ye·ste lee vee vyen·cha·nee
Jesi li ti vjenčan/ vjenčana? inf m/f	ye·see lee tee vyen·chan/ vyen·cha·na

farewells

Tomorrow is my last day here.
> *Sutra mi je zadnji*   *soo*·tra mee ye *zad*·nyee
> *dan ovdje.*   dan *awv*·dye

If you come to (Scotland) you can visit me.
> *Ako ikad dođete*   *a*·kaw ee·kad *daw*·je·te
> *u (Škotsku), možete*   oo (*shkawt*·skoo) *maw*·zhe·te
> *me posjetiti.* pol   me *paw*·sye·tee·tee
> *Ako ikad dođeš*   *a*·kaw ee·kad *daw*·jesh
> *u (Škotsku), možeš*   oo (*shkawt*·skoo) *maw*·zhesh
> *me posjetiti.* inf   me *paw*·sye·tee·tee

Keep in touch!
> *Ostanimo u vezi!*   *aw*·sta·nee·maw oo *ve*·zee

It's been great meeting you.
> *Bilo je lijepo*   *bee*·law ye lee·*ye*·paw
> *upoznati vas/te.* pol/inf   oo·*pawz*·na·tee vas/te

Here's my ...	*Ovo je moj ...* m	*aw*·vaw ye moy ...
	Ovo je moja ... f	*aw*·vaw ye *moy*·a ...
What's your ...?	*Koji je tvoj ...?* m	*koy*·ee ye tvoy ...
	Koja je tvoja ...? f	*koy*·a ye *tvoy*·a ...
address	*adresa* f	a·*dre*·sa
email address	*email adresa* f	ee·ma·eel a·*dre*·sa
phone number	*broj telefona* m	broy te·le·*faw*·na

well wishing

Bless you!	*Nazdravlje!*	naz·*drav*·lye
Bon voyage!	*Sretan put!*	*sre*·tan poot
Congratulations!	*Čestitke!*	*che*·steet·ke
Good luck!	*Sretno!*	*sret*·naw
Happy birthday!	*Sretan rođendan!*	*sre*·tan *raw*·jen·dan
Merry Christmas!	*Sretan božić!*	*sre*·tan *baw*·zheech

In this chapter phrases are given in the informal *ti* forms. If you're not sure what this means, see the **a-z phrasebuilder**, page 24.

common interests

česte zanimacije

What do you do in your spare time?

Što radiš u		shtaw *ra*·deesh oo
slobodno vrijeme?		slaw·bawd·naw vree·*ye*·me

Do you like …?	*Voliš li …?*	*vaw*·leesh lee …
I (don't) like …	*Ja (ne) volim …*	ya (ne) *vaw*·leem …
card games	*kartanje*	*kar*·ta·nye
computer games	*kompjuterske igre*	kawm·*pyoo*·ter·ske *ee*·gre
cooking	*kuhanje*	*koo*·ha·nye
dancing	*ples*	ples
drawing	*crtanje*	*tsr*·ta·nye
films	*filmove*	*feel*·maw·ve
gardening	*vrtlarstvo*	vrt·*lars*·tvaw
hiking	*rekreaciono pješačenje*	re·kre·a·tsee·aw·naw pye·*sha*·che·nye
music	*glazbu*	*glaz*·boo
painting	*slikanje*	*slee*·ka·nye
photography	*fotografiju*	faw·taw·*gra*·fee·yoo
reading	*čitanje*	*chee*·ta·nye
shopping	*kupovanje*	koo·*paw*·va·nye
socialising	*druženje*	*droo*·zhe·nye
sport	*sport*	spawrt
travelling	*putovanja*	poo·taw·*va*·nya

For more sporting activities, see **sport**, page 129.

music

What music do you like?
Koju vrstu glazbe voliš?   *koy*·oo *vr*·stoo *glaz*·be *vaw*·leesh

What bands do you like?
Koje grupe voliš?   *koy*·e *groo*·pe *vaw*·leesh

Do you …?	*Da li …?*	da lee …
dance	*plešeš*	*ple*·shesh
go to concerts	*ideš na*	*ee*·desh na
	koncerte	*kawn*·tser·te
listen to music	*slušaš glazbu*	*sloo*·shash *glaz*·boo
play an	*sviraš neki*	*svee*·rash *ne*·kee
instrument	*instrument*	een·stroo·*ment*
sing	*pjevaš*	*pye*·vash

blues	*bluz* m	blooz
classical music	*klasična glazba* f	*kla*·seech·na *glaz*·ba
electronic music	*elektronska*	e·*lek*·trawn·ska
	glazba f	*glaz*·ba
folk music	*folk glazba* f	fawlk *glaz*·ba
jazz	*džez* m	jez
opera	*opera* f	*aw*·pe·ra
operetta	*opereta* f	aw·pe·*re*·ta
pop	*pop* m	pawp
rock	*rock* m	rawk
traditional music	*tradicionalna*	*tra*·dee·tsee·aw·nal·na
	glazba f	*glaz*·ba
world music	*etno glazba* f	*et*·naw *glaz*·ba

Planning to go to a concert? See **going out**, page 113.

cinema & theatre

I feel like going to a ...	Htio/Htjela bih otići na ... m/f	htee·aw/htye·la beeh aw·tee·chee na ...
Did you like the ...?	Da li ti se dopao ...?	da lee tee se daw·pa·aw ...
ballet	balet	ba·let
film	film	feelm

I feel like going to a play.
Htio/Htjela bih otići na predstavu. m/f — htee·aw/htye·la beeh aw·tee·chee na pred·sta·voo

Did you like the play?
Da li ti se dopala predstava? — da lee tee se daw·pa·la pred·sta·va

What's showing at the cinema/theatre tonight?
Što se prikazuje u kinu/kazalištu večeras? — shtaw se pree·ka·zoo·ye oo kee·noo/ka·za·leesh·too ve·che·ras

Is it in English?
Da li je na engleskom? — da lee ye na en·gles·kawm

Does it have (English) subtitles?
Da li je film titlovan (na engleski)? — da lee ye feelm teet·law·van (na en·gle·skee)

Is this seat taken?
Je li ovo mjesto zauzeto? — ye lee aw·vaw mye·staw za·oo·ze·taw

This is my seat.
Ovo je moje mjesto. — aw·vaw ye moy·e mye·staw

Have you seen ...?
Da li si pogledao/pogledala ...? m/f — da lee see paw·gle·da·aw/paw·gle·da·la ...

Who's in it?
Tko glumi u tome? — tkaw gloo·mee oo taw·me

It stars ...
Glavnu ulogu igra ... — glav·noo oo·law·goo ee·gra ...

I thought it was ...	Ja mislim	ya *mee*·sleem
	da je bio ...	da ye *bee*·aw ...
excellent	*odličan*	*awd*·lee·chan
long	*dugačak*	*doo*·ga·chak
OK	*OK*	*aw*·key

I (don't) like ...	Ja (ne) volim ...	ya (ne) *vaw*·leem ...
action movies	*akcione*	*ak*·tsee·aw·ne
	filmove	*feel*·maw·ve
animated films	*animirane*	a·nee·*mee*·ra·ne
	filomove	*feel*·maw·ve
(Croatian) cinema	*(hrvatski) film*	(*hr*·vat·skee) feelm
comedies	*komedije*	*kaw*·me·dee·ye
documentaries	*dokumentarce*	daw·koo·men·*tar*·tse
drama	*drame*	*dra*·me
horror movies	*filmove strave*	*feel*·maw·ve *stra*·ve
	i užasa	ee *oo*·zha·sa
sci-fi	*filmove*	*feel*·maw·ve
	naučne	*na*·ooch·ne
	fantastike	fan·*ta*·stee·ke
short films	*kratkometražne*	*krat*·kaw·*me*·trazh·ne
	filmove	*feel*·maw·ve
thrillers	*trilere*	*tree*·le·re
war movies	*ratne filmove*	*rat*·ne *feel*·maw·ve

lost in translation

Croatians are proud of their rich literary heritage. It's a heritage that has absorbed the crosscurrents of Central European and Latin influence. Unfortunately though, little of Croatia's literary output is available in English translation.

The country's towering literary figure is undoubtedly the 20th-century novelist and playwright Miroslav Krleža. Always politcally active, Krleža broke with Tito in 1967 over the writer's campaign for equality between the Serbian and Croatian literary languages. He famously stated: 'Croatian and Serbian are one and the same language, which Croats call Croatian and Serbs Serbian'. His popular novel *The Return of Philip Latinovicz* which depicts the concerns of a changing Yugoslavia has been translated into English.

feelings

I'm (not) ...	Ja (ni)sam ...	ya (nee·)sam ...
annoyed	uznemiren/	ooz·ne·mee·ren/
	uznemirena m/f	ooz·ne·mee·re·na
disappointed	razočaran/	ra·zaw·cha·ran
	razočarana m/f	ra·zaw·cha·ra·na
embarrassed	posramljen/	paw·sram·lyen
	posramljena m/f	paw·sram·lye·na
happy	sretan/sretna m/f	sre·tan/sret·na
hungry	gladan/gladna m/f	gla·dan/glad·na
sad	tužan/tužna m/f	too·zhan/toozh·na
surprised	iznenađen/	eez·ne·na·jen/
	iznenađena m/f	eez·ne·na·je·na
thirsty	žedan/žedna m/f	zhe·dan/zhed·na
tired	umoran/	oo·maw·ran/
	umorna m/f	oo·mawr·na
worried	zabrinut/	za·bree·noot/
	zabrinuta m/f	za·bree·noo·ta

Are you hot/cold?
  Je li vam toplo/hladno? pol   ye lee vam *taw*·plaw/*hlad*·naw
  Je li ti toplo/hladno? inf   ye lee tee *taw*·plaw/*hlad*·naw

I'm (not) hot/cold.
  Meni (ni)je toplo/hladno.   *me*·nee (*nee*·)ye *taw*·plaw/*hlad*·naw

And how are you?
  A kako ste vi? pol   a *ka*·kaw ste vee
  A kako si ti? inf   a *ka*·kaw see tee

If feeling unwell, see **health**, page 177.

mixed emotions

a little	*malo*	*ma*·law
I'm a little sad.	*Malo sam tužan/ tužna.* m/f	*ma*·law sam *too*·zhan/ *toozh*·na
extremely	*krajnje*	*krai*·nye
I'm extremely sorry.	*Krajnje mi je žao.*	*krai*·nye mee ye *zha*·aw
very	*vrlo*	*vr*·law
I feel very lucky.	*Osjećam se vrlo sretno.*	*aw*·sye·cham se *vr*·law *sret*·naw

opinions

mišljenja

Did you like it?
Da li vam/ti se svidjelo? pol/inf — da lee vam/tee se *svee*·dye·law

I thought it was ...	*Mislio/Mislila sam da je bilo ...* m/f	*mee*·slee·aw/*mee*·slee·la sam da ye *bee*·law ...
It's ...	*Ovo je ...*	*aw*·vaw ye ...
awful	*užasno*	*oo*·zha·snaw
beautiful	*lijepo*	lee·*ye*·paw
boring	*dosadno*	*daw*·sad·naw
great	*odlično*	*awd*·leech·naw
interesting	*zanimljivo*	za·*neem*·lyee·vaw
OK	*OK*	*aw*·key
original	*originalno*	aw·ree·gee·*nal*·naw
strange	*neobično*	ne·aw·*beech*·naw

politics & social issues

You should anticipate being drawn into animated discussions on aspects of the recent conflict in the former Yugoslavia as the horrors of war are still very much alive in people's minds. Locals will seize the opportunity of converting you to the Croatian cause. Unless you enjoy very heated debates, you're best advised to stay in the role of nonjudgmental listener.

Who do you vote for?
   Za koga glasate/   za *kaw*·ga *gla*·sa·te/
   glasaš? pol/inf   *gla*·sash

I support the	*Ja sam pristaša*	ya sam *pree*·sta·sha
... party.	*... stranke.*	*... stran*·ke
I'm a member	*Ja sam član*	ya sam chlan
of the ... party.	*... stranke.*	*... stran*·ke
communist	*komunističke*	kaw·moo·*nee*·steech·ke
conservative	*konzervativne*	*kawn*·zer·va·teev·ne
democratic	*demokratske*	de·*maw*·krat·ske
farmers'	*seljačke*	se·lyach·ke
green	*zelene*	ze·le·ne
Istrian	*istarske*	ee·star·ske
regionalist	*regionalističke*	re·gee·aw·na·*lee*·steech·ke
liberal	*liberalne*	*lee*·be·ral·ne
(progressive)		
social	*socijal-*	saw·tsee·*yal*·
democratic	*demokratske*	de·*maw*·krat·ske
socialist	*socijalističke*	saw·tsee·ya·*lee*·steech·ke

Did you hear about ...?
   Jeste li čuli za ...? pol   ye·ste lee *choo*·lee za ...
   Jesi li čuo/čula za ...? inf m/f   ye·see lee *choo*·aw/*choo*·la za ...

Do you agree with it?
   Da li podržavate/   da lee paw·*dr*·zha·va·te/
   podržavaš to? pol/inf   paw·*dr*·zha·vash taw

I (don't) agree with ...
   Ja (ne) podržavam ...   ya (ne) paw·*dr*·zha·vam ...

How do people	Kako ljudi	ka·kaw lyoo·dee
feel about …?	gledaju na …?	gle·dai·oo na …
abortion	indicirani	een·dee·tsee·ra·nee
	abortus	a·bawr·toos
admission	primanje u	pree·ma·nye oo
into the EU	Europsku	e·oo·rawp·skoo
	uniju	oo·nee·yoo
animal rights	prava	pra·va
	životinja	zhee·vaw·tee·nya
crime	kriminal	kree·mee·nal
the economy	privredu	preev·re·doo
education	obrazovanje	aw·bra·zaw·va·nye
equal	jednake	yed·na·ke
opportunity	mogućnosti	maw·gooch·naw·stee
euthanasia	eutanaziju	e·oo·ta·na·zee·yoo
globalisation	globalizaciju	glaw·ba·lee·za·tsee·yoo
human rights	ljudska prava	lyood·ska pra·va
immigration	imigraciju	ee·mee·gra·tsee·yoo
racism	rasnu	ra·snoo
	netrpeljivost	ne·tr·pe·lyee·vawst
the return of	povratak ratnih	paw·vra·tak rat·neeh
war refugees	izbjeglica	eez·bye·glee·tsa
sexism	spolnu	spawl·noo
	diskriminaciju	dee·skree·mee·na·tsee·yoo
unemployment	nezaposlenost	ne·za·paw·sle·nawst

hot topics

If you really have a burning curiosity to learn more about Croatian attitudes to the recent conflict in the former Yugoslavia and its aftermath, you could try out the phrase below. Best not to trot it out in a slivovitz-fuelled context as the passions aroused could be strong enough on their own.

How do people feel about the extradition of generals to the international war-crimes tribunal in the Hague?

Kako ljudi gledaju na	ka·kaw lyoo·dee gle·dai·oo na
isporuku generala	ee·spaw·roo·koo ge·ne·ra·la
međunarodnom sudu	me·joo·na·rawd·nawm soo·doo
za ratne zločine u Hagu?	za rat·ne zlaw·chee·ne oo ha·goo

the environment

Is there a … problem here?
Postoji li ovdje   paw·stoy·ee lee awv·dye
problem …?   praw·blem …

What should be done about …?
Što bi trebalo   shtaw bee tre·ba·law
učiniti u vezi …?   oo·chee·nee·tee oo ve·zee …

acid rain	*kisele kiše* f pl	kee·se·le *kee*·she
conservation	*zaštita*	zash·tee·ta
	okoliša f	aw·kaw·lee·sha
drought	*suša* f	soo·sha
ecosystem	*ekosustav* m	e·kaw·soo·stav
endangered	*ugrožene*	oo·graw·zhe·ne
species	*vrste* n	vr·ste
hunting	*lov na životinje* m	lawv na zhee·*vaw*·tee·nye
hydroelectricity	*hidroelektrane* n	hee·draw·e·lek·*tra*·ne
irrigation	*navodnjavanje* n	na·vawd·*nya*·va·nye
nuclear energy/	*nuklearna energija/*	noo·kle·ar·na e·*ner*·gee·ya/
testing	*testiranja* f	te·*stee*·ra·nya
ozone layer	*ozonski*	aw·zawn·skee
	omotač m	aw·maw·*tach*
pesticides	*pesticidi* m pl	pe·stee·*tsee*·dee
marine algae	*pošast morskih*	paw·shast *mawr*·skeeh
	algi m	al·gee
pollution	*zagađenje* n	za·ga·*je*·nye
protection of	*zaštita morske*	zash·tee·ta *mawr*·ske
marine flora	*flore i faune* f	flaw·re ee fa·oo·ne
and fauna		
recycling	*plan za preradu*	plan za *pre*·ra·doo
program	*otpadaka* m	awt·pa·da·ka
subterranean	*podzemne*	pawd·zem·ne
waterways	*vode* f pl	vaw·de
toxic waste	*toksični otpad* m	tawk·seech·nee awt·pad
water supply	*vodovod* m	vaw·daw·vawd
timber	*djelatnosti drvne*	dye·*lat*·naw·stee drv·ne
industry	*industrije* f pl	een·*doo*·stree·ye

Is this a protected ...?	Je li ovo ...?	ye lee *aw*·vaw ...
forest	zaštićena šuma	*zash*·tee·che·na *shoo*·ma
park	zaštićen park	*zash*·tee·chen park
species	zaštićena vrsta	*zash*·tee·che·na *vr*·sta

colourful Croatian

Croatian speakers can draw on a rich variety of swear words and obscene expressions to make their feelings plainly felt.

Swearing in any language tends to be very idiomatic and difficult to translate, but even the most hardened Anglophone might blanch at the graphic nature of Croatian swearing. However, what might sound like a string of unbelievable obscenities to an English speaker is not quite as bad as it sounds to Croatian speakers for whom colourful swearing is an intrinsic part of the language.

If you're exposed to some colourful Croatian you may even find it quite amusing and it's best not to take offence, as this may not be the swearer's intention.

In this chapter phrases are given in the informal *ti* forms. If you're not sure what this means, see the **a-z phrasebuilder**, page 24.

where to go

gdje izaći

What's there to do in the evenings?
Što se može raditi   shtaw se *maw*·zhe ra·dee·tee
uvečer?   oo·ve·cher

What's on …?	*Što se događa …?*	shtaw se *daw*·ga·ja …
locally	*u ovom mjestu*	oo *aw*·vawm *mye*·stoo
this weekend	*ovoga vikenda*	aw·vaw·ga vee·ken·da
today	*danas*	da·nas
tonight	*večeras*	ve·che·ras

Where can I find …?	*Gdje mogu pronaći …?*	gdye *maw*·goo praw·*na*·chee …
clubs	*noćne klubove*	*nawch*·ne *kloo*·baw·ve
gay venues	*'gay' lokale*	gey law·*ka*·le
places to eat	*ugostiteljske lokale*	oo·*gaw*·stee·tel'·ske law·*ka*·le
pubs	*gostionice*	gaw·stee·*aw*·nee·tse

Is there a local … guide?	*Postoji li mjesni vodič kroz …?*	*paw*·stoy·ee lee *mye*·snee *vaw*·deech krawz …
entertainment	*zbivanja u svijetu razonode*	*zbee*·va·nya oo svee·*ye*·too ra·zaw·*naw*·de
event	*predstojeća zbivanja*	pred·*stoy*·e·cha *zbee*·va·nya
film	*filmske novosti*	*feelm*·ske *naw*·vaw·stee
gay	*'gay' aktivnosti*	gey ak·*teev*·naw·stee
music	*glazbu*	*glaz*·boo

I feel like going to a ...	Želim otići ...	zhe·leem aw·tee·chee ...
ballet	na balet	na ba·let
bar	u bar	oo bar
café	u kafić	oo ka·feech
concert	na koncert	na kawn·tsert
disco	u disko	oo dee·skaw
festival	na festival	na fe·stee·val
film	na prikazivanje filma	na pree·ka·zee·va·nye feel·ma
hotel for terrace dancing	u hotel sa plesnom terasom	oo haw·tel sa ple·snawm te·ra·sawm
karaoke bar	u karaoke bar	oo ka·ra·aw·ke bar
nightclub	u noćni klub	oo nawch·nee kloob
party	na zabavu	na za·ba·voo
performance	na priredbu	na pree·red·boo
play	na predstavu	na pred·sta·voo
pub	u gostionicu	oo gaw·stee·aw·nee·tsoo
restaurant	u restoran	oo re·staw·ran

For more on eateries, bars and drinks, see **eating out**, page 145.

invitations

pozivanje nekoga na nešto

Would you like to go (for a/an) ...? m/f	Da li bi htio/ htjela otići na ...?	da lee bee htee·aw/ htye·la aw·tee·chee na ...
I feel like going (for a/an) ...	Ja želim otići na ...	ya zhe·leem aw·tee·chee na ...
coffee	kavu	ka·voo
dancing	ples	ples
drink	piće	pee·che
ice cream	sladoled	sla·daw·led
meal	ručak	roo·chak

What are you doing …?	Što radiš …?	shtaw *ra*·deesh …
now	trenutno	*tre*·noot·naw
this weekend	ovoga vikenda	*aw*·vaw·ga vee·ken·da
tonight	večeras	ve·*che*·ras

I feel like going out somewhere.
Ja želim ići ya *zhe*·leem ee·chee
negdje vani. ne·gdye va·nee

I feel like going for a walk.
Ja želim ići u šetnju. ya *zhe*·leem ee·chee oo *shet*·nyoo

Do you know a good restaurant?
Da li znaš dobar da lee znash *daw*·bar
restoran? re·*staw*·ran

Do you want to come to the concert with me?
Da li bi htio/htjela ići da lee bee *htee*·aw/*htye*·la ee·chee
samnom na koncert. m/f *sam*·nawm na *kawn*·tsert

We're having a party.
Planiramo napraviti *pla*·nee·ra·maw *na*·pra·vee·tee
zabavu. za·ba·voo

You should come.
Ti si pozvan/pozvana. m/f tee see *pawz*·van/*pawz*·va·na

responding to invitations

Sure!
Svakako! *sva*·ka·kaw

Yes, I'd love to.
Da, volio/voljela bih. m/f da, *vaw*·lee·aw/*vaw*·lye·la beeh

That's very kind of you.
To je baš lijepo od tebe. taw ye bash lee·*ye*·paw awd *te*·be

Where shall we go?
Gdje bismo mogli otići? gdye *bee*·smaw *maw*·glee *aw*·tee·chee

going out

115

No, I'm afraid I can't.
  Ne, nažalost ne mogu.   ne, *na*·zha·lawst ne *maw*·goo

What about tomorrow?
  A kako bi bilo sutra?   a *ka*·kaw bee *bee*·law *soo*·tra

Sorry, I can't sing/dance.
  Oprosti, ali ja ne   aw·*praw*·stee, *a*·lee ya ne
  znam pjevati/plesati.   znam *pye*·va·tee/*ple*·sa·tee

arranging to meet

ugovaranje sastanka

What time will we meet?
  U koje vrijeme ćemo   oo *koy*·e vree·*ye*·me *che*·maw
  se naći?   se *na*·chee

Where will we meet?
  Gdje ćemo se naći?   gdye *che*·maw se *na*·chee

Let's meet …   *Hajde da*   *hai*·de da
                       se nađemo …   se *na*·je·maw …
  at (eight) o'clock   *u (osam) sati*   oo (*aw*·sam) *sa*·tee
  at (the entrance)   *na (ulazu)*   na (oo·la·zoo)

I'll pick you up.
  Ja ću te pokupiti.   ya choo te *paw*·koo·pee·tee

Are you ready?
  Jesi li spreman/spremna? m/f   *ye*·see lee *spre*·man/*sprem*·na

I'm ready.
  Ja sam spreman/   ya sam *spre*·man/
  spremna. m/f   *sprem*·na

I'll be coming later.
  Ja ću ti se   ya choo tee se
  pridružiti kasnije.   pree·*droo*·zhee·tee *ka*·snee·ye

SOCIAL

116

Croatian rhythms

dalmatinska a　　　　　dal·*ma*·teen·ska a
cappella klapa　　　　　ka·*pe*·la *kla*·pa

male a cappella choral singing from the Dalmatian coast
whose main motifs are love, wine and love of homeland.
Klapa is still very much a living tradition and is often sung
in company over food and wine.

diple i mih　　　　　　*dee*·ple ee meeh

traditional Istrian triangular bagpipes with a less piercing
sound than Scottish bagpipes

kolo　　　　　　　　　*kaw*·law

lively Slavic dance in which men and/or women hold hands
in either a circle or line and dance to the accompaniment of
an accordion, violins or the *tamburica*

roženice/sopile　　　　raw·zhe·*nee*·tse/saw·*pee*·le

traditional Istrian two-stem reed pipe with a very pene-
trating oboe-like sound

tamburica　　　　　　　tam·boo·*ree*·tsa

type of three-string or five-string mandolin popular in
inland Croatia which has also given its name to a musical
style centred around idyllic themes of love and village life

zagorske i　　　　　　　za·*gawr*·ske ee
međimurske popevke　me·jee·moor·ske paw·*pev*·ke

traditional melancholic folk songs from the regions of
Zagorje and Međimurje, with alternating monophonic
and polyphonic segments

Where will you be?
　Gdje ćeš ti biti?　　　　gdye chesh tee *bee*·tee

If I'm not there by (nine), don't wait for me.
　Ako ne budem tamo do　　*a*·kaw ne *boo*·dem *ta*·maw daw
　(devet), nemoj me čekati.　(*de*·vet) *ne*·moy me *che*·ka·tee

OK!
　OK!　　　　　　　　　　aw·*key*

I'll see you then.
　Vidimo se tada.　　　　*vee*·dee·maw se *ta*·da

See you later/tomorrow.
Vidimo se kasnije/
sutra.
vee·dee·maw se *ka*·snee·ye/
soo·tra

I'm looking forward to it.
Jedva čekam.
ye·dva *che*·kam

Sorry I'm late.
Oprosti što kasnim.
aw·*praw*·stee shtaw *ka*·sneem

Never mind.
Nije važno.
nee·ye *vazh*·naw

drugs

I don't take drugs.
Ja ne koristim droge.
ya ne *kaw*·ree·steem *draw*·ge

I take ... occasionally.
Ja koristim ... ponekad.
ya *kaw*·ree·steem ... *paw*·ne·kad

Do you want to have a smoke?
Hoćeš zapaliti?
haw·chesh za·*pa*·lee·tee

Do you have a light?
Imaš li vatre?
ee·mash lee *va*·tre

In this chapter phrases are given in the informal *ti* forms. If you're not sure what this means, see the **a–z phrasebuilder**, page 24.

asking someone out

kako nekoga pitati da sa vama izađe

Where would you like to go (tonight)?
Gdje bi htio/htjela gdye bee *htee*·aw/*htye*·la
izaći (večeras)? m/f ee·*za*·chee (ve·*che*·ras)

Would you like to do something (tomorrow)?
Da li bi htio/htjela da lee bee *htee*·aw/*htye*·la
samnom nešto raditi *sam*·nawm *nesh*·taw *ra*·dee·tee
(sutra)? m/f (*soo*·tra)

Yes, I'd love to.
Da, to bih baš volio/ da, taw beeh bash *vaw*·lee·aw/
voljela. m/f *vaw*·lye·la

Sorry, I can't.
Žao mi je, ali ne mogu. *zha*·aw mee ye *a*·lee ne *maw*·goo

pick-up lines

fraze udvaranja

Would you like a drink?
Mogu li ti kupiti *maw*·goo lee tee *koo*·pee·tee
piće? *pee*·che

You look like someone I know.
Ličiš na nekoga *lee*·cheesh na *ne*·kaw·ga
koga znam. *kaw*·ga znam

You're a fantastic dancer.
Krasno plešeš. *kra*·snaw *ple*·shesh

You were made for me.
  Stvoren/Stvorena   stvaw·ren/stvaw·re·na
  si za mene. m/f   see za *me*·ne

You blow me away.
  Obaraš me s nogu.   aw·ba·rash me s *naw*·goo

Can I …?   *Mogu li …?*   *maw*·goo lee …
  dance with you   *dobiti ovaj ples*   *daw*·bee·tee aw·vai ples
  sit here   *ovdje sjesti*   *awv*·dye *sye*·stee
  take you home   *te ispratiti*   te ee·spra·tee·tee
     kući   *koo*·chee

rejections

nepoželjno udvaranje

I'm here with my boyfriend.
  Ovdje sam sa   *awv*·dye sam sa
  svojom curom.   *svoy*·awm *tsoo*·rawm

I'm here with my girlfriend.
  Ovdje sam sa   *awv*·dye sam sa
  svojim dečkom.   *svoy*·eem *dech*·kawm

Excuse me, I have to go now.
  Oprosti, ali sada   aw·*praw*·stee *a*·lee sa·da
  stvarno žurim.   *stvar*·naw *zhoo*·reem

giving someone the flick

Leave me alone!
  Ostavi me na miru!   aw·sta·vee me na *mee*·roo

Don't touch me!
  Ne dodiruj me!   ne daw·*dee*·rooy me

Please control yourself.
  Molim te obuzdaj se.   *maw*·leem te aw·*booz*·dai se

Piss off!
  Odjebi!   aw·*dye*·bee

local talk

He's a babe.
On je super frajer.   awn ye *soo*-per *frai*-er

She's a babe.
Ona je super frajerica.   *aw*-na ye *soo*-per frai-e-ree-tsa

He's hot.
On je privlačan.   awn ye *preev*-lach-an

She's hot.
Ona je privlačna.   *aw*-na ye *preev*-lach-na

He's a bastard.
On je nitkov.   awn ye *neet*-kawv

She's a bitch.
Ona je pokvarena.   *aw*-na ye *pawk*-va-re-na

He gets around.
On je kurver.   awn ye *koor*-ver

She gets around.
Ona je drolja.   *aw*-na ye *draw*-lya

I'd rather not.
Radije nebih.   ra-dee-ye *ne*-beeh

No, thank you.
Ne, hvala ti.   ne, *hva*-la tee

Who do you think you are?
Što si ti umišljaš?   shtaw see tee oo-*meesh*-lyash

getting closer

zbližavanje

I like you very much.
Jako mi se sviđaš.   *ya*-kaw mee se *svee*-jash

You're great.
Super si.   *soo*-per see

Can I kiss you?
Smijem li te poljubiti?   *smee*-yem lee te paw-*lyoo*-bee-tee

romance

121

Do you want to come inside for a while?

Da li želiš ući   da lee *zhe*·leesh *oo*·chee
na kratko?   na *krat*·kaw

Do you want a massage?

Hoćeš masažu?   *haw*·chesh ma·*sa*·zhoo

Can I stay over?

Mogu li ostati kod   *maw*·goo lee *aw*·sta·tee kawd
tebe večeras?   *te*·be ve·*che*·ras

sex

Kiss me.

Poljubi me.   paw·*lyoo*·bee me

I want you.

Želim te.   *zhe*·leem te

Let's go to bed.

Idemo u krevet.   *ee*·de·maw oo *kre*·vet

Touch me here.

Dodirni me tu.   daw·*deer*·nee me too

Do you like this?

Da li ti se to sviđa?   da lee tee se taw *svee*·ja

I (don't) like that.

(Ne) sviđa mi se to.   (ne) *svee*·ja mee se taw

I think we should stop now.

Mislim da bi sada   *mee*·sleem da bee *sa*·da
trebali stati.   *tre*·ba·lee *sta*·tee

Do you have a (condom)?

Imaš li (prezervativ)?   *ee*·mash lee (pre·zer·va·*teev*)

Let's use a (condom).

Hajde da stavimo   *hai*·de da *sta*·vee·maw
(prezervativ).   (pre·zer·va·*teev*)

I won't do it without protection.

Ne želim dalje bez zaštite.   ne *zhe*·leem *da*·lye bez *zash*·tee·te

It's my first time.
   Ovo mi je prvi put.   *aw*·vaw mee ye *pr*·vee poot

It helps to have a sense of humour.
   Smisao za humor   *smee*·sa·aw za *hoo*·mawr
   pomaže.   *paw*·ma·zhe

Oh my god!
   O bože!   aw *baw*·zhe

That's great.
   To je predivno.   taw ye *pre*·deev·naw

Easy tiger!
   Lakše malo mačore!   *lak*·she *ma*·law *ma*·chaw·re

That was ...	*Bilo je ...*	*bee*·law ye ...
amazing	*prekrasno*	*pre*·kra·snaw
romantic	*romantično*	raw·*man*·teech·naw
wild	*strastveno*	*strast*·ve·naw

pillow talk

Whisper sweet nothings to your love with these terms of endearment. The words 'my fawn' and 'my little kitten' are usually reserved for women.

my candy	*slatkišu*	slat·*kee*·shoo
my dear	*dragi/draga* m/f	dra·gee/dra·ga
my fawn	*lane moje*	*la*·ne moy·e
my joy	*srećo moja*	*sre*·chaw moy·a
my little kitten	*mače moje malo*	*ma*·che moy·e *ma*·law
my love	*ljubavi moja*	lyoo·ba·vee moy·a
my soul	*dušo moja*	doo·shaw moy·a
my treasure	*zlato moje*	*zla*·taw moy·e

romance

love

I love you.
Volim te. vaw·leem te

I think we're good together.
Mislim da smo dobar par. mee·sleem da smaw daw·bar par

Will you …?	*Da li hoćeš …?*	da lee *haw*·chesh …
go out with me	samnom	*sam*·nawm
	izlaziti	*eez*·la·zee·tee
marry me	udati se	oo·da·tee se
	za mene	za *me*·ne
meet my	upoznati	oo·*pawz*·na·tee
parents	moje roditelje	*moy*·e *raw*·dee·te·lye

problems

Are you seeing someone else?
Viđaš li nekoga drugog? vee·jash lee *ne*·kaw·ga *droo*·gawg

You're just using me for sex.
Ti me samo koristiš za seks. tee me *sa*·maw *kaw*·ree·steesh za seks

I don't think it's working out.
Mislim da nam ne ide. mee·sleem da nam ne *ee*·de

We'll work it out.
Riješit ćemo probleme. ree·*ye*·sheet *che*·maw praw·*ble*·me

I never want to see you again.
Ne želim te više nikada vidjeti. ne *zhe*·leem te *vee*·she *nee*·ka·da *vee*·dye·tee

SOCIAL

beliefs & cultural differences

vjerovanja i kulturne razlike

religion

What's your religion?
Koje ste/si vjere? pol/inf   *kaw*·ye ste/see *vye*·re

I'm ...	*Ja sam ...*	ya sam ...
agnostic	*agnostik* m&f	ag·*naw*·steek
Buddhist	*budist(kinja)* m/f	boo·*deest*(·kee·nya)
Catholic	*katolik/*	ka·*taw*·leek/
	katolkinja m/f	ka·tawl·kee·nya
Christian	*kršćanin/*	krsh·cha·neen/
	kršćanka m/f	krsh·chan·ka
Hindu	*hindu* m&f	heen·*doo*
Jewish	*Židov(ka)* m/f	zhee·*dawv*(·ka)
Muslim	*musliman(ka)* m/f	moo·*slee*·man(·ka)
Orthodox	*pravoslavac/*	pra·vaw·*sla*·vats/
	pravoslavka m/f	pra·vaw·*slav*·ka
Protestant	*protestant(kinja)* m/f	praw·te·*stant*(·kee·nya)
Roman	*rimski katolik/*	*reem*·skee ka·*taw*·leek/
Catholic	*rimska katolkinja* m/f	*reem*·ska ka·tawl·kee·nya
Greek	*grko-katolik/*	gr·kaw·ka·*taw*·leek/
Catholic	*grko-katolkinja* m/f	gr·kaw·ka·tawl·kee·nya

I (don't) believe in ...	*Ja (ne) vjerujem u ...*	ya (ne) *vye*·roo·yem oo ...
astrology	*astrologiju*	a·straw·*law*·gee·yoo
fate	*sudbinu*	*sood*·bee·noo
God	*boga*	*baw*·ga

Where can I attend ...?	*Gdje mogu otići ...?*	gdye *maw*·goo aw·*tee*·che ...
mass	*na misu*	na *mee*·soo
a service	*na obred*	na *aw*·bred

Where can I pray/worship?
Gdje se mogu moliti? gdye se *maw*·goo *maw*·lee·tee

Can I pray/worship here?
Da li se mogu da lee se *maw*·goo
ovdje pomoliti? *awv*·dye paw·*maw*·lee·tee

I didn't mean to do anything wrong.
Nisam htio/htjela nee·sam *htee*·aw/*htye*·la
uraditi ništa krivo. m/f oo·*ra*·dee·tee *neesh*·ta *kree*·vaw

cultural differences

Is this a local or national custom?
Je li ovo mjesni ili ye lee *aw*·vaw *mye*·snee *ee*·lee
nacionalni običaj? na·tsee·aw·*nal*·nee *aw*·bee·chai

I don't want to offend you.
Ne želim vas/te ne *zhe*·leem vas/te
uvrijediti. pol/inf oo·vree·*ye*·dee·tee

I'm not used to this.
Nisam na ovo *nee*·sam na *aw*·vaw
navikao/navikla. m/f na·*vee*·ka·aw/na·*vee*·kla

I'd rather not join in.
Ja radije nebih ya *ra*·dee·ye *ne*·beeh
sudjelovao/ *soo*·dye·law·va·aw/
sudjelovala. m/f *soo*·dye·law·va·la

I'll try it.
Ja ću to probati. ya choo taw *praw*·ba·tee

I'm sorry, it's against my beliefs.
Žao mi je, ali to *zha*·aw mee ye *a*·lee taw
je protivno mojim ye *praw*·teev·naw *moy*·eem
vjerovanjima. vye·*raw*·va·nyee·ma

This is …	*Ovo je …*	*aw*·vaw ye …
different	*neobično*	ne·aw·*beech*·naw
fun	*zabavno*	*za*·bav·naw
interesting	*zanimljivo*	za·*neem*·lyee·vaw

When's the ... open?	Kada je ... otvoren/ otvorena? m/f	ka·da ye ... aw·tvaw·ren/ aw·tvaw·re·na
church	crkva f	tsr·kva
gallery	galerija f	ga·le·ree·ya
museum	muzej m	moo·zey

What kind of art are you interested in?
Koja vrsta umjetnosti vas/te zanima? pol/inf — kaw·ya vr·sta oo·myet·naw·stee vas/te za·nee·ma

What do you think of ...?
Kako doživljavate/ doživljavaš ...? pol/inf — ka·kaw daw·zheev·lya·va·te/ daw·zheev·lya·vash ...

What's in the collection?
Što sadrži ta zbirka? — shtaw sa·dr·zhee ta zbeer·ka

It's an exhibition of ...
Ova izložba je za ... — aw·va eez·lawzh·ba ye za ...

I'm interested in ...
Zainteresiran/ Zainteresirana sam za ... m/f — za·een·te·re·see·ran/ za·een·te·re·see·ra·na sam za ...

I like the works of ...
Sviđaju mi se djela koja spadaju pod ... — svee·ja·yoo mee se dye·la kaw·ya spa·dai·oo pawd ...

architecture	arhitektura f	ar·hee·tek·too·ra
artwork	umjetničko djelo n	oo·myet·neech·kaw dye·law
curator	kurator m	koo·ra·tawr
design	dizajn m	dee·zain
etching	gravura f	gra·voo·ra
exhibit	izložak predmet m	eez·law·zhak pred·met
exhibition hall	izložna dvorana f	eez·lawzh·na dvaw·ra·na

installation	instalacija f	een·sta·la·tsee·ya
opening	otvaranje n	awt·va·ra·nye
painter	slikar m	slee·kar
painting (the art)	slika f	slee·ka
painting (canvas)	slikanje n	slee·ka·nye
period	razdoblje n	raz·dawb·lye
permanent collection	stalna zbirka f	stal·na zbeer·ka
print	kopija f	kaw·pee·ya
sculptor	kipar m	kee·par
sculpture	skulptura f	skoolp·too·ra
statue	kip m	keep
studio	atelje m	a·te·lye
style	stil m	steel
technique	tehnika f	teh·nee·ka

... art	... umjetnost	... oo·myet·nawst
baroque	barokna	ba·rawk·na
Byzantine	bizantinska	bee·zan·teen·ska
expressionist	ekspresionistička	eks·pre·see·aw·nee·steech·ka
Gothic	gotička	gaw·teech·ka
graphic	grafička	gra·feech·ka
impressionist	impresionistička	eem·pre·see·aw·nee·steech·ka
minimalist	minimalistička	mee·nee·ma·lee·steech·ka
modern	moderna	maw·der·na
naive	naivna	na·eev·na
performance	kazališna	ka·za·leesh·na
pre-Romanesque	pred-Romanička	pred·raw·ma·neech·ka
Renaissance	Renesansna	re·ne·san·sna
Roman	Rimska	reem·ska
Romanesque	Romanička	raw·ma·neech·ka

In this chapter phrases are given in the informal *ti* forms. If you're not sure what this means, see the **a–z phrasebuilder**, page 24.

sporting interests

sportske zanimacije

What sport do you play?
Koji sport ti igraš?   koy·ee spawrt tee ee·grash

What sport do you follow?
Koji sport ti pratiš?   koy·ee spawrt tee pra·teesh

I play/do ...	Ja igram/	ya ee·gram/
	treniram ...	tre·nee·ram ...
I follow ...	Ja pratim ...	ya pra·teem ...
athletics	atletiku	at·le·tee·koo
basketball	košarku	kaw·shar·koo
football (soccer)	nogomet	naw·gaw·met
handball	rukomet	roo·kaw·met
scuba diving	ronjenje sa	raw·nye·nye sa
	bocama	baw·tsa·ma
tennis	tenis	te·nees
volleyball	odbojku	awd·boy·koo
water polo	vaterpolo	va·ter·paw·law

I ...	Ja ...	ya ...
cycle	vozim bicikl	vaw·zeem bee·tsee·kl
run	trčim	tr·cheem
walk	hodam	haw·dam

For more sports, see the **dictionary**.

Who's your favourite team?
Koja je tvoja   koy·a ye tvoy·a
omiljena ekipa?   aw·mee·lye·na e·kee·pa

Who's your favourite sportsman?
Koji je tvoj omiljeni   *koy*·ee ye tvoy *aw*·mee·lye·nee
sportaš?   *spawr*·tash

Who's your favourite sportswoman?
Koja je tvoja omiljena   *koy*·a ye tvoy·a *aw*·mee·lye·na
sportašica ?   spawr·*ta*·shee·tsa

Do you like (basketball)?
Voliš li (košarku)?   *vaw*·leesh lee (*kaw*·shar·koo)

Yes, very much.
Da, vrlo.   da, *vr*·law

Not really.
Ne baš.   ne bash

I like watching it.
Ja ga volim gledati.   ya ga *vaw*·leem *gle*·da·tee

going to a game

odlazak na utakmicu

Would you like to go to a game?
Da li bi išao/išla   da lee bee *ee*·sha·aw/*eesh*·la
na utakmicu? m/f   na *oo*·tak·mee·tsoo

Who are you supporting?
Za koga naviјaš?   za *kaw*·ga na·vee·yash

Who's playing/winning?
Tko igra/pobjeđuje?   tkaw *ee*·gra/paw·*bye*·joo·ye

scoring		
What's the score?		
Koji je rezultat?		*koy*·ee ye re·*zool*·tat
draw/even	*neodlučeno/*	ne·*awd*·loo·che·naw/
	neriješeno	ne·ree·ye·she·naw
match-point	*odlučujući*	awd·*loo*·choo·yoo·chee
	poen m	paw·*en*
nil (zero)	*nula* f	*noo*·la

That was a …	Bila je to …	bee·la ye taw …
game!	utakmica!	oo·tak·mee·tsa
bad	loša	law·sha
boring	dosadna	daw·sad·na
great	sjajna	syai·na

sports talk

What a …!	Kakav …!	ka·kav …
goal	gol	gawl
hit	pogodak	paw·gaw·dak
kick	šut	shoot
pass	dobačaj	daw·ba·chai
performance	nastup	na·stoop

playing sport

igranje sporta

Do you want to play?
Hoćeš igrati?
haw·ches ee·gra·te

Can I join in?
Mogu li se pridružiti?
maw·goo lee se pree·droo·zhee·tee

That would be great.
To bi bilo super.
taw bee bee·law soo·per

I can't.
Ja ne mogu.
ya ne maw·goo

My/Your point.
Mo/Tvoj poen.
moy/tvoy paw·en

Kick/Pass it to me!
Šutni/Dodaj meni!
shoot·nee/daw·dai me·nee

You're a good player.
Ti si dobar igrač. m
tee see daw·bar ee·grach
Ti si dobra igračica. f
tee see daw·bra ee·gra·chee·tsa

Thanks for the game.
Hvala na igri.
hva·la na ee·gree

Where's a good	Gdje je dobro	gdye ye *daw*·braw
place to go ...?	mjesto za ...?	*mye*·staw za ...
fishing	ribolov	*ree*·baw·lawv
horse riding	jahanje konja	*ya*·ha·nye *kaw*·nya
running	trčanje	*tr*·cha·nye
skiing	skijanje	*skee*·ya·nye
snorkeling	ronjenje s	*raw*·nye·nye s
	disalicom	*dee*·sa·lee·tsawm
surfing	daskanje na	*da*·ska·nye na
	valovima	*va*·law·vee·ma

Where's the	Gdje je ...	gdye ye ...
nearest ...?		
golf course	najbliži teren	*nai*·blee·zhee *te*·ren
	za golf	za gawlf
gym	najbliža teretana	*nai*·blee·zha te·re·*ta*·na
swimming pool	najbliži	*nai*·blee·zhee
	bazen za	*ba*·zen za
	plivanje	*plee*·va·nye
tennis court	najbliže tenisko	*nai*·blee·zhe *te*·nee·skaw
	igralište	ee·gra·*leesh*·te

What's the	Koja je cijena	*koy*·a ye tsee·*ye*·na
charge per ...?	po ...?	paw ...
day	danu	*da*·noo
game	utakmici	oo·*tak*·mee·tsee
hour	satu	*sa*·too
visit	posjeti	*paw*·sye·tee

Can I hire a ...?	Mogu li	*maw*·goo lee
	iznajmiti ...?	eez·*nai*·mee·tee ...
ball	loptu	*lawp*·too
bicycle	bicikl	bee·*tsee*·kl
court	igralište	ee·gra·*leesh*·te
racquet	reket	*re*·ket

Do I have to be a member to attend?

Da li moram biti član	da lee *maw*·ram *bee*·tee chlan
da bih prisustvovao/	da beeh *pree*·soost·vaw·va·aw/
prisustvovala? m/f	*pree*·soost·vaw·va·la

Is there a women-only session?
   Postoji li termin   paw·stoy·ee lee ter·meen
   samo za žene?   sa·maw za zhe·ne

Where are the changing rooms?
   Gdje su svlačionice?   gdye soo svla·chee·aw·nee·tse

diving

ronjenje

Is the visibility good?
   Da li je dobra vidljivost?   da lee ye daw·bra veed·lyee·vawst

How deep is the dive?
   Na koju se dubinu   na koy·oo se doo·bee·noo
   roni?   raw·nee

Is it a boat/shore dive?
   Da li je zaron sa   da lee ye za·rawn sa
   čamca/obale?   cham·tsa/aw·ba·le

I'd like to explore ...	*Želio/Željela bih ... istražiti* m/f	zhe·lee·aw/zhe·lye·la beeh ... ee·stra·zhee·tee
archaeological sites	*podvodna arheološka nalazišta*	pawd·vawd·na ar·he·aw·lawsh·ka na·la·zeesh·ta
caves/ wrecks	*podvodne spilje/olupine brodova*	pawd·vawd·ne spee·lye/aw·loo·pee·ne braw·daw·va
I'd like to go ...	*Želio/Željela bih ići ...* m/f	zhe·lee·aw/zhe·lye·la beeh ee·chee ...
night diving	*na noćno ronjenje*	na nawch·naw raw·nye·nye
scuba diving	*na ronjenje sa bocama*	na raw·nye·nye sa baw·tsa·ma
snorkelling	*na ronjenje sa disalicom*	na raw·nye·nye sa dee·sa·lee·tsawm
on a diving tour	*na ronilački izlet*	na raw·nee·lach·kee eez·let

sport

I'd like to ...	Želio/Željela bih ... m/f	zhe·lee·aw/zhe·lye·la beeh ...
learn to dive	naučiti roniti	na·oo·chee·tee raw·nee·tee
see sea walls	vidjeti morske nasipe	vee·dye·tee mawr·ske na·see·pe
I want to hire (a) ...	Želim iznajmiti ...	zhe·leem eez·nai·mee·tee ...
buoyancy vest	prsluk za spasavanje	pr·slook za spa·sa·va·nye
diving equipment	ronilačku opremu	raw·nee·lach·koo aw·pre·moo
flippers	peraje	pe·rai·e
mask	masku	ma·skoo
regulator	regulator	re·goo·la·tawr
snorkel	disalicu	dee·sa·lee·tsoo
tank	bocu	baw·tsoo
weight belt	olovni pojas	aw·lawv·nee poy·as
wetsuit	nepromočivo ronilačko odijelo	ne·praw·maw·chee·vaw raw·nee·lach·kaw aw·dee·ye·law
air fill	punjenje boca zrakom n	poo·nye·nye baw·tsa zra·kawm
dive (noun)	zaron m	za·rawn
dive (verb)	roniti	raw·nee·tee
diving boat	ronilački čamac m	raw·nee·lach·kee cha·mats
diving course	tečaj ronjenja m	te·chai raw·nye·nya

basketball

košarka

Who plays for (Cibona)?
Tko igra za (Cibonu)? tkaw ee·gra za (tsee·baw·noo)

He's a great (player).
On je odličan (igrač). awn ye awd·lee·chan (ee·grach)

Which team is the at the top of the league?
Koji je tim na čelu tablice? koy·ee ye teem na che·loo ta·blee·tse

back (position)	*bek* m	bek
ball	*lopta* f	*lawp*·ta
basket (structure)	*koš* m	kawsh
coach	*trener* m	*tre*·ner
double fault	*dupla greška* f	*doo*·pla *gresh*·ka
expulsion	*isključenje* n	ees·klyoo·*che*·nye
fan	*navijač* m	na·*vee*·yach
foul	*prekršaj* m	*pre*·kr·shai
free throw	*slobodno bacanje* n	*slaw*·bawd·naw *ba*·tsa·nye
jump-shot	*skok šut* m	skawk shoot
out	*aut* m	a·oot
player	*igrač* m	ee·grach
rebound	*odbitak* m	awd·*bee*·tak
referee	*sudac* m	soo·dats
skyhook shot	*horok* m	*haw*·rawk
slam-dunk	*zakucavanje* n	za·koo·*tsa*·va·nye
time-out	*pauza* f	*pa*·oo·za
travel	*koraci* m pl	*kaw*·ra·tsee

football/soccer

nogomet

Who plays for (Dinamo)?
Tko igra za (Dinamo)?   tkaw *ee*·gra za (*dee*·na·maw)

He's a great (goalkeeper).
On je odličan (vratar).   awn ye *awd*·lee·chan (*vra*·tar)

He played brilliantly in the match against (Italy).
On je sjajno odigrao utakmicu protiv (Italije).   awn ye *syai*·naw *aw*·dee·gra·aw *oo*·tak·mee·tsoo *praw*·teev (ee·*ta*·lee·ye)

sport

What a great/terrible team!
Kakav sjajan/užasan tim! ka·kav syai·an/oo·zha·san teem

ball	lopta f	lawp·ta
coach	trener m	tre·ner
corner (kick)	korner m	kawr·ner
expulsion	isključenje f	ees·klyoo·che·nye
fan	navijač m	na·vee·yach
foul	prekršaj m	pre·kr·shai
free kick	slobodni udarac m	slaw·bawd·nee oo·da·rats
goal	gol m	gawl
goalkeeper	vratar m	vra·tar
offside	ofsaid m	awf·sa·eed
penalty	penal m	pe·nal
player	igrač m	ee·grach
red card	crveni karton m	tsr·ve·nee kar·tawn
referee	sudac m	soo·dats
striker	napadač m	na·pa·dach
yellow card	žuti karton m	zhoo·tee kar·tawn

tennis

tenis

I'd like to play tennis.
Želim igrati tenis. zhe·leem ee·gra·tee te·nees

Can we play at night?
Možemo li igrati maw·zhe·maw lee ee·gra·tee
noću? naw·choo

I need my racquet restrung.
Trebam promjenu tre·bam praw·mye·noo
struna na mom reketu. stroo·na na mawm re·ke·too

SOCIAL

ace	*as* m	as
advantage	*prednost* f	*pred*·nawst
clay	*zemljana podloga* f	zem·lya·na *pawd*·law·ga
fault	*greška* f	*gresh*·ka
game, set, match	*gejm, set, meč* m	geym set mech
grass	*travnata podloga* f	*trav*·na·ta *pawd*·law·ga
hard court	*teniski teren sa*	te·nee·skee *te*·ren sa
	tvrdom	*tvr*·dawm
	podlogom m	*pawd*·law·gawm
net	*mreža* f	*mre*·zha
play doubles	*igrati u*	ee·gra·tee oo
	parovima	pa·raw·vee·ma
racquet	*reket* m	*re*·ket
serve	*servis* m	*ser*·vees
set	*set* m	set
tennis ball	*teniska loptica* f	te·nee·ska *lawp*·tee·tsa

water sports

sportovi na vodi

Can I book a lesson?
Mogu li zakazati — maw·goo lee za·*ka*·za·tee
sat obuke? — sat aw·boo·ke

Can I hire (a) …? *Mogu li* — maw·goo lee
iznajmiti …? — eez·*nai*·mee·tee …

boat	*čamac*	*cha*·mats
canoe	*kanu*	ka·*noo*
kayak	*kajak*	*kai*·ak
life jacket	*prsluk za*	*pr*·slook za
	spasavanje	spa·*sa*·va·nye
sea kayak	*morski kajak*	*mawr*·skee *kai*·ak
snorkelling	*ronilačku*	*raw*·nee·lach·koo
gear	*masku i*	*ma*·skoo ee
	disalicu	*dee*·sa·lee·tsoo
water-skis	*skije za vodu*	*skee*·ye za *vaw*·doo
wetsuit	*nepromočivo*	ne·praw·*maw*·chee·vaw
	podvodno	*pawd*·vawd·naw
	odijelo	aw·dee·*ye*·law

Are there any ...?	Da li ima kakvih ...?	da lee ee·ma kak·veeh ...
reefs	morskih grebenova	mawr·skeeh gre·be·naw·va
rips	jakih podvodnih struja	ya·keeh pawd·vawd·neeh stroo·ya
water hazards	opasnosti u vodi	aw·pa·snaw·stee oo vaw·dee

canoeing	kanuistika f	ka·noo·ee·stee·ka
guide	vodič m	vaw·deech
harbour master	lučki kapetan m	looch·kee ka·pe·tan
kayaking	kajakarenje n	kai·a·ka·re·nye
marina	marina f	ma·ree·na
motorboat	motorni čamac m	maw·tawr·nee cha·mats
oars	vesla n pl	ve·sla
port	luka f	loo·ka
sailing	jedrenje n	ye·dre·nye
sailing boat	jedrilica f	ye·dree·lee·tsa
surfboard	daska za surfanje f	da·ska za soor·fa·nye
surfing	daskanje na valovima n	da·ska·nye na va·law·vee·ma
swimming	plivanje n	plee·va·nye
wave	val m	val
water-skiing	skijanje na vodi n	skee·ya·nye na vaw·dee
windsurfing	jedrenje na dasci n	ye·dre·nye na das·tsee
yachting	krstarenje jahtom n	kr·sta·re·nye yah·tawm

For phrases about diving, see the **diving section**, page 133.
For phrases about hiking, see **outdoors**, page 139.

hiking

pješačenje

Where can I ...?	Gdje mogu ...?	gdye *maw*·goo ...
buy supplies	kupiti	koo·pee·tee
	namirnice	na·meer·nee·tse
find someone	naći nekoga	na·chee ne·kaw·ga
who knows	tko zna ovo	tkaw zna *aw*·vaw
this area	područje	paw·drooch·ye
get a map	nabaviti kartu	na·ba·vee·tee *kar*·too
hire hiking gear	iznajmiti	eez·*nai*·mee·tee
	opremu	*aw*·pre·moo
	za pješačenje	za pye·*sha*·che·nye

Do we need	Trebamo li	tre·ba·maw lee
to take ...?	ponijeti ...?	paw·nee·ye·tee ...
bedding	krevetninu	kre·vet·*nee*·noo
food	hranu	*hra*·noo
water	vodu	*vaw*·doo

How ...?	Koliko ...?	kaw·*lee*·kaw ...
high is the climb	je visok uspon	ye *vee*·sawk oo·spawn
long is the trail	dugačka staza	doo·gach·ka *sta*·za

Is there a hut?
Da li postoji   da lee *paw*·stoy·ee
planinarska koliba?   pla·*nee*·nar·ska *kaw*·lee·ba

When does it get dark?
Kada obično padne noć?   ka·da *aw*·beech·naw *pad*·ne nawch

Do we need a guide?
Treba li nam vodič?   tre·ba lee nam *vaw*·deech

Are there land mines in this area?
Da li ima mina   da lee *ee*·ma *mee*·na
na ovom području?   na *aw*·vawm *paw*·drooch·yoo

An unfortunate consequence of the recent war in the former Yugoslavia is the presence of land mines. Most mined areas are marked with warning signs which might have these words on them:

mine	*mee*·ne	**mines**
minirano	*mee*·nee·ra·naw	**mined**

Warning signs can be in the form of a red triangle with a black dot in the middle or depict a white skull and cross-bones against a red background. Unfortunately, warning signs are sometimes souvenired and mined areas may just be cordoned off with coloured plastic tape.

Less common improvised signs that you'll want to take close heed of if you venture off the beaten track include crossed tree branches or rock heaps by the road. Always be sure to check with the locals about the presence of land mines in their area and steer away from suspiciously deserted areas.

Is the track ...?	*Je li staza ...?*	ye lee *sta*·za ...
dangerous	*opasna*	*aw*·pa·sna
marked	*označena*	*aw*·zna·che·na
open	*otvorena*	*awt*·vaw·re·na
scenic	*panoramska*	pa·naw·*ram*·ska
Which is the ... route?	*Koji put je ...?*	*koy*·ee poot ye ...
easiest	*najlakši*	*nai*·lak·shee
shortest	*najkraći*	*nai*·kra·chee
Where can I find (a/the) ...?	*Gdje se ...?*	gdye se ...
campsite	*nalazi kamp*	na·la·zee kamp
nearest	*nalazi najbliže*	na·la·zee *nai*·blee·zhe
village	*selo*	*se*·law
showers	*nalaze tuševi*	na·la·ze *too*·she·vee
toilets	*nalaze zahodi*	na·la·ze *za*·haw·dee

Where have you come from?
Odakle dolazite/   aw·*da*·kle *daw*·la·zee·te/
dolaziš? pol/inf   *daw*·la·zeesh

How long did it take?
Koliko dugo je trebalo?   kaw·*lee*·kaw *doo*·gaw ye *tre*·ba·law

Does this path go to …?
Da li ovaj put vodi do …?   da lee *aw*·vai poot *vaw*·dee daw …

Is the water OK to drink?
Je li ova voda pitka?   ye lee *aw*·va *vaw*·da *peet*·ka

I'm lost.
Ja sam izgubljen/   ya sam eez·*goob*·lyen/
izgubljena. m/f   eez·*goob*·lye·na

beach

plaža

You may see a beach referred to as a *žal* (zhal) but the most common word is *plaža* (*pla*·zha). Beaches are an important focus for social life both day and night during the warmer months. Terrace dancing, *ples na terasama* (ples na te·*ra*·sa·ma), at beachside hotels is also a favourite summer pastime.

Where's the	*Gdje se nalazi*	gdye se *na*·la·zee
… beach?	*… plaža?*	… *pla*·zha
best	*najbolja*	*nai*·baw·lya
nearest	*najbliža*	*nai*·blee·zha
nudist	*nudistička*	noo·*dee*·steech·ka
public	*javna*	*yav*·na

signs

Zabranjen Ribolov	
za·bra·nyen *ree*·baw·lawv	**No Fishing**
Zabranjeno Plivanje	
za·bra·nye·naw *plee*·va·nye	**No Swimming**

141

bay	*uvala* f	*oo*·va·la
beach	*žal/plaža* f/m	zhal/*pla*·zha
cave	*spilja* f	*spee*·lya
channel	*kanal* m	*ka*·nal
cove	*dražica* f	dra·zhee·tsa
inlet	*draga* f	*dra*·ga
island	*otok* m	*aw*·tawk
lake	*jezero* n	*ye*·ze·raw
promontory	*rt* m	rt
reef	*morski greben* m	*mawr*·skee gre·ben

Is it safe to dive/swim here?

Da li je bezopasno   da lee ye *bez*·aw·pa·snaw
skakati/plivati ovdje?   *ska*·ka·tee/*plee*·va·tee *awv*·dye

What time is high/low tide?

U koliko sati je   oo kaw·*lee*·kaw *sa*·tee ye
plima/oseka?   *plee*·ma/*aw*·se·ka

Do we have to pay?

Trebamo li platiti?   *tre*·ba·maw lee *pla*·tee·tee

Could you put some sunscreen on my back, please?

Možete/Možeš li mi   *maw*·zhe·te/*maw*·zhesh lee mee
staviti kremu protiv   *sta*·vee·tee *kre*·moo *praw*·teev
sunca na leđa, molim? pol/inf   *soon*·tsa na *le*·ja *maw*·leem

How much for a/an …?	*Koliko stoji …?*	kaw·*lee*·kaw *stoy*·ee …
chair	*jedna stolica za sklapanje*	*yed*·na *staw*·lee·tsa za *skla*·pa·nye
hut	*jedna kućica*	*yed*·na *koo*·chee·tsa
umbrella	*jedan suncobran*	*ye*·dan *soon*·tsaw·bran

---

listen for …

aw·pa·snaw ye
    Opasno je!   **It's dangerous!**

pa·zee·te na *pawd*·vawd·noo pro·too·stroo·yoo
    Pazite na podvodnu   **Be careful of**
    protustruju!   **the undertow!**

weather

What's the weather like?
Kakvo je vrijeme? kak·vaw ye vree·ye·me

What will the weather be like tomorrow?
Kakvo će vrijeme kak·vaw che vree·ye·me
biti sutra? bee·tee soo·tra

It's ...   ... *je.*   ... ye
  cloudy   *Oblačno*   aw·blach·naw
  cold   *Hladno*   hlad·naw
  fine   *Vedro*   ve·draw
  freezing   *Ledeno*   le·de·naw
  hot   *Vruće*   vroo·che
  raining   *Kišovito*   kee·shaw·vee·taw
  snowing   *Snjegovito*   snye·gaw·vee·taw
  sunny   *Sunčano*   soon·cha·naw
  warm   *Toplo*   taw·plaw
  windy   *Vjetrovito*   vye·traw·vee·taw

flora & fauna

What ... is that?	... je to?	... ye taw
animal	Koja životinja	koy·a zhee·vaw·tee·nya
flower	Koji cvijet	koy·ee ts·vee·yet
plant	Koja biljka	koy·a beel'·ka
tree	Koje stablo	koy·e sta·blaw

Is it ...?	Je li ...?	ye lee ...
common	često	che·staw
dangerous	opasno	aw·pa·snaw
endangered	ugroženo	oo·graw·zhe·naw
poisonous	otrovno	aw·trawv·naw
protected	zaštićeno	zash·tee·che·naw

What is it used for?
Zašto se koristi? *zash·taw se kaw·ree·stee*

local plants & animals

almond tree	badem m	ba·dem
black bear	mrki medvjed m	mr·kee med·vyed
rosehip shrub	šipkov grm m	sheep·kawv grm
stone/pine	kuna bijelica/	koo·na bee·ye·lee·tsa/
marten	zlatica f	zla·tee·tsa
white-headed	bjeloglavi	bye·law·gla·vee
vulture	sup m	soop
wild goat	divokoza f	dee·vaw·kaw·za

Breakfast, *doručak* (*daw*-roo-chak), typically consists of toast with butter and rosehip jam, ham or prosciutto omelettes or bread rolls with a choice of toppings. Lunch, *ručak* (*roo*-chak), is usually taken between midday and 1pm, and in coastal regions in the summer months, is often followed by a siesta. Dinner, *večera* (*ve*-che-ra), is the main meal of the day and the time it's taken varies between 6 and 9pm.

breakfast	*doručak* m	*daw*-roo-chak
lunch	*ručak* m	*roo*-chak
dinner	*večera* f	*ve*-che-ra
snack	*užina* f	*oo*-zhee-na
eat	*jesti*	*ye*-stee
drink	*piti*	*pee*-tee
I'd like ...	*Želim* ...	*zhe*-leem ...
I'm starving!	*Gladan/Gladna*	*gla*-dan/*glad*-na
	sam kao vuk. m/f	sam *ka*-aw vook

finding a place to eat

pronalaženje mjesta za jelo

The word for café is both *kafić* (*ka*-feech) and *kavana* (ka-*va*-na), though *kafić* is much more commonly used. As restaurants don't usually display their menus outside you may need to go in and ask to have a look at the *jelovnik* (ye-*lawv*-neek).

Can you	*Možete/Možeš*	*maw*-zhe-te/*maw*-zhesh
recommend	*li preporučiti*	lee pre-paw-*roo*-chee-te
a ...	*neki ...* pol/inf	*ne*-kee ...
bar	*bar*	bar
café	*kafić*	*ka*-feech
restaurant	*restoran*	re-*staw*-ran

bistro bee·*straw*

lively venue catering mainly to a young crowd and serving a variety of alcoholic drinks as well as a limited range of food – popular in beachside areas

buffet bee·*fe*

small café – often with a lounge-style ambience including a TV – serving snacks and buffet-style foods, alcoholic and nonalcoholic beverages

gostionica gaw·stee·*aw*·nee·tsa

inn or pub that also operates as a no-frills, cheap restaurant

kafić/kavana ka·feech/ka·*va*·na

café – popular, usually licensed, social haunt that sometimes provides music and dancing in addition to a limited selection of dishes

konoba kaw·*naw*·ba

rustic establishment that serves wine and local peasant-style specialities

menza/kantina men·za/kan·tee·na

canteen usually for students or employees – for cheap eats as close to a home-cooked meal as one could hope

pekara pe·ka·ra

bakery and pastry shop serving the full range of delectable Croatian pastries and bread

pivnica peev·nee·tsa

pub or brewery-pub (pub attached to a brewery), often with an outdoor seating area during the warmer months, that sells a variety of draught and bottled beers and a limited selection of light meals

pizzeria pee·tse·*ree*·a

restaurant that specialises in delicious, often wood-fired, pizzas that rival their Italian cousins as cheap and tasty fare

restoran re·*staw*·ran

restaurant – serving a wide variety of dishes but often with a house speciality and usually licensed to sell alcohol

restoran sa   re·*staw*·ran sa
samoposluživanjem   sa·maw·paw·sloo·*zhee*·va·nyem
  quick and inexpensive self-service cafeteria with reasonably priced food of variable quality

slastičarnica   sla·stee·*char*·nee·tsa
  cake shop that serves ice cream, coffee, milk-based and other nonalcoholic drinks

taverna/birc   ta·*ver*·na/beerts
  tavern serving basic food as well as alcohol

Where would you go for ...?	*Gdje se može otići na ...?*	gdye se *maw*·zhe aw·*tee*·chee na ...
a celebration	*proslavu*	*praw*·sla·voo
a cheap meal	*jeftini obrok*	yef·tee·nee *aw*·brawk
local specialities	*mjesne specijalitete*	*mye*·sne spe·tsee·ya·lee·*te*·te
I'd like to reserve a table for ...	*Želim rezervirati stol za ...*	zhe·leem re·zer·*vee*·ra·tee stawl za ...
(two) people	*(dvoje) ljudi*	(dvoy·e) *lyoo*·dee
(eight) o'clock	*(osam) sati*	(*aw*·sam) sa·tee
I'd like ..., please.	*Mogu li dobiti ..., molim.*	*maw*·goo lee *daw*·bee·tee ... *maw*·leem
a children's menu	*dječji jelovnik*	*dyech*·yee ye·*lawv*·neek
the drink list	*cjenik pića*	*tsye*·neek *pee*·cha
a half portion	*pola obroka*	*paw*·la aw·*braw*·ka
the menu	*jelovnik*	ye·*lawv*·neek
a menu in English	*jelovnik na engleskom*	ye·*lawv*·neek na *en*·gle·skawm
nonsmoking	*nepušačko mjesto*	ne·poo·shach·kaw *mye*·staw
smoking	*pušačko mjesto*	poo·shach·kaw *mye*·staw
a table for (five)	*stol za (petero)*	stawl za (*pe*·taw·raw)

Are you still serving food?
Da li još servirate hranu?   da lee yawsh *ser*·vee·ra·te *hra*·noo

How long is the wait?
Koliko dugo se čeka?   kaw·lee·kaw *doo*·gaw se *che*·ka

at the restaurant

What would you recommend?
Što biste nam
preporučili?   shtaw *bee*·ste nam
pre·paw·*roo*·chee·lee

What's in that dish?
Od čega se
sastoji ovo jelo?   awd *che*·ga se
sa·stoy·ee *aw*·vaw ye·law

What's that called?
Kako se ono zove?   *ka*·kaw se *aw*·naw *zaw*·ve

I'll have that.
Ja bih to naručio/
naručila. m/f   ya beeh taw na·*roo*·chee·aw/
na·*roo*·chee·la

listen for ...	
zat·vaw·re·naw ye	
Zatvoreno je.	**We're closed.**
poo·nee smaw	
Puni smo.	**We're full.**
sam·aw tre·*noo*·tak	
Samo trenutak.	**One moment.**
gdye *zhe*·lee·te *sye*·stee	
Gdje želite sjesti?	**Where would you like to sit?**
shtaw vam *maw*·goo *paw*·noo·dee·tee	
Što vam mogu ponuditi?	**What can I get for you?**
eez·*vaw*·lee·te	
Izvolite!	**Here you go!**
pree·yat·naw/*daw*·bar tek	
Prijatno/Dobar tek.	**Enjoy your meal.**

Does it take long to prepare?

Da li priprema	da lee *pree*·pre·ma	
ovoga traje dugo?	*aw*·vaw·ga *trai*·e *doo*·gaw	

Is it self-serve?

Da li je ovdje	da lee ye *awv*·dye	
samoposluživanje?	sa·maw·paw·sloo·*zhee*·va·nye	

Is service included in the bill?

Da li je posluga	da lee ye *paw*·sloo·ga	
uključena	oo·klyoo·che·na	
u iznos na računu?	oo *eez*·naws na ra·*choo*·noo	

Are these complimentary?

Da li su ovi	da lee soo *aw*·vee	
besplatni?	be·splat·nee	

I'd like …	*Želim …*	*zhe*·leem …
a local	*neki mjesni*	ne·kee *mye*·snee
speciality	*specijalitet*	spe·tsee·ya·*lee*·tet
a meal fit	*kraljevski*	kra·lyev·skee
for a king	*obrok*	*aw*·brawk
the menu	*jelovnik*	ye·*lawv*·neek
that dish	*ono jelo*	*aw*·naw ye·*law*

I'd like it with …	*Želim to sa …*	*zhe*·leem taw sa …
pepper	*paprom*	*pa*·prawm
salt	*soli*	*saw*·lee
tomato sauce/	*ketchupom*	ke·cha·pawm
ketchup		
vinegar	*ocatom*	*aw*·tsa·tawm

I'd like it without …	*Želim to bez …*	*zhe*·leem taw bez …
cheese	*sira*	*see*·ra
chilli	*čilija*	*chee*·lee·ya
garlic	*češnjaka*	chesh·*nya*·ka
nuts	*raznih oraha*	*raz*·neeh *aw*·ra·ha
oil	*ulja*	*oo*·lya

For other specific meal requests, see **vegetarian & special meals**, page 161.

predjela	*pre·dye·la*	appetisers
juhe	*yoo·he*	soups
salate	*sa·la·te*	salads
glavna jela	*glav·na ye·la*	main courses
prilozi	*pree·law·zee*	side dishes
poslastice	*paw·sla·stee·tse*	desserts
laki obroci	*la·kee aw·braw·tsee*	light meals
aperitivi	*a·pe·ree·tee·vee*	apéritifs
pića	*pee·cha*	drinks
bezalkoholna pića	*be·zal·kaw·hawl·na pee·cha*	soft drinks
topli napitci	*taw·plee na·peet·tsee*	hot drinks
žestoka pića	*zhe·staw·ka pee·cha*	spirits
piva	*pee·va*	beers
vinjaci	*vee·nya·tsee*	brandies
domaća vina	*daw·ma·cha vee·na*	local wines
pjenušava vina	*pye·noo·sha·va vee·na*	sparkling wines
bijela vina	*bee·ye·la vee·na*	white wines
crna vina	*tsr·na vee·na*	red wines
desertna vina	*de·sert·na vee·na*	dessert wines

For more words you might see on a menu, see the **menu decoder**, page 163.

talking food

razgovor o hrani

I love this dish.
  Obožavam ovo jelo.   aw·baw·zha·vam aw·vaw ye·law

I love the local cuisine.
  Obožavam kuhinju   aw·baw·zha·vam koo·hee·nyoo
  ovoga područja.   aw·vaw·ga paw·drooch·ya

That was delicious!
  To je bilo izvrsno!   taw ye bee·law eez·vr·snaw

My compliments to the chef.
   Komplimenti   kawm·plee·*men*·tee
   šefu kuhinje.   she·foo koo·hee·nye

I'm full.
   Sit/Sita sam. m/f   seet/*see*·ta sam

This is ...	*Ovo je ...*	*aw*·vaw ye ...
(too) cold	*(pre)hladno*	(pre·)*hlad*·naw
spicy	*pikantno*	pee·*kant*·naw
superb	*odlično*	*awd*·leech·naw

at the table

za stolom

Please bring ...	*Molim vas*	*maw*·leem vas
	donesite ...	daw·*ne*·see·te ...
the bill	*račun*	*ra*·choon
a cloth	*stolnjak*	*stawl*·nyak
a menu	*jelovnik*	ye·*lawv*·neek
a serviette	*ubrus*	*oo*·broos

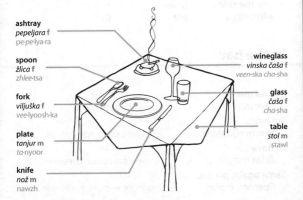

ashtray
pepeljara f
pe·*pe*·lya·ra

spoon
žlica f
zhlee·tsa

fork
viljuška f
vee·*lyoosh*·ka

plate
tanjur m
ta·nyoor

knife
nož m
nawzh

wineglass
vinska čaša f
veen·ska *cha*·sha

glass
čaša f
cha·sha

table
stol m
stawl

methods of preparation

način na koji je hrana pripremljena

I'd like it ...	Želim da bude ...	zhe·leem da boo·de ...
I don't want it ...	Ne želim	ne zhe·leem
	da bude ...	da boo·de ...
boiled	obareno	aw·ba·re·naw
deep-fried	prženo u	pr·zhe·naw oo
	dubokom ulju	doo·baw·kawm oo·lyoo
fried	prženo	pr·zhe·naw
grilled/broiled	pečeno na	pe·che·naw na
	roštilju	raw·shtee·lyoo
mashed	zdrobljeno	zdraw·blye·naw
	u kašu	oo ka·shoo
medium	srednje pečeno	sred·nye pe·che·naw
rare	nepotpuno	ne·pawt·poo·naw
	pečeno	pe·che·naw
reheated	podgrijano	pawd·gree·ya·naw
steamed	kuhano na pari	koo·ha·naw na pa·ree
well done	dobro pečeno	daw·braw pe·che·naw
with the dressing	sa začinima sa	sa za·chee·nee·ma sa
on the side	strane	stra·ne
without ...	bez ...	bez ...

in the bar

u baru

Excuse me!
Oprostite!
aw·praw·stee·te

I'm next.
Ja sam slijedeći/a. m/f
ya sam slee·ye·de·chee/a

I'll have ...
Želim naručiti ...
zhe·leem na·roo·chee·tee ...

Same again, please.
Opet isto, molim.
aw·pet ee·staw maw·leem

No ice, thanks.
   Bez leda, hvala.   bez *le*·da *hva*·la

I'll buy you a drink.
   Častim vas/te pićem. pol/inf   *cha*·steem vas/te *pee*·chem

What would you like?
   Što želite/želiš? pol/inf   shtaw *zhe*·lee·te/*zhe*·leesh

It's my round.
   Moj je red za čašćenje.   moy ye red za *chash*·che·nye

How much is that?
   Koliko to stoji?   kaw·*lee*·kaw taw *stoy*·ee

Do you serve meals here?
   Da li ovdje   da lee *awv*·dye
   poslužujete obroke?   paw·*sloo*·zhoo·ye·te *aw*·braw·ke

nonalcoholic drinks

bezalkoholna pića

... (mineral) water	... *(mineralna) voda* f	... *(mee*·ne·ral·na) *vaw*·da
sparkling	*gazirana*	ga·*zee*·ra·na
still	*obična*	*aw*·beech·na
apricot juice with	*sok od marelice*	sawk awd ma·*re*·lee·tse
whipped cream	*sa šlagom* m	sa *shla*·gawm
fizzy rosehip drink	*pašareta* f	pa·sha·*re*·ta
fresh lemonade	*slatka limunada* f	*slat*·ka lee·moo·*na*·da
(hot) water	*(topla) voda* f	*(taw*·pla) *vaw*·da
orange juice	*sok od naranče* m	sawk awd *na*·ran·che
rosehip and	*čaj od šipka*	chai awd *sheep*·ka
hibiscus tea	*i hibiscusa*	ee hee·*bee*·skoo·sa
soft drink	*bezalkoholno*	be·zal·kaw·hawl·naw
	piće m	*pee*·che
(cup of) tea ...	*(šalica) čaja* f ...	*(sha*·lee·tsa) *chai*·a ...
(cup of) coffee ...	*(šalica) kave* f ...	*(sha*·lee·tsa) *ka*·ve ...
with (milk)	*sa (mlijekom)*	sa (mlee·*ye*·kawm)
without (sugar)	*bez (šećera)*	bez (*she*·che·ra)

Croatians love their *kava* (ka·va), and you'll find coffee bars aplenty in towns and cities. Round tables are usually intended for those satisfied with just their daily fix, while rectangular tables are for those intending to eat as well.

black coffee	*crna kava* f	tsr·na ka·va
decaffeinated coffee	*kava bez kafeina* f	ka·va bez ka·fe·ee·na
iced coffee	*ledena kava* f	le·de·na ka·va
strong coffee	*jaka kava* f	ya·ka ka·va
Turkish coffee	*Turska kava*	toor·ska ka·va
weak coffee	*slaba kava* f	sla·ba ka·va
white coffee	*bijela kava* f	bee·ye·la ka·va

alcoholic drinks

alkoholna pića

beer	*pivo* n	pee·vaw
brandy	*rakija* f	ra·kee·ya
champagne	*šampanjac* m	sham·pa·nyats
cocktail	*koktel* m	kawk·tel
slivovitz (plum brandy)	*šljivovica* f	shlyee·vaw·vee·tsa
a shot of ...	*jedna čašica ...*	yed·na cha·shee·tsa ...
gin	*džina*	jee·na
rum	*ruma*	roo·ma
tequila	*tekile*	te·kee·le
vodka	*vodke*	vawd·ke
whisky	*viskija*	vee·skee·ya

a bottle/glass	boca/čaša	*baw*·tsa/*cha*·sha
of ... wine	... vina	... *vee*·na
dessert	desertnog	de·*sert*·nawg
red	crnog	*tsr*·nawg
rosé	rosea	raw·*se*·a
sparkling	pjenušavog	pye·*noo*·sha·vawg
white	bijelog	bee·*ye*·lawg
a ... of beer	jedna ... piva	*yed*·na ... *pee*·va
glass	čaša	*cha*·sha
large bottle	velika boca	ve·*lee*·ka *baw*·tsa
pint (500 ml)	krigla	*kree*·gla
small bottle	mala boca	*ma*·la *baw*·tsa

drinking up

If you're drinking in a threesome, don't at any price raise your thumb, index and middle finger all at once to signal another round. This is a Serbian gesture connected to Serbian nationalism and might see you swiftly ejected from your cosy bar-side nook.

Cheers!
   Živjeli! zhee·vye·lee

This is hitting the spot.
   Ovo mi baš prija. aw·vaw mee bash *pree*·ya

I feel fantastic!
   Osjećam se fantastično! aw·sye·cham se fan·*ta*·steech·naw

I think I've had one too many.
   Mislim da sam mee·sleem da sam
   popio/popila paw·pee·aw/*paw*·pee·la
   previše. m/f pre·vee·she

I'm feeling drunk.
   Osjećam se pijano. aw·sye·cham se *pee*·ya·naw

I'm pissed.
   Pijan/Pijana sam. m/f pee·yan/pee·ya·na sam

I feel ill.
   Muka mi je.   moo·ka mee ye

Where's the toilet?
   Gdje je zahod?   gdye ye za·hawd

Can you call a taxi for me?
   Možete/Možeš li mi   maw·zhe·te/maw·zhesh lee mee
   pozvati taksi? pol/inf   pawz·va·tee tak·see

I don't think you should drive.
   Mislim da nebi trebali   mee·sleem da ne·bee tre·ba·lee
   voziti. pol   vaw·zee·tee
   Mislim da nebi trebao/   mee·sleem da ne·bee tre·ba·aw/
   trebala voziti. m/f inf   tre·ba·la vaw·zee·tee

---

brandy reader

Croatia produces a great variety of wines but dearest to the hearts of most Croatians are the home-made brandies collectively known as *rakije* (ra·kee·ye) that come in a profusion of herbal and fruit flavours.

kruškovac	kroosh·ko·vats	pear-flavoured brandy
lozovača	law·zhaw·va·cha	herb-flavoured wine brandy
maraskino	ma·ra·skee·naw	sour-cherry brandy
orahovac	aw·ra·haw·vats	walnut brandy
pelinkovac	pe·leen·kaw·vats	herbal digestif brandy
šljivovica	shlyee·vaw·vee·tsa	plum brandy
travarica	tra·va·ree·tsa	bitter herbal brandy
vinjak	vee·nyak	wine brandy

buying food

kupovina hrane

What's the local speciality?
Što je ovdje
područni specijalitet?
shtaw ye *awv*·dye
paw·drooch·nee spe·tsee·ya·*lee*·tet

What's that?
Što je to?
shtaw ye taw

Can I taste it?
Mogu li to probati?
maw·goo lee taw *praw*·ba·tee

Can I have a bag, please?
Mogu li dobiti
vrećicu toga, molim?
maw·goo lee *daw*·bee·tee
vre·chee·tsoo *taw*·ga maw·leem

How much is (a kilo of cheese)?
Koliko stoji (kila sira)?
kaw·*lee*·kaw *stoy*·ee (*kee*·la *see*·ra)

How much?
Koliko?
kaw·*lee*·kaw

how would you like that?		
cooked	*kuhano*	*koo*·ha·naw
cured	*prerađeno*	*pre*·ra·je·naw
dried	*sušeno*	*soo*·she·naw
fresh	*svježe*	*svye*·zhe
frozen	*zaleđeno*	*za*·le·je·naw
raw	*sirovo*	*see*·raw·vaw
smoked	*dimljeno*	*deem*·lye·naw

I'd like …	Želim …	zhe·leem …
(200) grams	(dvijesto) grama	(dvee·ye·staw) gra·ma
half a dozen	pola tuceta	paw·la too·tse·ta
a dozen	tucet	too·tset
half a kilo	pola kile	paw·la kee·le
a kilo	kilu	kee·loo
(two) kilos	(dvije) kile	(dvee·ye) kee·le
a bottle	bocu	baw·tsoo
a jar	staklenku	sta·klen·koo
a packet	kutiju	koo·tee·yoo
a piece	komad	kaw·mad
(three) pieces	(tri) komada	(tree) kaw·ma·da
a slice	krišku	kreesh·koo
(six) slices	(šest) krišaka	(shest) kree·sha·ka
a tin	limenku	lee·men·koo
(just) a little	(samo) malo	(sa·maw) ma·law
more	više	vee·she
some …	malo …	ma·law …
that one	onaj/onu/	aw·nai/aw·noo/
	ono m/f/n	aw·naw
this one	ovaj/ovu/	aw·vai/aw·voo/
	ovo m/f/n	aw·vaw

Less.	Manje.	ma·nye
A bit more.	Malo više.	ma·law vee·she
Enough.	Dosta.	daw·sta

listen for …

maw·goo lee vam paw·maw·chee	
Mogu li vam pomoći?	**Can I help you?**
shtaw zhe·lee·te	
Što želite?	**What would you like?**
nesh·taw droo·gaw	
Nešto drugo?	**Anything else?**
ne·ma taw·ga	
Nema toga.	**There isn't any.**
taw ye (pet) koo·na	
To je (pet) kuna.	**That's (five) kuna.**

FOOD

Do you have …?	Da li imate …?	da lee *ee*·ma·te …
anything	nešto	*nesh*·taw
cheaper	jeftinije?	yef·*tee*·nee·ye
other kinds	druge vrste	*droo*·ge vr·ste
Where can I find	Gdje se nalazi dio	gdye se *na*·la·zee *dee*·aw
the … section?	prodavaonice	praw·da·va·*aw*·nee·tse
	za …?	za …
dairy	mliječne	mlee·*yech*·ne
	proizvode	praw·*eez*·vaw·de
fish	ribu	*ree*·boo
frozen goods	zaleđenu	za·le·je·noo
	hranu	*hra*·noo
fruit and	voće i	*vaw*·che ee
vegetable	povrće	*paw*·vr·che
meat	meso	*me*·saw
poultry	meso od	*me*·saw awd
	peradi	pe·ra·dee

pekara f	*pe*·ka·ra	bakery
prodavaonica	praw·da·va·*aw*·nee·tsa	bottle shop/
alkohola f	*al*·kaw·haw·la	liquor store
mesnica f	*me*·snee·tsa	butcher's shop
delikatese f pl	de·lee·ka·*te*·se	delicatessen
trgovac	*tr*·gaw·vats	greengrocer
povrćem m	*paw*·vr·chem	
tržnica f	*trzh*·nee·tsa	market
supermarket m	soo·per·*mar*·ket	supermarket

cooking utensils

pribor i posuđe za kuhanje

Could I please borrow a ...?	*Mogu li posuditi jedan/ jednu ... molim?* m/f	*maw*·goo lee paw·*soo*·dee·tee ye·dan/ yed·noo ... *maw*·leem
I need a ...	*Trebam jedan/ jednu ...* m/f	*tre*·bam ye·dan/ yed·noo ...
chopping board	*dasku za rezanje* f	*da*·skoo za re·za·nye
frying pan	*tavu* f	*ta*·voo
knife	*nož* m	nawzh
saucepan	*lonac* m	*law*·nats

For more cooking implements, see the **dictionary**.

vegetarian & special meals
posebni obroci i vegetarijanska hrana

ordering food

naručivanje hrane

Is there a ...	*Da li znate za ...*	da lee *zna*·te za ...
restaurant near	*restoran ovdje*	re·*staw*·ran *awv*·dye
here?	*blizu?*	*blee*·zoo
Do you have ...	*Da li imate ...*	da lee *ee*·ma·te ...
food?	*obrok?*	*aw*·brawk
halal	*halal*	*ha*·lal
kosher	*košer*	*kaw*·sher
vegetarian	*vegetarijanski*	ve·ge·ta·*ree*·yan·skee

I don't eat ...		
Ja ne jedem ...		ya ne *ye*·dem ...
Is it cooked in/with ...?		
Je li to kuhano u/sa ...?		ye lee taw *koo*·ha·naw oo/sa ...

Could you	*Možete li*	*maw*·zhe·te lee
prepare a	*prirediti*	pree·*re*·dee·tee
meal without ...?	*obrok koji*	*aw*·brawk *koy*·ee
	ne sadrži ...?	ne *sa*·dr·zhee ...
butter	*maslac*	*ma*·slats
eggs	*jaja*	*yai*·a
fish	*ribu*	*ree*·boo
fish stock	*riblji bujon*	*reeb*·lyee *boo*·yawn
meat stock	*mesni bujon*	*mes*·nee *boo*·yawn
oil	*ulje*	*oo*·lye
pork	*svinjetinu*	*svee*·nye·tee·noo
poultry	*meso od peradi*	*me*·saw awd *pe*·ra·dee
red meat	*crveno meso*	*tsr*·ve·naw *me*·saw

Is this ...?	Da li je ovo ...?	da lee ye aw·vaw ...
decaffeinated	bez kafeina	bez ka·fe·ee·na
free of	bez	bez
animal	životinjskih	zhe·vaw·teen'·skeeh
produce	sastojaka	sa·stoy·a·ka
free range	domaće	daw·ma·che
genetically	genetski	ge·net·skee
modified	modificirano	maw·dee·fee·tsee·ra·naw
gluten free	bez glutena	bez gloo·te·na
low fat	s malo masnoće	s ma·law ma·snaw·che
low in sugar	s malo šećera	s ma·law she·che·ra
organic	organski	awr·gan·skee
	proizvedeno	praw·eez·ve·de·naw
salt free	bez soli	bez saw·lee

special diets & allergies

posebna ishrana i alergije

I'm on a special diet.

Ja sam na posebnoj dijeti.   ya sam na paw·seb·noy dee·ye·tee

I'm allergic	Ja sam alergičan/	ya sam a·ler·gee·chan/
to ...	alergična na ... m/f	a·ler·geech·na na ...
dairy	mliječne	mlee·yech·ne
produce	proizvode	praw·eez·vaw·de
eggs	jaja	yai·a
gelatine	želatinu	zhe·la·tee·noo
gluten	gluten	gloo·ten
honey	med	med
MSG	glutaminat	gloo·ta·mee·nat
nuts	razne orahe	raz·ne aw·ra·he
peanuts	kikiriki	kee·kee·ree·kee
seafood	morske plodove	mawr·ske plaw·daw·ve
shellfish	školjke i rakove	shkawl'·ke ee ra·kaw·ve

To explain your dietary restrictions with reference to religious beliefs, see **beliefs & cultural differences**, page 125.

FOOD

This miniguide to Croatian cuisine lists dishes and ingredients in alphabetical order in Croatian. It's designed to help you get the most out of your gastronomic experience by providing you with food terms that you may see on menus etc. Adjectives on their own are given in the masculine form only. For an explanation of how to form feminine and neuter adjectives see the **a–z phrasebuilder**, page 16.

A

ajvar ⓜ *ai*·var *relish made from minced roast eggplant & capsicum & flavoured with lemon juice, garlic, olive oil & parsley*

ananas ⓜ *a*·na·nas *pineapple*

arambašići ⓜ pl *a*·ram·ba·shee·chee *mincemeat parcels rolled in vine or silver beet leaves (also called* **japraci***)*

artičoka ⓕ ar·tee·*chaw*·ka *artichoke*

artičoke na dalmatinski način ⓕ pl ar·tee·*chaw*·ke na dal·*ma*·teen·skee *na*·cheen *artichokes stuffed with breadcrumbs soaked in milk & lemon juice, seasoned with parsley & garlic then drizzled with olive oil & oven baked*

B

bakalar ⓜ ba·ka·*lar dried salted cod that is reconstituted in water before cooking*
— **s krumpirom** s kroom·*pee*·rawm *dried salted cod simmered with oil, bay leaves & lemon slices – served with diced boiled potatoes & parsley*

baklava ⓕ ba·*kla*·va *filo pastry squares stuffed with chopped nuts, sugar & cinnamon & drenched in melted butter & rose-water flavoured syrup*

banana ⓕ ba·*na*·na *banana*

bečki odrezak ⓜ *bech*·kee aw·dre·zak *Wiener schnitzel*

bijeli mekani sir ⓜ bee·*ye*·lee *me*·ka·nee seer *cottage cheese*

blatina ⓕ *bla*·tee·na *well-known red wine*

blitva ⓕ *bleet*·va *silver beet • Swiss chard – green leafy vegetable indigenous to Croatia*

— **s krumpirom** s kroom·*pee*·rawm *boiled potatoes served with silver beet fried in garlic & drizzled with olive oil*

bola ⓕ *baw*·la *refreshing chilled drink made from sugar & fruit or herbs soaked in white wine*

borgonja ⓕ bawr·*gaw*·nya *Istrian red wine*

borovnica ⓕ baw·*rawv*·nee·tsa *blueberry*

brancin ⓜ bran·*tseen sea bass*

breskva ⓕ *bres*·kva *peach*

brodet ⓜ braw·det *tasty fish stew often served with polenta*
— **na dalamatinski način** na dal·*ma*·teen·skee *na*·cheen *Dalmatian-style mixed fish stew with rice*

bubreg ⓜ *boo*·breg *kidney*

bučice ⓕ pl boo·*chee*·tse *courgette • zucchini*

burek ⓜ *boo*·rek *oily flaky pastry stuffed with cheese or minced meat – popular breakfast food or snack of Turkish origin*
— **s mesom** s me·sawm *fried minced beef & onion layered between filo pastry sheets then topped with beaten eggs & milk & baked*
— **sa sirom** sa see·rawm *filo pastry layered with a mixture of beaten eggs, cottage cheese, sour cream & dill then oven baked*

burgundac ⓜ boor·*goon*·dats *premium red wine*

C

celer ⓜ tse·ler *celery*

cikla ⓕ *tsee*·kla *beetroot*

crna maslina ⓕ *tsr*·na *ma*·slee·na *black olive*

crni rižoto ⓜ tsr·nee ree·zhaw·taw *'black risotto' – highly prized risotto containing cuttlefish, squid, olive oil, onion, garlic, parsley & red wine & given its black colour by the addition of squid ink*

crvena paprika ⓕ tsr·ve·na pa·pree·ka *red capsicum • red bell pepper*

cvjetača ⓕ tsvye·ta·cha *cauliflower*
— s kiselim vrhnjem s kee·se·leem vrh·nyem *boiled cauliflower topped with sour cream, melted butter, cheese & breadcrumbs then oven baked*

Č

čajno pecivo ⓜ chai·naw pe·tsee·vaw *cookie • sweet biscuit*

češnjak ⓜ chesh·nyak *garlic*

ćevapčići ⓜ pl che·vap·chee·chee *skinless minced beef & lamb sausages flavoured with garlic, parsley, pepper & salt – served grilled*

čokoladna krema ⓕ chaw·kaw·lad·na kre·ma *chocolate cream dessert*

D

dagnja ⓕ dag·nya *mussel*

Dalmatinska salata od hobotnice ⓕ dal·ma·teen·ska sa·la·ta awd haw·bawt·nee·tse *octopus salad – a Dalmatian speciality*

dimljen deem·lyen *smoked*

dimljena riba ⓕ deem·lye·na ree·ba *smoked fish*

dimljeni losos ⓜ deem·lye·nee law·saws *smoked salmon*

dimljeni sir ⓜ deem·lye·nee seer *smoked cheese*

dingač ⓜ deen·gach *Dalmatian red wine*

dinja ⓕ dee·nya *honeydew melon*

divlji deev·lyee *wild*

divlja šparoga ⓕ deev·lya shpa·raw·ga *wild asparagus*

dnevni meni ⓜ dnev·nee me·nee *daily special*

doboš torta ⓕ do·bosh tawr·ta *rich layered cake of Hungarian origin garnished with coffee cream & caramel*

dobro pečen daw·braw pe·chen *well done*

domaći daw·ma·chee *home-made • home-style*

domaći rezanci ⓜ pl daw·ma·chee re·zan·tsee *home-style egg noodles – often served in soups*

dunja ⓕ doo·nya *quince*

Dž

džem ⓜ jem *jam*

džuveč ⓜ joo·vech *casserole made from mixed vegetables pork cutlets & rice – flavoured with parsley, celery leaves, chilli & tomato paste*

F

fazan ⓜ fa·zan *pheasant*

fileki ⓕ pl fee·le·kee *tripe*

francuska salata ⓕ fran·tsoo·ska sa·la·ta *salad of diced potato, carrot & peas smothered in a lemony mayonnaise sauce*

fuži ⓜ pl foo·zhee *pasta twirls*

G

gljiva ⓕ glyee·va *mushroom*

golub ⓜ gaw·loob *pigeon*

govedina ⓕ gaw·ve·dee·na *beef*

goveđa juha ⓕ gaw·ve·ja yoo·ha *beef bouillon*

goveđi gulaš ⓜ gaw·ve·jee goo·lash *diced beef & pork braised with onion, sauerkraut, sour cream & paprika*

grah ⓜ grah *dried beans*

graševina ⓕ gra·she·vee·na *white riesling-style wine*

grožđe ⓕ grawzh·je *grape*

gulaš od divljači ⓜ goo·lash od deev·lya·chee *game goulash*

gulaš-juha ⓕ goo·lash·yoo·ha *'goulash soup' – thick hearty soup containing red pepper, potatoes, diced beef flavoured with red wine, bay leaf, tomato paste, caraway seed, chilli, onion & garlic*

guska ⓕ goo·ska *goose*

H

heljda ⓕ hel'·da *buckwheat*

hladetina ⓕ hla·de·tee·na *brawn prepared from boiled pigs' hocks or trotters & cubed pork shoulder with the addition of*

vegetables, boiled eggs, garlic, parsley & paprika – a special-occasion treat
hladni pladanj ⓜ hlad·nee pla·dan' *cold cuts – might include thin slices of delicious Istrian or Dalmatian pršut & goat's cheese, all garnished with olives*
hobotnica ⓕ haw·bawt·nee·tsa *octopus*
hrenovka ⓕ hre·nawv·ka *frankfurter*

I

inćun ⓜ een·choon *anchovy*
Istarska jota ⓕ ee·star·ska yaw·ta *Istrian stew prepared from sauerkraut, beans, potatoes & smoked dried meats – seasoned with garlic & bay leaves*
Istarski kaneloni ⓜ pl ee·star·skee ka·ne·law·nee *pancakes filled with a mixture of fried cubed prosciutto & ham, cottage cheese & mushrooms then dipped in beaten egg & breadcrumbs, fried & topped with a tomato sauce*
Istarski lonac ⓜ ee·star·skee law·nats *Istrian hotpot of diced lamb, carrot, cabbage, garlic, tomato, onion & olive oil – flavoured with bay leaves & sometimes white wine*

J

jabuka ⓕ ya·boo·ka *apple*
jagoda ⓕ ya·gaw·da *strawberry*
jaje ⓝ yai·e *egg*
— **na oko** na aw·kaw *fried egg*
janjeća čorba ⓕ ya·nye·cha chawr·ba *lamb stew of parsley root, celeriac, Brussels sprouts & carrot – flavoured with tomato paste, sour cream, paprika, bay leaves, lemon juice & parsley*
janjeća juha ⓕ ya·nye·cha yoo·ha *soup made from lamb, root vegetables, rice, cabbage, egg yolk, garlic, onion, bay leaf, peppercorns, lemon juice, sour cream, parsley & spices*
janjetina ⓕ ya·nye·tee·na *lamb*
— **na ražnju** na razh·nyoo *lamb cooked on a spit*
japraci ⓜ pl ya·pra·tsee *mincemeat parcels rolled in vine or silver beet leaves (also called **arambašići**)*
jastog ⓜ ya·stawg *lobster*
ječam ⓜ ye·cham *barley*

jegulja ⓕ ye·goo·lya *eel*
jetrena pašteta ⓕ ye·tre·na pash·te·ta *liverwurst (pâté)*
jogurt ⓜ yaw·goort *yoghurt*
juha ⓕ yoo·ha *soup*
— **od bujače** awd boo·ya·che *pumpkin soup*
— **od cvjetače** awd tsvye·ta·che *cauliflower soup with sour cream & egg yolk – thickened with a roux*
— **od gljiva s heljdinom kašom** awd glyee·va s hel'·dee·nawm ka·shawm *rich buckwheat & mushroom soup containing beef stock & sour cream & seasoned with cloves & parsley*
— **od graha** awd gra·ha *soup made from dried kidney or borlotti beans, smoked bacon bones (or smoked pork hock), onion, carrot, bay leaf & garlic*
— **od graška** awd grash·ka *pea soup*
— **od heljdine kaše i krumpira** awd hel'·dee·ne ka·she ee kroom·pee·ra *buckwheat & potato soup containing sour cream, onion & minced parsley*
— **od kisele repe i graha** awd kee·se·le re·pe ee gra·ha *sour turnip & bean soup*
— **od kiselog kupusa i graha** awd kee·se·lawg koo·poo·sa ee gra·ha *sauerkraut & bean soup*
— **od krastavca** awd kra·stav·tsa *cucumber soup*
— **od krumpira** awd kroom·pee·ra *potato soup containing smoked bacon, garlic, sour cream, spices, marjoram, bay leaves, parsley, vinegar & paprika*
— **od krumpira na Zagorski način** awd kroom·pee·ra na za·gawr·skee na·cheen *Zagorje potato soup containing smoked bacon & onion – flavoured with marjoram, bay leaves, paprika, parsley & vinegar*
— **od mahuna** awd ma·hoo·na *runner-bean soup*
— **od piletine i povrća** awd pee·le·tee·ne ee paw·vr·cha *chicken & vegetable soup with carrot, celery, parsnip & peas – served with **noklice** (dumplings)*
— **od povrća** awd paw·vr·cha *vegetable soup*
— **od rajčica** awd rai·chee·tsa *tomato soup*
— **od repe i kupusa** awd re·pe ee koo·poo·sa *turnip & cabbage soup*

juha od špinata i krumpira yoo·ha awd shpee·na·ta ee kroom·pee·ra *spinach & potato soup containing puréed spinach, diced potatoes & beef bouillon – thickened with a sour cream & egg yolk roux*

K

kajgana ① kai·ga·na *scrambled eggs*
kalamari ⓜ pl ka·la·ma·ree *calamari • squid*
kapar ⓜ ka·par *caper*
kaša ① ka·sha *gruel • porridge*
　— **od zobi** awd zaw·bee *oatmeal porridge*
kaštradina ① kash·tra·dee·na *dried mutton soup with vegetables*
kavijar ⓜ ka·vee·yar *caviar*
kesten ⓜ ke·sten *chestnut*
　— **pire** pee·re *dessert prepared from chestnut purée, sugar, vanilla, rum & cream & garnished with chocolate shavings*
kiflice ⓜ pl kee·flee·tse *delicate crescent-shaped biscuits that come in a variety of flavours including vanilla*
　— **od badema** awd ba·de·ma *almond biscuits dusted with icing sugar made from butter, flour, ground almonds & vanilla sugar*
　— **od oraha** awd aw·ra·ha *biscuits made from a dough of butter, egg yolks, cream cheese, flour & sugar – stuffed with an egg white, sugar & ground-walnut filling*
kiseli kupus ⓜ kee·se·lee koo·poos *sauerkraut – dear to the hearts of Croatians, sauerkraut is prepared from whole cored cabbage heads layered with horseradish, bay leaves, garlic, dried red pepper & salt*
klinčić ⓜ kleen·cheech *clove*
knedle ① pl kned·le *dumplings made from butter, semolina flour, eggs & milk – often served in soups*
kobasica ① kaw·ba·see·tsa *sausage*
kolač ⓜ kaw·lach *cake*
komorač ⓜ kaw·maw·rach *fennel*
kompot ⓜ kawm·pawt *stewed fruit*
kotlovina ① kawt·law·vee·na *fried pork chops simmered in a piquant sauce containing onions, garlic, tomato, mustard,*

chillies, white wine & paprika – traditionally prepared outdoors over an open fire
kozji sir ⓜ kawz·yee seer *goat's milk cheese*
krastavac ⓜ kra·sta·vats *cucumber*
krema ① kre·ma *cream • filling*
krempita ① krem·pee·ta *layered puff pastry filled with a custard-like cream*
krepka juha od mesa ① krep·ka yoo·ha awd me·sa *broth • consommé*
kroštule ⓜ pl krawsh·too·le *similar to Italian crostoli, these are bow-shaped pastries flavoured with lemon rind & vanilla then deep fried in oil & sprinkled with icing sugar*
kruh ⓜ krooh *bread*
krumpir ⓜ kroom·peer *potato*
　— **salata** sa·la·ta *potato salad*
kruška ① kroosh·ka *pear*
krvavica ① kr·va·vee·tsa *blood sausage*
kuglice od ruma ① pl koo·glee·tse awd roo·ma *rum balls made from egg whites, ground walnuts, sugar, grated chocolate & rum – a rich treat*
kuglof ⓜ koo·glawf *ring-shaped sponge cake sometimes flavoured with lemon or containing raisins soaked in rum*
kuhan koo·han *boiled • cooked*
　— **na pari** na pa·ree *steamed*
kuhana govedina ① koo·ha·na gaw·ve·deena *boiled beef*
kuhana škrpina ① koo·ha·na shkr·pee·na *boiled scorpion fish – a Dalmatian speciality*
kuhana šunka ① koo·ha·na shoon·ka *boiled ham*
kuhani krumpir ⓜ koo·ha·nee kroom·peer *boiled potatoes*
kukuruz ⓜ koo·koo·rooz *corn*
kulen ⓜ koo·len *paprika-flavoured sausage*
kumin ⓜ koo·meen *caraway – popular spice used in savoury dishes*
kupina ① koo·pee·na *blackberry*
kupus ⓜ koo·poos *cabbage*

L

leća ① le·cha *lentil*
ledene kocke ⓜ pl le·de·ne kawts·ke *coffee-flavoured or chocolate-flavoured sponge cake layered with chocolate cream*

lička kisela čorba ① leech·ka kee·se·la chor·ba 'Lika-style sour stew' – stew prepared with cubed meat, mixed vegetables & cabbage – flavoured with garlic, vinegar, sour cream & parsley

lignje ① pl leeg·nye calamari • squid
— **s krumpirom** s kroom·pee·rawm traditional Dalmatian dish consisting of squid cooked between layers of potato seasoned with mixed herbs, garlic & parsley & doused with olive oil

limun ⓜ lee·moon lemon

lišće maslačka ⓝ leesh·che ma·slach·ka dandelion leaves – popular salad greens with a slightly bitter taste

losos ⓜ law·saws salmon

lovorov list ⓜ law·vaw·rawv leest bay leaf

lubenica ① loo·be·nee·tsa watermelon

lubin ⓜ loo·been sea bass

luk ⓜ look onion

M

mađarica ① ma·ja·ree·tsa layers of a rich sweet baked dough interspersed with a chocolate cream filling & topped with melted chocolate

mahuna ① ma·hoo·na green bean

majoneza ① mai·aw·ne·za mayonnaise

makov kolač ⓜ ma·kawv kaw·lach poppy-seed cake

makovnjača ① ma·kawv·nya·cha poppy-seed roll

makovo sjeme ⓝ ma·kaw·vaw sye·me poppy seed – often used in pastries

malina ① ma·lee·na raspberry

malvazija ① mal·va·zee·ya white Istrian wine with a yellowy-gold colour

maneštra ① ma·nesh·tra vegetable & bean soup sometimes containing meat – similar to Italian minestrone
— **od bobi** awd baw·bee broad-bean soup with fresh maize

maraska voćna salata ① ma·ra·ska vawch·na sa·la·ta fruit salad containing sour & sweet cherries, pear & quince macerated in **maraskino** liqueur & dusted with sugar

maraskino ⓜ ma·ra·skee·naw liqueur made from Dalmatian sour cherries & flavoured with the kernels, giving it a slightly bitter aftertaste – known in English as 'maraschino'

marelica ① ma·re·lee·tsa apricot

mariniran ma·ree·nee·ran marinated

maslac ⓜ ma·slats butter

maslina ① ma·slee·na olive

maslinovo ulje ⓝ ma·slee·naw·vaw oo·lye olive oil

masnoća ① ma·snaw·cha fat

med ⓜ med honey

medovina ① me·daw·vee·na mead (mildly alcoholic fermented honey drink)

Međimurska salata od luka ① me·jee·moor·ska sa·la·ta awd loo·ka salted onions with the excess liquid removed & dressed with pumpkinseed oil – served as a side dish

Međimurski gulaš ⓜ me·jee·moor·skee goo·lash veal stewed with onion, garlic, hot peppers, pickled peppers & **ajvar**

mesna jela ⓝ me·sna ye·la meat dishes

meso ⓝ me·saw meat

miješana salata ① mee·ye·sha·na sa·la·ta mixed salad

miješano meso ⓝ mee·ye·sha·naw me·saw mixed grill – popular menu item as Croatians love their meat

mlijeko ⓝ mlee·ye·kaw milk

mlinci ⓜ pl mleen·tsee pasta tatters made from flour, eggs & dripping & sometimes coated with butter, cream or cottage cheese – typical accompaniment to roasted meats or **bakalar**

mortadela ① mawr·ta·de·la mortadella – type of aromatic pork sausage with small squares of fat & served thinly sliced as an appetiser

moruna ① maw·roo·na sturgeon (fish)

musaka ① moo·sa·ka moussaka – layered lasagne-style dish containing meat & vegetables
— **od zelenih i crvenih paprika** awd ze·le·neeh ee tsr·ve·neeh pa·pree·ka moussaka made from peeled, grilled green & red capsicums layered with fried ground beef with onion & a sauce made from feta, sour cream & eggs
— **s patlidžanima i tikvicama** s pat·lee·ja·nee·ma ee teek·vee·tsa·ma eggplant & zucchini moussaka made from layered eggplant & zucchini interspersed with ground beef & a sauce made from feta, eggs & sour cream

muškatov oraščić ⓜ moosh·ka·tawv aw·rash·cheech nutmeg

N

na ražnju na *razh*-nyoo *roasted on a spit*
na žaru na *zha*-roo *barbecued • grilled (broiled)*
nabujak od riže ⓜ na·*boo*·yak awd *ree*·zhe *rice pudding*
nadjev ⓜ *nad*·yev *stuffing*
naranča ⓕ *na*·ran·cha *orange*
naravni odrezak ⓜ *na*·rav·nee aw·dre·zak *veal escalope*
narodna jela ⓝ *na*·rawd·na *ye*·la *traditional Croatian dishes*
nepotpuno pečen ne·pawt·poo·naw *pe*·chen *rare*
noklice ⓕ pl *naw*·klee·tse *dumplings for soup made from breadcrumbs, milk-soaked bread, eggs & parsley – there are variations containing minced liver & meat*

Nj

njoki ⓜ pl *nyaw*·kee *gnocchi (dumplings made from semolina or potato)*

O

ocat ⓜ *aw*·tsat *vinegar*
odojak na ražnju ⓜ aw·doy·ak na *razh*·nyoo *suckling pig roasted on a spit*
okruglice ⓕ pl aw·*kroo*·glee·tse *dumplings made from semolina or potato – served as a savoury accompaniment or, stuffed with plums or jam, as a dessert*
omlet ⓜ *aw*·mlet *omelette*
    — sa sirom sa *see*·rawm *cheese omelette*
opolo ⓜ *aw*·paw·law *Dalmatian red wine*
orada ⓕ aw·*ra*·da *gilthead (fish)*
orah ⓜ *aw*·rah *walnut*
orahnjača ⓕ aw·*rah*·nya·cha *walnut roll – ground walnut, butter, cinnamon & sugar mixture encased in a yeasty dough & then baked*
oslić ⓜ *aw*·sleech *hake*
oštriga ⓕ *awsh*·tree·ga *oyster*
ovčji sir *awv*·chyee seer *sheep's milk cheese*

P

palačinka ⓕ pa·la·*cheen*·ka *pancake – often served filled with jam or ground nuts then topped with chocolate, may also come with savoury fillings as a main course*
    — sa sirom sa *see*·rawm *dessert pancake filled with cottage cheese, sugar, raisins, egg & sour cream then oven baked*
palenta ⓕ pa·*len*·ta *polenta*
papar ⓜ *pa*·par *pepper*
    — od ljutih papričica awd *lyoo*·teeh pa·*pree*·chee·tsa *cayenne pepper*
paprika ⓕ pa·*pree*·ka *paprika*
paprikaš ⓜ pa·*pree*·kash *paprikash – beef or fish stew heavily flavoured with paprika*
pastičada ⓕ pa·stee·*cha*·da *Dalmatian speciality consisting of beef rounds larded with smoked bacon then stewed with fried vegetables flavoured with rosemary, bay leaves & peppercorns & served with a white wine, olive, lemon juice & beef stock sauce. Another version has a sauce made from dried fruit & apples, tomato paste & red wine.*
pastirska juha ⓕ pa·*steer*·ska *yoo*·ha *'shepherd's soup' – soup made from cubed lamb, veal chops & pork neck also containing onion, garlic, chilli, bay leaves, paprika, tomato, potato & wine*
pastrva ⓕ *pas*·tr·va *trout*
paški sir ⓜ *pash*·kee seer *sheep's milk cheese from the island of Pag*
pašta fažol ⓕ *pash*·ta fa·*zhawl* *bean soup with pasta*
patka ⓕ *pat*·ka *duck*
    — s maslinama s ma·slee·*na*·ma *duck rubbed with salt & garlic then marinated in a mixture of wine, lemon juice, thyme, oil & pepper & roasted in the oven*
patlidžan ⓜ pat·*lee*·jan *eggplant*
pečen *pe*·chen *baked • roasted*
    — na žaru na *zha*·roo *grilled*
    — u tavi oo *ta*·vee *pan-roasted*
pečena orada s prokulicom ⓕ *pe*·che·na aw·*ra*·da s *praw*·koo·lee·tsawm *roast gilthead (fish) with silver beet – a Dalmatian speciality*
pečena svinjetina ⓕ *pe*·che·na svee·nye·*tee*·na *roast pork*

pečurka ① *pe*-choor-ka *field mushroom*
pečurke na žaru ① pl *pe*-choor-ke na *zha*-roo *grilled field mushrooms*
peršin ⑩ *per*-sheen *parsley*
pikantan pee-*kan*-tan *hot (spicy) • savoury*
pile na dalmatinski način ⑥ *pee*-le na dal-*ma*-teen-skee na-cheen *'Dalmatian-style chicken' – boiled chicken pieces covered with a sauce of olive oil, onion, capers, parsley & anchovies then baked in the oven*
pileća krem-juha ① *pee*-le-cha krem-*yoo*-ha *cream of chicken soup*
piletina ① *pee*-le-tee-na *chicken*
pirjan *peer*-yan *stewed*
pita sa špinatom ① *pee*-ta sa shpee-*na*-tawm *spinach pie made from flaky pastry & boiled seasoned spinach layered with cottage-style cheese*
pizza ① *pee*-tsa *pizza – often wood-fired, Croatian pizzas rival their Italian cousins as cheap delicious meals*
plavac ⑩ *pla*-vats *Dalmatian red wine*
pljeskavice od blitve ① pl *plye*-ska-vee-tse awd *bleet*-ve *patties made from silver beet, grated cheese, breadcrumbs, eggs & olive oil then seasoned with garlic & mint, fried & topped with sour cream*
podlanica ① *pawd*-la-nee-tsa *gilthead seabream (fish)*
podravski lonac ⑩ *paw*-drav-skee *law*-nats *layer of cooked dried beans, topped with pork cubes (or pork chops), a layer of cabbage, a layer of capsicum, bacon, green beans & cabbage then baked in a sealed dish*
pohan *paw*-han *fried in a breadcrumb batter*
pomfrit ⑩ *pawm*-freet *French fries • chips*
poriluk ⑩ *paw*-ree-look *leek*
poslastice ① pl *paw*-sla-stee-tse *desserts*
posutice ① pl *paw*-soo-tee-tse *type of pasta served with various side dishes (eg, salted pilchards)*
poširan paw-*shee*-ran *poached*
povrće ⑥ *paw*-vr-che *vegetable(s)*
prepržen pre-*pr*-zhen *prepared au gratin*
prilozi ⑩ pl *pree*-law-zee *side dishes*
prokupac ⑩ *praw*-koo-pats *well-known red wine similar to Pinot Noir*
prošek ⑩ *praw*-shek *sweet Dalmatian dessert wine*

prstac ⑩ pr-*stats* *date mussel – popular on the Adriatic Coast*
pršut ⑩ pr-*shoot* *prized smoke-dried ham similar to Italian prosciutto*
pržen pr-zhen *fried*
pržen u dubokom ulju pr-zhen oo *doo*-baw-kawm oo-lyoo *deep-fried*
prženi krumpiri ⑩ pl pr-zhe-nee kroom-pee-ree *pan-fried potatoes*
pržolica s lukom ① pr-*zhaw*-lee-tsa s loo-kawm *pan-fried steak with onions*
pšenica ① pshe-nee-tsa *wheat*
puding ⑩ *poo*-deeng *pudding*
punjen poo-nyen *stuffed*
punjena teleća prsa ① poo-nye-na te-le-cha pr-sa *stuffed breast of veal*
punjene paprike ① pl poo-nye-ne pa-pree-ke *capsicums stuffed with rice, tomato paste, parsley, onion & mincemeat then oven baked*
punjene rajčice ① pl poo-nye-ne rai-chee-tse *tomatoes stuffed with breadcrumbs, garlic & herbs then oven baked*
punjene sipe ① pl poo-nye-ne see-pe *squid fried with onions & garlic, stuffed with a mixture of breadcrumbs, parsley & egg, then baked in the oven in a tomato, garlic, rosemary & wine sauce*
punjenje ⑥ poo-nye-nye *stuffing*
puran ⑩ poo-ran *turkey cock*
purica ① poo-ree-tsa *turkey hen*
  — s mlincima s mleen-tsee-ma *turkey with mlinci – a Zagorje speciality often served at festive gatherings*
puževi na Vrbovečki način ⑩ pl poo-zhe-vee na vr-baw-vech-kee na-cheen *snails sautéed with onions then cooked in a sauce made from flour, paprika, meat stock & sour cream*

R

rajčica ① rai-chee-tsa *tomato*
rak ⑩ rak *crab*
rak (slatkovodni) ⑩ rak (slat-kaw-vawd-nee) *crayfish*
raž ① razh *rye*
ražanj ⑩ ra-zhan' *grill with a spit*
ražnjići ⑩ pl razh-nyee-chee *shish kebabs*
rebarca ⑥ pl re-bar-tsa *ribs*
repa ① re-pa *turnip*

restani krumpir ⓜ *re*·sta·nee kroom·*peer* roast potato

rezanci ⓜ pl *re*·zan·tsee pasta

riba ① *ree*·ba fish

riblja juha ① *reeb*·lya yoo·ha fish chowder made with freshwater fish cooked with onion, chilli, bay leaves & peppercorns to which tomato paste, paprika, vinegar & chopped parsley are added

riblji paprikaš ⓜ *reeb*·lyee pa·pree·kash carp or pike stewed in a paprika sauce & served with home-made noodles

ričet ⓜ *ree*·chet hearty winter soup containing barley, kidney beans, smoked meat & vegetables – flavoured with parsley root, bay leaf & garlic

riža ① *ree*·zha rice

rižoto ⓜ ree·*zhaw*·taw risotto – cooked rice dish made from arborio rice & often served with seafood dishes
— **od liganja** awd lee·ga·nya risotto containing squid, celery root, white wine, tomato paste, olive oil & fish stock – topped with parmesan cheese before serving

rotkvica ① *rawt*·kvee·tsa radish

rožata ① *raw*·zha·ta Croatian crème caramel with the zing of lemon zest

Ruska salata ① *roo*·ska sa·*la*·ta 'Russian salad' – salad of boiled potato, carrots, peas, chicken or ham, pickles & boiled eggs smothered in a sauce containing mayonnaise, lemon juice & parsley

ruzmarin ⓜ *rooz*·ma·reen rosemary

S

salama ① sa·*la*·ma salami

salata ① sa·*la*·ta salad
— **od cikle i kupusa** awd *tsee*·kle ee koo·poo·sa beetroot & cabbage salad containing horseradish, green capsicum, onion, garlic, oil & vinegar
— **od krastavaca** awd kra·sta·va·tsa cucumber salad
— **od patlidana i rajčica** awd pat·lee·ja·na ee rai·chee·tsa eggplant & tomato salad
— **od pečenih paprika** awd pe·che·neeh pa·pree·ka peeled roasted red peppers sprinkled with garlic, parsley, oil & vinegar
— **od prokulica** awd *praw*·koo·lee·tse boiled Brussels sprouts tossed with minced garlic, oil, lemon juice & vinegar
— **od rajčica** awd rai·chee·tsa tomato salad

salo ⓜ sa·law lard
— **na slavonski način** na *sla*·vawn·skee na·cheen carp pieces layered with sliced potato, sprinkled with paprika, smoked bacon & parsley then baked in the oven

sardela ① sar·de·la pilchard

sardina ① sar·*dee*·na sardine

sardine u ulju ① pl sar·*dee*·ne oo oo·lyoo sardines in oil

sarma ① *sar*·ma sour cabbage leaves stuffed with a mixture of ground meat (beef, pork & bacon), rice & garlic & flavoured with paprika, chilli & bay leaves then topped with a roux
— **od lišća od loze** awd *leesh*·cha awd *law*·ze vine leaves wrapped around a filling of minced beef & lamb (or beef & pork), egg & rice flavoured with parsley, paprika & pepper then simmered in water, wine or beef consommé

savijača ① sa·vee·ya·cha strudel see **štrudla**

savijena teletina ① sa·vee·ye·na te·le·tee·na pounded veal cutlets rolled around a filling of bacon, carrot & dill pickles then coated in flour & fried

seljački ručak ⓜ se·lyach·kee roo·chak fried diced veal combined with eggplant, tomatoes, capsicum, mushrooms & parsley & seasoned with paprika

sendvić ⓜ send·veech sandwich

senf ⓜ senf mustard

silvanac ⓜ seel·va·nats well-known white wine from Orahovica

sipa ① see·pa cuttlefish
— **punjen pršutom i rižom** poo·nyen pr·shoo·tawm ee ree·zhawm cuttlefish stuffed with prosciutto & rice – a Dalmatian speciality

sipica ⓜ see·pee·tsa squid

sir ⓜ seer cheese

skuhan ⓜ skoo·han done (cooked)

skuša ① skoo·sha mackerel

sladak sla·dak sweet

sladoled ⓜ sla·daw·led ice cream
— **od jagoda** od ya·gaw·da strawberry ice cream
— **sa šlagom** sa shla·gawm ice cream with whipped cream

slano ⓝ *sla*·naw salty • savoury
slanutak ⓜ sla·*noo*·tak chickpea
slastičarna ⓕ sla·stee·*char*·na cake shop
slatki kupus ⓜ *slat*·kee koo·poos sweet cabbage
slavonska riblja salata ⓕ *sla*·vawn·ska reeb·lya sa·*la*·ta Slavonian fish salad containing a number of different types of fish (pike, carp etc) poached with herbs & peppercorns then combined with vegetables sautéed in oil & white wine, lemon juice & parsley & served with sour cream
sleđ ⓜ slej herring
smokva ⓕ *smawk*·va fig
sok ⓜ sawk juice
sol ⓕ sawl salt
som ⓜ sawm catfish
— **na dunavski način** na *doo*·nav·skee na·cheen catfish fillets flavoured with lemon juice then rolled in flour, fried & baked with a mixture of fried onions, capsicum, chilli & tomato
sos ⓜ saws dip • gravy • sauce
srednje pečen ⓜ *sred*·nye pe·chen medium
srnetina ⓕ sr·ne·*tee*·na venison
stolno vino ⓝ *stawl*·naw vee·naw table wine
sušen soo·shen dried
sušena svinjska nožica ⓕ *soo*·she·na sveen′·ska naw·zhee·tsa dried pork hock
svinjetina ⓕ svee·nye·*tee*·na pork
— **na Đurđevački način** na *joor*·je·vach·kee na·cheen pork shanks cooked with tomato, green capsicum, smoked sausage, wine & sour cream & garnished with parsley
svinjski gulaš ⓜ *sveen′*·skee goo·lash pork goulash
svinjski kotlet ⓜ *sveen′*·skee *kawt*·let pork cutlet
— **na samoborski način** ⓜ na sa·*maw*·bawr·skee na·cheen pork chop served with garlic sauce & potato
svinjsko koljeno ⓝ *sveen′*·skaw kaw·lye·naw pork knuckle
svjež svyezh fresh

Š

šampinjon ⓜ sham·pee·*nyawn* button mushroom
šaran ⓜ *sha*·ran carp

šaumrole ⓕ pl sha·oom·*raw*·le puff pastry horns baked in the oven then filled with a mixture of whipped egg white, sugar & lemon juice
šećer ⓜ *she*·cher sugar
škampi ⓜ pl *shkam*·pee scampi (large prawns)
— **na buzaru** na boo·za·roo scampi stew – a Dalmatian speciality
— **na gradele** na gra·*de*·le grilled scampi – a Dalmatian speciality
školjke i rakovi ⓕ pl & ⓜ pl *shkawl′*·ke ee ra·kaw·vee 'shellfish & crabs' – equivalent to the collective term 'shellfish'
šljiva ⓕ *shlye*·va plum
šljivovica ⓕ *shlye*·vaw·vee·tsa slivovitz (plum brandy)
špageti ⓜ pl shpa·*ge*·tee spaghetti
šparoga ⓕ shpa·*raw*·ga asparagus
špinat ⓜ *shpee*·nat spinach
štrudla ⓕ *shtroo*·dla strudel – Croatian speciality containing a variety of sweet or savoury fillings such as cheese, buckwheat, potato, pumpkin, walnuts, poppy seed, nettles or fruit
— **s kupusum** s koo·poo·sawm savoury strudel-like pastry filled with shredded cabbage sautéed in oil
štrukle ⓕ pl *shtroo*·kle biscuit-sized boiled pastry parcels containing fruit fillings
— **s jabukama** s ya·boo·ka·ma **štrukle** filled with apple
— **s trešnjama** s tresh·nya·ma **štrukle** filled with sour cherries
štuka ⓕ *shtoo*·ka pike
šumska jagoda ⓕ *shoom*·ska ya·gaw·da wild strawberry
šunka ⓕ *shoon*·ka cured bacon
šunkarica ⓕ *shoon*·ka·ree·tsa type of salami made of rolled cured offal

T

tartuf ⓜ tar·*toof* truffle – delicacy from the region of Istria sometimes served shaved over scrambled eggs or risotto
teleća jetra na žaru ⓕ *te*·le·cha ye·tra na zha·roo grilled calf liver
teleća ragu-juha ⓕ *te*·le·cha ra·*goo*·yoo·ha veal ragout
teleće pečenje ⓝ *te*·le·che pe·*che*·nye roast veal

teletina ① te·le·tee·na *veal*

teran ⓜ te·ran *Istrian red wine*

tlačenica ① tla·che·nee·tsa *brawn • headcheese*

topljeni sir ⓜ taw·plye·nee seer *melted soft cheese*

torta od oraha ① tawr·ta awd aw·ra·ha *walnut layer cake*

traminac ⓜ tra·mee·nats *well-known dry white wine*

trapist ⓜ tra·peest *type of tasty cheese similar to Port Salut (French cheese)*

travarica ① tra·va·ree·tsa *herbal brandy purportedly with health giving properties*

trešnja ① tresh·nya *cherry*

tripice ① pl tree·pee·tse *tripe*

tučeno vrhnje ① too·che·naw vrh·nye *whipped cream*

tunjevina ① too·nye·vee·na *tuna*

turska kava ① toor·ska ka·va *Turkish coffee – strong brewed coffee popular in Croatia*

tvrdo kuhano jaje ① tvr·daw koo·ha·no yai·ye *hard-boiled egg*

U

ukiseljena svinjetina ① oo·kee·se·lye·na svee·nye·tee·na *pickled pork*

umak ⓜ oo·mak *dip • gravy • sauce*
  — od hrena awd hre·na *horseradish sauce with sour cream, egg yolk, mustard & lemon juice*
  — od rajčice awd rai·chee·tse *tomato sauce*

uštipci ⓜ pl oosh·teep·tsee *savoury doughnuts*

V

voće ⓝ vaw·che *fruit*

voćna salata ① vawch·na sa·la·ta *fruit salad*

voćni sladoled ⓜ vawch·nee sla·daw·led *fruit-flavoured ice cream*

Z

začin ⓜ za·cheen *seasoning*

Zagorska pita od tikvica s makom ① za·gawr·ska pee·ta awd teek·vee·tsa s ma·kawm *pumpkin pie with poppy seeds served in Zagorje*

Zagorska svatovska juha ① za·gawr·ska sva·tawv·ska yoo·ha *'Zagorje-style wedding soup' – soup containing veal shanks, celery & parsley roots, kohlrabi, cabbage, onion & carrot flavoured with peppercorns & parsley, with rice, egg yolks & sour cream added*

Zagorske štrukle ① pl za·gawr·ske shtroo·kle *strudel stuffed with a mixture of cottage cheese, butter, cream & eggs – an appetiser popular in the Zagorje region*

Zagorski džuveč ⓜ za·gawr·skee joo·vech *chicken pieces baked with mixed vegetables stewed in chicken stock, parsley, celery leaves, garlic, chilli & rice*

Zagorski pureći odrezak ⓜ za·gawr·skee poo·re·chee aw·dre·zak *turkey cutlets rolled around an omelette-like filling made from fried onions, mushrooms, turkey liver & eggs then dipped in beaten eggs & breadcrumbs & fried*

Zagrebački odrezak ⓜ za·gre·bach·kee aw·dre·zak *veal stuffed with ham & cheese then fried in breadcrumbs*

zec na hvarski način ⓜ zets na hvar·skee na·cheen *from the island of Hvar, this dish contains rabbit marinated in a mixture of vinegar, oil, red wine, celery, garlic, minced onion, thyme, rosemary, peppercorns & cloves then browned & braised in port*

zelena maslina ① ze·le·na ma·slee·na *green olive*

zelena paprika ① ze·le·na pa·pree·ka *green capsicum • green bell pepper*

zelena salata ① ze·le·na sa·la·ta *green salad • lettuce*

zubatac ⓜ zoo·ba·tats *dentex (fish)*

Ž

žaba ① zha·ba *frog – frogs legs are a popular delicacy sometimes found in a* **brodet** *or stew with eels*

žemička ① zhe·meech·ka *type of bread roll*

žgvacet od purana ⓜ zhgva·tset awd poo·ra·na *fried cubed turkey combined with onion, garlic & tomato then simmered until tender in white wine, marjoram & basil – an Istrian specialty*

emergencies

hitni slučajevi

English	Croatian	Pronunciation
Help!	*Upomoć!*	*oo*·paw·mawch
Stop!	*Stanite!*	*sta*·nee·te
Go away!	*Maknite se!*	*mak*·nee·te se
Thief!	*Lopov!*	*law*·pawv
Fire!	*Požar!*	*paw*·zhar
Watch out!	*Pazite!*	*pa*·zee·te

It's an emergency.
Imamo hitan slučaj.
ee·ma·maw *hee*·tan *sloo*·chai

There's been an accident.
Desila se nezgoda.
de·see·la se *nez*·gaw·da

Call the police.
Nazovite policiju.
na·zaw·vee·te paw·*lee*·tsee·yoo

Call a doctor.
Zovite liječnika.
zaw·vee·te lee·*yech*·nee·ka

Call an ambulance.
Zovite hitnu pomoć.
zaw·vee·te *heet*·noo paw·mawch

Could you please help?
*Molim vas, možete li
mi pomoći?*
maw·leem vas *maw*·zhe·te lee
mee *paw*·maw·chee

Can I use your phone?
*Mogu li koristiti vaš
telefon?*
maw·goo lee kaw·*ree*·stee·tee vash
te·*le*·fawn

I'm lost.
*Izgubio/Izgubila
sam se.* m/f
eez·*goo*·bee·aw/eez·*goo*·bee·la
sam se

Where are the toilets?
Gdje se nalaze nužnici?
gdye se *na*·la·ze *noozh*·nee·tsee

Is it safe at night?
Je li bezopasno noću?
ye lee *bez*·aw·pa·snaw *naw*·choo

police

Where's the police station?
  Gdje se nalazi   gdye se *na*·la·zee
  policijska stanica?   paw·*lee*·tseey·ska *sta*·nee·tsa

I want to report an offence.
  Želim prijaviti prekršaj.   zhe·leem pree·*ya*·vee·tee *pre*·kr·shai

It was him.
  On je to uradio.   awn ye taw oo·*ra*·dee·aw

It was her.
  Ona je to uradila.   *aw*·na ye taw oo·*ra*·dee·la

I've been ...	Ja sam	ya sam
	bio/bila ... **m/f**	bee·aw/bee·la ...
He's been ...	On je bio ...	awn ye bee·aw ...
She's been ...	Ona je bila ...	aw·na ye bee·la ...
assaulted	napadnut/	na·pad·noot
	napadnuta **m/f**	na·pad·noo·ta
raped	silovan/	see·law·van
	silovana **m/f**	see·law·va·na
robbed	opljačkan/	awp·lyach·kan
	opljačkana **m/f**	awp·lyach·ka·na

He tried to	On me je	awn me ye
... me.	pokušao ...	paw·koo·sha·aw ...
She tried to	Ona me je	aw·na me ye
... me.	pokušala ...	paw·koo·sha·la ...
assault	napasti	na·pa·stee
rape	silovati	see·law·va·tee
rob	opljačkati	awp·lyach·ka·tee

I've lost my ...	*Izgubio/*	eez·*goo*·bee·aw/
	Izgubila sam ... m/f	eez·*goo*·bee·la sam ...
backpack	*svoj ranac*	svoy *ra*·nats
bags	*svoje torbe*	svoy·e *tawr*·be
credit card	*svoju kreditnu*	svoy·oo *kre*·deet·noo
	karticu	*kar*·tee·tsoo
jewellery	*svoj nakit*	svoy *na*·keet
money	*svoj novac*	svoy *naw*·vats
passport	*svoju*	svoy·oo
	putovnicu	poo·*tawv*·nee·tsoo
travellers	*svoje putničke*	svoy·e *poot*·neech·ke
cheques	*čekove*	*che*·kaw·ve

My ... was/were stolen.

Ukrali su mi ... oo·kra·lee soo mee ...

the police may say ...

You're charged with ...	*Optuženi ste ...*	awp·*too*·zhe·nee ste ...
He/She is charged with ...	*On/Ona je*	awn/*aw*·na ye
	optužen/	awp·*too*·zhen/
	optužena ... m/f	awp·*too*·zhe·na ...
assault	*tvornim*	*tvawr*·neem
	napadom	*na*·pa·dawm
disturbing the peace	*narušavanjem*	na·roo·*sha*·va·nyem
	reda	*re*·da
not having a visa	*nedostatkom*	ne·daw·*stat*·kawm
	vize	*vee*·ze
overstaying your visa	*ostankom u*	aw·*stan*·kawm oo
	zemlji po	*zem*·lyee paw
	isteku vize	ee·*ste*·koo *vee*·ze
possession (of illegal substances)	*posjedovanjem*	paw·*sye*·daw·va·nyem
	(ilegalnih tvari)	(ee·le·*gal*·neeh *tva*·ree)
shoplifting	*krađom u*	*kra*·jawm oo
	prodavaonici	praw·da·va·*aw*·nee·tsee
theft	*krađom*	*kra*·jawm

essentials

175

What am I accused of?
> *Čime me teretite?*   *chee·me me te·re·tee·te*

I'm sorry.
> *Žao mi je.*   *zha·aw mee ye*

I (don't) understand.
> *Ja (ne) razumijem.*   *ya (ne) ra·zoo·mee·yem*

I didn't realise I was doing anything wrong.
> *Nisam bio svjesan*   *nee·sam bee·aw svye·san*
> *da radim išta krivo.* m   *da ra·deem eesh·ta kree·vaw*
> *Nisam bila svjesna*   *nee·sam bee·la svyes·na*
> *da radim išta krivo.* f   *da ra·deem eesh·ta kree·vaw*

I didn't do it.
> *Ja to nisam uradio/*   *ya taw nee·sam oo·ra·dee·aw/*
> *uradila.* m/f   *oo·ra·dee·la*

Can I pay an on-the-spot fine?
> *Mogu li platiti*   *maw·goo lee pla·tee·te*
> *novčanu globu na*   *nawv·cha·noo glaw·boo na*
> *licu mjesta?*   *lee·tsoo mye·sta*

I want to contact my embassy/consulate.
> *Želim stupiti u*   *zhe·leem stoo·pee·tee oo*
> *kontakt sa svojom*   *kawn·takt sa svoy·awm*
> *ambasadom/*   *am·ba·sa·dawm/*
> *konzulatom.*   *kawn·zoo·la·tawm*

Can I make a phone call?
> *Mogu li obaviti*   *maw·goo lee aw·ba·vee·tee*
> *telefonski poziv?*   *te·le·fawn·skee paw·zeev*

Can I have a lawyer (who speaks English)?
> *Mogu li dobiti*   *maw·goo lee daw·bee·tee*
> *odvjetnika (koji*   *awd·vyet·nee·ka (koy·ee*
> *govori engleski)?*   *gaw·vaw·ree en·gle·skee)*

This drug is for personal use.
> *Ova droga je za*   *aw·va draw·ga ye za*
> *osobnu upotrebu.*   *aw·sawb·noo oo·paw·tre·boo*

I have a prescription for this drug.
> *Ja imam recept*   *ya ee·mam re·tsept*
> *za ovaj lijek.*   *za aw·vai lee·yek*

doctor

liječnik

Where's the nearest ...?	*Gdje je najbliži/a ...?* m/f	gdye ye nai·blee·zhee/a ...
(night) chemist	*(noćna) ljekarna* f	*(nawch·*na) lye·kar·na
dentist	*zubar* m	zoo·bar
doctor	*liječnik* m	lee·yech·neek
emergency department	*odjel hitne pomoći* m	aw·dyel heet·ne paw·maw·chee
hospital	*bolnica* f	bawl·nee·tsa
medical centre	*medicinski centar* m	me·dee·tseen·skee tsen·tar
optometrist	*optičar* m	awp·tee·char

I need a doctor (who speaks English).
Trebam liječnika   tre·bam lee·yech·nee·ka
(koji govori engleski).   (koy·ee gaw·vaw·ree en·gle·skee)

Could I see a female doctor?
Mogu li dobiti   maw·goo lee daw·bee·tee
ženskog liječnika?   zhen·skawg lee·yech·nee·ka

Could the doctor come here?
Može li liječnik   maw·zhe lee lee·yech·neek
doći ovamo?   daw·chee aw·va·maw

Is there an after-hours emergency number?
Postoji li noćni broj   paw·stoy·ee lee nawch·nee broy
telefona za hitne   te·le·faw·na za heet·ne
slučajeve?   sloo·chai·e·ve

I've run out of my medication.
Nestalo mi je lijekova.   ne·sta·law mee ye lee·*ye*·kaw·va

This is my usual medicine.
Ovo je moj   *aw*·vaw ye moy
uobičajeni lijek.   oo·aw·*bee*·chai·e·nee lee·*yek*

My child weighs (20 kilos).
Moje dijete teži   *moy*·e dee·*ye*·te te·zhee
(dvadeset kila).   (*dva*·de·set *kee*·la)

What's the correct dosage?
Koja je točna doza?   *koy*·a ye *tawch*·na *daw*·za

I don't want a blood transfusion.
Ne želim transfuziju krvi.   ne *zhe*·leem trans·*foo*·zee·yoo *kr*·vee

Please use a new syringe.
Molim upotrijebite   *maw*·leem oo·paw·tree·*ye*·bee·te
novu špricu.   *naw*·voo shpree·tsoo

I have my own syringe.
Ja imam svoju špricu.   ya *ee*·mam svoy·oo shpree·tsoo

I've been vaccinated against (tetanus).
Cijepljen/Cijepljena sam   tsee·*ye*·plyen/tsee·*ye*·plye·na sam
protiv (tetanusa). **m/f**   *praw*·teev (*te*·ta·noo·sa)

He's been vaccinated against (hepatitis A/B/C).
On je cijepljen protiv   awn ye tsee·*ye*·plyen *praw*·teev
(hepatitisa A/B/C).   (he·pa·*tee*·tee·sa a/be/tse)

She's been vaccinated against (typhoid).
Ona je cijepljena   *aw*·na ye tsee·*ye*·plye·na
protiv (tifusa).   *praw*·teev *tee*·foo·sa

My prescription is …
Moj recept je za …   moy *re*·tsept ye za …

How much will it cost?
Koliko će to stajati?   kaw·*lee*·kaw che taw *stai*·a·tee

Can I have a receipt for my insurance?
Mogu li dobiti račun   *maw*·goo lee *daw*·bee·tee *ra*·choon
za moje osiguranje?   za *moy*·e aw·see·goo·*ra*·nye

I need new …	*Trebam nove …*	*tre*·bam *naw*·ve …
contact lenses	*kontakt leće*	*kawn*·takt *le*·che
glasses	*naočale*	*na*·aw·cha·le

symptoms & conditions

I'm sick.
Ja sam bolestan/
bolesna. m/f
ya sam *baw*·le·stan/
baw·le·sna

My friend is (very) sick.
Moj prijatelj
je (vrlo) bolestan. m
moy *pree*·ya·tel'
ye (*vr*·law) *baw*·le·stan

Moja prijateljica
je (vrlo) bolesna. f
moy·a *pree*·ya·te·lyee·tsa
ye (*vr*·law) *baw*·les·na

My child is (very) sick.
Moje dijete
je (vrlo) bolesno.
moy·e dee·*ye*·te
ye (*vr*·law) *baw*·le·snaw

He/She is having a/an ...	On/Ona trenutno ima ...	awn/*aw*·na tre·noot·naw ee·ma ...
allergic reaction	alergičnu reakciju	a·*ler*·geech·noo re·*ak*·tsee·yoo
asthma attack	napad astme	na·pad *ast*·me
baby	trudove	troo·daw·ve
epileptic fit	napad epilepsije	na·pad e·pee·*lep*·see·ye
heart attack	srčani napad	sr·cha·nee na·pad

I've been ...	Ja sam ...	ya sam ...
He's been ...	On je ...	awn ye ...
She's been ...	Ona je ...	*aw*·na ye ...
injured	povrijeđen/ povrijeđena m/f	paw·vree·*ye*·jen paw·vree·*ye*·je·na
vomiting	povraćao/ povraćala m/f	paw·vra·cha·aw/ paw·vra·cha·la

179

What's the problem?
Što nije u redu? shtaw *nee*·ye oo *re*·doo

Where does it hurt?
Gdje vas boli? gdye vas *baw*·lee

Do you have a temperature?
Da li imate temperaturu? da lee ee·*ma*·te tem·pe·ra·*too*·roo

How long have you been like this?
Koliko dugo ste kaw·*lee*·kaw *doo*·gaw ste
u ovom stanju? oo *aw*·vawm *sta*·nyoo

Have you had this before?
Da li ste patili od da lee ste *pa*·tee·lee awd
ovoga u prošlosti? aw·*vaw*·ga oo *prawsh*·law·stee

Are you sexually active?
Da li ste spolno aktivni? da lee ste *spawl*·naw *ak*·teev·nee

Have you had unprotected sex?
Da li ste imali da lee ste ee·*ma*·lee
nezaštićeni ne·*zash*·tee·che·nee
spolni odnos? *spawl*·nee *awd*·naws

How long are you travelling for?
Koliko dugo ćete kaw·*lee*·kaw *doo*·gaw *che*·te
putovati? poo·*taw*·va·tee

You need to be admitted to hospital.
Trebate ići u *tre*·ba·te ee·*chee* oo
bolnicu. *bawl*·nee·tsoo

Do you ...?	*Da li ...?*	da lee ...
drink	*pijete*	*pee*·ye·te
smoke	*pušite*	*poo*·shee·te
take drugs	*uzimate droge*	oo·zee·*ma*·te *draw*·ge

Are you ...?	*Jeste li ...?*	*ye*·ste lee ...
allergic to	*alergični*	a·*ler*·geech·nee
anything	*na išta*	na *eesh*·ta
on medication	*na nekim*	na *ne*·keem
	lijekovima	lee·*ye*·kaw·vee·ma

the doctor may say ...

You should have it checked when you go home.
Trebate otići na
kontrolu kada
odete kući.
tre·ba·te aw·tee·chee na
kawn·traw·loo ka·da
aw·dete koo·chee

You should return home for treatment.
Trebate se vratiti
kući na liječenje.
tre·ba·te se vra·tee·tee
koo·chee na lee·ye·che·nye

You're a hypochondriac.
Vi ste hipohondar.
vee ste hee·paw·hawn·dar

I feel ...	Osjećam se ...	aw·sye·cham se ...
anxious	napeto	na·pe·taw
better	bolje	baw·lye
depressed	potišteno	paw·teesh·te·naw
dizzy	ošamućeno	aw·sha·moo·che·naw
hot and cold	toplo i hladno	taw·plaw ee hlad·naw
nauseous	mučno u želudcu	mooch·naw oo zhe·lood·tsoo
shivery	drhtavo	drh·ta·vaw
strange	čudno	chood·naw
weak	slabo	sla·baw
worse	gore	gaw·re

It hurts here.
Boli me ovdje.
baw·lee me awv·dye

I'm dehydrated.
Ja sam dehidrirao/
dehidrirala. m/f
ya sam de·hee·dree·ra·aw/
de·hee·dree·ra·la

I can't sleep.
Ne mogu spavati.
ne maw·goo spa·va·tee

I think it's the medication I'm on.
Mislim da je to od
lijekova koje uzimam.
mee·sleem da ye taw awd
lee·ye·kaw·va koy·e oo·zee·mam

I'm on medication for ...
Ja sam na
lijekovima za ...
ya sam na
lee·ye·kaw·vee·ma za ...

He/She is on medication for …

On/Ona je na lijekovima za …	awn/*aw*·na ye na lee·*ye*·kaw·vee·ma za …

I have (a/an) …

Imam …	*ee*·mam …

He/She has (a/an) …

On/Ona ima …	awn/*aw*·na ee·ma …

I've recently had (a/an) …

Nedavno sam imao/imala … m/f	ne·dav·naw sam ee·ma·aw/*ee*·ma·la …

He/She has recently had (a/an) …

On/Ona je nedavno imao/imala … m/f	awn/*aw*·na ye ne·dav·naw ee·ma·aw/*ee*·ma·la …

asthma	astma f	*ast*·ma
cold (noun)	prehlada f	pre·hla·da
constipation	zatvorenje n	zat·vaw·*re*·nye
cough (noun)	kašalj m	*ka*·shal'
dehydration	dehidratacija f	de·hee·dra·*ta*·tsee·ya
diabetes	dijabetes m	dee·ya·*be*·tes
diarrhoea	proljev m	*pro*·lyev
ear infection	upala uha f	oo·pa·la *oo*·ha
fever	groznica f	*graw*·znee·tsa
flu	gripa f	*gree*·pa
headache	glavobolja f	gla·*vaw*·baw·lya
heatstroke	sunčanica f	sun·*cha*·nee·tsa
hypothermia	hipotermija f	hee·paw·*ter*·mee·ya
jellyfish sting	opeklina od meduze f	*aw*·pe·klee·na awd me·*doo*·ze
muscle cramps	grčenje mišića n	gr·che·nye mee·*shee*·cha
nausea	mučnina f	mooch·*nee*·na
sore throat	grlobolja f	gr·*law*·baw·lya
sunburn	opekline od sunca f pl	*aw*·pe·klee·ne awd *soon*·tsa

I've been ...	Mene je ujela ...	me·ne ye oo·ye·la ...
bitten by a snake	zmija	zmee·ya
stung by a bee	pčela	pche·la
stung by a wasp	osa	aw·sa

I ...	Ja sam ...	ya sam ...
removed a tick	odstranio/ odstranila krpelja m/f	awd·stra·nee·aw/ awd·stra·nee·la kr·pe·lya
stepped on a sea urchin	stao/stala na morskog ježa m/f	sta·aw/sta·la na mawr·skawg ye·zha

women's health

(I think) I'm pregnant.
Ja (mislim da) sam trudna. ya (mee·sleem da) sam trood·na

I'm on the pill.
Ja sam na
antibaby-pilulama.
ya sam na
an·tee·bey·bee·pee·loo·la·ma

I haven't had my period for (six) weeks.
Nisam imala
mjesečnicu već
(šest) tjedana.
nee·sam ee·ma·la
mye·sech·nee·tsoo vech
(shest) tye·da·na

I've noticed a lump here.
Primjetila sam
izraslinu ovdje.
pree·mye·tee·la sam
eez·ra·slee·noo awv·dye

I need ...	Trebam ...	tre·bam ...
contraception	sredstvo za sprječavanje trudnoće	sreds·tvaw za sprye·cha·va·nye trood·naw·che
the morning-after pill	hitnu kontracepciju	heet·noo kawn·tra·tsep·tsee·yoo
a pregnancy test	test na trudnoću	test na trood·naw·choo

SAFE TRAVEL

the doctor may say ...

Are you using contraception?

Da li koristite sredstva	da lee *kaw*·ree·stee·te *sreds*·tva
za sprječavanje	za sprye·*cha*·va·nye
trudnoće?	trood·*naw*·che

Are you menstruating?

Da li menstruirate?	da lee men·stroo·*ee*·ra·te

Are you pregnant?

Jeste li trudni?	*ye*·ste lee *trood*·nee

When did you last have your period?

Kada ste zadnji put	*ka*·da ste *zad*·nyee poot
imali mjesečnicu?	ee·ma·lee *mye*·sech·nee·tsoo

You're pregnant.

Vi ste trudni.	vee ste *trood*·nee

alternative treatments

alternativni oblici liječenja

I prefer ...	*Ja bih radije ...*	ya beeh *ra*·dee·ye ...
Can I see	*Mogu li*	*maw*·goo lee
someone who	*posjetiti*	*paw*·sye·tee·tee
practices ...?	*nekoga tko*	*ne*·kaw·ga tkaw
	vrši praksu ...?	*vr*·shee *prak*·soo ...
acupuncture	*akopunkture*	a·kaw·*poonk*·*too*·re
naturopathy	*naturopatije*	*na*·too·raw·pa·tee·ye
reflexology	*refleksologije*	re·flek·saw·*law*·gee·ye

I don't use (Western medicine).

Ja ne koristim	ya ne kaw·*ree*·steem
(Zapadnjačku medicinu).	(*za*·pad·nyach·koo me·dee·*tsee*·noo)

allergies

I'm allergic to ...	Ja sam alergičan/ alergična na ... m/f	ya sam a·ler·gee·chan/ a·ler·geech·na na ...
He/She is allergic to ...	On/Ona je alergičan/ alergična na ... m/f	awn/aw·na ye a·ler·gee·chan/ a·ler·geech·na na ...
antibiotics	antibiotike	an·tee·bee·aw·tee·ke
anti-inflammatories	lijekove protiv upale	lee·ye·kaw·ve praw·teev oo·pa·le
aspirin	aspirin	a·spee·reen
bees	pčele	pche·le
codeine	kodein	kaw·de·een
penicillin	penicilin	pe·nee·tsee·leen
pollen	pelud	pe·lood
sulphur-based drugs	lijekove koji sadrže sumpor	lee·ye·kaw·ve koy·ee sa·dr·zhe soom·pawr

I have a skin allergy.
  Ja imam kožnu alergiju.   ya ee·mam kawzh·noo a·ler·gee·yoo

I'm on a special diet.
  Ja sam na posebnoj dijeti.   ya sam na paw·seb·noy dee·ye·tee

I'm allergic to (gluten).
  Ja sam alergičan/   ya sam a·ler·gee·chan/
  alergična na (gluten). m/f   a·ler·geech·na na (gloo·ten)

antihistamines	antihistaminici m pl	an·tee·hee·sta·mee·nee·tsee
inhaler	inhalator m	een·ha·la·tawr
injection	injekcija f	ee·nyek·tsee·ya

For more food-related allergies, see **vegetarian & special meals**, page 162.

parts of the body

My ... hurts.
   Moj/Moja/Moje ... boli. m/f/n   moy/*moy*·a/*moy*·e ... *baw*·lee

I can't move my ...
   Moj ... je nepomičan. m   moy ... ye *ne*·paw·mee·chan
   Moja ... je nepomična. f   *moy*·a ... ye *ne*·paw·meech·na
   Moje ... je nepomično. n   *moy*·e ... ye *ne*·paw·meech·naw

I have a cramp in my ...
   Grči mi se ...   *gr*·chee mee se ...

My ... is swollen.
   Moj ... je natekao. m   moy ... ye *na*·te·ka·aw
   Moja ... je natekla. f   *moy*·a ... ye *na*·te·kla
   Moje ... je nateklo. n   *moy*·e ... ye *na*·te·klaw

eye
oko n
aw·kaw

nose
nos m
naws

mouth
usta f
oo·sta

ear
uho n
oo·haw

head
glava f
gla·va

hand
ruka f
roo·ka

arm
ruka f
roo·ka

chest
prsa f
pr·sa

stomach
želudac m
zhe·*loo*·dats

bum
stražnjica f
strazh·nyee·tsa

leg
noga f
naw·ga

foot
stopalo n
staw·pa·law

chemist

I need something for (a headache).
Trebam nešto za   tre·bam nesh·taw za
(glavobolju).   (gla·vaw·baw·lyoo)

Do I need a prescription for (antihistamines)?
Da li mi treba recept   da lee mee tre·ba re·tsept
za (antihistaminike)?   za (an·tee·hee·sta·mee·nee·ke)

I have a prescription.
Ja imam recept.   ya ee·mam re·tsept

How many times a day?
Koliko puta na dan?   kaw·lee·kaw poo·ta na dan

Will it make me drowsy?
Hoće li me to napraviti   haw·che lee me taw na·pra·vee·tee
pospanim/pospanom? m/f   paw·spa·neem/paw·spa·nawm

antiseptic	*antiseptik* m	an·tee·sep·teek
contraceptives	*sredstva za*	sreds·tva za
	sprječavanje	sprye·cha·va·nye
	neželjene	ne·zhe·lye·ne
	trudnoće n pl	trood·naw·che
painkillers	*tablete protiv*	ta·ble·te praw·teev
	bolova f pl	baw·law·va
rehydration salts	*soli za*	saw·lee za
	rehidrataciju f	re·hee·dra·ta·tsee·yoo
thermometer	*toplomjer* m	taw·plaw·myer

listen for ...

dva poo·ta dnev·naw (ooz hra·noo)
Dva puta dnevno (uz hranu).   **Twice a day (with food).**

maw·ra·te oo·ze·tee chee·ta·voo praw·pee·sa·noo daw·zoo
lee·ye·ka paw oo·poo·ta·ma
Morate uzeti čitavu propisanu   **You must complete**
dozu lijeka po uputama.   **the course.**

health

dentist

I have a ...	Ja imam ...	ya ee·mam ...
broken tooth	razbijen zub	ra·zbee·yen zoob
cavity	karijes	ka·ree·yes
toothache	zubobolju	zoo·baw·baw·lyoo

I've lost a filling.
Ispala mi je plomba.   ee·spa·la mee ye plawm·ba

My dentures are broken.
Razbilo mi se   ra·zbee·law mee se
umjetno zubalo.   oo·myet·naw zoo·ba·law

My gums hurt.
Bole me desni.   baw·le me de·snee

I don't want it extracted.
Ne želim da ga vadite.   ne zhe·leem da ga va·dee·te

Ouch!
Jao!   ya·aw

I need (a/an) ...	Treba mi ...	tre·ba mee ...
anaesthetic	anestetik	a·ne·ste·teek
filling	plomba	plawm·ba

listen for ...

shee·rawm awt·vaw·ree·te oo·sta
Širom otvorite usta.   **Open wide.**

aw·vaw ne·che nee·ma·law baw·lye·tee
Ovo neće nimalo boljeti.   **This won't hurt a bit.**

za·gree·zee·te aw·vaw
Zagrizite ovo.   **Bite down on this.**

ne·moy·te se mee·tsa·tee
Nemojte se micati.   **Don't move.**

ee·spe·ree·te
Isperite!   **Rinse!**

SAFE TRAVEL

Nouns in the dictionary have their gender indicated by ⓜ, ⓕ or ⓝ. If it's a plural noun you'll also see pl. When a word that could be either a noun or a verb has no gender indicated, it's a verb.

Nouns and adjectives are in the nominative case. You'll be understood if you just pick words out of this dictionary, but if you'd like to know more about case, see the **a–z phrasebuilder**, page 21.

Adjectives in the dictionary are given in the masculine form only. For an explanation of how to form feminine and neuter adjectives, refer to the **a–z phrasebuilder**, page 16.

Verbs are mostly given in two forms: perfective and imperfective. See the **a–z phrasebuilder**, page 17 for an explanation of these terms and when to use which form. Perfective and imperfective forms are either separated by a slash (with the perfective form given first) or consist of a root imperfective form to which a bracketed prefix is added to form the perfective. For example, the verb 'give' has the forms dati/davati da·tee/da·va·tee with the first form being the perfective form and the second the imperfective. The verb 'call' is represented as (po)zvati (paw·)zva·tee which has the perfective form pozvati and the imperfective form zvati. Where two syllables are stressed in the transliteration, eg (paw·)zva·tee it means that once you add the prefix to form the perfective, the stress shifts to the prefix.

Where only one form of a verb is given (not all verbs have both forms) the abbreviations perf and imp have been used to identify whether they are perfective or imperfective.

A

aboard (boat, plane) ukrcan na
oo·kr·tsan na
aboard (train, bus) u oo
abortion pobačaj ⓜ paw·ba·chai
about o · oko · u vezi · zbog aw · aw·kaw ·
oo ve·zee · zbawg
above iznad eez·nad
abroad u inozemstvu oo ee·naw·zemst·voo
accident nezgoda ⓕ nez·gaw·da
accommodation smještaj ⓜ smye·shtai
account (bank) račun ⓜ ra·choon
across kroz · preko krawz · pre·kaw
activist aktivist ⓜ ak·tee·veest
actor glumac ⓜ gloo·mats
acupuncture akopunktura ⓕ
a·kaw·poonk·too·ra
adaptor konverter ⓜ kawn·ver·ter
addiction ovisnost ⓕ aw·vee·snawst
address adresa ⓕ a·dre·sa

administration uprava ⓕ oo·pra·va
admission (price) ulaznica (cijena) ⓕ
oo·laz·nee·tsa (tsee·ye·na)
admit (allow) dozvoliti/dozvoljavati
dawz·vaw·lee·tee/
dawz·vaw·lya·va·tee
admit (confess) priznati/priznavati
pree·zna·tee/pree·zna·va·tee
Adriatic Coast Jadranska obala ⓕ
ya·dran·ska aw·ba·la
Adriatic Sea Jadransko more ⓝ
ya·dran·skaw maw·re
adult odrasla osoba ⓕ aw·dra·sla
aw·saw·ba
advertisement oglas ⓜ aw·glas
advice savjet ⓜ sa·vyet
aerobics aerobik ⓜ a·e·raw·beek
aeroplane zrakoplov ⓜ zra·kaw·plawv
Africa Afrika ⓕ a·free·ka
after iza · po · poslije ee·za · paw ·
paw·slee·ye

(this) afternoon *(ovo) poslijepodne* ⓝ (aw·vaw) paw·slee·ye·pawd·ne
aftershave *losion za upotrebu poslije brijanja* ⓝ law·see·awn za oo·paw·tre·boo paw·slee·ye bree·ya·nya
again *opet* aw·pet
age (person) *uzrast* ⓜ ooz·rast
(three days) ago *(tri dana) prije* (tree da·na) pree·ye
agree *složiti/slagati se* slaw·zhee·tee/sla·ga·tee se
agriculture *poljodjelstvo* ⓝ paw·lyaw·dyel·stvaw
ahead *naprijed* na·pree·yed
AIDS *SIDA* ⓕ see·da
air *zrak* ⓜ zrak
air-conditioned *klimatiziran* klee·ma·tee·zee·ran
air-conditioning *klima* ⓕ klee·ma
airline *zrakoplovna tvrtka* ⓕ zra·kaw·plawv·na tvr·tka
airmail *zračna pošta* ⓕ zrach·na pawsh·ta
airplane *zrakoplov* ⓜ zra·kaw·plawv
airport *zračna luka* ⓕ zrach·na loo·ka
airport tax *porez na zračni prijevoz* ⓜ paw·rez na zrach·nee pree·ye·vawz
aisle (plane etc) *prolaz između sjedišta* ⓜ praw·laz eez·me·joo sye·deesh·ta
alarm clock *budilica* ⓕ boo·dee·lee·tsa
alcohol *alcohol* ⓜ al·kaw·hawl
all *sve* sve
allergy *alergija* ⓕ a·ler·gee·ya
alley *uska ulica* ⓕ oo·ska oo·lee·tsa
almond *badem* ⓜ ba·dem
almost *skoro* skaw·raw
alone *sam* sam
already *već* vech
also *također* ta·kaw·jer
altar *oltar* ⓜ awl·tar
altitude *visina* ⓕ vee·see·na
always *uvijek* oo·vee·yek
ambassador *veleposlanik* ⓜ ve·le·paw·sla·neek
ambulance *hitna pomoć* ⓕ heet·na paw·mawch
American football *američki nogomet* ⓜ a·me·reech·kee naw·gaw·met
amphitheatre *amfiteatar* ⓜ am·fee·te·a·tar
anaemia *anemija* ⓕ a·ne·mee·ya
anarchist *anarhist* ⓜ a·nar·heest
ancient *antički* an·teech·kee
and *i* ee
angry *ljutit* lyoo·teet

animal *životinja* ⓕ zhee·vaw·tee·nya
ankle *gležanj* ⓜ gle·zhan'
another *drugi* droo·gee
answer *odgovor* ⓜ awd·gaw·vawr
ant *mrav* ⓜ mrav
antibiotics *antibiotici* ⓜ pl an·tee·bee·aw·tee·tsee
antinuclear *antinuklearni* an·tee·noo·kle·ar·nee
antique *antikvitet* ⓜ an·tee·kvee·tet
antiseptic *antiseptik* ⓜ an·tee·sep·teek
any *bilo koji* bee·law koy·ee
apartment *stan* ⓜ stan
appendix (body) *slijepo crijevo* ⓝ slee·ye·paw tsree·ye·vaw
apple *jabuka* ⓕ ya·boo·ka
appointment *sastanak* ⓜ sa·sta·nak
apricot *kajsija* ⓕ kai·see·ya
April *travanj* ⓜ tra·van'
apse *apsida* ⓕ a·psee·da
archaeological *arheološki* ⓜ ar·he·aw·lawsh·kee
architect *arhitekt* ⓜ ar·hee·tekt
architecture *arhitektura* ⓕ ar·hee·tek·too·ra
argue *(po)svađati se* (paw·)sva·ja·tee se
arm *ruka* ⓕ roo·ka
aromatherapy *aromaterapija* ⓕ a·raw·ma·te·ra·pee·ya
arrest *uhititi* perf oo·hee·tee·tee
arrivals *dolasci* ⓜ pl daw·las·tsee
arrive *stići/stizati* stee·chee/stee·za·tee
art *umjetnost* ⓕ oo·myet·nawst
art gallery *galerija* ⓕ ga·le·ree·ya
artist *umjetnik/umjetnica* ⓜ/ⓕ oo·myet·neek/oo·myet·nee·tsa
ashtray *pepeljara* ⓕ pe·pe·lya·ra
Asia *Azija* ⓕ a·zee·ya
ask (a question) *(u)pitati* (oo·)pee·ta·tee
ask (for something) *(za)tražiti* (za·)tra·zhee·tee
asparagus *šparoga* ⓕ shpa·raw·ga
aspirin *aspirin* ⓜ a·spee·reen
asthma *astma* ⓕ ast·ma
at *kod · pri · na · u* kawd · pree · na · oo
athletics *atletika* ⓕ at·le·tee·ka
atmosphere *atmosfera* ⓕ at·maw·sfe·ra
aubergine *patlidžan* ⓜ pa·tlee·jan
August *kolovoz* ⓜ kaw·law·vawz
aunt *tetka* ⓕ tet·ka
Australia *Australija* ⓕ a·oo·stra·lee·ya
Australian Rules Football *Australski nogomet* ⓜ a·oo·stral·skee naw·gaw·met

Austria Austrija ① a-oo-stree-ya
Austro-Hungarian Empire
   Austru-Ugarsko carstvo ⓝ
   a-oo-straw-oo-gar-skaw tsar-stvaw
automated teller machine (ATM)
   bankovni automat ⓜ ban-kawv-nee
   a-oo-*taw*-mat
autumn jesen ① ye-sen
avenue avenija ① a-ve-nee-ya
awful užasan oo-zha-san

B

B&W (film) crno-bijeli (film)
   tsr-naw-bee-ye-lee (feelm)
baby beba ① be-ba
baby food hrana za bebe ① hra-na za be-be
baby powder puder za bebe ⓜ poo-der
   za be-be
baby-sitter dadilja ① da-dee-lya
back (body) leđa ① le-ja
back (position) pozadina ①
   paw-za-dee-na
backpack ranac ⓜ ra-nats
bacon slanina ① sla-nee-na
bad loš lawsh
bag torba ① tawr-ba
baggage prtljaga ① prt-lya-ga
baggage allowance dozvoljena
   količina prtljage ① dawz-vaw-lye-na
   kaw-lee-chee-na prt-lya-ge
baggage claim šalter za podizanje
   prtljage ⓜ shal-ter za paw-dee-za-nye
   prt-lya-ge
bakery pekara ① pe-ka-ra
balance (account) saldo ⓜ sal-daw
balcony balkon ⓜ bal-kawn
(the) Balkans Balkan ⓜ bal-kan
ball lopta ① lawp-ta
ballet balet ⓜ ba-let
banana banana ① ba-na-na
band (music) grupa ① groo-pa
bandage zavoj ⓜ za-voy
Band-aid flaster ⓜ fla-ster
bank (institution) banka ① ban-ka
bank account bankovni račun ⓜ
   ban-kawv-nee ra-choon
banknote novčanica ① nawv-cha-nee-tsa
baptism krštenje ① krsh-te-nye
bar bar ⓜ bar
barber brijač ⓜ bree-yach
baseball bejzbol ⓜ beyz-bawl

basket koš ⓜ kawsh
basketball košarka ① kaw-shar-ka
bath kupka ① koop-ka
bathing suit kupaći kostim ⓜ
   koo-pa-chee kaw-steem
bathroom kupaonica ①
   koo-pa-aw-nee-tsa
battery (for car) akumulator ⓜ
   a-koo-moo-la-tawr
battery (general) baterija ① ba-te-ree-ya
bay uvala ① oo-va-la
be biti/bivati bee-tee/bee-va-tee
beach plaža ① pla-zha
beach volleyball odbojka na pjesku ①
   awd-boy-ka na pye-skoo
bean grah ⓜ grah
beansprout klica graha ① klee-tsa gra-ha
beautiful lijep lee-yep
beauty salon kozmetički salon ⓜ
   kawz-me-teech-kee sa-lawn
because zato za-taw
bed krevet ⓜ kre-vet
bed linen posteljina ① paw-ste-lyee-na
bedding krevetnina ① kre-vet-nee-na
bedroom spavaća soba ① spa-va-cha
   saw-ba
bee pčela ① pche-la
beef govedina ① gaw-ve-dee-na
beer pivo ⓝ pee-vaw
beer hall pivnica ① peev-nee-tsa
beetroot cikla ① tsee-kla
before prije pree-ye
beggar prosjak ⓜ praw-syak
behind iza ee-za
Belgium Belgija ① bel-gee-ya
bell pepper paprika ① pa-pree-ka
below ispod ee-spawd
beside pored · kraj · do · uz paw-red · krai
   · daw · ooz
best najbolji nai-baw-lyee
bet oklada ① aw-kla-da
better bolji baw-lyee
between između ee-zme-joo
Bible biblija ① bee-blee-ya
bicycle bicikl ⓜ bee-tsee-kl
big velik ve-leek
bigger veći ve-chee
biggest najveći nai-ve-chee
bike bicikl ⓜ bee-tsee-kl
bike chain lanac na biciklu ⓜ la-nats na
   bee-tsee-kloo
bike lock lokot na biciklu ⓜ law-kawt na
   bee-tsee-kloo

bike path *biciklistička staza* ①
bee·tsee·klee·steech·ka *sta·za*
bike shop *prodavaonica bicikala* ①
praw·da·va·*aw*·nee·tsa bee·*tsee*·ka·la
bill (account) *račun* ⓜ *ra*·choon
binoculars *dalekozor* ⓜ *da*·le·kaw·zawr
bird *ptica* ① *ptee*·tsa
birth certificate *izvod iz matične knjige
rođenih* ⓜ *eez*·vawd eez *ma*·teech·ne
knye·ge raw·je·neeh
birthday *rođendan* ⓜ *raw*·jen·dan
biscuit *keks* ⓜ keks
bite (dog) *ugriz* ⓜ *oo*·greez
bite (insect) *ubod* ⓜ *oo*·bawd
bitter *gorak* *gaw*·rak
black *crn* tsrn
bladder *mjehur* ⓜ *mye*·hoor
blanket *deka* ① *de*·ka
blind *slijep* slee·*yep*
blister *žulj* zhool'
blocked *zaglavljen* za·glav·*lyen*
blood *krv* ① krv
blood group *krvna grupa* ① *krv*·na groo·pa
blood pressure *tlak krvi* ⓜ tlak *kr*·vee
blood test *krvne pretrage* ① pl
krv·ne pre·*tra*·ge
blue *plav* plav
board (a plane, ship etc) *ukrcati/ukrca-
vati se* oo·*kr*·tsa·tee/oo·kr·*tsa*·va·tee se
boarding house *pansion* *pan*·see·awn
boarding pass *zrakoplovna ulaznica* ①
zra·kaw·plawv·na oo·*laz*·nee·tsa
boat (ship) *brawd* ⓜ brawd
boat (smaller/private) *čamac* ⓜ *cha*·mats
body *tijelo* ① *tee*·ye·law
boiled *obaren* aw·*ba*·ren
bone *kost* ① kawst
book *knjiga* ① *knyee*·ga
book (make a booking) *rezervirati* perf
re·zer·*vee*·ra·tee
booked out *popunjen* *paw*·poo·nyen
bookshop *knjižara* ① *knyee*·zha·ra
boot(s) (footwear) *čizma/e* ①/① pl
chee·zma/e
border *granica* ① *gra*·nee·tsa
bored *koji se dosađuje* koy·ee se
daw·*sa*·joo·ye
boring *dosadan* *daw*·sa·dan
borrow *posuditi/posuđivati*
paw·*soo*·dee·tee/paw·soo·*jee*·va·tee
Bosnia-Hercegovina *Bosna i
Hercegovina* ① *baw*·sna ee
her·tse·gaw·vee·na

botanic garden *botanički vrt* ⓜ
baw·*ta*·neech·kee vrt
both *oba/obje* ⓜ&①/① *aw*·ba/*aw*·bye
bottle *boca* ① *baw*·tsa
bottle opener *otvarač za boce* ⓜ
awt·*va*·rach za *baw*·tse
bottle shop *prodavaonica alkohola* ①
praw·da·va·*aw*·nee·tsa al·*kaw*·haw·la
bottom (body) *stražnjica* ①
strazh·*nyee*·tsa
bottom (position) *dno* ⓜ dnaw
bowl *zdjela* ① *zdye*·la
box *kutija* ① *koo*·tee·ya
boxer shorts *bokserice* ① pl
bawk·se·ree·tse
boxing *boks* ⓜ bawks
boy *dječak* ⓜ *dye*·chak
boyfriend *dečko* ⓜ *dech*·kaw
bra *grudnjak* ⓜ *grood*·nyak
brakes *kočnice* ① pl *kawch*·nee·tse
brandy *rakija* ① *ra*·kee·ya
brave *hrabar* *hra*·bar
bread *kruh* ⓜ krooh
bread rolls *žemičke* ① pl zhe·*meech*·ke
break (s)lomiti (s)*law*·mee·tee
break down (po)kvariti se (paw·)
kva·ree·tee se
breakfast *doručak* ⓜ *daw*·roo·chak
breast (body) *prsa* ⓜ *pr*·sa
breathe *dahnuti/disati* *dah*·noo·tee/
dee·sa·tee
bribe *mito* ⓜ *mee*·taw
bridge *most* ⓜ mawst
briefcase *aktovka* ① *ak*·tawv·ka
brilliant *briljantan* bree·*lyan*·tan
bring *donijeti/donositi* *daw*·nee·ye·tee/
daw·naw·see·tee
broccoli *brokula* ① *braw*·koo·la
brochure *brošura* ① *braw*·shoo·ra
broken *razbijen* ra·*zbee*·yen
broken down *pokvaren* paw·*kva*·ren
bronchitis *bronhitis* ⓜ *brawn*·hee·tees
brother *brat* ⓜ brat
brown *smeđ* smej
bruise *modrica* ① *maw*·dree·tsa
brush *četka* ① *chet*·ka
bucket *kanta* ① *kan*·ta
Buddhist *Budist* ⓜ boo·*deest*
budget *budžet* ⓜ *boo*·jet
buffet *bife* ⓜ bee·*fe*
bug (insect) *stjenica* ① *stye*·nee·tsa
build (iz)graditi (eez·)*gra*·dee·tee
builder *građevinar* ⓜ gra·je·*vee*·nar

building *zgrada* ① *zgra*-da
bumbag *torbica nošena oko struka* ①
    tawr-bee-tsa *naw*-she-na *aw*-kaw *stroo*-ka
burn *opeklina* ① *aw*-pe-klee-na
burnt *izgoren* eez-*gaw*-ren
bus (city) *gradski autobus* ⓜ *grad*-skee
    a-oo-*taw*-boos
bus (intercity) *međugradski autobus* ⓜ
    me-joo-*grad*-skee a-oo-*taw*-boos
bus station *autobuska stanica* ①
    a-oo-*taw*-boo-ska *sta*-nee-tsa
bus stop *autobuska stanica* ①
    a-oo-*taw*-boo-ska *sta*-nee-tsa
business *biznis* ⓜ *beez*-nees
business class *prvi razred* ⓜ pr-vee *ra*-zred
business man/woman *biznismen* ⓜ&①
    beez-nees-men
business person *poslovna osoba* ①
    paw-slawv-na *aw*-saw-ba
business trip *službeno putovanje* ⓝ
    sloozh-be-naw poo-*taw*-*va*-nye
busker *ulični zabavljač* ⓜ oo-leech-nee
    za-*bav*-lyach
busy *zauzet* za-*oo*-zet
but *osim* aw-seem
butcher *mesar* ⓜ *me*-sar
butcher's shop *mesnica* ① *me*-snee-tsa
butter *maslac* ⓜ *ma*-slats
butterfly *leptir* ⓜ *le*-pteer
button *dugme* ⓝ *doog*-me
buy *kupiti/kupovati* koo-*pee*-tee/
    koo-*paw*-va-tee

C

cabbage *kupus* ⓜ *koo*-poos
cable car *uspinjača* ① oo-*spee*-nya-cha
café *kafić/kavana* ⓜ/① ka-*feech*/ka-*va*-na
cake *kolač* ⓜ *kaw*-lach
cake shop *slastičarnica* ①
    sla-stee-*char*-nee-tsa
calculator *digitron* ⓜ *dee*-gee-trawn
calendar *kalendar* ⓜ ka-*len*-dar
call *(po)zvati* (paw-)*zva*-tee
camera *foto-aparat* ⓜ *faw*-taw-a-*pa*-rat
camera shop *prodavaonica foto-aparata* ①
    praw-da-va-*aw*-nee-tsa faw-taw-a-*pa*-ra-ta
camp *kampirati* imp kam-*pee*-ra-tee
camping ground *kamp* ⓜ kamp
camping store *prodavaonica opreme za*
    kampiranje ① praw-da-va-*aw*-nee-tsa
    aw-pre-me za kam-*pee*-ra-nye

campsite *mjesto za kampiranje* ⓝ
    mye-staw za kam-*pee*-ra-nye
can (be able) *moći* imp *maw*-chee
can (have permission) *smjeti* imp *smye*-tee
can (tin) *limenka* ① *lee*-men-ka
can opener *otvarač za limenke* ⓜ
    awt-*va*-rach za *lee*-men-ke
Canada *Kanada* ① *ka*-na-da
cancel *poništiti/poništavati*
    paw-*nee*-shtee-tee/paw-nee-*shta*-va-tee
cancer *rak* ⓜ rak
candle *svijeća* ① svee-*ye*-cha
candy *slatkiši* ⓜ pl slat-*kee*-shee
cantaloupe *dinja* ① *dee*-nya
cape (promontory) *rt* ⓜ rt
capsicum *paprika* ① *pa*-pree-ka
car *automobil* ⓜ a-oo-taw-*maw*-beel
car hire *najam automobila* ⓜ *nai*-am
    a-oo-taw-maw-*bee*-la
car owner's title *potvrda vlasništva automobila* ①
    paw-tvr-da *vlas*-neesh-tva
    a-oo-taw-maw-*bee*-la
car park *parkiralište* ⓝ par-*kee*-ra-leesh-te
car registration *registracija* ①
    re-gee-*stra*-tsee-ya
caravan *karavana* ① ka-ra-*va*-na
cardiac arrest *srčani udar* ⓜ
    sr-cha-nee oo-dar
cards (playing) *karte za igranje* ① pl
    kar-te za ee-*gra*-nye
care (for someone) *(po)brinuti se* (paw-)
    bree-noo-tee se
Careful! *Oprez!* aw-prez
carpenter *tesar* ⓜ *te*-sar
carrot *mrkva* ① *mrk*-va
carry *nositi* imp *naw*-see-tee
carton *kartonska kutija* ① *kar*-tawn-ska
    koo-tee-ya
cash *gotovina* ① gaw-*taw*-vee-na
cash (a cheque) *unovčiti/unovčavati*
    oo-*nawv*-chee-tee/oo-nawv-*cha*-va-tee
cash register *blagajna* ① bla-*gai*-na
cashier *blagajnik* ⓜ bla-*gai*-neek
casino *kasino* ⓜ ka-*see*-naw
cassette *kazeta* ① ka-ze-ta
castle *dvorac* ⓜ *dvaw*-rats
casual work *povremeni posao* ⓜ
    paw-vre-me-nee paw-sa-aw
cat *mačka* ① *mach*-ka
cathedral *katedrala* ① ka-te-*dra*-la
Catholic *katolik* ⓜ *ka*-taw-leek
Catholicism *Katoličanstvo* ⓝ
    ka-taw-lee-*chan*-stvaw

cauliflower *cvjetača* ① *tsvye*·ta·cha
cave *spilja* ① *spee*·lya
CD *CD* ⓜ tse de
celebration *proslava* ① *praw*·sla·va
cemetery *groblje* ⓝ *graw*·blye
cent *cent* ⓜ tsent
centimetre *centimetar* ① tsen·tee·*me*·tar
centre *centar* ① *tsen*·tar
ceramics *keramika* ① ke·*ra*·mee·ka
cereal *žitarica* ① zhee·ta·ree·tsa
certificate *svjedodžba* ① svye·*dawj*·ba
chain *lanac* ⓜ *la*·nats
chair *stolica za sklapanje* ① *staw*·lee·tsa za *skla*·pa·nye
chairlift (skiing) *žičara* ① *zhee*·cha·ra
champagne *šampanjac* ⓜ sham·*pa*·nyats
championships *prvenstvo* ⓝ pr·*vens*·tvaw
chance *šansa* ① *shan*·sa
change *promjena* ① *praw*·mye·na
change (coins) *kusur* ⓜ koo·soor
change (money) *zamijeniti/ zamjenjivati* za·mee·ye·nee·tee/ za·mee·ye·*nyee*·va·tee
changing room *kabina za presvlačenje* ① pl ka·*bee*·na za pres·*vla*·che·nye
charming *šarmantan* shar·*man*·tan
chat up *udvarati se* imp oo·*dva*·ra·te se
cheap *jeftino* ① *yef*·tee·naw
cheat *varalica* ① va·ra·lee·tsa
check (bill) *račun* ⓜ *ra*·choon
check *provjeriti/provjeravati praw*·vye·ree·tee/praw·vye·*ra*·va·te
check-in (airport) *prijemni šalter* ⓜ *pree·yem*·nee *shal*·ter
checkpoint *mjesto kontrole* ⓝ *mye*·staw kawn·*traw*·le
cheese *sir* ⓜ seer
cheese shop *prodavaonica sira* ① praw·da·va·*aw*·nee·tsa see·ra
chef *šef kuhinje* ⓜ shef koo·*hee*·nye
chemist (pharmacist) *ljekarnik* ⓜ *lye*·kar·neek
chemist (pharmacy) *ljekarna* ① lye·*kar*·na
cheque *ček* ⓜ chek
cherry *trešnja* ① *tresh*·nya
chess *šah* ⓜ shah
chess board *šahovska ploča* ① *sha*·hawv·ska *plaw*·cha
chest (body) *prsa* ⓜ *pr*·sa
chestnut *kesten* ⓜ *ke*·sten
chewing gum *žvakača guma* ① *zhva*·ka·cha *goo*·ma

chicken (as food) *piletina* ① *pee*·le·tee·na
chickenpox *vodene kozice* ① pl *vaw*·de·ne *kaw*·zee·tse
chickpea *slanutak* ⓜ sla·*noo*·tak
child *dijete* ⓝ dee·ye·te
child seat *sjedalo za dijete* ⓝ *sye*·da·law za dee·ye·te
childminding *čuvanje djece* ⓝ *choo*·va·nye *dye*·tse
children *djeca* ① pl *dye*·tsa
chilli *čili* ⓜ *chee*·lee
chilli sauce *umak od čilija* ⓜ *oo*·mak awd *chee*·lee·ya
chiropractor *kiropraktor* ⓜ kee·*raw*·prak·tawr
chocolate *čokolada* ① chaw·kaw·*la*·da
choose *izabrati/izabirati* ee·za·*bra*·tee/ ee·za·bee·ra·tee
chopping board *daska za sjeckanje* ① *da*·ska za *syets*·ka·nye
chopsticks *štapići za jelo* ⓜ pl *shta*·pee·chee za ye·law
Christian *kršćanin/kršćanka* ⓜ/① *krsh*·cha·neen/krsh·chan·ka
Christmas *božić* ⓜ *baw*·zheech
Christmas Day *božićni dan* ⓜ *baw*·zheech·nee dan
Christmas Eve *badnjak* ⓜ *bad*·nyak
church *crkva* ① *tsr*·kva
cider *jabukovača* ① ya·boo·kaw·*va*·cha
cigar *cigara* ① *tsee*·ga·ra
cigarette *cigareta* ① tsee·ga·*re*·ta
cigarette lighter *upaljač* ⓜ oo·*pa*·lyach
cinema *kino* ⓝ *kee*·naw
circle dance *kolo* ⓝ *kaw*·law
circus *cirkus* ⓜ *tseer*·koos
citizenship *državljanstvo* ⓝ dr·zhav·*lyan*·stvaw
city *grad* ⓜ grad
city centre *gradski centar* ⓜ *grad*·skee *tsen*·tar
civil rights *građanska prava* ⓝ pl *gra*·jan·ska *pra*·va
class (category) *klasa* ① *kla*·sa
classical *klasičan kla*·see·chan
clean *čist* cheest
clean *(o)čistiti* (aw·)chee·stee·tee
cleaning *čišćenje* ⓝ *cheesh*·che·nye
client *stranka* ① *stran*·ka
cliff *litica* ① *lee*·tee·tsa
climb *popeti/penjati se* paw·*pe*·tee/ *pe*·nya·tee se
cloakroom *garderoba* ① gar·de·*raw*·ba

clock *sat* ⓜ sat
close (nearby) *blizak* blee-zak
close (shut) *zatvoriti/zatvarati* zat-vaw-ree-tee/zat-va-ra-tee
closed *zatvoren* zat-vaw-ren
clothesline *konop za sušenje rublja* ⓜ kaw-nawp za soo-she-nye roob-lya
clothing *odjeća* ① awd-ye-cha
clothing store *prodavaonica odjeće* ① praw-da-va-aw-nee-tsa aw-dye-che
cloud *oblak* ⓜ aw-blak
cloudy *oblačan* aw-bla-chan
clutch (car) *kvačilo* ① kva-chee-law
coach (sports) *trener* ⓜ tre-ner
coast *obala* ① aw-ba-la
coat *kaput* ⓜ ka-poot
cocaine *kokain* ⓜ kaw-ka-een
cockroach *žohar* ⓜ zhaw-har
cocktail *koktel* ⓜ kawk-tel
cocoa *kakao* ⓜ ka-ka-aw
coffee *kava* ① ka-va
coins *novčići* ⓜ pl nawv-chee-chee
cold *prehlada* ① pre-hla-da
cold *hladan* hla-dan
(have a) cold *imati prehladu* imp ee-ma-tee pre-hla-doo
colleague *kolega/kolegica* ⓜ/① kaw-le-ga/kaw-le-gee-tsa
collect call *poziv na račun nazvane osobe* ⓜ paw-zeev na ra-choon naz-va-ne aw-saw-be
college *koledž* ⓜ kaw-lej
colour *boja* ① boy-a
comb *češalj* ⓜ che-shal'
come *doći/dolaziti* daw-chee/daw-la-zee-tee
comedy *komedija* ① kaw-me-dee-ya
comfortable *ugodan* oo-gaw-dan
commission *komisija* ① kaw-mee-see-ya
communications (profession) *komunikacije* ① pl kaw-moo-nee-ka-tsee-ye
communion *pričest* ① pree-chest
communism *komunizam* ⓜ kaw-moo-nee-zam
communist *komunista* ⓜ kaw-moo-nee-sta
companion *drug* ⓜ droog
company *društvo* ① droosh-tvaw
compass *kompas* ⓜ kawm-pas
complain *(po)žaliti se* (paw-)zha-lee-tee se
complaint *prigovor* ⓜ pree-gaw-vawr
complimentary (free) *besplatan* be-spla-tan
computer *računalo* ⓜ ra-choo-na-law

computer game *kompjuterska igra* ① kawm-pyoo-ter-ska ee-gra
concert *koncert* ⓜ kawn-tsert
concussion *potres mozga* ⓜ paw-tres maw-zga
conditioner (hair) *omekšivač (za kosu)* aw-mek-shee-vach (za kaw-soo)
condom *prezervativ* ① pre-zer-va-teev
conference (big) *konferencija* ① kon-fe-ren-tsee-ya
conference (small) *vjećanje* ⓝ vye-cha-nye
confession (admission) *priznanje* ⓝ pree-zna-nye
confession (at church) *ispovijed* ① ee-spaw-vee-yed
confirm (a booking) *potvrditi/potvrđivati* pawt-vr-dee-tee/pawt-vr-jee-va-tee
congratulations *čestitke* ① pl che-steet-ke
conjunctivitis *konjunktivitis* ⓜ kaw-nyoonk-tee-vee-tees
connection *veza* ① ve-za
conservative *konzervativan* kawn-zer-va-tee-van
constipation *zatvorenje* ⓝ zat-vaw-re-nye
consulate *konzulat* ⓜ kawn-zoo-lat
contact-lens solution *tekućina za kontakt leće* ① te-koo-chee-na za kawn-takt le-che
contact lenses *kontakt leće* ① pl kawn-takt le-che
contraceptives *sredstva za sprječavanje neželjene trudnoće* ⓝ pl sreds-tva za sprye-cha-va-nye ne-zhe-lye-ne trood-naw-che
contract *ugovor* ⓜ oo-gaw-vawr
convenience store *prodavaonica sa produženim radnim vremenom* ① praw-da-va-aw-nee-tsa sa praw-doo-zhe-neem rad-neem vre-me-nawm
convent *samostan* ⓜ sa-maw-stan
cook *kuhar/kuharica* ⓜ/① koo-har/koo-ha-ree-tsa
cook *(s)kuhati (s)koo-ha-tee*
cookie *keks* ⓜ keks
cooking *kuhanje* ⓝ koo-ha-nye
cool *hladan* hla-dan
coral *koralj* ⓜ kaw-ral'
corkscrew *vadičep* ⓜ va-dee-chep
corn *kukuruz* ⓜ koo-koo-rooz
corner *ugao* ⓜ oo-ga-aw
cornflakes *kukuruzne pahuljice* ① pl koo-koo-rooz-ne pa-hoo-lyee-tse

corrupt *pokvaren* paw-kva-ren
cost *stajati* imp staī-a-tee
cotton *pamuk* ⓜ pa-mook
cotton balls *kuglice vate* ① pl koo-glee-tse
va-te
cotton buds *vatene čačkalice za uši* ① pl
va-te-ne chach-ka-lee-tse za oo-shee
cough *(za)kašljati* (za-)kash-lya-tee
cough medicine *sirup za kašalj* ⓜ
see-roop za ka-shal'
count *(iz)brojati* (eez-)broy-a-tee
counter (at bar) *šank* ⓜ shank
country (land) *zemlja* ① zem-lya
country (nation state) *država* ① dr-zha-va
countryside *seosko područje* ⓝ
se-aw-skaw paw-drooch-ye
county *okrug* ⓜ aw-kroog
coupon *kupon* ⓜ koo-pawn
courgette *bučice* ① pl boo-chee-tse
court (legal) *sud* ⓜ sood
court (tennis) *igralište* ⓝ ee-gra-leesh-te
cove *dražica* ① dra-zhee-tsa
cover charge (nightclub) *cijena*
ulaznice ① tsee-ye-na oo-laz-nee-tse
cow *krava* ① kra-va
crafts (handicrafts) *umjetnički obrti* ⓜ pl
oo-myet-neech-kee aw-br-tee
crash *sudar* ⓜ soo-dar
crazy *lud* lood
cream (cosmetic) *krema* ① kre-ma
cream (food) *vrhnje* ⓝ vrh-nye
creche *jaslice* ① pl ya-slee-tse
credit *kredit* ⓜ kre-deet
credit card *kreditna kartica* ① kre-deet-na
kar-tee-tsa
cricket (sport) *kriket* ⓜ kree-ket
Croat *Hrvat/Hrvatica* ⓜ/① hr-vat/
hr-va-tee-tsa
Croatia *Hrvatska* ① hr-vat-ska
crop *urod* ⓜ oo-rawd
cross *križ* ⓜ kreezh
crowded *prepun* pre-poon
cucumber *krastavac* ⓜ kra-sta-vats
cup *šalica* ① sha-lee-tsa
cupboard *ormar* ⓜ awr-mar
currency exchange *tečaj stranih valuta* ⓜ
te-chai stra-neeh va-loo-ta
current (electricity) *struja* ① stroo-ya
current affairs *aktuelna zbivanja* ⓝ pl
ak-too-el-na zbee-va-nya
custom *običaj* ⓜ aw-bee-chai
customs *carinarnica* ①
tsa-ree-nar-nee-tsa

cut *(na)rezati* (na-)re-za-tee
cutlery *pribor za jelo* ⓜ pree-bawr za ye-law
CV *kratak životopis* ⓜ kra-tak
zhee-vaw-taw-pees
cycle *voziti bicikl* imp vaw-zee-tee bee-tsee-kl
cycling *vožnja biciklom* ① vawzh-nya
bee-tsee-klawm
cyclist *biciklist* ⓜ bee-tsee-kleest
cystitis *cistitis* ⓜ tsee-stee-tees

D

dad *tata* ⓜ ta-ta
daily *dnevni* dnev-nee
dance *ples* ⓜ ples
dance *(za)plesati* (za-)ple-sa-tee
dancing *plesanje* ⓝ ple-sa-nye
dangerous *opasan* aw-pa-san
dark *mračan* mra-chan
dark (of colour) *taman* ta-man
date (appointment) *spoj* ⓜ spoy
date (day) *datum* ⓜ da-toom
date (fruit) *datulja* ① da-too-lya
date (a person) *izaći/izlaziti* ee-za-chee/
ee-zla-zee-tee
date of birth *datum rođenja* ⓝ da-toom
raw-je-nya
daughter *kći* ① kchee
dawn *zora* ① zaw-ra
day *dan* ⓜ dan
day after tomorrow *prekosutra* ⓜ
pre-kaw-soo-tra
day before yesterday *prekjučer* ⓜ
prek-yoo-cher
dead *mrtav* mr-tav
deaf *gluh* glooh
deal (cards) *(po)dijeliti* (paw-)
dee-ye-lee-tee
December *prosinac* ⓜ praw-see-nats
decide *odlučiti/odlučivati*
awd-loo-chee-tee/awd-loo-chee-va-tee
deck chairs *ležaljka* ① le-zhal'-ka
deep *dubok* ⓜ doo-bawk
deforestation *krčenje šuma* ⓝ kr-che-nye
shoo-ma
degrees (temperature) *stupnjevi* pl
stoop-nye-vee
delay *zakašnjenje* ⓝ za-kash-nye-nye
delicatessen *delikatese* ① pl de-lee-ka-te-se
deliver *dostaviti/dostavljati*
daw-sta-vee-tee/daw-stav-lya-tee
democracy *demokracija* ①
de-maw-kra-tsee-ya

demonstration (protest) *demonstracija* ①
de-mawn-*stra*-tsee-ya

Denmark *Danska* ① *dan*-ska

dental floss *konac za čišćenje zubi* ⑩
kaw-nats za *cheesh*-che-nye *zoo*-bee

dentist *zubar* ⑩ *zoo*-bar

deodorant *dezodorans* ⑩ de-zaw-*daw*-rans

depart (leave) *otići/odlaziti* aw-tee-chee/
awd-la-zee-tee

department store *robna kuća* ① *rawb*-na
koo-cha

departure *odlazak* ⑩ *awd*-la-zak

departure gate *izlaz* ⑩ *eez*-laz

deposit (bank) *depozit* ⑩ de-paw-zeet

deposit (surety) *jamstvo* ⑩ *yam*-stvaw

derailleur *mjenjač brzina na biciklu* ⑩
mye-nyach br-zee-na na bee-*tsee*-kloo

descendant *potomak* ⑩ *paw*-taw-mak

desert *pustinja* ① *poo*-stee-nya

design *dizajn* ⑩ *dee*-zain

dessert *poslastice* ① pl *paw*-sla-stee-tse

destination *odredište* ① *aw*-dre-deesh-te

details *podatci* ⑩ pl *paw*-dat-tsee

diabetes *dijabetes* ⑩ dee-ya-*be*-tes

dial tone *znak slobodnog biranja na
telefonu* ⑩ znak *slaw*-bawd-nawg
bee-ra-nya na te-le-*faw*-noo

diaper *pelene* ① pl *pe*-le-ne

diaphragm (body part) *dijafragma* ①
dee-ya-*frag*-ma

diarrhoea *proljev* ⑩ *praw*-lyev

diary *dnevnik* ⑩ *dnev*-neek

dice *kockice* ① pl *kawts*-kee-tse

dictionary *rječnik* ⑩ *ryech*-neek

die *umrijeti/umirati* oo-mree-ye-tee/
oo-*mee*-ra-tee

diet *dijeta* ① dee-*ye*-ta

different (not this one) *drugačiji*
droo-*ga*-chee-yee

difficult *težak* te-zhak

dining car *kola za ručavanje* ① *kaw*-la za
roo-*cha*-va-nye

dinner *večera* ① *ve*-che-ra

direct *direktan* dee-*rek*-tan

direct-dial *direktan poziv* ⑩ dee-*rek*-tan
paw-zeev

direction *smjer* ⑩ *smyer*

director *director* ⑩ dee-*rek*-tawr

dirty *prljav* pr-lyav

disabled *onesposobljen*
aw-ne-*spaw*-sawb-lyen

disco *disko* ⑩ *dee*-skaw

discount *popust* ⑩ *paw*-poost

discrimination *diskriminacija* ①
dee-skree-mee-na-tsee-ya

disease *bolest* ① *baw*-lest

dish (food item) *jelo* ⑩ *ye*-law

dish (plate) *posuda* ① *paw*-soo-da

disk (CD-ROM) *disk (CD-ROM)* ⑩ deesk
(tse de rawm)

disk (floppy) *disketa* ① dee-*ske*-ta

diving (underwater) *ronjenje* ⓝ
raw-nye-nye

diving equipment *ronilačka oprema* ①
raw-nee-lach-ka aw-*pre*-ma

divorced (of man) *razveden* raz-ve-den

divorced (of woman) *razvedena*
raz-ve-de-na

dizzy *ošamućen* aw-*sha*-moo-chen

do *(u)činiti* (oo-)*chee*-nee-tee

doctor (medical) *liječnik* ⑩ lee-*yech*-neek

documentary *dokumentarac* ⑩
daw-koo-men-*ta*-rats

dog *pas* ⑩ pas

dole (unemployment benefit) *potpora
za nezoposlene* ① *pawt*-paw-ra za
ne-*za*-paw-sle-ne

doll *lutka* ① *loot*-ka

dollar *dolar* ⑩ *daw*-lar

door *vrata* ① *vra*-ta

dope (drugs) *trava* ① *tra*-va

double *dvostruk* dvaw-strook

double bed *dupli krevet* ⑩ *doo*-plee *kre*-vet

double room *dvokrevetna soba* ①
dvaw-kre-vet-na *saw*-ba

down *dolje* daw-lye

downhill *nizbrdo* neez-br-daw

dozen *tucet* ⑩ *too*-tset

drama *drama* ① *dra*-ma

dream *san* ⑩ san

dress *haljina* ① *ha*-lyee-na

dried *sušeni* soo-she-nee

drink *piće* ⑩ *pee*-che

drink (alcoholic) *alkoholno piće* ⑩
al-kaw-hawl-naw *pee*-che

drink (po)piti *(paw-)pee*-tee

drive *voziti* imp *vaw*-zee-tee

driving licence *vozačka dozvola* ①
vaw-zach-ka *dawz*-vaw-la

drug (illicit) *droga* ① *draw*-ga

drug addiction *ovisnost o drogama* ①
aw-vee-snawst aw *draw*-ga-ma

drug dealer *trgovac drogama* ⑩
tr-*gaw*-vats *draw*-ga-ma

drug trafficking *trgovina drogama* ①
tr-*gaw*-vee-na *draw*-ga-ma

drug user *korisnik droga* ⑩
kaw·ree·sneek draw·ga

drugs (illicit) *droge* ① pl draw·ge

drum (instrument) *bubanj* ⑩ boo·ban'[]

drunk *pijan* pee·yan

dry *suh* sooh

dry *(o)sušiti* (aw·)soo·shee·tee

duck *patka* ① pa·tka

dummy (pacifier) *duda* ① doo·da

DVD *DVD* ⑩ de ve de

E

each *svaki* ⑩ sva·kee

ear *uho* ⑪ oo·haw

early *rani* ra·nee

earn *zaraditi/zarađivati* za·ra·dee·tee/
za·ra·jee·va·tee

earplugs *čepovi za uši* ⑩ pl che·paw·vee
za oo·shee

earrings *naušnice* ① pl na·oosh·nee·tse

Earth *zemlja* ① zem·lya

earthquake *potres* ⑩ paw·tres

east *istok* ⑩ ee·stawk

Easter *uskrs* oos·krs

easy *jednostavan* yed·naw·sta·van

eat *(po)jesti* (paw·)ye·stee

economy class *drugi razred* ⑩ droo·gee
raz·red

ecstasy (drug) *ekstasi* ① ek·sta·see

eczema *ekcem* ① ek·tsem

editor *urednik* ⑩ oo·red·neek

education *obrazovanje* ⑪
aw·bra·zaw·va·nye

egg *jaje* ⑪ yai·e

eggplant *patlidžan* ⑩ pat·lee·jan

election *izbori* ① pl eez·baw·ree

electricity *struja* ① stroo·ya

elevator *dizalo* ① dee·za·law

email *e-mail* ① ee·me·eel

embarrassed *posramljen* paw·sram·lyen

embassy *ambasada* ① am·ba·sa·da

emergency *hitan slučaj* ⑩ hee·tan sloo·chai

emergency department (hospital)
Odjel hitne pomoći ⑩ aw·dyel heet·ne
paw·maw·chee

emotional *emocionalan*
e·maw·tsee·aw·na·lan

employee *zaposlenik/zaposlenica* ⑩/①
za·paw·sle·neek/za·paw·sle·nee·tsa

employer *poslodavac* ⑩
paw·slaw·da·vats

empty *prazan* pra·zan

end *kraj* ⑩ krai

endangered species *ugrožene vrste* ① pl
oo·graw·zhe·ne vr·ste

engaged (marriage) *vjeren* vye·ren

engaged (phone) *zauzet* za·oo·zet

engagement *vjerenje* ⑪ vye·re·nye

engine *motor* ⑩ maw·tawr

engineer *inženjer* ⑩ een·zhe·nyer

engineering *inženjerstvo* ⑪
een·zhe·nyer·stvaw

England *Engleska* ① en·gle·ska

English *engleski* en·gle·skee

enjoy (oneself) *provesti/provoditi se*
praw·ve·stee/praw·vaw·dee·tee se

enough *dosta* daw·sta

enter *ući/ulaziti* oo·chee/oo·la·zee·tee

entertainment guide *vodič o zbivan-
jima u svijetu razonode* ⑩ vaw·deech
aw zbee·va·nye·ma oo svee·ye·too
ra·zaw·naw·de

entry *ulaz* ⑩ oo·laz

envelope *omotnica* ① aw·mawt·nee·tsa

environment *prirodna okolina* ①
pree·rawd·na aw·kaw·lee·na

epilepsy *padavica* ① pa·da·vee·tsa

equal opportunity *jednake
mogućnosti* ① pl yed·na·ke
maw·gooch·naw·stee

equality *ravnopravnost* ①
rav·naw·prav·nawst

equipment *oprema* ① aw·pre·ma

escalator *pokretne stepenice* ① pl
paw·kret·ne ste·pe·nee·tse

estate agency *agencija za prodaju
nekretnina* ① a·gen·tsee·ya za
praw·dai·oo ne·kret·nee·na

euro *euro* ⑩ e·oo·raw

Europe *Europa* ① e·oo·raw·pa

evening *večer* ① ve·cher

every *svaki* ⑩ sva·kee

everyone *svatko* svat·kaw

everything *sve* sve

exactly *točno* tawch·naw

excellent *odličan* awd·lee·chan

excess (baggage) *višak prtljage* ⑩
vee·shak prt·lya·ge

exchange *razmjena* ① raz·mye·na

exchange *razmijeniti/razmjenjivati*
raz·mee·ye·nee·tee/raz·mye·nyee·va·tee

exchange rate *tečaj razmjene* ⑩ te·chai
raz·mye·ne

excluded *isključen* ees·klyoo·chen

E

exhaust (car) *ispušni plinovi* ⓜ
ee·spoosh·nee plee·naw·vee
exhibition *izložba* ⓕ eez·lawzh·ba
exit *izlaz* ⓜ eez·laz
expensive *skup* skoop
experience *iskustvo* ⓝ ees·koost·vaw
exploitation *iskorištavanje* ⓝ
ee·skaw·reesh·ta·va·nye
express *brzi* br·zee
express (mail) *ekspres pušta* ⓕ cks·pres
pawsh·ta
express mail *poslano expres poštom* ⓕ
paw·sla·naw eks·pres pawsh·tawm
extension (visa) *produženje* ⓝ
praw·doo·zhe·nye
eye *oko* ⓝ aw·kaw
eye drops *kapi za oči* ⓕ pl ka·pee za
aw·chee
eyes *oči* ⓕ pl aw·chee

F

fabric *tkanina* ⓕ tka·nee·na
face *lice* ⓝ lee·tse
face cloth *ručnik za lice* ⓜ rooch·neek
za lee·tse
factory *tvornica* ⓕ tvawr·nee·tsa
factory worker *radnik u tvornici* ⓜ
rad·neek oo tvawr·nee·tsee
fall *pad* ⓜ pad
fall (autumn) *jesen* ⓕ ye·sen
family *obitelj* ⓕ aw·bee·tel'
family name *prezime* ⓝ pre·zee·me
fan (machine) *ventilator* ⓜ ven·tee·la·tawr
fan (sport, etc) *navijač* ⓜ na·vee·yach
fanbelt *remen za ventilator* ⓜ re·men za
ven·tee·la·tawr
far *daleko* da·le·kaw
fare *cijena vožnye* ⓕ tsee·ye·na vawzh·nye
farm *farma* ⓕ far·ma
farmer *poljodjelac* ⓜ paw·lyaw·dye·lats
fashion *moda* ⓕ maw·da
fast *brz* brz
fat *debeo* de·be·aw
father *otac* ⓜ aw·tats
father-in-law (of husband) *punac* ⓜ
poo·nats
father-in-law (of wife) *svekar* sve·kar
faucet *slavina* ⓕ sla·vee·na
faulty *pokvaren* pawk·va·ren
fax machine *telefaks* ⓜ te·le·faks
February *veljača* ⓕ ve·lya·cha

feed (na)*hraniti* (na·)hra·nee·tee
feel (touch) *dirnuti/dirati* deer·noo·tee/
dee·ra·tee
feeling *osjećaj* ⓜ aw·sye·chai
feelings *osjećaji* ⓜ pl aw·sye·chai·ee
female *ženski* zhen·skee
fence *ograda* ⓕ aw·gra·da
fencing (sport) *mačevanje* ⓝ
ma·che·va·nye
ferry *trajekt* ⓜ trai·ekt
festival *festival* ⓝ fe·stee·val
fever *groznica* ⓕ graw·znee·tsa
few *nekoliko* ne·kaw·leek·aw
fiancé *vjerenik* ⓜ vye·re·neek
fiancée *vjerenica* ⓕ vye·re·nee·tsa
fiction (genre) *fikcija* ⓕ feek·tsee·ya
fig *smokva* ⓕ smaw·kva
fight (battle) *borba* ⓕ bawr·ba
fight (fisticuffs) *tuča* ⓕ too·cha
fill (na)*puniti* (na·)poo·nee·tee
film (cinema) *film* ⓝ feelm
film (for camera) *film za foto-aparat* ⓜ
feelm za faw·taw·a·pa·rat
film speed *brzina filma* ⓕ br·zee·na feel·ma
filtered *filtriran* feel·tree·ran
find *naći/nalaziti* na·chee/na·la·zee·tee
fine (penalty) *novčana globa* ⓕ
nawv·cha·na glaw·ba
fine (delicate) *sitan* see·tan
fine (weather) *vedar* ve·dar
finger *prst* ⓜ prst
finish *završiti/završavati* za·vr·shee·tee/
za·vr·sha·va·tee
Finland *Finska* ⓕ feen·ska
fire *požar* ⓜ paw·zhar
firewood *drvo za ogrijev* ⓝ dr·vaw za
aw·gryev
first *prvi* pr·vee
first class *prvi razred* ⓜ pr·vee raz·red
first-aid kit *pribor za prvu pomoć* ⓜ
pree·bawr za pr·voo paw·mawch
fish *riba* ⓕ ree·ba
fish shop *prodavaonica ribe* ⓕ
praw·da·va·aw·nee·tsa ree·be
fisherman *ribar* ⓜ ree·bar
fishing *ribolov* ⓜ ree·baw·lawv
fishing village *ribarsko selo* ⓝ
ree·bar·skaw se·law
fishmonger *trgovac ribom* ⓜ tr·gaw·vats
ree·bawm
flag *zastava* ⓕ za·sta·va
flannel *flanel* ⓜ fla·nel
flash (camera) *blic* ⓜ bleets

flashlight *(ručna) svjetiljka* ⓕ *(rooch·*na) *svye·teel'·ka*
flat *plosnat plaw·snat*
flat (apartment) *stan* ⓜ *stan*
flea *buha* ⓕ *boo·ha*
flea market *buvljak* ⓜ *boov·lyak*
flight *let* ⓜ *let*
flood *poplava* ⓕ *paw·pla·va*
floor (ground) *pod* ⓜ *pawd*
floor (storey) *kat* ⓜ *kat*
florist *cvjećara* ⓕ *tsvye·cha·ra*
flour *brašno* ⓝ *brash·naw*
flower *cvijet* ⓜ *tsvee·yet*
flu *gripa* ⓕ *gree·pa*
fly *(po)letjeti* *(paw·)let·ye·tee*
foggy *maglovit* ma·*glaw·*veet
follow *pratiti* imp *pra·tee·tee*
food *hrana* ⓕ *hra·na*
food supplies *zalihe hrane* ⓕ pl *za·*lee·he *hra·*ne
foot *stopalo* ⓝ *staw·pa·law*
football (soccer) *nogomet* ⓜ *naw·gaw·met*
footpath *pločnik* ⓜ *plawch·neek*
foreign *strani stra·nee*
forest *šuma* ⓕ *shoo·ma*
forever *zauvijek za·*oo·vee·yek
forget *zaboraviti/zaboravljati* za·*baw·ra·*vee·tee/za·*baw·*rav·lya·tee
forgive *oprostiti/opraštati* aw·*praw·*stee·tee/aw·*prash·*ta·tee
fork *viljuška* ⓕ *vee·*lyoosh·ka
fortnight *dva tjedna* ⓕ dva *tyed·*na
fortune-teller *vrač* ⓜ vrach
foul *prekršaj* ⓜ *pre·kr·*shai
foyer *foaje* ⓝ *faw·a·*i·e
fragile *lomljiv lawm·lyeev*
France *Francuska* ⓕ *fran·*tsoo·ska
free (available) *slobodan slaw·baw·dan*
free (gratis) *besplatan be·*spla·tan
free (not bound) *nevezan ne·*ve·zan
freeze *zamrznuti/zamrzavati* za·*mr·*znoo·tee/za·*mr·*za·va·tee
fresh *svjež svyezh*
Friday *petak* ⓜ *pe·*tak
fridge *hladnjak* ⓜ *hlad·*nyak
fried *prženi pr·*zhe·nee
friend *prijatelj/prijateljica* ⓜ/ⓕ *pree·*ya·tel'/*pree·*ya·te·lyee·tsa
from *iz • od eez • awd*
frost *mraz* ⓜ mraz
frozen *zaleđen za·*le·jen
fruit *voće* ⓝ *vaw·*che

fruit picking *branje voća* ⓝ *bra·*nye *vaw·*cha
fry *(is)pržiti* *(ees·)pr·*zhee·tee
frying pan *tava* ⓕ *ta·*va
full *pun* poon
full-time *punim radnim vremenom* *poo·*neem *rad·*neem *vre·*me·nawm
fun *zabavan za·*ba·van
(have) fun *uživati* imp oo·*zhee·*va·tee
funeral *pogreb* ⓜ *paw·*greb
funny *smješan smye·*shan
furniture *namještaj* ⓜ *na·*mye·shtai
future *budućnost* ⓕ boo·*dooch·*nawst

G

game *igra* ⓕ *ee·*gra
game (football) *utakmica* ⓕ oo·*tak·*mee·tsa
garage *garaža* ⓕ ga·*ra·*zha
garbage *smeće* ⓝ *sme·*che
garbage can *kanta za smeće* ⓕ *kan·*ta za *sme·*che
garden *vrt* ⓜ vrt
gardener *vrtlar* ⓜ *vrt·*lar
gardening *vrtlarstvo* ⓝ *vrt·*lars·tvaw
garlic *češnjak* ⓜ *chesh·*nyak
gas (for cooking) *plin* ⓜ pleen
gas (petrol) *benzin* ⓜ *ben·*zeen
gas cartridge *plinski uložak* ⓜ *pleen·*skee oo·*law·*zhak
gastroenteritis *gastroenteritis* ⓜ *ga·*straw·en·te·ree·tees
gate (airport, etc) *izlaz* ⓜ *eez·*laz
gauze *gaza* ⓕ *ga·*za
gay *homoseksualan* haw·maw·sek·soo·a·lan
Germany *Njemačka* ⓕ *nye·*mach·ka
get *dobiti/dobivati* daw·*bee·*tee/daw·*bee·*va·tee
get off (a train, etc) *sići/silaziti sa* *see·*chee/*see·*la·zee·tee sa
gift *dar* ⓜ dar
gig *nastup* ⓜ *na·*stoop
gin *džin* ⓜ jeen
girl *djevojčica* ⓕ *dye·*voy·chee·tsa
girlfriend *cura* ⓕ *tsoo·*ra
give *dati/davati* *da·*tee/da·*va·tee
given name *krsno ime* ⓝ *kr·*snaw *ee·*me
glandular fever *mononukleoza* ⓕ *maw·*naw·nook·le·aw·za
glass (material) *staklo* ⓝ *sta·*klo
glass (receptacle) *čaša* ⓕ *cha·*sha

glasses (spectacles) *naočale* ① pl
na·aw·cha·le

glove(s) *rukavica/e* ① sg/① pl
roo·ka·vee·tsa/e

glue *ljepilo* ① lye·pee·law

go *ići* imp ee·chee

go out *izaći/izlaziti* ee·za·chee/eez·la·zee·tee

go out with *izaći/izlaziti sa* ee·za·chee/
eez·la·zee·tee sa

goal *gol* ⑩ gawl

goalkeeper *vratar* ⑩ vra·tar

goat *jarac* ⑩ ya·rats

god (general) *bog* ⑩ bawg

goggles (skiing) *naočale za skijanje* ① pl
na·aw·cha·le za skee·ya·nye

goggles (swimming) *zaštitne naočale za
plivanje* ① pl zash·teet·ne na·aw·cha·le
za plee·va·nye

gold *zlato* ⑩ zla·taw

golf *golf* ⑩ gawlf

golf ball *loptica za golf* ① lawp·tee·tsa
za gawlf

golf course *teren za golf* ① te·ren za gawlf

good *dobar* daw·bar

Goodbye. *Zbogom.* zbaw·gawm

government *vlada* ① vla·da

gram *gram* ⑩ gram

grandchild *unuk/unuka* ⑩/①
oo·nook/oo·noo·ka

grandfather *djed* ⑩ dyed

grandmother *baka* ① ba·ka

grapefruit *grejpfrut* ⑩ greyp·froot

grapes *grožđe* ⑩ grawzh·je

grass (lawn) *trava* ① tra·va

grateful *zahvalan* za·hva·lan

grave (tomb) *grob* ⑩ grawb

gray *siv* seev

great (fantastic) *krasno* kra·snaw

green *zelen* ze·len

greengrocer *trgovac povrćem* ⑩
tr·gaw·vats paw·vr·chem

grey *siv* seev

grocery *namirnica* ① na·meer·nee·tsa

groundnut *kikiriki* ⑩ kee·kee·ree·kee

grow (po)rasti (paw·)ra·stee

g-string *g-string* ⑩ ge·streeng

guaranteed *garantiran* ga·ran·tee·ran

guess *pogoditi/pogađati*
paw·gaw·dee·tee/paw·ga·ja·tee

guesthouse *privatni smještaj za najam* ①
pree·vat·nee smyesh·tai za nai·am

guide (audio) *audio vodič* ⑩ a·oo·dee·aw
vaw·deech

guide (person) *vodič* ⑩ vaw·deech

guide dog *pas vodič* ⑩ pas vaw·deech

guidebook *vodič* ⑩ vaw·deech

guided tour *ekskurzija s vodičem* ①
ek·skoor·zee·ya s vaw·dee·chem

guilty *kriv* kreev

guitar *gitara* ① gee·ta·ra

gums (teeth) *desni* ① pl de·snee

gun *puška* ① poosh·ka

gym (place) *teretana* ① te·re·ta·na

gymnastics *gimnastika* ① geem·na·stee·ka

gynaecologist *ginekolog* ⑩
gee·ne·kaw·lawg

H

hair (body) *dlaka* ① dla·ka

hair (head) *kosa* ① kaw·sa

hairbrush *četka za kosu* ① chet·ka za
kaw·soo

haircut *šišanje* ⑩ shee·sha·nye

hairdresser *frizer* ⑩ free·zer

halal *halal* ha·lal

half *polovina* ① paw·law·vee·na

ham *šunka* ① shoon·ka

hammer *čekić* ⑩ che·keech

hammock *viseća mreža za ležanje* ①
vee·se·cha mre·zha za le·zha·nye

hand *ruka* ① roo·ka

handbag *ručna torbica* ① rooch·na
tawr·bee·tsa

handball *rukomet* ⑩ roo·kaw·met

handicrafts *ručni radovi* ① pl rooch·nee
ra·daw·vee

handkerchief *rupčić* ⑩ roop·cheech

handlebars *volan bicikla* ⑩ vaw·lan
bee·tsee·kla

handmade *ručno izrađen* rooch·naw
eez·ra·jen

handsome *zgodan* zgaw·dan

happy *sretan* sre·tan

harassment *uznemiravanje* ⑩
ooz·ne·mee·ra·va·nye

harbour *luka* ① loo·ka

hard (not easy) *težak* te·zhak

hard (not soft) *tvrd* tvrd

hardware store *prodavaonica metalne i
tehničke robe* ① praw·da·va·aw·nee·tsa
me·tal·ne ee teh·neech·ke raw·be

hash *hašiš* ⑩ ha·sheesh

hat *šešir* ⑩ she·sheer

have *imati* imp ee·ma·tee

hay fever *peludna groznica* ① pe·lood·na grawz·nee·tsa
hazelnut *lješnjak* ⑩ lyesh·nyak
he *on* ⑩ awn
head *glava* ① gla·va
headache *glavobolja* ① gla·vaw·baw·lya
headlights *prednje svjetlo* ⑩ pred·nye svyet·law
health *zdravlje* ⑩ zdrav·lye
hear *čuti* perf choo·tee
hearing aid *slušni aparat* ⑩ sloosh·nee a·pa·rat
heart *srce* ⑩ sr·tse
heart attack *srčani udar* ⑩ sr·cha·nee oo·dar
heart condition *poremećaj srca* ⑩ paw·re·me·chai sr·tsa
heat *vrućina* ① vroo·chee·na
heated *zagrijan* za·gree·yan
heater *grijač* ⑩ gree·yach
heating *grijanje* ⑩ gree·ya·nye
heavy *težak* te·zhak
Hello. (answering telephone) *Halo.* ha·law
Hello. (not answering telephone) *Zdravo.* zdra·vaw
helmet *kaciga* ① ka·tsee·ga
help *pomoć* ① paw·mawch
help *pomoći/pomagati* paw·maw·chee/ paw·ma·ga·tee
Help! *Upomoć!* oo·paw·mawch
hepatitis *hepatitis* ⑩ he·pa·tee·tees
her *njen/njena/njeno* ⑩/①/⑩ nyen/ nye·na/nyen·naw
herb *biljka* ① beel'·ka
herbalist *travar* ⑩ tra·var
here *ovdje* awv·dye
heroin *heroin* ⑩ he·raw·een
high *visok* vee·sawk
high school *srednja škola* ① sred·nya shkaw·la
highchair *visoka stolica za bebe* ① vee·saw·ka staw·lee·tsa za be·be
highway *autoput* ⑩ a·oo·taw·poot
hike *(pro)pješačiti* (praw·) pye·sha·chee·tee
hiking *pješačenje* ⑩ pye·sha·che·nye
hiking boots *gležnjače* ① pl glezh·nya·che
hiking route *pješački put* ⑩ pye·shach·kee poot
hill *brežuljak* ⑩ bre·zhoo·lyak
hire *iznajmiti/iznajmljivati* eez·nai·mee·tee/eez·naim·lye·va·tee
his *njegov/njegova/negovo* ⑩/①/⑩ nye·gawv/nye·gawv·va/nye·gawv·vaw

historical *povijesni* paw·vee·ye·snee
history *povijest* ① paw·vee·yest
hitchhike *stopirati* imp staw·pee·ra·tee
HIV *HIV* ⑩ heev
hockey *hokej* ⑩ haw·key
holiday (day off) *blagdan* ⑩ blag·dan
holidays *praznici* ⑩ pl praz·nee·tsee
Holy Week *veliki tjedan* ⑩ ve·lee·kee tye·dan
home *dom* ⑩ dawm
(at) home *kući* koo·chee
homeless *koji je bez doma* ⑩ koy·ee ye bez daw·ma
homemaker *domaćica* ① daw·ma·chee·tsa
homeopathy *homeopatija* ① haw·me·aw·pa·tee·ya
homosexual *homoseksualac/ homoseksualka* ⑩/① haw·maw·sek·soo·a·lats/ haw·maw·sek·soo·a·lka
honey *med* ⑩ med
honeymoon *medeni mjesec* ⑩ me·de·nee mye·sets
horoscope *horoskop* ⑩ haw·raw·skawp
horse *konj* ⑩ kawn'
horse riding *jahanje konja* ① ya·ha·nye kaw·nya
hospital *bolnica* ① bawl·nee·tsa
hospitality *gostoprimstvo* ⑩ gaw·staw·preems·tvaw
hot *vruć* vrooch
hot water *topla voda* ① taw·pla vaw·da
hotel *hotel* ⑩ haw·tel
hour *sat* ⑩ sat
house *kuća* ① koo·cha
housework *kućni poslovi* ⑩ pl kooch·nee paw·slaw·vee
how *kako* ka·kaw
how much *koliko* kaw·lee·kaw
hug *(za)grliti* (za·)gr·lee·tee
huge *ogroman* aw·graw·man
human resources *ljudski resursi* ⑩ pl lyood·skee re·soor·see
human rights *ljudska prava* ⑩ pl lyood·ska pra·va
humanities *društvene znanosti* ① pl droosht·ve·ne zna·naw·stee
hundred *sto* staw
Hungary *Mađarska* ① ma·jar·ska
hungry (to be) *biti gladan/gladna* ⑩/① bee·tee gla·dan/gla·dna
hunting *lov na životinje* ⑩ lawv na zhee·vaw·tee·nye

hurt (emotionally) *uvrijediti/vrijeđati*
oo·vree·ye·dee·tee/vree·ye·ja·tee
hurt (physically) *raniti/ranjavati*
ra·nee·tee/ra·nya·va·tee
husband *muž* ⓜ moozh

I

I *ja* ya
ice *led* ⓜ led
ice cream *sladoled* ⓜ sla·daw·led
ice hockey *hokej na ledu* ⓜ haw·key
na le·doo
ice-cream parlour *sladoledarna* ⓕ
sla·daw·le·dar·na
identification *identifikacija* ⓕ
ee·den·tee·fee·ka·tsee·ya
identification card (ID) *osobna iskaznica* ⓕ
aw·sawb·na ee·skaz·nee·tsa
idiot *budala* ⓕ boo·da·la
if *ako* a·kaw
ill *bolestan* baw·le·stan
Illyrians *Iliri* ⓜ pl ee·lee·ree
immigration *imigracija* ⓕ
ee·mee·gra·tsee·ya
important *važan* va·zhan
impossible *nemoguć* ne·maw·gooch
in *u · na · po · kroz* oo · na · paw · krawz
in a hurry *užurban* oo·zhoor·ban
in front of *pred* pred
included *uključen* ook·lyoo·chen
income tax *porez na dohodak* ⓜ paw·rez
na daw·haw·dak
independence *nezavisnost* ⓕ
ne·za·vee·snawst
India *Indija* ⓕ een·dee·ya
indicator (car) *žmigavac* ⓜ zhme·ga·vats
indigestion *probavne smetnje* ⓕ pl
praw·bav·ne smet·nye
indoor *unutrašnji* oo·noo·trash·nyee
industry *industrija* ⓕ een·doo·stree·ya
infection *zaraza* ⓕ za·ra·za
inflammation *upala* ⓕ oo·pa·la
influenza *gripa* ⓕ gree·pa
information *informacije* ⓕ pl
een·fawr·ma·tsee·ye
ingredient *sastojak* ⓜ sa·stoy·ak
inject *ubrizgati/ubrizgavati*
oo·breez·ga·tee/oo·breez·ga·va·tee
injection *injekcija* ⓕ ee·nyek·tsee·ya
injured *povrijeđen* ⓜ paw·vree·ye·jen
injury *povreda* ⓕ paw·vre·da

inner tube *zračnica* ⓕ zrach·nee·tsa
innocent *nevin* ⓜ ne·veen
inside *unutra* oo·noo·tra
instructor *instruktor* ⓜ een·strook·tawr
insurance *osiguranje* ⓕ aw·see·goo·ra·nye
interesting *zanimljiv* za·neem·lyeev
intermission *prekid* ⓜ pre·keed
international *međunarodan*
me·joo·na·raw·dan
Internet *internet* ⓜ een·ter·net
Internet café *internet kafić* ⓜ een·ter·net
ka·feech
interpreter *tumač* ⓜ too·mach
interview *intervju* ⓜ een·ter·vyoo
invite *pozvati/pozivati* pawz·va·tee/
paw·zee·va·tee
Ireland *Irska* ⓕ eer·ska
iron (for clothes) *pegla* ⓕ pe·gla
island *otok* ⓜ aw·tawk
Israel *Izrael* ⓜ ee·zra·el
it *ovo/to* ⓜ aw·vaw/taw
IT *Informacijska tehnologija* ⓕ
een·fawr·ma·tseey·ska
teh·naw·law·gee·ya
Italy *Italija* ⓕ ee·ta·lee·ya
itch *svrbež* svr·bezh
itemised *nabrojan* ⓜ na·broy·an
itinerary *plan puta* ⓜ plan poo·ta
IUD *spirala* ⓕ spee·ra·la

J

jacket *jakna* ⓕ yak·na
jail *zatvor* ⓜ zat·vawr
jam *džem* ⓜ jem
January *siječanj* ⓜ see·ye·chan'
Japan *Japan* ⓜ ya·pan
jar *staklenka* ⓕ sta·klen·ka
jaw *čeljust* ⓕ che·lyoost
jealous *ljubomoran* lyoo·baw·maw·ran
jeans *traperice* ⓕ pl tra·pe·ree·tse
jeep *džip* ⓜ jeep
jet lag *umor poslije dugog leta* ⓜ
oo·mawr paw·slee·ye doo·gawg le·ta
jewellery *nakit* ⓜ na·keet
Jewish *Židovski* zhee·dawv·skee
job *posao* ⓜ paw·sa·aw
jogging *trčanje* ⓜ tr·cha·nye
joke *šala* ⓕ sha·la
journalist *novinar/novinarka* ⓜ/ⓕ
naw·vee·nar/naw·vee·nar·ka
journey *putovanje* ⓜ poo·taw·va·nye

judge *sudac* ⓜ soo·dats
juice *sok* ⓜ sawk
July *srpanj* ⓜ sr·pan'
jump *skočiti/skakati* skaw·chee·tee/ ska·ka·tee
jumper (sweater) *džemper* ⓜ jem·per
jumper leads *kablovi za punjenje akumulatora* ⓜ pl ka·blaw·vee za poo·nye·nye a·koo·moo·la·taw·ra
June *lipanj* ⓜ lee·pan'

K

karst *krš* ⓜ krsh
ketchup *ketchup* ⓜ ke·chap
key *ključ* klyooch
keyboard (computer) *tastatura* ⓕ ta·sta·too·ra
keyboard (instrument) *klavijatura* ⓕ kla·vee·ya·too·ra
kick *šutnuti/šutirati* shoot·noo·tee/ shoo·tee·ra·tee
kidney *bubreg* ⓜ boo·breg
kilo *kila* ⓕ kee·la
kilogram *kilogram* ⓜ kee·law·gram
kilometre *kilometar* ⓜ kee·law·me·tar
kind (nice) *prijazan* pree·ya·zan
kindergarten *vrtić za djecu* ⓜ vr·teech za dye·tsoo
king *kralj* ⓜ kral'
kiosk *kiosk* ⓜ kee·awsk
kiss *poljubac* ⓜ paw·lyoo·bats
kiss *(po)ljubiti* (paw·)lyoo·bee·tee
kitchen *kuhinja* ⓕ koo·hee·nya
knee *koljeno* ⓝ kaw·lye·naw
knife *nož* ⓜ nawzh
know *(sa)znati* (sa·)zna·tee
kosher *košer* ⓜ kaw·sher

L

labourer *radnik* ⓜ rad·neek
lace *čipka* ⓕ cheep·ka
lake *jezero* ⓝ ye·ze·raw
lamb (animal) *janje* ⓝ ya·nye
lamb (meat) *janjetina* ⓕ ya·nye·tee·na
land *zemlja* zem·lya
landlady *gazdarica* ⓕ gaz·da·ree·tsa
landlord *gazda* ⓜ gaz·da
language *jezik* ⓜ ye·zeek
laptop *prenosivi računar* ⓜ pre·naw·see·vee ra·choo·nar

large *krupan* kroo·pan
last (previous) *predhodni* pred·hawd·nee
last (week) *prošli* prawsh·lee
late *kasan* ka·san
late *kasnije* ka·snee·ye
laugh *(na)smijati se* (na·)smee·ya·tee se
laundrette *automatska praonica* ⓕ a·oo·taw·mat·ska pra·aw·nee·tsa
laundry (clothes) *pranje rublja* ⓝ pra·nye roob·lya
laundry (place) *praonica* ⓕ pra·aw·nee·tsa
laundry (room) *soba za pranje rublja* ⓕ saw·ba za pra·nye roob·lya
law *zakon* ⓜ za·kawn
law (study, professsion) *pravo* ⓝ pra·vaw
lawyer *pravnik* ⓜ prav·neek
laxative *laksativ* ⓜ lak·sa·teev
lazy *lijen* lee·yen
leader *čelnik* ⓜ chel·neek
leaf *list* ⓜ leest
learn *(na)učiti* (na·)oo·chee·tee
leather *koža* ⓕ kaw·zha
lecturer *nastavnik* ⓜ na·stav·neek
ledge *izbočina* ⓕ eez·baw·chee·na
leek *poriluk* ⓜ paw·ree·look
left (direction) *lijevi* lee·ye·vee
left luggage *odložena prtljaga* ⓕ awd·law·zhe·na prt·lya·ga
left luggage (office) *ured za odlaganje prtljage* ⓜ oo·red za awd·la·ga·nye prt·lya·ge
left-wing *ljevičarski* ⓜ lye·vee·char·skee
leg *noga* ⓕ naw·ga
legal *zakonit* za·kaw·neet
legislation *zakonodavstvo* ⓝ za·kaw·naw·davs·tvaw
legume *mahunar* ⓜ ma·hoo·nar
lemon *limun* ⓜ lee·moon
lemonade *limunada* ⓕ lee·moo·na·da
lens *leća* ⓕ le·cha
Lent *post* ⓜ pawst
lentil *leća* ⓕ le·cha
lesbian *lezbijka* ⓕ lez·beey·ka
less *manje* ma·nye
letter (mail) *pismo* ⓝ pee·smaw
lettuce *zelena salata* ⓕ ze·le·na sa·la·ta
liar *lažljivac/lažljivica* ⓜ/ⓕ lazh·lyee·vats/lazh·lyee·vee·tsa
library *knjižnica* ⓕ knyeezh·nee·tsa
lice *uši* ⓕ pl oo·shee
licence *dozvola* ⓕ dawz·vaw·la
licence-plate number *broj registarske tablice* ⓜ broy re·gee·star·ske ta·blee·tse

lie (not stand) *leći/ležati* le-chee/le-zha-tee
life *život* ⓜ zhee-vawt
life jacket *prsluk za spasavanje* ⓜ
  pr-slook za spa-sa-va-nye
lift (elevator) *dizalo* ⓝ dee-za-law
light (illumination) *svjetlost* ⓕ svyet-lawst
light (lamp) *svjetiljka* ⓕ svye-teel'-ka
light (not heavy) *lagan* la-gan
light (of colour) *svijetao* svye-ta-aw
light bulb *žarulja* ⓕ zha-roo-lya
light meter *svjetlomjer* ⓜ svyet-law-myer
lighter *peniš* ⓝ pe-nee-sha
lighter (cigarette) *upaljač* ⓜ oo-pa-lyach
like (appeal to) *dopasti/dopadati se*
  daw-pa-stee/daw-pa-da-tee se
like (a person) *voljeti* imp vaw-lye-tee
like (want) *(po)željeti* (paw-)zhe-lye-tee
linen (material) *laneno platno* ⓝ
  la-ne-naw plat-naw
linen (sheets etc) *posteljina* ⓕ
  paw-ste-lyee-na
lip balm *balzam za usne* ⓜ bal-zam za
  oo-sne
lips *usne* ⓕ pl oo-sne
lipstick *ruž za usne* ⓜ roozh za oo-sne
liquor store *prodavaonica alkohola* ⓕ
  praw-da-va-aw-nee-tsa al-kaw-haw-la
listen (to) *(po)slušati* (paw-)sloo-sha-tee
little *mali* ma-lee
little (not much) *malo* ma-law
live (somewhere) *stanovati* imp
  sta-naw-va-tee
liver *jetra* ⓕ ye-tra
lizard *gušter* ⓜ goosh-ter
local *mjesni* mye-snee
lock *brava* ⓕ bra-va
lock *zaključati/zaključavati*
  zak-lyoo-cha-tee/zak-lyoo-cha-va-tee
locked *zaključan* zak-lyoo-chan
lollies *bomboni* ⓜ pl bawm-baw-nee
long *dugačak* doo-ga-chak
look *(po)gledati* (paw-)gle-da-tee
look after *(po)brinuti se za* (paw-)
  bree-noo-tee se za
look for *(po)tražiti* (paw-)tra-zhee-tee
lookout *vidik* ⓜ vee-deek
loose *labav* ⓜ la-bav
loose change *sitniš* ⓜ seet-neesh
lose *(iz)gubiti* (eez-)goo-bee-tee
lost *izgubljen* eez-goob-lyen
lost property office *ured za izgubljene*
  stvari ⓜ oo-red za eez-goob-lye-ne
  stva-ree

(a) lot *puno* ⓝ poo-naw
loud *glasan* ⓜ gla-san
love *ljubav* ⓕ lyoo-bav
love *voljeti* imp vaw-lye-tee
lover *ljubavnik/ljubavnica* ⓜ/ⓕ
  lyoo-bav-neek/lyoo-bav-nee-tsa
low *nizak* nee-zak
lubricant *lubrikant* ⓜ loo-bree-kant
luck *sreća* ⓕ sre-cha
lucky *sretan* sre-tan
luggage *prtljaga* ⓕ prt-lya-ga
luggage lockers *pretinac za*
  odlaganje prtljage ⓜ pre-tee-nats za
  awd-la-ga-nye prt-lya-ge
luggage tag *etiketa za prtljagu* ⓕ
  e-tee-ke-ta za prt-lya-goo
lump *grumen* ⓜ groo-men
lunch *ručak* ⓜ roo-chak
lung *pluća* ⓝ pl ploo-cha
luxury *raskošan* ra-skaw-shan

M

Macedonia *Makedonija* ⓕ
  ma-ke-daw-nee-ya
machine *stroj* ⓜ stroy
magazine *magazin* ⓜ ma-ga-zeen
mail (letters, postal system) *pošta* ⓕ
  pawsh-ta
mailbox *poštanski sanducić* ⓜ
  pawsh-tan-skee san-doo-cheech
main *glavni* glav-nee
main road *glavna ulica* ⓕ glav-na oo-lee-tsa
make (bring about) *(na)praviti* (na-)
  pra-vee-tee
make (fabricate) *(u)činiti* (oo-)chee-nee-tee
make-up *šminka* ⓕ shmeen-ka
mammogram *mamogram* ⓜ
  ma-maw-gram
man (human) *čovjek* ⓜ chaw-vyek
man (male person) *muškarac* ⓜ
  moosh-ka-rats
manager *menadžer* ⓜ me-na-jer
mandarin *mandarina* ⓕ man-da-ree-na
mandolin *mandolina* ⓕ man-daw-lee-na
manual worker *fizički radnik* ⓜ
  fee-zeech-kee rad-neek
many *mnogi* mnaw-gee
map (of country) *karta* ⓕ kar-ta
map (of town) *plan grada* ⓜ plan gra-da
March *ožujak* ⓜ aw-zhoo-yak
margarine *margarin* ⓜ mar-ga-reen

marijuana *marihuana* ① ma-ree-hoo-*a*-na
marina *marina* ① ma-*ree*-na
marital status *bračno stanje* ⑩
  brach-naw *sta*-nye
market *tržnica* ① *trzh*-nee-tsa
marmalade *marmelada* ① mar-me-*la*-da
marriage *brak* ⑩ brak
married (of man) *vjenčan vyen*-chan
married (of woman) *vjenčana vyen*-cha-na
marry *udati/udavati se* oo-da-tee/
  oo-*da*-va-tee se
martial arts *borilačke vještine* ① pl
  baw-ree-lach-ke vye-*shtee*-ne
mass (Catholic) *misa* ① *mee*-sa
massage *masaža* ① ma-*sa*-zha
masseur/masseuse *maser/maserka* ⑩/①
  ma-*ser*/ma-*ser*-ka
mat *otirač* ⑩ aw-*tee*-rach
match (sports) *utakmica* ① oo-*tak*-mee-tsa
matches (for lighting) *šibice* ① pl
  shee-bee-tse
mattress *madrac* ⑩ *mad*-rats
May *svibanj* ⑩ *svee*-ban'
maybe *možda mawzh*-da
mayonnaise *majoneza* ① mai-aw-*ne*-za
mayor *gradonačelnik* ⑩
  gra-daw-*na*-chel-neek
me *me* mee
meal *ručak* ⑩ *roo*-chak
measles *ospice* ① pl aw-*spee*-tse
meat *meso* ⑩ *me*-saw
mechanic *automehaničar* ⑩
  a-oo-taw-me-*ha*-nee-char
media *mediji* ⑩ pl *me*-dee-yee
medicine (medication) *lijekovi* ⑩ pl
  lee-*ye*-kaw-vee
medicine (profession) *medicina* ①
  me-dee-*tsee*-na
meditation *meditacija* ① me-dee-*ta*-tsee-ya
meet (for first time) *upoznati/upoznavati*
  oo-*pawz*-na-tee/oo-pawz-*na*-va-tee
meet (run into) *sresti/sretati* sre-*stee*/
  sre-*ta*-tee
melon *dinja* ① *dee*-nya
member *član/članica* ⑩/① *chlan*/
  chlan-ee-tsa
menstruation *mjesečnica* ①
  mye-*sech*-nee-tsa
menu *jelovnik* ⑩ ye-*lawv*-neek
message *poruka* ① paw-*roo*-ka
metal *metal* ⑩ *me*-tal
metre *metar* ⑩ *me*-tar
metro (train) *metro* ⑩ *me*-traw

metro station *metro stanica* ① *me*-traw
  sta-nee-tsa
microwave (oven) *mikrovalna pećnica* ①
  mee-kraw-val-na *pech*-nee-tsa
midday *podne* ⑩ *pawd*-ne
midnight *ponoć* ① paw-*nawch*
migraine *migrena* ① mee-*gre*-na
military *vojska* ① *voy*-ska
military service *vojna obveza* ① *voy*-na
  awb-ve-za
milk *mlijeko* ⑩ mlee-*ye*-kaw
millimetre *milimetar* ① *mee*-lee-me-tar
million *milijun* ⑩ *mee*-lee-yoon
mince *mljeveno meso* ① *mlye*-ve-naw
  me-saw
mineral water *mineralna voda* ①
  mee-ne-ral-na *vaw*-da
minute *minuta* ① *mee*-noo-ta
mirror *ogledalo* ⑩ aw-*gle*-da-law
miscarriage *pobačaj* ⑩ *paw*-ba-chai
Miss *Gospodica* ① *gaw*-spaw-jee-tsa
miss (feel absence of) *nedostajati* imp
  ne-*daw*-stai-a-tee
mistake *pogreška* ① *paw*-gresh-ka
mix (po)miješati (paw-)mee-*ye*-sha-tee
mobile phone *mobilni telefon* ⑩
  maw-beel-nee te-le-fawn
modem *modem* ⑩ *maw*-dem
modern *suvremen* soo-vre-men
moisturiser *hidratantna krema* ①
  hee-dra-*tant*-na *kre*-ma
monastery *samostan* ⑩ *sa*-maw-stan
Monday *ponedjeljak* ⑩ paw-ne-*dye*-lyak
money *novac* ⑩ *naw*-vats
monk *redovnik* ⑩ re-*dawv*-neek
Montenegro *Crna Gora* ① *tsr*-na *gaw*-ra
month *mjesec* ⑩ *mye*-sets
monument *spomenik* ⑩ *spaw*-me-neek
moon *mjesec* ⑩ *mye*-sets
more *više vee*-she
morning *jutro* ⑩ *yoo*-traw
morning sickness *trudnička jutarnja*
  mučnina ① *trood*-neech-ka yoo-tar-nya
  mooch-*nee*-na
mosque *džamija* ① *ja*-mee-ya
mosquito *komarac* ⑩ *kaw*-ma-rats
mosquito coil *zapaljivo sredstvo protiv*
  komaraca ① za-*pa*-lye-vaw sreds-*tvaw*
  praw-teev kaw-*ma*-ra-tsa
mosquito net *mreža za komarce* ①
  mre-zha za kaw-*mar*-tse
motel *motel* ⑩ *maw*-tel
mother *majka* ① *mai*-ka

mother-in-law (of husband) *punica* ① *poo*-nee-tsa
mother-in-law (of wife) *svekrva* ① *sve*-kr-va
motorbike *motocikl* ⑩ maw-taw-*tsee*-kl
motorboat *motorni čamac* ⑩ *maw*-tawr-nee *cha*-mats
motorcycle *motocikl* ⑩ maw-taw-*tsee*-kl
motorway (tollway) *autoput na kojem se plaća cestarina* ⑩ *a*-oo-*taw*-poot na *koy*-em se *pla*-cha tse-*sta*-ree-na
mountain *planina* ① pla-*nee*-na
mountain bike *brdski bicikl* ⑩ *brd*-skee bee-*tsee*-kl
mountain path *brdska staza* ① *brd*-ska *sta*-za
mountain range *gorski lanac* ⑩ *gawr*-skee *la*-nats
mountaineering *alpinizam* ⑩ al-pee-*nee*-zam
mouse *miš* ⑩ meesh
mouth *usta* ① *oo*-sta
movie *film* ⑩ feelm
Mr *Gospodin* ⑩ gaw-*spaw*-deen
Mrs *Gospođa* ① gaw-spaw-ja
Ms *G'đa* ① *g*-ja
mud *blato* ⑩ *bla*-taw
muesli *muesli* ⑩ pl *moo*-zlee
mum *mama* ① *ma*-ma
mumps *zaušnjaci* ⑩ pl za-oosh-nya-tsee
murder *ubojstvo* ⑩ oo-*boys*-tvaw
murder *ubiti/ubijati* oo-bee-tee/ oo-*bee*-ya-tee
muscle *mišić* ⑩ mee-sheech
museum *muzej* ⑩ *moo*-zey
mushroom *gljiva* ① *glyee*-va
music *glazba* ① *glaz*-ba
music shop *prodavaonica muzike* ① praw-da-va-*aw*-nee-tsa moo-*zee*-ke
musician *muzičar* ⑩ moo-zee-char
Muslim *musliman/muslimanka* ⑩/① moo-*slee*-man/moo-*slee*-man-ka
mussel *dagnja* ① *dag*-nya
mustard *senf* ⑩ senf
mute *nijem* nee-*yem*
my *moj/moja/moje* ⑩/①/⑩ moy/moy-a/ moy-e

N

nail clippers *škarice za nokte* ① pl *shka*-ree-tse za *nawk*-te
name (given) *ime* ⑩ *ee*-me

napkin *salveta* ① sal-*ve*-ta
nappy *pelene* ① pl pe-*le*-ne
nappy rash *osip od pelena* ⑩ *aw*-seep awd pe-*le*-na
national park *nacionalni park* ⑩ na-tsee-aw-nal-nee park
nationality *nacionalnost* ① na-tsee-aw-*nal*-nawst
nature *priroda* ① pree-raw-da
naturopathy *naturoterapije* ① pl *na*-too-raw-te-*ra*-pee-ye
nausea *mučnina* ① mooch-*nee*-na
nave *srednja lađa crkve* ① *sred*-nya *la*-ja *tsr*-kve
navigation *navigacija* ① na-vee-ga-*tsee*-ya
near *blizu* blee-zoo
nearby *obližnji* aw-bleezh-nyee
nearest *najbliži* nai-blee-zhee
necessary *potreban* paw-tre-ban
necklace *ogrlica* ① *aw*-gr-lee-tsa
nectarine *nektarinka* ① nek-ta-*reen*-ka
need (za) *(za)trebati* (za-)tre-ba-tee
needle (sewing) *igla za šivenje* ① *ee*-gla za shee-ve-nye
needle (syringe) *igla injekcije* ① *ee*-gla ee-*nyek*-tsee-ye
negative *negativan* ne-ga-tee-van
neither *niti* nee-tee
net *mreža* ① mre-zha
Netherlands *Nizozemska* ① nee-zaw-zem-ska
never *nikada* nee-ka-da
new *nov* nawv
New Year's Day *novogodišnji dan* ⑩ naw-vaw-*gaw*-deesh-nyee dan
New Year's Eve *doček nove godine* ⑩ *daw*-chek naw-ve gaw-dee-ne
New Zealand *Novi Zeland* ⑩ *naw*-vee ze-land
news *vijesti* ① pl vee-*ye*-stee
newsstand *kiosk za prodaju novina* ⑩ *kee*-awsk za praw-dai-oo naw-vee-na
newsagency *prodavaonica novina i časopisa* ① praw-da-va-*aw*-nee-tsa naw-vee-na ee cha-saw-pee-sa
newspaper *novine* ① pl *naw*-vee-ne
next (month) *slijedeći* slee-ye-*de*-chee
next to *pored* paw-red
nice *lijep* lee-yep
nickname *nadimak* ⑩ *na*-dee-mak
night *noć* ⑩ nawch
nightclub *noćni klub* ⑩ nawch-nee kloob
no (response) *ne* ne

no (absence of something) *ništa* neesh-ta
no vacancy *bez slobodnih mjesta*
   bez slaw-bawd-neeh mye-sta
noisy *bučan* boo-chan
none *nikakav* nee-ka-kav
nonsmoking *nepušački* ⓜ
   ne-poo-shach-kee
noodles *rezanci* ⓜ pl re-zan-tsee
noon *podne* ⓝ pawd-ne
north *sjever* ⓜ sye-ver
Norway *Norveška* ① nawr-vesh-ka
nose *nos* ⓜ naws
not ne ne
notebook *bilježnica* ① bee-lyezh-nee-tsa
nothing *ništa* ⓝ neesh-ta
November *studeni* ⓜ stoo-de-nee
now *sada* sa-da
nuclear energy *nuklearna energija* ①
   noo-kle-ar-na e-ner-gee-ya
nuclear testing *nuklearna testiranja* ① pl
   noo-kle-ar-na te-stee-ra-nya
nuclear waste *nuklearni otpad* ⓜ
   noo-kle-ar-nee awt-pad
number (figure) *broj* ⓜ broy
number (quantity) *količina* ①
   kaw-lee-chee-na
numberplate *registarska tablica* ①
   re-gee-star-ska ta-blee-tsa
nun *opatica* ① aw-pa-tee-tsa
nurse *medicinska sestra* ①
   me-dee-tseen-ska se-stra
nut *orah* ⓜ aw-rah

O

oats *zob* ① zawb
ocean *ocean* ⓜ aw-tse-an
October *listopad* ⓜ lee-staw-pad
off (spoiled) *pokvaren* pawk-va-ren
office *ured* ⓜ oo-red
office worker *službenik/službenica* ⓜ/①
   sloozh-be-neek/sloozh-be-nee-tsa
often *često* che-staw
oil *ulje* ⓝ oo-lye
oil (petrol) *nafta* ① naf-ta
old *star* star
olive *maslina* ① ma-slee-na
olive oil *maslinovo ulje* ⓝ ma-slee-naw-vaw
   oo-lye
Olympic Games *Olimpijske igre* ① pl
   aw-leem-peey-ske ee-gre
omelette *omlet* ⓜ aw-mlet

on *na · pri · o · u* na · pree · aw · oo
on time *na vrijeme* na vree-ye-me
once *jednom* yed-nawm
one *jedan* ⓜ ye-dan
one-way (ticket) *jednosmjeran*
   yed-naw-smye-ran
onion *luk* ⓜ look
only *samo* sa-maw
open *otvoren* awt-vaw-ren
open *otvoriti/otvarati* awt-vaw-ree-tee/
   awt-va-ra-tee
opening hours *početak radnog vremena* ⓜ
   paw-che-tak rad-nawg vre-me-na
opera *opera* ① aw-pe-ra
opera house *operna dvorana* ①
   aw-per-na dvaw-ra-na
operation *operacija* ① aw-pe-ra-tsee-ya
operator *operator* ⓜ aw-pe-ra-tawr
opinion *mišljenje* ① meesh-lye-nye
opposite *nasuprot* na-soo-prawt
optometrist *optičar* ⓜ awp-tee-char
or *ili* ee-lee
orange (colour) *narančast* na-ran-chast
orange (fruit) *naranča* ① na-ran-cha
orange juice *sok od naranče* ⓜ sawk awd
   na-ran-che
orchestra *orkestar* ⓜ awr-ke-star
order *poredak* ⓜ paw-re-dak
order (demand) *narediti/naređivati*
   na-re-dee-tee/na-re-jee-va-tee
order (request) *naručiti/naručivati*
   na-roo-chee-tee/na-roo-chee-va-tee
ordinary *običan* ① aw-bee-chan
orgasm *orgazam* ⓜ awr-ga-zam
original *originalan* aw-ree-gee-na-lan
other *drugi* droo-gee
our *naš/naša/naše* ⓜ/①/ⓝ nash/nash-a/
   na-she
out of order *pokvaren* ⓜ pawk-va-ren
outside *vani* va-nee
ovarian cyst *cista na jajniku* ① tsee-sta na
   yai-nee-koo
ovary *jajnik* ⓜ yai-neek
oven *pečnica* ① pech-nee-tsa
overcoat *zimski kaput* ⓜ zeem-skee ka-poot
overdose *prevelika doza* ① pre-ve-leeka
   daw-za
overnight *preko noći* pre-kaw naw-chee
overseas *inostranstvo* ①
   ee-naw-strans-tvaw
owe *dugovati* imp doo-gaw-va-tee
owner *vlasnik* ⓜ vla-sneek
oxygen *kisik* ⓜ kee-seek

oyster *oštrige* ① pl awsh·tree·ge
ozone layer *ozonski omotač* ⓜ
  aw·zawn·skee aw·maw·tach

P

pacemaker *elekronski stimulator srca* ⓜ
  e·lek·trawn·skee stee·moo·la·tawr sr·tsa
pacifier *duda* ① doo·da
package *paket* ⓜ pa·ket
packet (general) *kutija* ① koo·tee·ya
padlock *lokot* ⓜ law·kawt
page *stranica* ① stra·nee·tsa
pain *bol* ① bawl
painful *bolan* baw·lan
painkiller *tableta protiv bolova* ①
  ta·ble·ta praw·teev baw·law·va
painter *slikar* ⓜ slee·kar
painting (a work) *slika* ① slee·ka
painting (the art) *slikarstvo* ⓜ
  slee·kars·tvaw
pair (couple) *par* ⓜ par
Pakistan *Pakistan* ⓜ pa·kee·stan
palace *palača* ① pa·la·cha
pan *tava* ① ta·va
pants (trousers) *hlače* ① pl hla·che
panty liners *ulošci za žensko donje
  rublje* ⓜ pl oo·lawsh·tsee za zhen·skaw
  daw·nye roob·lye
pantyhose *hulahopke* ① pl hoo·la·hawp·ke
pap smear *PAPA test* ⓜ pa·pa test
paper *papir* ⓜ pa·peer
paperwork *dokumentacija* ①
  daw·koo·men·ta·tsee·ya
paraplegic *paraplegičar* ⓜ
  pa·ra·ple·gee·char
parcel *paket* ⓜ pa·ket
parents *roditelji* ⓜ pl raw·dee·te·lyee
park *park* ⓜ park
park (a car) *parkirati* imp par·kee·ra·tee
parliament *sabor* ⓜ sa·bawr
part (component) *dio* ⓜ dee·aw
part-time *honorarni* ⓜ haw·naw·rar·nee
party (night out) *provod* ⓜ praw·vawd
party (politics) *stranka* ① stran·ka
pass *dobaciti/dobacivati* daw·ba·tsee·tee/
  daw·ba·tsee·va·tee
passenger *putnik* ⓜ poot·neek
passport *putovnica* ① poo·tawv·nee·tsa
passport number *broj putovnice* ⓜ broy
  poo·tawv·nee·tse
past *prošlost* ① prawsh·lawst

pasta *tjestenina* ① tye·ste·nee·na
pastry *fino pecivo* ⓝ fee·naw pe·tsee·vaw
path *staza* ① sta·za
pay (u)platiti* (oo)pla·tee·tee
payment (by someone) *uplata* ① oo·pla·ta
payment (to someone) *isplata* ① ees·pla·ta
pea *grašak* ⓜ gra·shak
peace *mir* ⓜ meer
peach *breskva* ① bresk·va
peak (mountain) *vrh* ⓜ vrh
peanut *kikiriki* ⓜ kee·kee·ree·kee
pear *kruška* ① kroosh·ka
pedal *pedala* ① pe·da·la
pedestrian *pješak* ⓜ pye·shak
pen (ballpoint) *kemijska* ① ke·meey·ska
pencil *olovka* ① aw·lawv·ka
penis *penis* ⓜ pe·nees
penknife *džepni nožić* ⓜ jep·nee
  naw·zheech
pensioner *umirovljenik* ⓜ
  oo·mee·rawv·lye·neek
people *ljudi* ⓜ pl lyoo·dee
pepper *papar* ⓜ pa·par
pepper (bell) *paprika* ① pa·pree·ka
per (day) *na* na
per cent *postotak* ⓜ paw·staw·tak
perfect *savršen* sa·vr·shen
performance *priredba* ① pree·red·ba
perfume *parfem* ⓜ par·fem
period pain *menstrualni bolovi* ⓜ pl
  men·stroo·al·nee baw·law·vee
permission *dopuštenje* ⓝ daw·poosh·te·nye
permit *dozvola* ① dawz·vaw·la
person *osoba* ① aw·saw·ba
petrol *benzin* ⓜ ben·zeen
petrol station *benzinska stanica* ①
  ben·zeen·ska sta·nee·tsa
pharmacy *ljekarna* ① lye·kar·na
phone book *telefonski imenik* ⓜ
  te·le·fawn·skee ee·me·neek
phone box *telefonska govornica* ①
  te·le·fawn·ska gaw·vawr·nee·tsa
phonecard *telefonska kartica* ①
  te·le·fawn·ska kar·tee·tsa
photo *fotografija* ① faw·taw·gra·fee·ya
photograph *slikati* perf slee·ka·tee
photographer *fotograf* ⓜ faw·taw·graf
photography *fotografija* ①
  faw·taw·gra·fee·ya
phrasebook *zbirka fraza* ① zbeer·ka fra·za
pickaxe *pijuk* ⓜ pee·yook
pickles *kiseli krastavci* ⓜ pl kee·se·lee
  kra·stav·tsee

english–croatian

P

209

picnic *piknik* ⓜ *peek*-neek
pie *pita* ⓕ *pee*-ta
piece *komad* ⓜ *kaw*-mad
pig *svinja* ⓕ *svee*-nya
pill *tableta* ⓕ ta-*ble*-ta
(the) Pill (contraceptive) *antibaby-pilula* ⓕ an-tee-bey-bee-*pee*-loo-la
pillow *jastuk* ⓜ *ya*-stook
pillowcase *jastučnica* ⓕ *ya*-stooch-nee-tsa
pineapple *ananas* ⓜ a-na-nas
pink *ružičast* roo-zhee-chast
pistachio *trišlja* ⓕ *treesh*-lya
place *mjesto* ⓝ *mye*-staw
place of birth *mjesto rođenja* ⓝ *mye*-staw raw-*je*-nya
plaited ornamentation *pletenasti ukras* ⓜ *ple*-te-na-stee oo-kras
plane *zrakoplov* ⓜ *zra*-kaw-plawv
planet *planeta* ⓕ pla-*ne*-ta
plant *biljka* ⓕ *beel'*-ka
plastic *plastičan* pla-stee-chan
plate *tanjur* ⓜ *ta*-nyoor
plateau *plato* ⓕ pla-*taw*
platform *peron* ⓜ *pe*-rawn
play (board games) *igrati* imp ee-gra-tee
play (instrument) (od)*svirati* (awd-)*svee*-ra-tee
play (theatre) *predstava* ⓕ *pred*-sta-va
plug (bath) *čep* ⓜ chep
plug (electricity) *utikač* ⓜ oo-tee-kach
plum *šljiva* ⓕ *shlyee*-va
poached *poširan* paw-*shee*-ran
pocket *džep* ⓜ jep
pocket knife *džepni nožič* ⓜ *jep*-nee naw-zheech
poetry *poezija* ⓕ paw-e-zee-ya
point (logic) *svrha* ⓕ *svr*-ha
point *pokazati/pokazivati* paw-ka-za-tee/ paw-ka-zee-va-tee
poisonous *otrovan* aw-traw-van
police *policija* ⓕ paw-*lee*-tsee-ya
police officer *policajac* ⓜ paw-lee-*tsai*-ats
police station *policijska stanica* ⓕ paw-*lee*-tsey-ska sta-nee-tsa
politician *političar* ⓜ paw-*lee*-tee-char
politics *politika* ⓕ paw-*lee*-tee-ka
pollen *pelud* ⓕ *pe*-lood
pollution *zagađenje* ⓝ za-ga-je-nye
pool (game) *bilijar* ⓜ *bee*-lee-yar
pool (swimming) *bazen za plivanje* ⓜ *ba*-zen za *plee*-va-nye
poor *siromašan* see-raw-ma-shan
popular *popularan* paw-*poo*-la-ran

pork *svinjetina* ⓕ svee-nye-tee-na
pork sausage *svinjska kobasica* ⓕ *sveen'*-ska kaw-*ba*-see-tsa
port (sea) *luka* ⓕ *loo*-ka
positive *pozitivan* paw-zee-tee-van
possible *moguć* maw-gooch
post office *poštanski ured* ⓜ *pawsh*-tan-skee oo-red
postage *poštarina* ⓕ pawsh-*ta*-ree-na
postcard *dopisnica* ⓕ *daw*-pee-snee-tsa
postcode *poštanski broj* ⓜ *pawsh*-tan-skee broy
poster *poster* ⓜ *paw*-ster
pot (ceramics) *posuda* ⓕ *paw*-soo-da
pot (dope) *trava* ⓕ *tra*-va
potato *krumpir* ⓜ *kroom*-peer
pottery *grnčarija* ⓕ grn-*cha*-ree-ya
pound (money, weight) *funta* ⓕ *foon*-ta
poverty *siromaštvo* ⓝ see-raw-*mash*-tvaw
powder *prah* ⓜ prah
power *snaga* ⓕ *sna*-ga
prawn *škamp* ⓜ shkamp
prayer *molitva* ⓕ *maw*-leet-va
prefer *pretpostaviti/pretpostavljati* pret-*paw*-sta-vee-tee/ pret-*paw*-stav-lya-tee
pregnancy test kit *test na trudnoću* ⓜ test na trood-*naw*-choo
pregnant *trudna* ⓕ *trood*-na
premenstrual tension *predmenstrualna napetost* ⓕ pred-*men*-stroo-al-na na-pe-tawst
prepare *pripremiti/pripremati* pree-pre-*mee*-tee/pree-pre-*ma*-tee
prescription *recept za lijekove* ⓜ *re*-tsept za lee-ye-kaw-ve
present (gift) *poklon* ⓜ *paw*-klawn
present (time) *sadašnjost* ⓕ sa-dash-nyawst
president *predsjednik* ⓜ *pred*-syed-neek
pressure *pritisak* ⓜ *pree*-tee-sak
pretty *zgodan* zgaw-dan
price *cijena* ⓕ *tsee*-ye-na
priest *svećenik* ⓜ sve-che-neek
prime minister *ministar predsjednik* ⓜ *mee*-nee-star *pred*-syed-neek
printer (computer) *pisač* ⓜ *pee*-sach
prison *zatvor* ⓜ *zat*-vawr
prisoner *zatvorenik* ⓜ zat-vaw-re-neek
private *privatan* pree-va-tan
profit *dobitak* ⓜ *daw*-bee-tak
program *program* ⓜ *praw*-gram
projector *projektor* ⓜ proy-*ek*-tawr

promise *obećati/obećavati* aw-*be*-cha-tee/
aw-be-*cha*-va-tee
promontory rt ⓜ rt
prostitute *prostitutka* ⓕ praw-stee-*toot*-ka
protect *(za)štititi* (za-)*shtee*-tee-tee
protected (species) *zaštićen* zash-tee-chen
protest *prosvjed* ⓜ praws-vyed
protest *prosvjedovati* imp
praw-svye-daw-va-tee
provisions *namirnice* ⓕ pl na-meer-nee-tse
pub (bar) *gostionica* ⓕ gaw-stee-*aw*-nee-tsa
public gardens *javni parkovi* ⓜ pl
yav-nee *par*-kaw-vee
public relations *odnosi s javnošću* ⓜ pl
awd-naw-see s yav-*nawsh*-choo
public telephone *javni telefon* ⓜ *yav*-nee
te-*le*-fawn
public toilet *javni zahod* ⓜ *yav*-nee za-hawd
publishing *izdavanje* ⓝ eez-*da*-va-nye
pull *(po)vući* (paw-)*voo*-chee
pump *pumpa* ⓕ *poom*-pa
pumpkin *bundeva* ⓕ *boon*-de-va
puncture *(pro)bušiti* (praw-)*boo*-shee-tee
pure *čist* cheest
purple *ljubičast* lyoo-bee-chast
purse *novčarka* ⓕ nawv-char-ka
push *gurnuti/gurati* goor-noo-tee/*stav*-lya-tee
put *staviti/stavljati* sta-vee-tee/*stav*-lya-tee

Q

quadriplegic *potpuno paralizirana
osoba* ⓕ *pawt*-poo-naw
pa-ra-*lee*-zee-ra-na aw-*saw*-ba
qualifications *kvalifikacije* ⓕ pl
kva-lee-fee-*ka*-tsee-ye
quality *kvaliteta* ⓕ kva-lee-*te*-ta
quarantine *karantena* ⓕ ka-ran-*te*-na
quarter *četvrtina* ⓕ chet-vr-*tee*-na
queen *kraljica* ⓕ *kra*-lyee-tsa
question *pitanje* ⓝ *pee*-ta-nye
queue *red* ⓜ red
quick *brz* brz
quiet *tih* teeh
quit *ostaviti/ostavljati* aw-sta-vee-tee/
aw-stav-lya-tee

R

rabbit *zec* ⓜ zets
race (sport) *utrka* ⓕ *oo*-tr-ka
racetrack *trkalište* ⓝ *tr*-ka-leesh-te

racing bike *trkaći bicikl* ⓜ *tr*-ka-chee
bee-tsee-kl
racism *rasna netrpeljivost* ⓕ *ra*-sna
ne-tr-pe-lyee-vawst
racquet *reket* ⓜ *re*-ket
radiator *radijator* ⓜ ra-dee-*ya*-tawr
radio *radio* ⓜ *ra*-dee-aw
radish *rotkva* ⓕ *rawt*-kva
railway station *željeznička stanica* ⓕ
zhe-lyez-nee-chka *sta*-nee-tsa
rain *kiša* ⓕ *kee*-sha
raincoat *kabanica* ⓕ ka-*ba*-nee-tsa
raisin *grožđica* ⓕ *grawzh*-jee-tsa
rape *silovanje* ⓝ see-*law*-va-nye
rape *silovati* perf see-*law*-va-tee
rare (uncommon) *rijedak* ree-*ye*-dak
rare (meat) *nepotpuno pečen*
ne-*pawt*-poo-naw *pe*-chen
rash *osip* ⓜ *aw*-seep
raspberry *malina* ⓕ ma-*lee*-na
rat *štakor* ⓜ *shta*-kawr
rave *rejv parti* ⓜ reyv *par*-tee
raw *sirov* ⓜ *see*-rawv
razor *brijač* ⓜ *bree*-yach
razor blade *britva* ⓕ *breet*-va
read *(pro)čitati* (praw-)*chee*-ta-tee
reading *čitanje* ⓝ *chee*-ta-nye
ready *spreman* *spre*-man
real-estate agent *posrednik za prodaju
nekretnina* ⓜ *paw*-sred-neek za
praw-*dai*-oo ne-kret-*nee*-na
rear (seat etc) *stražnji* strazh-nyee
reason *razlog* ⓜ *raz*-lawg
receipt *račun* ⓜ *ra*-choon
recently *nedavno* ne-dav-naw
recommend *preporučiti/preporučivati*
pre-paw-roo-chee-tee/
pre-paw-roo-chee-va-tee
record (music etc) *snimiti/snimati*
snee-mee-tee/snee-ma-tee
recording *snimak* ⓜ *snee*-mak
recyclable *koji se mogu reciklirati* ⓝ
koy-ee se maw-goo re-tsee-*klee*-ra-tee
recycle *reciklirati* perf re-tsee-*klee*-ra-tee
red *crven* tsr-ven
referee *sudac* ⓜ *soo*-dats
reference *preporuka* ⓕ pre-paw-*rooka*
reflexology *refleksologija* ⓕ
re-flek-saw-*law*-gee-ya
refrigerator *hladnjak* ⓜ *hlad*-nyak
refugee *izbjeglica* ⓕ eez-byeg-lee-tsa
refund *povrat novca* ⓜ *pawv*-rat
nawv-tsa

refuse *odbiti/odbijati* awd-bee-tee/
awd-*bee*-ya-tee
regional *područni* paw-drooch-nee
registered mail (by) *preporučenom
poštom* pre-paw-roo-che-nawm
pawsh-tawm
rehydration salts *soli za rehidrataciju* ①
saw-lee za re-hee-dra-*ta*-tsee-yoo
reiki *reiki* ⑩ re-ee-kee
relationship (not family) *odnos* ⑩
awd-naws
relationship (family) *srodstvo* ⑩
srawd-stvaw
relax *opustiti/opuštati se* aw-poo-stee-tee/
aw-*poosh*-ta-tee se
relic *relikvija* ① re-*leek*-vee-ya
religion *vjera* ① vye-ra
religious (concerning religion) *vjerski*
vyer-skee
religious (person) *pobožan* paw-baw-zhan
remote *udaljen* oo-da-lyen
remote control *daljinski upravljač* ⑩
da-lyeen-skee oo-*prav*-lyach
rent *iznajmiti/iznajmljivati*
eez-*nai*-mee-tee/eez-naim-*lyee*-va-tee
repair *popraviti/popravljati*
paw-pra-vee-tee/paw-prav-lya-tee
republic *republika* ① re-poo-blee-ka
reservation (booking) *rezervacija* ①
re-zer-va-tsee-ya
rest *odmoriti/odmarati se*
awd-*maw*-ree-tee/awd-*ma*-ra-tee se
restaurant *restoran* ⑩ re-staw-ran
restaurant (family run) *gostiona* ①
gaw-stee-*aw*-na
résumé *rezime* ⑩ re-zee-*me*
retired *umirovljen* oo-*mee*-rawv-lyen
return (come back) *vratiti/vraćati se*
vra-tee-tee/vra-cha-tee se
return (ticket) *povratan* paw-vra-tan
reverse charge call *poziv na račun
nazvane osobe* ⑩ paw-zeev na
ra-choon naz-va-ne aw-saw-be
review (article) *pregled* ⑩ pre-gled
rhythm *ritam* ⑩ ree-tam
rib *rebro* ⑩ re-braw
rice *riža* ① ree-zha
rich (wealthy) *bogat* baw-gat
ride (trip) *vožnja* ① vawzh-nya
ride (horse) *jahati* imp ya-ha-tee
right (correct) *ispravan* ee-spra-van
right (direction) *desno* de-snaw
right-wing *desničarski* de-snee-char-skee

ring (on finger) *prsten* ⑩ pr-sten
ring (of phone) *nazvati/nazivati*
naz-va-tee/na-zee-va-tee
rip-off *prekomjerna cijena* ①
pre-kawm-yer-na tsee-ye-na
river *rijeka* ① ree-ye-ka
road *cesta* ① tse-sta
road map *putna karta* ① poot-na *kar*-ta
rob (o)pljačkati (aw)-plyach-ka-tee
rock (music) *rock* ⑩ rawk
rock *stijena* ① stee-ye-na
rock climbing *alpinističko penjanje* ⑩
al-pee-*nee*-steech-kaw pe-nya-nye
rock group *rock grupa* ① rawk groo-pa
rockmelon *dinja* ① dee-nya
roll (bread) *žemička* ① zhe-*meech*-ka
rollerblading *rošulanje* ⑩ raw-*shoo*-la-nye
romantic *romantičan* raw-man-tee-chan
room *soba* ① saw-ba
room number *broj sobe* ① broy saw-be
rope *uže* ① oo-zhe
round *okrugao* aw-kroo-ga-aw
roundabout *kružni tok* ⑩ kroozh-nee tawk
route *put* ⑩ poot
rowing *veslanje* ⑩ ve-sla-nye
rubbish *smeće* ⑩ sme-che
rubbish bin *kanta za smeće* ① kan-ta
za sme-che
rubella *rubeola* ① roo-be-*aw*-la
rug *tepih* ⑩ te-peeh
rugby *ragbi* ⑩ rag-bee
ruins *ruševine* ① pl roo-she-vee-ne
rule *pravilo* ① pra-vee-law
rum *rum* ⑩ room
run (po)trčati (paw-)tr-cha-tee
running *trčanje* ⑩ tr-cha-nye
runny nose *šmrkav nos* ⑩ shmr-kav naws

S

sad *tužan* too-zhan
saddle *sedlo* ⑩ sed-law
safe *sef* ⑩ sef
safe *siguran* see-goo-ran
safe sex *siguran seks* ⑩ see-goo-ran seks
saint *svetac/svetica* ⑩/① sve-tats/sve-tee-tsa
salad *salata* ① sa-*la*-ta
salami *salama* ① sa-la-ma
salary *plaća* ① pla-cha
sale *rasprodaja* ① ra-spraw-dai-a
sales tax *porez na promet* ⑩ paw-rez na
praw-met

salmon *losos* ⓜ *law*·saws
salt *sol* ⓘ sawl
same *isti* ⓜ *ee*·stee
sand *pijesak* ⓜ pee·ye·sak
sandal *sandala* ⓘ san·*da*·la
sanitary napkin *higijenski uložak* ⓜ
  hee·gee·yen·skee oo·law·zhak
sardine *sardina* ⓘ sar·*dee*·na
Saturday *subota* ⓘ soo·*baw*·ta
sauce *umak* ⓜ *oo*·mak
saucepan *lonac* ⓜ *law*·nats
sauna *sauna* ⓘ *sa*·oo·na
sausage *kobasica* ⓘ kaw·*ba*·see·tsa
say *kazati/kazivati* ka·za·tee/ka·*zee*·va·tee
scalp *skalp* ⓜ skalp
scarf *šal* ⓜ shal
school *škola* ⓘ *shkaw*·la
science *znanost* ⓘ *zna*·nawst
scientist *znanstvenik* ⓜ *znanst*·ve·neek
scissors *škare* ⓘ pl *shka*·re
score *postići/postizati* paw·stee·chee/
  paw·stee·za·tee
scoreboard *semafor* ⓜ *se*·ma·fawr
Scotland *Škotska* ⓘ *shkawt*·ska
scuba diving *ronjenje sa bocama* ⓝ
  raw·nye·nye sa *baw*·tsa·ma
sculpture *skulptura* ⓘ skoolp·*too*·ra
sea *more* ⓝ *maw*·re
seasick *koji pati od morske bolesti* koy·ee
  pa·tee awd mawr·ske baw·le·stee
seaside *primorje* ⓝ pree·*mawr*·ye
season (winter etc) *godišnje doba* ⓝ
  gaw·deesh·nye *daw*·ba
season (for activities) *sezona* ⓘ se·*zaw*·na
seat (place) *sjedište* ⓝ *sye*·deesh·te
seatbelt *sigornosni pojas* ⓜ
  see·goor·naw·snee *poy*·as
second (clock) *sekunda* ⓘ se·*koon*·da
second *drugi* droo·gee
second class *drugi razred* ⓜ *droo*·gee
  raz·red
second-hand *polovni* paw·*lawv*·nee
second-hand shop *prodavaonica*
  polovne robe ⓘ praw·da·va·*aw*·ne·tsa
  paw·lawv·ne raw·be
secretary *tajnik/tajnica* ⓜ/ⓘ tai·neek/
  tai·nee·tsa
see *vidjeti/viđati* vee·dye·tee/vee·ja·tee
self-service *samoposluga* ⓘ
  sa·maw·*paw*·sloo·ga
self-employed *samostalno zaposlen*
  sa·maw·stal·naw za·*paw*·slen
selfish *sebičan* ⓜ *se*·bee·chan

sell *prodati/prodavati* praw·da·tee/
  praw·*da*·va·tee
send (po)*slati* (paw·)*sla*·tee
sensible *razuman* ra·zoo·man
sensual *razbludan* raz·*bloo*·dan
separate *odvojen* awd·*voy*·en
September *rujan* ⓜ roo·yan'
Serbia *Srbija* ⓘ sr·bee·ya
serious *ozbiljan* aw·zbee·lyan'
service *usluga* ⓘ oo·*sloo*·ga
service charge *naplata za usluge* ⓘ
  na·pla·ta za oo·sloo·ge
service station *benziska stanica* ⓘ
  ben·zeen·ska *sta*·nee·tsa
serviette *salveta* ⓘ sal·*ve*·ta
several *nekoliko* ne·kaw·lee·kaw
sew *sašiti/šivati* sa·shee·tee/*shee*·va·tee
sex *seks* ⓜ seks
sexism *spolna diskriminacija* ⓘ *spawl*·na
  dee·skree·mee·*na*·tsee·ya
sexy *privlačan* pree·vla·chan
shade *hladovina* ⓘ hla·*daw*·vee·na
shadow *sjena* ⓘ *sye*·na
shampoo *šampon* ⓜ sham·*pawn*
shape *oblik* ⓜ *aw*·bleek
share (a dorm etc) *dijeliti* imp dee·ye·lee·tee
share (with) *podijeliti* perf
  paw·dee·ye·lee·tee
shave (o)*brijati se* (aw·)*bree*·ya·tee se
shaving cream *pjena za brijanje* ⓘ *pye*·na
  za *bree*·ya·nye
she *ona* ⓘ *aw*·na
sheep *ovca* ⓘ *awv*·tsa
sheet (bed) *plahta* ⓘ *pla*·hta
shelf *polica* ⓘ *paw*·lee·tsa
shiatsu *shiatsu* ⓘ shee·*a*·tsoo
shingles (illness) *osip u struku* ⓜ *aw*·seep
  oo *stroo*·koo
ship *brod* ⓜ brawd
shirt *košulja* ⓘ *kaw*·shoo·lya
shoe(s) *cipela/e* ⓘ sg/ⓘ pl *tsee*·pe·la/e
shoe shop *prodavaonica cipela*
  praw·da·va·aw·ne·tsa *tsee*·pe·la
shoot (u)*pucati* (oo·)*poo*·tsa·tee
shop *prodavaonica* ⓘ
  praw·da·va·*aw*·ne·tsa
shop *kupovati* imp koo·*paw*·va·tee
shopping *kupovina* ⓘ koo·*paw*·vee·na
shopping centre *trgovački centar* ⓜ
  tr·gaw·vach·kee *tsen*·tar
short (duration) *kratak* kra·tak
short (height) *nizak* nee·zak
shortage *nedostatak* ⓜ ne·daw·*sta*·tak

shorts *kratke hlače* ① pl *krat*·ke *hla*·che

shoulder *rame* ⓝ *ra*·me

shout *viknuti/vikati* *veek*·noo·tee/*vee*·ka·tee

show *predstava* ① *pred*·sta·va

show *pokazati/pokazivati* paw·ka·za·tee/
paw·ka·zee·va·tee

shower (bathroom) *tuš* ⓜ toosh

shrine *moćnica* ① *mawch*·nee·tsa

shut *zatvoren* zat·vaw·ren

shy *stidljiv* steed·lyeev

sick *bolestan* baw·les·tan

side *strana* ① *stra*·na

sign *znak* ⓜ znak

signature *potpis* ⓜ *pawt*·pees

silk *svila* ① *svee*·la

silver *srebro* ⓝ *sre*·braw

similar *sličan* slee·chan

simple *jednostavan* yed·naw·sta·van

since (May etc) *od • otkako* awd •
awt·ka·kaw

sing *(za)pjevati* (za·)*pye*·va·tee

Singapore *Singapur* ⓜ *seen*·ga·poor

singer *pjevač/pjevačica* ⓜ/① *pye*·vach/
pye·va·chee·tsa

single (man) *neoženjen* ne·aw·zhen·yen

single (woman) *neudata* ne·oo·da·ta

single room *jednokrevetna soba* ①
yed·naw·kre·vet·na *saw*·ba

singlet *potkošulja* ① *pawt*·kaw·shoo·lya

sister *sestra* ① *se*·stra

sit *sjesti/sjedati* sye·stee/*sye*·da·tee

size (general) *veličina* ① *ve*·lee·chee·na

skate *rošulati se* imp raw·*shoo*·la·tee se

skateboarding *vožnja na skateboardu* ①
vawzh·nya na *skeyt*·bawr·doo

ski *skijati* imp *skee*·ya·tee

skiing *skijanje* ⓝ *skee*·ya·nye

skim milk *obrano mlijeko* ⓝ *aw*·bra·naw
mlee·ye·kaw

skin *koža* ① *kaw*·zha

skirt *suknja* ① *sook*·nya

skull *lubanja* ① *loo*·ba·nya

sky *nebo* ⓝ *ne*·baw

sleep *(od)spavati* (awd·)*spa*·va·tee

sleeping bag *vreća za spavanje* ①
vre·cha za *spa*·va·nye

sleeping berth *spavaća kola* ①
spa·va·cha *kaw*·la

sleeping car *spavaći kupe* ⓜ *spa*·va·chee
koo·pe

sleeping pills *tableta za spavanje* ①
tab·le·ta za *spa*·va·nye

(to be) sleepy *pospan* paw·span

slice *kriška* ① *kreesh*·ka

slide (film) *dijapozitiv* ⓜ
dee·ya·paw·zee·teev

Slovakia *Slovačka* ① *slaw*·vach·ka

Slovenia *Slovenija* ① *slaw*·ve·nee·ya

slow *spor* spawr

slowly *sporo* *spaw*·raw

small *mali* *ma*·lee

smaller *manji* *ma*·nyee

smallest *najmanji* nai·*ma*·nyee

smell (pleasant) *miris* ⓜ *mee*·rees

smell (unpleasant) *smrad* ⓜ smrad

smile *(na)smiješiti se* (na·)*smee*·ye·shee·tee se

smoke (is)pušiti (ees·)*poo*·shee·tee

snack *laki obrok* ⓜ *la*·kee *aw*·brawk

snail *puž* ⓜ poozh

snake *zmija* ① *zmee*·ya

snorkelling *ronjenje s disalicom* ⓝ
raw·nye·nye s *dee*·sa·lee·tsawm

snow *snijeg* ⓜ snee·*yeg*

snowboarding *daskanje na snijegu* ⓝ
da·ska·nye na snee·*ye*·goo

soap *sapun* ⓜ sa·*poon*

soccer *nogomet* ⓜ *naw*·gaw·met

social welfare *socijalna skrb* ①
saw·tsee·yal·na skrb

socialist *socijalistički* ⓜ
saw·tsee·ya·*lee*·steech·kee

sock(s) *čarapa/e* ① sg/① pl *cha*·ra·pa/e

soft drink *bezalkoholno piće* ⓝ
be·zal·kaw·hawl·naw *pee*·che

soldier *vojnik* ⓜ *voy*·neek

some *malo* *ma*·law

someone *netko* *net*·kaw

something *nešto* *nesh*·taw

sometimes *ponekad* paw·*ne*·kad

son *sin* ⓜ seen

song *pjesma* ① *pye*·sma

soon *uskoro* oo·*skaw*·raw

sore *bolan* baw·lan

soup *juha* ① *yoo*·ha

sour cream *kiselo vrhnje* ⓝ *kee*·se·law
vrh·nye

south *jug* ⓜ yoog

souvenir *suvenir* ⓜ soo·ve·*neer*

souvenir shop *prodavaonica suvenira* ①
praw·da·va·aw·nee·tsa soo·ve·*nee*·ra

soy milk *sojino mlijeko* ⓝ *soy*·ee·naw
mlee·ye·kaw

soy sauce *soja* ① *soy*·a

spa *toplice* ① pl *taw*·plee·tse

space *prostor* ⓜ *praw*·stawr

Spain *Španjolska* ① *shpa*·nyawl·ska

sparkling wine *pjenušavo vino* ⓝ
  pye·noo·sha·vaw vee·naw
speak *(pro)govoriti* (praw)·gaw·vaw·ree·tee
special *poseban* ⓜ paw·se·ban
specialist *stručnjak* ⓜ strooch·nyak
speed *brzina* ⓕ br·zee·na
speed limit *brzinsko ograničenje* ⓝ
  br·zeen·skaw aw·gra·nee·che·nye
speedometer *brzinomjer* ⓜ
  br·zee·naw·myer
spider *pauk* ⓜ pa·ook
spinach *špinat* ⓜ shpee·nat
spoiled *razmažen* raz·ma·zhen
spoke *žbica* ⓕ zhbee·tsa
spoon *žlica* ⓕ zhlee·tsa
sport *sport* ⓜ spawrt
sports store *prodavaonica sportske robe* ⓕ
  praw·da·va·aw·nee·tsa spawrt·ske raw·be
sportsperson *sportaš/sportašica* ⓜ/ⓕ
  spawr·tash/spawr·ta·shee·tsa
sprain *uganuće* ⓝ oo·ga·noo·che
spring (coil) *opruga* ⓕ aw·proo·ga
spring (season) *proljeće* ⓝ praw·lye·che
square (town) *trg* ⓜ trg
stadium *stadion* ⓜ sta·dee·awn
stairway *stepenište* ⓝ ste·pe·neesh·te
stale *ustajao* oo·stai·a·aw
stamp (mail) *poštanska marka* ⓕ
  pawsh·tan·ska mar·ka
stand-by ticket *uvjetna karta* ⓕ
  oo·vyet·noo kar·ta
star *zvjezda* ⓕ zvyez·da
(four-)star *(sa četiri) zvjezdice* ⓕ pl
  (sa che·tee·ree) zvye·zdee·tse
start *početak* ⓜ paw·che·tak
start *započeti/započinjati* za·paw·che·tee/
  za·paw·chee·nya·tee
station *stanica* ⓕ sta·nee·tsa
stationer's (shop) *prodavaonica uredskog*
  materijala ⓕ praw·da·va·aw·nee·tsa
  oo·reds·kawg ma·te·ree·ya·la
statue *kip* ⓜ keep
stay (at a hotel) *odsjesti/odsjedati*
  awd·sye·stee/awd·sye·da·tee
stay (in one place) *ostati/ostajati* imp
  aw·sta·tee/aw·sta·ya·tee
steak (beef) *odrezak* ⓜ aw·dre·zak
steal *(u)krasti* (oo·)kra·stee
steep *strm* strm
step *stepenica* ⓕ ste·pe·nee·tsa
stereo *linija* ⓕ lee·nee·ya
still water *obična voda* ⓕ aw·beech·na
  vaw·da

stock (food) *bujon* ⓜ boo·yawn
stockings *visoke čarape* ⓕ pl vee·saw·ke
  cha·ra·pe
stolen *ukraden* ⓜ oo·kra·den
stomach *želudac* ⓜ zhe·loo·dats
stomachache (to have a) *imati trbobolju*
  ee·ma·tee tr·baw·baw·lyoo
stone *kamen* ⓜ ka·men
stoned (drugged) *napljugan* nap·lyoo·gan
stop (bus, tram) *stanica* ⓕ sta·nee·tsa
stop (cease) *zaustaviti/zaustavljati*
  za·oo·sta·vee·tee/za·oo·stav·lya·tee
stop (prevent) *spriječiti/sprječavati*
  spree·ye·chee·tee/spree·ye·cha·va·tee
Stop! *Stanite/Stani!* pol/inf sta·nee·te/sta·nee
storm *oluja* ⓕ aw·loo·ya
story *priča* ⓕ pree·cha
stove *pećnica* ⓕ pech·nee·tsa
straight (not crooked) *ravan* ra·van
strange *neobičan* ne·aw·bee·chan
stranger *stranac* ⓜ stra·nats
strawberry *jagoda* ⓕ ya·gaw·da
stream *struja* ⓕ stroo·ya
street *ulica* ⓕ oo·lee·tsa
street market *ulična tržnica* ⓕ oo·leech·na
  trzh·nee·tsa
strike *štrajk* ⓜ shtraik
string *struna* ⓕ stroo·na
stroke (health) *moždani udar* ⓜ
  mawzh·da·nee oo·dar
stroller *dječja hodalica* ⓕ dyech·ya
  haw·da·lee·tsa
strong (physically) *jak* yak
stubborn *tvrdoglav* tvr·daw·glav
student *student* ⓜ stoo·dent
studio *atelje* ⓝ a·te·lye
stupid *glup* gloop
style *stil* ⓜ steel
subtitles *titlovi* ⓜ pl teet·law·vee
suburb *predgrađe* ⓝ pred·gra·je
subway *podzemna željeznica* ⓕ
  pawd·zem·na zhe·lye·znee·tsa
sugar *šećer* ⓜ she·cher
suitcase *kofer* ⓜ kaw·fer
sultana (vrsta velikih grožđica ⓕ vr·sta
  ve·lee·keeh grawzh·jee·tsa
summer *ljeto* ⓝ lye·taw
summit *vrh* ⓜ vrh
sun *sunce* ⓝ soon·tse
sunblock *losion za zaštitu od sunca* ⓜ
  law·see·awn za zash·tee·too awd soon·tsa
sunburn *opekline od sunca* ⓕ pl
  aw·pe·klee·ne awd soon·tsa

Sunday *nedjelja* ① *ne*-dye-lya
sunglasses *naočale za sunce* ① pl *na*-aw-cha-le (za *soon*-tse)
sunny *sunčan* soon-chan
sunrise *izlazak sunca* ⑩ *eez*-la-zak soon-tsa
sunset *zalazak sunca* ⑩ *za*-la-zak soon-tsa
sunstroke *sunčanica* ① soon-cha-nee-tsa
supermarket *supermarket* ⑩ soo-per-mar-ket
superstition *praznovjerje* ⑩ praz-naw-vyer-ye
supporter (politics) *pristaša* ⑩ pree-sta-sha
supporter (sport) *navijač* ⑩ na-vee-yach
surf *daskati na valovima* da-ska-tee na *va*-law-vee-ma
surface mail (land) *obična pošta* ① aw-beech-na pawsh-ta
surface mail (sea) *prekomorska pošta* ① pre-kaw-mawr-ska pawsh-ta
surfboard *daska za surfanje* ① *da*-ska za soor-fa-nye
surfing *daskanje na valovima* ⑩ *da*-ska-nye na *va*-law-vee-ma
surname *prezime* ⑩ pre-zee-me
surprise *iznenađen* ⑩ eez-ne-na-jen
sweater *džemper* ⑩ jem-per
Sweden *Švedska* ① shved-ska
sweet *sladak* sla-dak
sweets *bomboni* ⑩ pl bawm-baw-nee
swelling *oteklina* ① aw-te-klee-na
swim *(za)plivati* (za-)plee-va-tee
swimming (sport) *plivanje* ⑩ plee-va-nye
swimming pool *bazen za plivanje* ⑩ *ba*-zen za plee-va-nye
swimsuit *kupaći kostim* ⑩ koo-pa-chee *kaw*-steem
Switzerland *Švicarska* ① shvee-tsar-ska
synagogue *sinagoga* ① see-na-*gaw*-ga
synthetic *sintetičan* ⑩ seen-te-tee-chan
syringe *štrcaljka* ① shtr-tsal'-ka

T

table *stol* ⑩ stawl
table tennis *stolni tenis* ⑩ *stawl*-nee te-nees
tablecloth *stolnjak* ⑩ *stawl*-nyak
tail *rep* ⑩ rep
tailor *krojač* ⑩ kroy-ach
take *uzeti/uzimati* oo-ze-tee/oo-zee-ma-tee
talk *(pro)govoriti* (praw-)gaw-*vaw*-ree-tee
tall *visok* vee-sawk
tampon *tampon* ⑩ tam-pawn

tanning lotion *losion za dobijanje tena* ⑩ law-*see*-awn za daw-bee-ya-nye *te*-na
tap *slavina* ① sla-vee-na
tap water *obična voda* ① *aw*-beech-na vaw-da
tasty *ukusan* oo-koo-san
tax *porez* ⑩ paw-rez
taxi *taksi* ⑩ tak-see
taxi stand *taksi stanica* ① tak-see sta-nee-tsa
tea *čaj* ⑩ chai
teacher *učitelj* ⑩ oo-chee-tel'
team *momčad* ① mawm-chad
teaspoon *žličica* ① zhlee-chee-tsa
technique *tehnika* ① teh-nee-ka
teeth *zubi* ⑩ pl zoo-bee
telegram *telegram* ⑩ te-le-gram
telephone *telefon* ⑩ te-le-fawn
telephone *telefonirati* imp te-le-faw-*nee*-ra-tee
telephone box *telefonska govornica* ① te-le-fawn-ska gaw-*vawr*-nee-tsa
telephone centre *telefonska centrala* ① te-le-fawn-ska tsen-*tra*-la
telescope *teleskop* ⑩ te-le-skawp
television (general) *televizija* ① te-le-*vee*-zee-ya
television set *televizor* ⑩ te-le-*vee*-zawr
tell *reći* perf re-chee
temperature (fever) *groznica* ① grawz-nee-tsa
temperature (weather) *temperatura* ① tem-pe-ra-*too*-ra
temple *hram* ⑩ hram
tennis *tenis* ⑩ te-nees
tennis court *tenisko igralište* ⑩ te-nee-skaw ee-gra-leesh-te
tent *šator* ⑩ sha-tawr
tent peg *šatorski kolčić* ⑩ *sha*-tawr-skee kawl-cheech
terrible *strašan* stra-shan
test *test* ⑩ test
thank *zahvaliti/zahvaljivati* za-hva-lee-tee/za-hva-*lyee*-va-tee
thank you *hvala vam/ti* pol/inf *hva*-la vam/tee
that (one) *ono* ⑩ *aw*-naw
theatre *kazalište* ⑩ *ka*-za-leesh-te
their *njihov/njihova/njihovo* ⑩/①/⑩ nyee-hawv/nyee-haw-va/nyee-haw-vaw
there *tamo* ta-maw
they *oni/one/ona* ⑩/①/⑩ aw-nee/aw-ne/aw-na

thick (liquid) *gust* goost
thick (object) *debeo* de·be·aw
thief *lopov* ⓜ law·pawv
thin *tanak* ⓜ ta·nak
think *(po)misliti* (paw·)mee·slee·tee
third *treći* tre·chee
(to be) thirsty *žedan* zhe·dan
this *ovaj/ova/ovo* ⓜ/①/ⓝ aw·vai/aw·va/ aw·vaw
this (one) *ovo* ⓝ aw·vaw
thread *konac* ⓜ kaw·nats
throat *grlo* ⓝ gr·law
thrush (illness) *infekcija kandide* ① een·fek·tsee·ya kan·dee·de
thunderstorm *grmljavina* ① grm·lya·vee·na
Thursday *četvrtak* ⓜ chet·vr·tak
ticket *karta* ① kar·ta
ticket collector *osoblje koje uzima odrezak karte* ⓝ aw·sawb·lye koy·e oo·zee·ma aw·dre·zak kar·te
ticket machine *automat za prodaju karata* ⓜ a·oo·taw·mat za praw·dai·oo ka·ra·ta
ticket office *šalter* ⓜ shal·ter
tide *plima i oseka* ① plee·ma ee aw·se·ka
tight *tijesan* tee·ye·san
time *vrijeme* ⓝ vree·ye·me
time difference *razlika u vremenu* ① raz·lee·ka oo vre·me·noo
timetable *vozni red* ⓜ vawz·nee red
tin (can) *limenka* ① lee·men·ka
tin opener *otvarač za limenke* ⓜ awt·va·rach za lee·men·ke
tiny *sićušan* ⓜ see·choo·shan
tip (gratuity) *bakšiš* bak·sheesh
tire (car) *guma na automobile* ① goo·ma na a·oo·taw·maw·bee·le
tire (general) *guma* ① goo·ma
tired *umoran* oo·maw·ran
tissues *papirnati rupčići* ⓜ pl pa·peer·na·tee roop·chee·chee
to *do* · *nad* · *prema* · *u* · *za* daw · nad · pre·ma · oo · za
toast *tost* ⓜ tawst
toaster *toster* ⓜ taw·ster
tobacco *duhan* ⓜ doo·han
tobacconist *prodavač duhana* ⓜ praw·da·vach doo·ha·na
tobogganing *sanjkanje* ⓝ san'·ka·nye
today *danas* da·nas
toe *nožni prst* ⓜ nawzh·nee prst
together *zajedno* zai·ed·naw
toilet *zahod* ⓜ za·hawd

toilet paper *toaletni papir* ⓜ taw·a·let·nee pa·peer
tomato *rajčica* ① rai·chee·tsa
tomato sauce *umak od rajčica* ⓜ oo·mak awd rai·chee·tsa
tomorrow *sutra* soo·tra
tomorrow afternoon *sutra popodne* soo·tra paw·pawd·ne
tomorrow evening *sutra uvečer* soo·tra oo·ve·cher
tomorrow morning *sutra ujutro* soo·tra oo·yoo·traw
tonight *večeras* ve·che·ras
too (expensive etc) *suviše* soo·vee·she
tooth *zub* ⓜ zoob
toothache *zubobolja* ① zoo·baw·baw·lya
toothbrush *četkica za zube* ① chet·kee·tsa za zoo·be
toothpaste *pasta za zube* ① pa·sta za zoo·be
toothpick *čačkalica* ① chach·ka·lee·tsa
torch (flashlight) *(ručna) svjetiljka* ① (rooch·na) svye·teel'·ka
touch (sense) *dirnuti/dirati* deer·noo·tee/ dee·ra·tee
tour *ekskurzija* ① ek·skoor·zee·ya
tourist *turist* ⓜ too·reest
tourist office *turistička agencija* ① too·ree·steech·ka a·gen·tsee·ya
towards (direction) *prema* pre·ma
towel *ručnik* ⓜ rooch·neek
tower *toranj* ⓜ taw·ran'
toxic waste *toksični otpad* ⓜ tawk·seech·nee awt·pad
toy shop *prodavaonica igračaka* ① praw·da·va·aw·nee·tsa ee·gra·cha·ka
track (path) *put* ⓜ poot
track (sport) *staza* ① sta·za
trade *trgovina* ① tr·gaw·vee·na
tradesperson *obrtnik* ⓜ aw·brt·neek
traffic *promet* ⓜ praw·met
traffic light *semafor* ⓜ se·ma·fawr
trail *put* ⓜ poot
train *vlak* ⓜ vlak
train station *željeznička stanica* ① zhe·lyez·neech·ka sta·nee·tsa
tram *tramvaj* ⓜ tram·vai
transit lounge *tranzitna čekaonica* ① tran·zeet·na che·ka·aw·nee·tsa
translate *prevesti/prevoditi* pre·ve·stee/ pre·vaw·dee·tee
transport *prijevoz* ⓜ pree·ye·vawz
travel *(pro)putovati* (praw·)poo·taw·va·tee

travel agency *putna agencija* ① *poot*-na
a-*gen*-tsee-ya
travel sickness *mučnina od vožnje* ①
mooch-*nee*-na awd *vawzh*-nye
travellers cheque *putnički čekovi* ⑩ pl
poot-neech-kee che-*kaw*-vee
tree *stablo* ⑪ *sta*-blaw
trip (journey) *izlet* ⑩ *eez*-let
trolley *kolica za prtljagu* ① kaw-*lee*-tsa za
prt-*lya*-goo
trousers *hlače* ① pl *hla*-che
truck *kamion* ⑩ ka-*mee*-awn
trust (*po*)*vjerovati* (paw-)vye-raw-va-tee
try *probati/probavati* praw-ba-tee/
praw-*ba*-va-tee
try (attempt) *pokušati/pokušavati*
paw-koo-sha-tee/paw-koo-*sha*-va-tee
T-shirt *majica* ① *mai*-ee-tsa
tube (tyre) *zračnica* ① *zrach*-nee-tsa
Tuesday *utorak* ⑩ oo-*taw*-rak
tumour *tumor* ⑩ *too*-mawr
tuna (as food) *tunjevina* ① *too*-nye-vee-na
tuna (fish) *tuna* ① *too*-na
tune *melodija* ① me-*law*-dee-ya
turkey *puran* ⑩ *poo*-ran
turn *okrenuti/okretati* aw-*kre*-noo-tee/
aw-*kre*-ta-tee
TV (set) *televizor* ⑩ te-le-*vee*-zawr
tweezers *pinceta* ① peen-*tse*-ta
twice *dvaput* dva-poot
twin room *dvokrevetna soba* ①
dvaw-kre-vet-na *saw*-ba
twins *blizanci* ⑩ pl blee-*zan*-tsee
two *dva* dva
type *vrsta* ① *vr*-sta
typical *tipičan* tee-*pee*-chan
tyre (car) *guma na automobile* ① *goo*-ma
na a-oo-taw-maw-*bee*-le
tyre (general) *guma* ① *goo*-ma

U

ultrasound *ultrazvuk* ⑩ *ool*-tra-zvook
umbrella *suncobran* ⑩ *soon*-tsaw-bran
uncomfortable *neudoban* ne-oo-*daw*-ban
underground railway *podzemna
željeznica* ① *pawd*-zem-na
zhe-lye-znee-tsa
understand *razumjeti/razumijevati*
ra-*zoo*-mye-tee/ra-zoo-mee-ye-va-tee
underwear *donje rublje* ① *daw*-nye roob-lye
unemployed *nezaposlen* ne-*za*-paw-slen

unfair *nepravedan* ne-*pra*-ve-dan
uniform *uniforma* ① oo-nee-*fawr*-ma
universe *svemir* ⑩ *sve*-meer
university *sveučilište* ⑪ sve-oo-chee-leesh-te
unleaded *bezolovni* be-zaw-*lawv*-nee
unsafe *nesiguran* ne-see-*goo*-ran
until (Friday, etc) *do* daw
unusual *neobičan* ne-*aw*-bee-chan
up *gore* *gaw*-re
urgent *hitan* *hee*-tan
urinary infection *infekcija mokraćnih
kanala* ① een-*fek*-tsee-ya
maw-krach-neeh ka-*na*-la
USA *SAD* ① pl es a de
useful *koristan* kaw-*ree*-stan

V

vacancy *slobodno mjesto* ⑪ *slaw*-bawd-naw
mye-staw
vacant *prazan* *pra*-zan
vacation *praznici* ⑩ pl *praz*-nee-tsee
vaccination *cijepljenje* ⑪ tsee-*yep*-lye-nye
vagina *vagina* ① va-*gee*-na
validate *potvrditi/potvrđivati*
pawt-vr-dee-tee/pawt-vr-*jee*-va-tee
valley *dolina* ① daw-*lee*-na
valuable *dragocjen* dra-*gaw*-tsyen
value (price) *vrijednost* ① vree-*yed*-nawst
van *kombi* ⑩ *kawm*-bee
veal *teletina* ① te-le-*tee*-na
vegetable *povrće* ⑪ *paw*-vr-che
vegetarian *vegetarijanac* ⑩
ve-ge-ta-ree-*ya*-nats
vein *vena* ① *ve*-na
venereal disease *spolna bolesta* ①
spawl-na *baw*-les-ta
Venetian *venecijanski* ve-ne-*tsee*-yan-skee
Venice *Venecija* ① ve-ne-tsee-ya
venue *lokal* ⑩ *law*-kal
very *vrlo* *vr*-law
video recorder *video rekorder* ⑩
vee-de-aw re-*kawr*-der
video tape *video kazeta* ① vee-de-aw
ka-ze-ta
view *prizor* ⑩ *pree*-zawr
village *selo* ⑪ *se*-law
vine *vinova loza* ① vee-naw-va *law*-za
vinegar *ocat* ⑩ *aw*-tsat
vineyard *vinograd* ⑩ vee-naw-grad
virus *virus* ① *vee*-roos
visa *viza* ① *vee*-za

visit *posjetiti/posjećivati* paw·sye·tee·tee/
paw·sye·chee·va·tee

vitamins *vitamini* ⓜ pl vee·ta·mee·nee

vodka *vodka* ⓕ vawd·ka

voice *glas* ⓜ glas

volleyball (sport) *odbojka* ⓕ awd·boy·ka

volume *ton* ⓜ tawn

vote *glasovati* imp gla·saw·va·tee

W

wage *plaća* ⓕ pla·cha

wait (for) *(pri)čekati nekoga* (pree·)
che·ka·tee ne·kaw·ga

waiter *konobar* ⓜ kaw·naw·bar

waiting room *čekaonica* ⓕ
che·ka·aw·nee·tsa

wake (someone) up *(pro)buditi nekoga*
(praw·)boo·dee·tee ne·kaw·ga

walk *hodati* imp haw·da·tee

walkway *hodnik* ⓜ hawd·neek

wall (outer) *zid* ⓜ zeed

walled city *citadela* ⓕ tsee·ta·de·la

want *(po)željeti* (paw·)zhe·lye·tee

war *rat* ⓜ rat

wardrobe *ormar za odjeću* ⓜ awr·mar za
aw·dye·choo

warm *topao* ⓜ taw·pa·aw

warn *upozoriti/upozoravati*
oo·paw·zaw·ree·tee/
oo·paw·zaw·ra·va·tee

wash (oneself) *(o)prati se* (aw·)pra·tee se

wash (something) *(o)prati* (aw·)pra·tee

wash cloth (flannel) *ručnik* ⓜ rooch·neek

washing machine *stroj za pranje rublja* ⓜ
stroy za pra·nye roob·lya

watch *(po)gledati* (paw·)gle·da·tee

watch *sat* ⓜ sat

water *voda* ⓕ vaw·da

water bottle *boca za vodu* ⓕ baw·tsa
za vaw·doo

water bottle (hot) *termofor* ⓜ ter·maw·fawr

water taxi *taksi na vodi* ⓜ tak·see na
vaw·dee

waterfall *vodopad* ⓜ vaw·daw·pad

waterfront *riva* ⓕ ree·va

watermelon *lubenica* ⓕ loo·be·nee·tsa

waterproof *nepromočiv*
ne·praw·maw·cheev

water-skiing *skijanje na vodi* ⓝ skee·ya·nye
na vaw·dee

wave *val* ⓜ val

way (manner) *način* ⓜ na·cheen

we *mi* mee

weak *slab* slab

wealthy *bogat* baw·gat

wear *nositi* imp naw·see·tee

weather *vremenski uvjeti* ⓜ pl
vre·men·skee oo·vye·tee

wedding *vjenčanje* ⓝ vyen·cha·nye

wedding cake *svadbena torta* ⓕ
svad·be·na tawr·ta

wedding present *svadbeni dar* ⓜ
svad·be·nee dar

Wednesday *srijeda* ⓕ sree·ye·da

week *tjedan* ⓜ tye·dan

(this) week *(ovaj) tjedan* ⓜ (aw·vai) tye·dan

weekend *vikend* ⓜ veek·end

weigh *(iz)vagati* (eez·)va·ga·tee

weight *težina* ⓕ te·zhee·na

weights *tegovi* ⓜ pl te·gaw·vee

welcome *dočekati/dočekivati*
daw·che·ka·tee/daw·che·kee·va·tee

welfare *socijalna skrb* ⓕ saw·tsee·yal·na
skrb

well *dobro* daw·braw

west *zapad* ⓜ za·pad

wet *mokar* ⓜ maw·kar

what *koji/koja/koje* ⓜ/ⓕ/ⓝ
koy·ee/koy·a/koy·e

wheel *kotač* ⓜ kaw·tach

wheelchair *invalidska kolica* ⓕ pl
een·va·leed·ska kaw·lee·tsa

when *kada* ka·da

where *gdje* gdye

which *koji* koy·ee

whisky *viski* ⓜ vee·skee

white *bijel* bee·yel

who *tko* tkaw

wholemeal bread *crni kruh* ⓜ tsr·nee
krooh

why *zašto* zash·taw

wide *širok* shee·rawk

wife *žena* ⓕ zhe·na

win *pobijediti/pobjeđivati*
paw·bee·ye·dee·tee/paw·bye·jee·va·tee

wind *vjetar* ⓜ vye·tar

window *prozor* ⓜ praw·zawr

windscreen *vjetrobran* ⓜ vye·traw·bran

windsurfing *jedrenje na dasci* ⓝ
ye·dre·nye na das·tsee

wine *vino* ⓝ vee·naw

wings *krila* ⓝ pl kree·la

winner *pobjednik* ⓜ paw·byed·neek

winter *zima* ⓕ zee·ma

wire *žica* ① zhee·tsa
wish *(po)željeti* (paw·)zhe·lye·tee
with *kod · od · sa · za·* kawd · awd · sa · za
within (an hour) *u roku od* oo raw·koo awd
without *bez* bez
wok *duboka posuda za prženje* ①
  doo·baw·ka paw·soo·da za pr·zhe·nye
woman *žena* ① zhe·na
wonderful *divan* dee·van
wood *drvo* ⑩ dr·vaw
wool *vuna* ① voo·na
word *riječ* ① ree·yech
work *rad* ⑩ rad
work *raditi* imp ra·dee·tee
work experience *radno iskustvo* ⑩
  rad·naw ee·skoos·tvaw
work permit *radna dozvola* ① rad·na
  dawz·vaw·la
workout *tjelovježba* ① tye·law·vyezh·ba
workshop *radionica* ① ra·dee·aw·nee·tsa
world *svijet* ⑩ svee·yet
World Cup *svjetski kup* ⑩ svyet·skee koop
worried *zabrinut* ⑩ za·bree·noot
worship *(po)moliti se* (paw·)maw·lee·tee
  (se)
wrist *ručni zglob* rooch·nee zglawb
write *(na)pisati* (na·)pee·sa·tee
writer *pisac* ⑩ pee·sats
wrong *kriv* kreev

Y

yacht *jahta* ① yah·ta
year *godina* ① gaw·dee·na
(this) year *(ova) godina* ① (aw·va)
  gaw·dee·na
yellow *žut* zhoot
yes *da* da
yesterday *jučer* yoo·cher
(not) yet *(ne) još* (ne) yawsh
yoga *joga* ① yaw·ga
yogurt *jogurt* ⑩ yaw·goort
you inf *ti* tee
you pol sg & pl *vi* vee
young *mlad* mlad
your *tvoj/tvoja/tvoje* ⑩/①/⑩ tvoy/
  tvoy·a/tvoy·e
youth hostel *prenoćište za mladež* ⑩
  pre·naw·cheesh·te za mla·dezh
Yugoslavia *Jugoslavija* ①
  yoo·gaw·sla·vee·ya

Z

zip/zipper *šlic* ⑩ shleets
zodiac *zodijak* ⑩ zaw·dee·yak
zoo *zoološki vrt* ⑩ zaw·lawsh·kee vrt
zucchini *bučice* ① pl boo·chee·tse

A

Nouns in the dictionary have their gender indicated by ⓜ, ⓕ or ⓝ. If it's a plural noun you'll also see pl. When a word that could be either a noun or a verb has no gender indicated, it's a verb.

Nouns and adjectives are in the nominative case. You'll be understood if you just pick words out of this dictionary, but if you'd like to know more about case, see the **a–z phrasebuilder**, page 21.

Adjectives in the dictionary are given in the masculine form only. For an explanation of how to form feminine and neuter adjectives, refer to the **a–z phrasebuilder**, page 16.

Verbs are mostly given in two forms: perfective and imperfective. See the **a–z phrasebuilder,** page 17 for an explanation of these terms and when to use which form. Perfective and imperfective forms are either separated by a slash (with the perfective form given first) or consist of a root imperfective form to which a bracketed prefix is added to form the perfective. For example, the verb 'give' has the forms *dati/ davati* da·tee/da·va·tee with the first form being the perfective form and the second the imperfective. The verb 'call' is represented as *(po)zvati* (paw·)zva·tee which has the perfective form *pozvati* and the imperfective form *zvati*. Where two syllables are stressed in the transliteration, eg *(paw·)zva·tee* it means that once you add the prefix to form the perfective, the stress shifts to the prefix. Verbs are listed alphabetically according to their root (unprefixed) form.

Where only one form of a verb is given (not all verbs have both forms) the abbreviations perf and imp have been used to identify whether they are perfective or imperfective.

A

adresa ⓕ a·dre·sa *address*
aerobik ⓜ a·e·raw·beek *aerobics*
Afrika ⓕ a·free·ka *Africa*
agencija za prodaju nekretnina ⓕ
  a·gen·tsee·ya za praw·dai·oo
  ne·kret·nee·na *estate agency*
ako a·kaw *if*
akopunktura ⓕ a·kaw·poonk·too·ra
  acupuncture
aktivist ⓜ ak·tee·veest *activist*
aktovka ⓕ ak·tawv·ka *briefcase*
aktuelna zbivanja ⓝ pl ak·too·el·na
  zbee·va·nya *current affairs*
akumulator ⓜ a·koo·moo·la·tawr
  battery (for car)
alcohol ⓜ al·kaw·hawl *alcohol*
alergija ⓕ a·ler·gee·ya *allergy*
alkoholno piće ⓝ al·kaw·hawl·naw
  pee·che *drink (alcoholic)*

alpinističko penjanje ⓝ
  al·pee·nee·steech·kaw pe·nya·nye *rock
  climbing*
alpinizam ⓜ al·pee·nee·zam
  mountaineering
ambasada ⓕ am·ba·sa·da *embassy*
amfiteatar ⓜ am·fee·te·a·tar
  amphitheatre
amfora ⓕ am·faw·ra *amphora*
ananas ⓜ a·na·nas *pineapple*
anarhist ⓜ a·nar·heest *anarchist*
anemija ⓕ a·ne·mee·ya *anaemia*
antibaby-pilula ⓕ an·tee·bey·bee·pee·
  loo·la *the Pill (contraceptive)*
antibiotici ⓜ pl an·tee·be·aw·tee·tsee
  antibiotics
antički an·teech·kee *ancient*
antikvitet ⓜ an·tee·kvee·tet *antique*
antinuklearni an·tee·noo·kle·ar·nee
  antinuclear
antiseptik ⓜ an·tee·sep·teek *antiseptic*

arheološki ⓜ ar·he·*aw*·lawsh·kee *archaeological*

arhitekt ⓜ ar·hee·*tekt* *architect*

arhitektura ⓕ ar·hee·tek·*too*·ra *architecture*

aromaterapija ⓕ a·*raw*·ma·te·ra·pee·ya *aromatherapy*

aspirin ⓜ a·*spee*·reen *aspirin*

astma ⓕ *ast*·ma *asthma*

atelje ⓜ a·te·*lye* *studio*

atletika ⓕ at·*le*·tee·ka *athletics*

atmosfera ⓕ at·maw·*sfe*·ra *atmosphere*

audio vodič ⓜ a·oo·dee·aw *vaw*·deech *guide (audio)*

Australija ⓕ a·oo·*stra*·lee·ya *Australia*

Austrija ⓕ a·oo·*stree*·ya *Austria*

Austru-Ugarsko carstvo ⓜ a·oo·*straw*·oo·*gar*·skaw *tsar*·stvaw *Austro-Hungarian Empire*

autobus a·oo·*taw*·boos *bus*

autobuska stanica ⓕ a·oo·*taw*·boo·ska *sta*·nee·tsa *bus station • bus stop*

automat za prodaju karata ⓜ a·oo·*taw*·mat za *praw*·dai·oo *ka*·ra·ta *ticket machine*

automatska praonica ⓕ a·oo·*taw*·mat·ska pra·*aw*·nee·tsa *launderette*

automehaničar ⓜ a·oo·taw·me·*ha*·nee·char *mechanic*

automobil ⓜ a·oo·taw·*maw*·beel *car*

autoput ⓜ a·oo·taw·*poot* *highway*

avenija ⓕ a·ve·nee·ya *avenue*

Azija ⓕ *a*·zee·ya *Asia*

badem ⓜ *ba*·dem *almond*

badnjak ⓜ *bad*·nyak *Christmas Eve*

baka ⓕ *ba*·ka *grandmother*

bakšiš ⓜ *bak*·sheesh *tip (gratuity)*

balet ⓜ *ba*·let *ballet*

Balkan ⓜ *bal*·kan *the Balkans*

balkon ⓜ *bal*·kawn *balcony*

banana ⓕ *ba*·*na*·na *banana*

banka ⓕ *ban*·ka *bank (institution)*

bankovni automat ⓜ *ban*·kawv·nee a·oo·*taw*·mat *automated teller machine (ATM)*

bankovni račun ⓜ *ban*·kawv·nee *ra*·choon *bank account*

bar ⓜ bar *bar*

baterija ⓕ ba·te·ree·ya *battery (general)*

bazen za plivanje ⓜ *ba*·zen za *plee*·va·nye *swimming pool*

beba ⓕ *be*·ba *baby*

bejzbol ⓜ *beyz*·bawl *baseball*

Belgija ⓕ *bel*·gee·ya *Belgium*

benzin ⓜ ben·*zeen* *gasoline • petrol*

benziska stanica ⓕ ben·zeen·ska *sta*·nee·tsa *gas station • petrol station*

besplatan be·*spla*·tan *free (gratis)*

bez bez *without*

— slobodnih mjesta *slaw*·bawd·neeh *mye*·sta *no vacancy*

bezalkoholno piće ⓝ be·zal·kaw·hawl·naw *pee*·che *soft drink*

bezolovni be·zaw·*lawv*·nee *unleaded*

biblija ⓕ *bee*·blee·ya *Bible*

bicikl ⓜ bee·*tsee*·kl *bicycle*

biciklist ⓜ bee·tsee·*kleest* *cyclist*

bife ⓜ bee·*fe* *buffet*

bijel bee·*yel* *white*

bilijar ⓜ bee·*lee*·yar *pool (game)*

bilježnica ⓕ bee·*lyezh*·nee·tsa *notebook*

biljka ⓕ *beel*·ka *herb • plant*

biti/bivati bee·*tee*/bee·*va*·tee *be*

biznis ⓜ *beez*·nees *business*

biznismen ⓜ&ⓕ *beez*·nees·men *business man/woman*

blagajna ⓕ bla·*gai*·na *cash register*

blagajnik ⓜ bla·*gai*·neek *cashier*

blagdan ⓜ *blag*·dan *holiday (day off)*

blato ⓝ *bla*·taw *mud*

blic ⓜ bleets *flash (camera)*

blizak *blee*·zak *close (nearby)*

blizanci ⓜ pl blee·*zan*·tsee *twins*

blizu *blee*·zoo *near*

boca ⓕ *baw*·tsa *bottle*

— za vodu za *vaw*·doo *water bottle*

bog ⓜ bawg *god (general)*

bogat *baw*·gat *wealthy*

boja ⓕ *boy*·a *colour*

boks ⓜ bawks *boxing*

bokserice ⓕ pl *bawk*·se·ree·tse *boxer shorts*

bol ⓕ bawl *pain*

bolan *baw*·lan *painful*

bolest ⓕ *baw*·lest *disease*

bolestan *baw*·les·tan *sick*

bolji *baw*·lyee *better*

bolnica ⓕ *bawl*·nee·tsa *hospital*

bomboni ⓜ pl bawm·*baw*·nee *candy • lollies • sweets*

borba ⓕ *bawr*·ba *fight (battle)*

ekspres pošta ① eks·pres pawsh·ta express (mail)
ekstasi ① ek·sta·see ecstasy (drug)
e-mail ⓜ ee·me·eel email
emocionalan e·maw·tsee·aw·na·lan emotional
Engleska ① en·gle·ska England
engleski en·gle·skee English
euro ⓜ e·oo·raw euro
Europa ① e·oo·raw·pa Europe

F

farma ① far·ma farm
festival ⓜ fe·stee·val festival
fikcija ① feek·tsee·ya fiction (genre)
film ⓜ feelm film • movie
— **za foto-aparat** za faw·taw·a·pa·rat film (for camera)
filtriran feel·tree·ran filtered
fino pecivo ⓝ fee·naw pe·tsee·vaw pastry
Finska ① feen·ska Finland
fizički radnik ⓜ fee·zeech·kee rad·neek manual worker
[fl]anel fla·nel flannel
[fl]aster fla·ster Band-aid
[fo]aje ① fwa·ai·e foyer
[fot]o-aparat ⓜ faw·taw·a·pa·rat camera
[foto]graf ⓜ faw·taw·graf photographer
[fotogr]afija ① faw·taw·gra·fee·ya
...to • photography
[Francu]ska ① fran·tsoo·ska France
[frizer] free·zer hairdresser
[funta] ① foon·ta pound (money, weight)

...ga·le·re·ya art gallery
...a·ran·tee·ran guaranteed
...ra·zha garage
...gar·de·raw·ba cloakroom
... ga·straw·en·te·ree·tees
...landlord
...da·ree·tsa landlady

...n·na·stee·ka
...kaw·lawg

gladan/gladna ⓜ/① gla·dan/gla·dna hungry
glas ⓜ glas voice
glasan gla·san loud
glasovati imp ① gla·saw·va·tee vote
glava ① gla·va head
— **ulica** oo·lee·tsa main road
glavni glav·nee main
glavobolja ① gla·vaw·baw·lya headache
glazba ① glaz·ba music
(po)gledati (paw)gle·da·tee look • watch
gležanj ⓜ gle·zhan' ankle
gležnjače ① pl glezh·nya·che hiking boots
gljiva ① glyee·va mushroom
gluh glooh deaf
glumac ⓜ gloo·mats actor
glup gloop stupid
godišnje doba ⓝ gaw·deesh·nye daw·ba season (winter etc)
gol ⓜ gawl goal
golf ⓜ gawlf golf
gorak gaw·rak bitter
gore gaw·re up
gorski lanac ⓜ gawr·skee la·nats mountain range
Gospodin ⓜ gaw·spaw·deen Mr
Gospođa ① gaw·spaw·ja Mrs
Gospođica ① gaw·spaw·jee·tsa Miss
gostiona ① gaw·stee·aw·na restaurant (family run)
gostionica ① gaw·stee·aw·nee·tsa pub (bar)
gostoprimstvo gaw·staw·preems·tvaw hospitality
gotovina ① gaw·taw·vee·na cash
govedina ① gaw·ve·dee·na beef
(pro)govoriti (praw)gaw·vaw·ree·tee speak • talk
grad ⓜ grad city
(iz)graditi (eez)gra·dee·tee build
gradski autobus ⓜ grad·skee a·oo·taw·boos bus (city)
gradski centar ⓜ grad·skee tsen·tar city centre
građanska prava ⓝ pl gra·jan·ska pra·va civil rights
građevinar ⓜ gra·je·vee·nar builder
gram ⓜ gram gram
granica ① gra·nee·tsa border
grijač ⓜ gree·yach heater
grijanje ⓝ gree·ya·nye heating
gripa ① gree·pa influenza

borilačke vještine ⓝ pl baw·ree·lach·ke vye·shtee·ne martial arts
Bosna i Hercegovina ① baw·sna ee her·tse·gaw·vee·na Bosnia-Hercegovina
botanički vrt baw·ta·neech·kee vrt botanic garden
božić ⓜ baw·zheech Christmas
božićni dan ⓜ baw·zheech·nee dan Christmas Day
bračno stanje ⓝ brach·naw sta·nye marital status
brak ⓜ brak marriage
brašno ① brash·naw flour
brat ⓜ brat brother
brava ① bra·va lock
brdska staza ① brd·ska sta·za mountain path
brdski bicikl ⓜ brd·skee bee·tsee·kl mountain bike
breskva ① bresk·va peach
brežuljak ⓜ bre·zhoo·lyak hill
brijač ⓜ bree·yach barber • razor
(o)brijati se (aw)bree·ya·tee se shave
briljantan bree·lyan·tan brilliant
(po)brinuti se (paw)bree·noo·tee se care (for someone)
(po)brinuti se za (paw)bree·noo·tee se za look after
britva ① breet·va razor blade
brod ⓜ brawd ship
broj ⓜ broy number (figure)
— **putovnice** poo·tawv·nee·tse passport number
— **registarske tablice** re·gee·star·ske ta·blee·tse licence-plate number
— **sobe** saw·be room number
(iz)brojati (eez)broy·a·tee count
brokula ① braw·koo·la broccoli
bronhitis ⓜ brawn·hee·tees bronchitis
brošura ① braw·shoo·ra brochure
brz brz fast
brzi br·zee express
brzina ① br·zee·na speed
— **filma** feel·ma film speed
brzinomjer ⓜ br·zee·naw·myer speedometer
brzinsko ograničenje ⓝ br·zeen·skaw aw·gra·nee·che·nye speed limit
bučan boo·chan noisy
bučice ① pl boo·chee·tse courgette • zucchini
budala ① boo·da·la idiot
budilica ① boo·dee·lee·tsa alarm clock

Budist ⓜ boo·deest Buddhist
(pro)buditi nekoga (praw)boo·dee·tee ne·kaw·ga wake (someone) up
budućnost ① boo·dooch·nawst future
budžet ⓜ boo·jet budget
buha ① boo·ha flea
bundeva ① boon·de·va pumpkin
(pro)bušiti (praw)boo·shee·tee puncture
buvljak ⓜ boov·lyak flea market

C

carinarnica ① tsa·ree·nar·nee·tsa customs
CD ⓜ tse de CD
cent ⓜ tsent cent
centar ⓜ tsen·tar centre
centimetar ⓜ tsen·tee·me·tar centimetre
cesta ① tse·sta road
cigara ① tsee·ga·ra cigar
cigareta ① tsee·ga·re·ta cigarette
cijena ① tsee·ye·na price
— **ulaznice** oo·laz·nee·tse cover charge (nightclub etc)
— **vožnje** vawzh·nye fare
cijepljenje ⓝ tsee·yep·lye·nye vaccination
cipela/e ① sg/① pl tsee·pe·la/e shoe(s)
cirkus ⓜ tseer·koos circus
cistitis ⓜ tsee·stee·tees cystitis
citadela ① tsee·ta·de·la walled city
crkva ① tsr·kva church
crn tsrn black
Crna Gora ① tsr·na gaw·ra Montenegro
crno-bijeli (film) tsr·naw·bee·ye·lee (feelm) B&W (film)
crven tsr·ven red
crvi ⓜ pl tsr·vee worms
cura ① tsoo·ra girlfriend
cvijet ⓜ tsvee·yet flower
cvjećara ① tsvye·cha·ra florist

Č

čačkalica ① chach·ka·lee·tsa toothpick
čaj ⓜ chai tea
čamac ⓜ cha·mats boat
čarapa/e ① sg/① pl cha·ra·pa/e sock(s)
čaša ① cha·sha glass (receptacle)
ček ⓜ chek cheque
čekaonica ① che·ka·aw·nee·tsa waiting room

croatian–english

(pri)čekati nekoga (pree-)che-ka-tee ne-kaw-ga *wait (for)*
čekić ⓜ che-keech *hammer*
čeljust ⓕ che-lyoost *jaw*
čelnik ⓜ chel-neek *leader*
čep ⓜ chep *plug (bath)*
čepovi za uši ⓜ pl che-paw-vee za oo-shee *earplugs*
čestitke ⓕ pl che-steet-ke *congratulations*
često che-staw *often*
češalj ⓜ che-shal' *comb*
češnjak ⓜ chesh-nyak *garlic*
četka ⓕ chet-ka *brush*
— **za kosu** ⓕ za kaw-soo *hairbrush*
četkica za zube ⓕ chet-kee-tsa za zoo-be *toothbrush*
četvrtak ⓜ chet-vr-tak *Thursday*
četvrtina ⓕ chet-vr-tee-na *quarter*
(u)činiti (oo-)chee-nee-tee *do · make*
čipka ⓕ cheep-ka *lace*
čist cheest *clean · pure*
(o)čistiti (aw-)chee-stee-tee *clean*
čišćenje ⓝ cheesh-che-nye *cleaning*
čitanje ⓝ chee-ta-nye *reading*
(pro)čitati (praw-)chee-ta-tee *read*
čizma/e ⓕ sg/ⓕ pl cheez-ma/e *boot(s) (footwear)*
član(ica) ⓜ/ⓕ chlan(-ee-tsa) *member*
čokolada ⓕ chaw-kaw-la-da *chocolate*
čovjek ⓜ chaw-vyek *man (human)*
čuti perf choo-tee *hear*
čuvanje djece ⓝ choo-va-nye dye-tse *childminding*

D

da da *yes*
dadilja ⓕ da-dee-lya *baby-sitter*
dahnuti/disati dah-noo-tee/dee-sa-tee *breathe*
daleko da-le-kaw *far*
dalekozor ⓜ da-le-kaw-zawr *binoculars*
daljinski upravljač ⓜ da-lyeen-skee oo-prav-lyach *remote control*
dan ⓜ dan *day*
danas da-nas *today*
Danska ⓕ dan-ska *Denmark*
dar ⓜ dar *gift*
daska ⓕ da-ska *board*
— **za surfanje** za soor-fa-nye *surfboard*

daskanje na snijegu ⓝ da-ska-nye na snee-ye-goo *snowboarding*
daskanje na valovima ⓝ da-ska-nye na va-law-vee-ma *surfing*
dati/davati da-tee/da-va-tee *give*
datulja ⓕ da-too-lya *date (fruit)*
datum ⓜ da-toom *date (day)*
— **rođenja** raw-je-nya *date of birth*
debeo de-be-aw *fat · thick (object)*
dečko ⓜ dech-kaw *boyfriend*
deka ⓕ de-ka *blanket*
delikatese ⓕ pl de-lee-ka-te-se *delicatessen*
demokracija ⓕ de-maw-kra-tsee-ya *democracy*
demonstracija ⓕ de-mawn-stra-tsee-ya *demonstration (protest)*
depozit ⓜ de-paw-zeet *deposit (bank)*
desni ⓜ pl de-snee *gum (teeth)*
desničarski de-snee-char-skee *right-wing*
desno de-snaw *right (direction)*
dezodorans ⓜ de-zaw-daw-rans *deodorant*
digitron ⓜ dee-gee-trawn *calculator*
dijabetes ⓜ dee-ya-be-tes *diabetes*
dijafragma ⓕ dee-ya-frag-ma *diaphragm (body part)*
dijapozitiv ⓜ dee-ya-paw-zee-teev *slide (film)*
dijeliti imp dee-ye-lee-tee *share (a dorm etc)*
(po)dijeliti (paw-)dee-ye-lee-tee *deal (cards)*
dijeta ⓕ dee-ye-ta *diet*
dijete ⓝ dee-ye-te *child*
dinja ⓕ dee-nya *cantaloupe · melon · rockmelon*
dio ⓜ dee-aw *part (component)*
director ⓜ dee-rek-tawr *director*
direktan dee-rek-tan *direct*
— **poziv** paw-zeev *direct-dial*
dirnuti/dirati deer-noo-tee/dee-ra-tee *feel · touch*
disk (CD-ROM) ⓜ deesk (tse de rawm) *disk (CD-ROM)*
disketa ⓕ dee-ske-ta *disk (floppy)*
disko ⓜ dee-skaw *disco*
diskriminacija ⓕ dee-skree-mee-na-tsee-ya *discrimination*
divan dee-van *wonderful*
dizajn ⓜ dee-zain *design*
dizalo ⓝ dee-za-law *elevator · lift*

djeca ⓝ pl dye-tsa *children*
dječak ⓜ dye-chak *boy*
dječja hodalica ⓕ dyech-ya haw-da-lee-tsa *stroller*
djed ⓜ dyed *grandfather*
djevojčica ⓕ dye-voy-chee-tsa *girl*
dlaka ⓕ dla-ka *hair (body)*
dnevni dnev-nee *daily*
dnevnik ⓜ dnev-neek *diary*
dno ⓝ dnaw *bottom (position)*
do daw *beside · to*
dobaciti/dobacivati daw-ba-tsee-tee/daw-ba-tsee-va-tee *pass*
dobar daw-bar *good*
dobitak ⓜ daw-bee-tak *profit*
dobiti/dobivati daw-bee-tee/daw-bee-va-tee *get*
dobro daw-braw *well*
doček nove godine ⓜ daw-chek naw-ve gaw-dee-ne *New Year's Eve*
dočekati/dočekivati daw-che-ka-tee/daw-che-kee-va-tee *welcome*
doći/dolaziti daw-chee/daw-la-zee-tee *come*
dokumentacija ⓕ daw-koo-men-ta-tsee-ya *paperwork*
dokumentarac ⓜ daw-koo-men-ta-rats *documentary*
dolar ⓜ daw-lar *dollar*
dolasci ⓜ pl daw-las-tsee *arrivals*
dolina ⓕ daw-lee-na *valley*
dolje daw-lye *down*
dom ⓜ dawm *home*
donijeti/donositi daw-nee-ye-tee/daw-naw-see-tee *bring*
donje rublje ⓝ daw-nye roob-lye *underwear*
dopasti/dopadati se daw-pa-stee/daw-pa-da-tee se *like (appeal to)*
dopisnica ⓕ daw-pee-snee-tsa *postcard*
dopuštenje ⓝ daw-poosh-te-nye *permission*
doručak ⓜ daw-roo-chak *breakfast*
dosadan daw-sa-dan *boring*
dosta daw-sta *enough*
dostaviti/dostavljati daw-sta-vee-tee/daw-stav-lya-tee *deliver*
dozvola ⓕ dawz-vaw-la *licer...*
dozvoliti/dozvoljavati daw... dawz-vaw-lya-va-tee *admit (a...*
dozvoljena količina prtljage ⓕ dawz-vaw-lye-na kaw-lee-chee-na prt-lya-ge *baggage allowance*

dragocjen dra-gaw-tsyen *valuable*
drama ⓕ dra-ma *drama*
dražica ⓕ dra-zhee-tsa *cove*
droga/e ⓕ sg/ⓕ pl draw-ga/e *drug(s) (illicit)*
drug ⓜ droog *companion*
drugačiji droo-ga-chee-yee *different (another)*
drugi droo-gee *another · other · second*
— **razred** raz-red *economy class · second class*
društvene znanosti ⓕ pl droosht-ve-ne zna-naw-stee *humanities*
društvo ⓝ droosh-tvaw *company*
drvo ⓝ dr-vaw *wood*
— **za ogrjev** za aw-gryev *firewood*
država ⓕ dr-zha-va *country (nation stat...*
državljanstvo ⓝ dr-zhav-lyan-stvaw... *citizenship*
dubok ⓜ doo-bawk *deep*
dugačak doo-ga-chak *long*
dugme ⓝ doog-me *button*
dugovati imp doo-gaw-va-tee...
duhan ⓜ doo-han *tobacco...*
dupli krevet ⓜ doo-plee... *double bed*
dva dva *two*
— **tjedna** ⓕ tyed...
dvaput dva-poot...
DVD ⓜ de ve d...
dvokrevetna s... saw-ba dou...
dvorac ⓜ...
dvostruk...

Dž

djeca...

galerija ⓕ...
garantiran...
garaža ⓕ ga...
garderoba ⓕ...
gastroenterit...
gazda ⓜ...
gazdarica ⓕ gcz-da...
gdje gdye *where*
G'da gya Ms
gimnastika ⓕ gee...*gymnastics*
ginekolog ⓜ gee-ne...*gynecologist*
gitara ⓕ gee-ta-ra gu...

(za)grliti (za-)gr-lee-tee hug
grlo ⓝ gr-law throat
grmljavina ⓕ grm-lya-vee-na thunderstorm
grnčarija ⓕ grn-cha-ree-ya pottery
grob ⓜ grawb grave (tomb)
groblje ⓝ graw-blye cemetery
groznica ⓕ grawz-nee-tsa fever
grožđica ⓕ grawzh-jee-tsa raisin
grudnjak ⓜ grood-nyak bra
grumen ⓜ groo-men lump
grupa ⓕ groo-pa band (music)
g-string ⓜ ge-streeng g-string
guma ⓕ goo-ma gum (substance) •
   tire • tyre
   — na automobile na
   a-oo-taw-maw-bee-le tire (car)
gurnuti/gurati goor-noo-tee/goo-ra-tee
   push
gust goost thick (liquid)
gušter ⓜ goosh-ter lizard

H

halal ha-lal halal
haljina ⓕ ha-lyee-na dress
Halo. ha-law Hello. (answering telephone)
halucinacija ⓕ ha-loo-tsee-na-tsee-ya
   hallucination
hašiš ⓜ ha-sheesh hash
hepatitis ⓜ he-pa-tee-tees hepatitis
heroin ⓜ he-raw-een heroin
hidratantna krema ⓕ hee-dra-tant-na
   kre-ma moisturiser
higijenski uložak ⓜ hee-gee-yen-skee
   oo-law-zhak sanitary napkin
Hinduist ⓜ heen-doo-eest Hindu
hitan hee-tan urgent
   — slučaj sloo-chai emergency
hitna pomoć ⓕ heet-na paw-mawch
   ambulance
HIV ⓜ heev HIV
hlače ⓕ pl hla-che trousers
hladan hla-dan cold • cool
hladnjak ⓜ hlad-nyak refrigerator
hladovina ⓕ hla-daw-vee-na shade
hodati imp haw-da-tee walk
hodnik ⓜ hawd-neek walkway
hokej ⓜ haw-key hockey
   — na ledu na le-doo ice hockey
homeopatija ⓕ haw-me-aw-pa-tee-ya
   homeopathy

homoseksualac/homoseksualka ⓜ/ⓕ
   haw-maw-sek-soo-a-lats/
   haw-maw-sek-soo-al-ka homosexual
homoseksualan haw-maw-sek-soo-a-lan gay
honorarni ⓜ haw-naw-rar-nee part-time
horoskop ⓜ haw-raw-skawp horoscope
hotel ⓜ haw-tel hotel
hrabar hra-bar brave
hram ⓜ hram temple
hrana ⓕ hra-na food
   — za bebe za be-be baby food
(na)hraniti (na-)hra-nee-tee feed
Hrvat/Hrvatica ⓜ/ⓕ hr-vat/hr-va-tee-tsa
   Croat
Hrvatska ⓕ hr-vat-ska Croatia
hvala vam/ti pol/inf hva-la vam/tee
   thank you

I

i ee and
ići imp ee-chee go
   — u kupovinu imp oo
   koo-paw-vee-noo go shopping
identifikacija ⓕ ee-den-tee-fee-ka-tsee-ya
   identification
igla injekcije ⓕ ee-gla ee-nyek-tsee-ye
   syringe
igla za šivenje ⓕ ee-gla za shee-ve-nye
   sewing needle
igra ⓕ ee-gra game
igralište ⓝ ee-gra-leesh-te court (tennis)
igrati imp ee-gra-tee play (board games)
ili ee-lee or
Iliri ⓜ pl ee-lee-ree Illyrians
imati imp ee-ma-tee have
ime ⓝ ee-me name (given)
imigracija ⓕ ee-mee-gra-tsee-ya
   immigration
Indija ⓕ een-dee-ya India
indijski oraščić ⓜ een-deey-skee
   aw-rash-cheech cashew
industrija ⓕ een-doo-stree-ya industry
infekcija ⓕ een-fek-tsee-ya infection
   — kandide kan-dee-de thrush (illness)
   — mokraćnih kanala maw-krach-neeh
   ka-na-la urinary infection
informacije ⓕ pl een-fawr-ma-tsee-ye
   information
Informacijska tehnologija ⓕ
   een-fawr-ma-tseey-ska
   teh-naw-law-gee-ya IT

injekcija ⓕ ee-*nyek*-tsee-ya *injection*
inostranstvo ⓝ ee-naw-*strans*-tvaw *overseas*
instruktor ⓜ een-*strook*-tawr *instructor*
internet ⓜ een-ter-net *Internet*
— **kafić** ka-feech *Internet café*
intervju ⓜ een-ter-*vyoo* *interview*
invalidska kolica ⓕ pl een-*va*-leed-ska *kaw*-*lee*-tsa *wheelchair*
inženjer ⓜ een-*zhe*-nyer *engineer*
inženjerstvo ⓝ een-zhe-*nyer*-stvaw *engineering*
Irska ⓕ *eer*-ska *Ireland*
isključen ees-klyoo-chen *excluded*
iskustvo ⓝ ees-*koost*-vaw *experience*
isplata ⓕ ees-*pla*-ta *payment (to someone)*
ispod ee-*spawd* *below*
ispovijed ⓕ ee-*spaw*-vee-yed *confession (at church)*
ispravan ee-*spra*-van *right (correct)*
isti ⓜ ee-*stee* *same*
istok ee-*stawk* *east*
Italija ⓕ ee-*ta*-lee-ya *Italy*
iz eez *from*
iza ee-za *after • behind*
izabrati/izabirati ee-*za*-bra-tee/ ee-za-bee-ra-tee *choose*
izaći/izlaziti ee-za-chee/ee-zla-zee-tee *go out*
izaći/izlaziti sa ee-*za*-chee/ eez-la-zee-tee sa *go out with (date) a person*
izbjeglica ⓕ *eez*-byeg-lee-tsa *refugee*
izbočina ⓕ eez-baw-chee-na *ledge*
izbori pl *eez*-baw-ree *election*
izdavanje ⓝ eez-*da*-va-nye *publishing*
izgoren eez-gaw-ren *burnt*
(iz)gubiti (eez-)*goo*-bee-tee *lose*
izgubljen eez-goob-lyen *lost*
izlaz ⓜ eez-laz *departure gate • exit*
izlazak ⓜ eez-la-zak *night out*
izlazak sunca ⓜ eez-la-zak *soon*-tsa *sunrise*
izlet ⓜ eez-let *trip (journey)*
izložba ⓕ eez-*lawzh*-ba *exhibition*
između ee-zme-joo *between*
iznad eez-nad *above*
iznajmiti/iznajmljivati eez-*nai*-mee-tee/ eez-naim-*lyee*-va-tee *hire • rent*
iznenađen ⓜ eez-ne-na-jen *surprise*
Izrael ⓜ ee-zra-el *Israel*

J

ja ya *I*
jabuka ⓕ *ya*-boo-ka *apple*
jabukovača ⓕ *ya*-boo-kaw-va-cha *cider*
Jadranska obala ⓕ *ya*-dran-ska *aw*-ba-la *Adriatic Coast*
Jadransko more ⓝ *ya*-dran-skaw *maw*-re *Adriatic Sea*
jagoda ⓕ *ya*-gaw-da *strawberry*
jahanje konja ⓝ ya-ha-nye *kaw*-nya *horse riding*
jahati imp *ya*-ha-tee *ride (horse)*
jahta ⓕ *yah*-ta *yacht*
jaje ⓝ *yai*-e *egg*
jajnik ⓜ *yai*-neek *ovary*
jak yak *strong (physically)*
jakna ⓕ *yak*-na *jacket*
janje ⓝ *ya*-nye *lamb (animal)*
janjetina ⓕ *ya*-nye-tee-na *lamb (meat)*
Japan ⓜ *ya*-pan *Japan*
jarac ⓜ *ya*-rats *goat*
jaslice ⓕ pl *ya*-slee-tse *creche*
jastučnica ⓕ *ya*-stooch-nee-tsa *pillowcase*
jastuk ⓜ *ya*-stook *pillow*
javni *yav*-nee *public*
— **parkovi** ⓜ pl *par*-kaw-vee *public gardens*
— **telefon** ⓜ te-*le*-fawn *public telephone*
— **zahod** ⓜ *za*-hawd *public toilet*
je ⓕ ye *her*
jedan ⓜ *ye*-dan *one*
jednake mogućnosti ⓕ pl *yed*-na-ke maw-*gooch*-naw-stee *equal opportunity*
jednokrevetna soba ⓕ *yed*-naw-*kre*-vet-na *saw*-ba *single room*
jednom *yed*-nawm *once*
jednosmjeran *yed*-naw-*smye*-ran *one-way (ticket)*
jednostavan *yed*-naw-sta-van *easy*
jedrenje na dasci ⓝ *ye*-dre-nye na *das*-tsee *windsurfing*
jeftino ⓝ *yef*-tee-naw *cheap*
jelo ⓝ *ye*-law *dish (food item)*
jelovnik ⓜ ye-*lawv*-neek *menu*
jesen ⓕ *ye*-sen *autumn • fall*
(po)jesti (*paw*-)ye-stee *eat*
jetra ⓕ *ye*-tra *liver*
jezero ⓝ *ye*-ze-raw *lake*
jezik ⓜ *ye*-zeek *language*
joga ⓕ *yaw*-ga *yoga*

jogurt ⓜ *yaw*-goort *yogurt*
(ne) još (ne) yawsh *(not) yet*
jučer *yoo*-cher *yesterday*
jug ⓜ yoog *south*
Jugoslavija ⓕ *yoo*-gaw-*sla*-vee-ya *Yugoslavia*
juha ⓕ *yoo*-ha *soup*
jutro ⓝ *yoo*-traw *morning*

K

kabanica ⓕ ka-*ba*-nee-tsa *raincoat*
kabina za presvlačenje ⓕ pl ka-*bee*-na za pres-*vla*-che-nye *changing room*
kablovi za punjenje akumulatora ⓜ pl *ka*-blaw-vee za poo-nye-nye a-koo-moo-*la*-taw-ra *jumper leads*
kaciga ⓕ ka-tsee-ga *helmet*
kada ka-da *when*
kafić ⓜ ka-feech *café*
kajsija ⓕ kai-see-ya *apricot*
kakao ka-*ka*-aw *cocoa*
kako ka-kaw *how*
kalendar ⓜ ka-*len*-dar *calendar*
kamen ⓜ ka-men *stone*
kamion ⓜ ka-mee-awn *truck*
kamp ⓜ kamp *camping ground*
kampirati imp kam-*pee*-ra-tee *camp*
Kanada ⓕ ka-na-da *Canada*
kanta ⓕ kan-ta *bucket*
 — za smeće za sme-che *garbage can*
kapi za oči ⓕ pl ka-pee za aw-chee *eye drops*
kaput ⓜ ka-poot *coat*
karantena ⓕ ka-ran-te-na *quarantine*
karavana ⓕ ka-ra-va-na *caravan*
karta ⓕ kar-ta *map (of country)* • *ticket*
karte za igranje ⓕ pl kar-te za ee-gra-nye *cards (playing)*
kartonska kutija ⓕ kar-tawn-ska koo-tee-ya *carton*
kasan ka-san *late*
kasino ⓜ ka-see-naw *casino*
kasnije ka-snee-ye *later*
(za)kašljati (za-)kash-lya-tee *cough*
kat ⓜ kat *floor (storey)*
katedrala ⓕ ka-te-*dra*-la *cathedral*
Katoličanstvo ⓝ ka-taw-lee-*chan*-stvaw *Catholicism*
katolik ⓜ ka-taw-leek *Catholic*
kava ⓕ ka-va *coffee*
kazalište ⓝ ka-za-leesh-te *theatre*

kazati/kazivati ka-za-tee/ka-*zee*-va-tee *say*
kazeta ⓕ ka-ze-ta *cassette*
kći ⓕ kchee *daughter*
keks ⓜ keks *biscuit*
kemijska ⓕ ke-meey-ska *pen (ballpoint)*
keramika ⓕ ke-ra-mee-ka *ceramics*
kikiriki ⓜ kee-kee-*ree*-kee *groundnut* • *peanut*
kila ⓕ kee-la *kilo*
kilogram ⓜ kee-law-gram *kilogram*
kilometar ⓜ kee-law-me-tar *kilometre*
kino ⓝ kee-naw *cinema*
kiosk ⓜ kee-awsk *kiosk*
 — za prodaju novina za praw-dai-oo naw-vee-na *newsstand*
kip ⓜ keep *statue*
kiropraktor ⓜ kee-raw-prak-tawr *chiropractor*
kiseli krastavci ⓜ pl kee-se-lee kra-stav-tsee *pickles*
kiselo vrhnje ⓝ kee-se-law vrh-nye *sour cream*
kisik ⓜ kee-seek *oxygen*
kiša ⓕ kee-sha *rain*
kivi ⓜ kee-vee *kiwifruit*
klasa ⓕ kla-sa *class (category)*
klasičan kla-see-chan *classical*
klasni sistem ⓜ kla-snee see-stem *class system*
klavijatura ⓕ kla-vee-ya-too-ra *keyboard (instrument)*
klima ⓕ klee-ma *air-conditioning*
klimatiziran klee-ma-tee-zee-ran *air-conditioned*
ključ ⓜ klyooch *key*
knjiga ⓕ knyee-ga *book*
knjižara ⓕ knyee-zha-ra *bookshop*
knjižnica ⓕ knyeezh-nee-tsa *library*
kockice ⓕ pl kawts-kee-tse *dice*
kočnice ⓕ pl kawch-nee-tse *brakes*
kod kawd *at* • *with*
kofer ⓜ kaw-fer *suitcase*
koji koy-ee *which*
koji/koja/koje ⓜ/ⓕ/ⓝ koy-ee/koy-a/koy-e *what*
kokain ⓜ kaw-ka-een *cocaine*
kokos ⓜ kaw-kaws *coconut*
koktel ⓜ kawk-tel *cocktail*
kola za ručavanje ⓝ kaw-la za roo-cha-va-nye *dining car*
kolač ⓜ kaw-lach *cake*
kolačić ⓜ kaw-la-cheech *biscuit* • *cookie*

K

croatian–english

229

koledž ⓜ *kaw·*lej *college*

kolega/kolegica ⓜ/ⓕ kaw·*le·ga/ kaw·*le·*gee·tsa *colleague*

koliba ⓕ *kaw·*lee·*ba *lodge*

kolica za prtljagu ⓕ *kaw·*lee·tsa za prt·*lya·goo *trolley*

količina ⓕ *kaw·*lee·*chee·na *number (quantity)*

koliko kaw·*lee·*kaw *how much*

koljeno ⓝ *kaw·*lye·naw *knee*

kolo ⓝ *kaw·*law *circle dance*

kolovoz ⓜ *kaw·*law·vawz *August*

komad ⓜ *kaw·*mad *piece*

komarac ⓜ *kaw·*ma·rats *mosquito*

kombi ⓜ *kawm·*bee *van*

komedija ⓕ *kaw·*me·*dee·ya *comedy*

komisija ⓕ *kaw·*mee·*see·ya *commission*

kompas ⓜ *kawm·*pas *compass*

kompjuterska igra ⓕ *kawm·*pyoo·*ter·ska ee·gra *computer game*

komunikacije ⓕ pl kaw·*moo·nee·*ka·tsee·ye *communications (profession)*

komunista ⓜ *kaw·*moo·*nee·sta *communist*

komunizam ⓜ *kaw·*moo·*nee·zam *communism*

konac ⓜ *kaw·*nats *thread*
  — **za čišćenje zubi** ⓜ za cheesh·*che·nye zoo·bee *dental floss*

koncert ⓜ *kawn·*tsert *concert*

konferencija ⓕ kon·fe·*ren·*tsee·ya *conference (big)*

konj ⓜ *kawn' *horse*

konjunktivitis ⓜ kaw·nyoonk·tee·*vee·*tees *conjunctivitis*

konobar ⓜ *kaw·*naw·bar *waiter*

konop za sušenje rublja ⓜ *kaw·*nawp za soo·she·nye roob·lya *clothesline*

kontakt leće ⓕ pl *kawn·*takt *le·*che *contact lenses*

konverter ⓜ kawn·*ver·*ter *adaptor*

konzervativan *kawn·*zer·va·tee·van *conservative*

konzulat ⓜ *kawn·*zoo·lat *consulate*

koralj ⓜ *kaw·*ral' *coral*

korisnik droga ⓜ *kaw·*ree·sneek *draw·*ga *drug user*

koristan *kaw·*ree·*stan *useful*

kosa ⓕ *kaw·*sa *hair (head)*

kost ⓕ *kawst *bone*

koš ⓜ *kawsh *basket*

košarka ⓕ *kaw·*shar·ka *basketball*

košer ⓜ *kaw·*sher *kosher*

košulja ⓕ *kaw·*shoo·lya *shirt*

kotač ⓜ *kaw·*tach *wheel*

kozmetički salon ⓜ kawz·*me·*teech·kee sa·lawn *beauty salon*

koža ⓕ *kaw·*zha *leather • skin*

kraj ⓜ krai *end*

kraj krai *beside*

kralj ⓜ kral' *king*

kraljica ⓕ kra·*lyee·*tsa *queen*

krasno kra·snaw *great (fantastic)*

(u)krasti (oo·)kra·stee *steal*

kratak kra·tak *short*
  — **životopis** ⓜ zhee·vaw·taw·pees *CV*

kratke hlače ⓕ pl krat·ke hla·che *shorts*

krava ⓕ kra·va *cow*

krčenje šuma ⓝ kr·che·nye shoo·ma *deforestation*

kredit ⓜ kre·deet *credit*

kreditna kartica ⓕ kre·deet·na kar·tee·tsa *credit card*

kreker ⓜ kre·ker *cracker*

krema ⓕ kre·ma *cream (cosmetic)*

krevet ⓜ kre·vet *bed*

krevetnina ⓕ kre·vet·nee·na *bedding*

kriket ⓜ kree·ket *cricket (sport)*

krila ⓝ pl kree·la *wings*

kriška ⓕ kreesh·ka *slice*

kriv kreev *guilty • wrong*

krivnja ⓕ kreev·nya *fault (someone's)*

križ ⓜ kreezh *cross*

krojač ⓜ kroy·ach *tailor*

kroz krawz *across • in*

krsno ime ⓝ kr·snaw ee·me *given name*

krš ⓜ krsh *karst*

kršćanin/kršćanka ⓜ/ⓕ krsh·cha·neen/ krsh·chan·ka *Christian*

krštenje ⓝ krsh·te·nye *baptism*

kruh ⓜ krooh *bread*

krumpir ⓜ kroom·peer *potato*

krupan kroo·pan *large*

kruška ⓕ kroosh·ka *pear*

kružni tok ⓜ kroozh·nee tawk *roundabout*

krv ⓕ krv *blood*

krvna grupa ⓕ krv·na groo·pa *blood group*

krvne pretrage ⓕ pl krv·ne pre·tra·ge *blood test*

kuća ⓕ koo·cha *house*

kući koo·chee *(at) home*

kućni poslovi ⓜ pl kooch·nee paw·slaw·vee *housework*

kuglice vate ① pl *koo·glee·tse va·te* cotton balls

kuhanje ⓝ *koo·ha·nye* cooking

kuhar/kuharica ⓜ/① *koo·har/koo·ha·ree·tsa* cook

(s)kuhati *(s)koo·ha·tee* cook

kuhinja ① *koo·hee·nya* kitchen

kukuruz ⓜ *koo·koo·rooz* corn

kukuruzne pahuljice ① pl *koo·koo·rooz·ne pa·hoo·lyee·tse* cornflakes

kupaći kostim ⓜ *koo·pa·chee kaw·steem* bathing suit · swimsuit

kupaonica ① *koo·pa·aw·nee·tsa* bathroom

kupiti/kupovati *koo·pee·tee/koo·paw·va·tee* buy

kupka ① *koop·ka* bath

kupon ⓜ *koo·pawn* coupon

kupovati imp *koo·paw·va·tee* shop

kupovina ① *koo·paw·vee·na* shopping

kupus ⓜ *koo·poos* cabbage

kusur ⓜ *koo·soor* change (coins)

kutija ① *koo·tee·ya* box · packet

kvačilo ⓝ *kva·chee·law* clutch (car)

kvalifikacije ① pl *kva·lee·fee·ka·tsee·ye* qualifications

kvaliteta ① *kva·lee·te·ta* quality

(po)kvariti se *(paw·)kva·ree·tee se* break down

L

labav ⓜ *la·bav* loose

lagan *la·gan* light (not heavy)

laki obrok ⓜ *la·kee aw·brawk* snack

laksativ ⓜ *lak·sa·teev* laxative

lanac ⓜ *la·nats* chain

laneno platno ⓝ *la·ne·naw plat·naw* linen (material)

lažljivac/lažljivica ⓜ/① *lazh·lyee·vats/lazh·lyee·vee·tsa* liar

leća ① *le·cha* lens · lentil

leći/ležati *le·chee/le·zha·tee* lie (not stand)

led ⓜ *led* ice

leđa ⓝ *le·ja* back (body)

leptir ⓜ *le·pteer* butterfly

let ⓜ *let* flight

(po)letjeti *(paw·)let·ye·tee* fly

lezbijka ① *lez·beey·ka* lesbian

ležaljka ① *le·zhal'·ka* deck chairs

lice ⓝ *lee·tse* face

liječnik ⓜ *lee·yech·neek* doctor (medical)

lijekovi ⓜ pl *lee·ye·kaw·vee* medicine (medication)

lijen *lee·yen* lazy

lijep *lee·yep* beautiful · nice

lijevi *lee·ye·vee* left (direction)

limenka ① *lee·men·ka* can (tin)

limun ⓜ *lee·moon* lemon

limunada ① *lee·moo·na·da* lemonade

linija ① *lee·nee·ya* stereo

lipanj ⓜ *lee·pan'* June

list ⓜ *leest* leaf

listopad ⓜ *lee·staw·pad* October

litica ① *lee·tee·tsa* cliff

lokal ⓜ *law·kal* venue

lokot ⓜ *law·kawt* padlock

(s)lomiti *(s)law·mee·tee* break

lomljiv *lawm·lyeev* fragile

lonac ⓜ *law·nats* saucepan

lopov ⓜ *law·pawv* thief

lopta ① *lawp·ta* ball

loptica za golf ① *lawp·tee·tsa za gawlf* golf ball

losion *law·see·awn* lotion
— **za dobijanje tena** *za daw·bee·ya·nye te·na* tanning lotion
— **za upotrebu poslije brijanja** *za oo·paw·tre·boo paw·slee·ye bree·ya·nya* aftershave
— **za zaštitu od sunca** *za zash·tee·too awd soon·tsa* sunblock

losos ⓜ *law·saws* salmon

loš *lawsh* bad

lov na životinje ⓜ *lawv na zhee·vaw·tee·nye* hunting

lubanja ① *loo·ba·nya* skull

lubenica ① *loo·be·nee·tsa* watermelon

lubrikant ⓜ *loo·bree·kant* lubricant

lud *lood* crazy

luk ⓜ *look* onion

luka ① *loo·ka* harbour · port (sea)

lutka ① *loot·ka* doll

Lj

(po)ljubiti *(paw·)lyoo·bee·tee* kiss

ljubomoran *lyoo·baw·maw·ran* jealous

ljudi ⓜ pl *lyoo·dee* people

ljudska prava ⓝ pl *lyood·ska pra·va* human rights

ljudski resursi ⓜ pl *lyood·skee re·soor·see* human resources

ljutit *lyoo·teet* angry

M

mačevanje ⓝ ma·che·va·nye
fencing (sport)
mačka ⓕ mach·ka *cat*
madrac ⓜ mad·rats *mattress*
Mađarska ⓕ ma·jar·ska *Hungary*
magazin ⓜ ma·ga·zeen *magazine*
maglovit ma·glaw·veet *foggy*
majica ⓕ mai·ee·tsa *T-shirt*
majka ⓕ mai·ka *mother*
Makedonija ⓕ ma·ke·daw·nee·ya
Macedonia
mali ma·lee *small*
malo ma·law *little (not much)* • *some*
mama ⓕ ma·ma *mum*
mandarina ⓕ man·da·ree·na *mandarin*
mandolina ⓕ man·daw·lee·na *mandolin*
mango ⓜ man·gaw *mango*
manje ma·nye *less*
manji ma·nyee *smaller*
marakuja ⓕ ma·ra·koo·ya *passionfruit*
margarin ⓜ mar·ga·reen *margarine*
marihuana ⓕ ma·ree·hoo·a·na
marijuana
marina ⓕ ma·ree·na *marina*
marmelada ⓕ mar·me·la·da *marmalade*
masaža ⓕ ma·sa·zha *massage*
maser/maserka ⓜ/ⓕ ma·ser/ma·ser·ka
masseur/masseuse
maslac ⓜ ma·slats *butter*
maslina ⓕ ma·slee·na *olive*
maslinovo ulje ⓝ ma·slee·naw·vaw
oo·lye *olive oil*
me(ne) me(·ne) *me*
med ⓜ med *honey*
medeni mjesec ⓜ me·de·nee mye·sets
honeymoon
medicina ⓕ me·dee·tsee·na *medicine*
(profession)
medicinska sestra ⓕ me·dee·tseen·ska
se·stra *nurse*
mediji ⓜ pl me·dee·yee *media*
meditacija ⓕ me·dee·ta·tsee·ya
meditation
međugradski autobus ⓜ
me·joo·grad·skee a·oo·taw·boos
bus (intercity)
međunarodan me·joo·na·raw·dan
international
melodija ⓕ me·law·dee·ya *tune*
menadžer ⓜ me·na·jer *manager*

menstrualni bolovi ⓜ pl
men·stroo·al·nee baw·law·vee
period pain
mesar ⓜ me·sar *butcher*
mesnica ⓕ me·snee·tsa *butcher's shop*
meso ⓝ me·saw *meat*
metal ⓜ me·tal *metal*
metar ⓜ me·tar *metre*
metro ⓜ me·traw *metro (train)*
— **stanica** ⓕ sta·nee·tsa *metro station*
mi mee *we*
migrena ⓕ mee·gre·na *migraine*
(po)miješati (paw)mye·sha·tee *mix*
mikrovalna pećnica ⓕ mee·kraw·val·na
pech·nee·tsa *microwave (oven)*
milijun ⓜ mee·lee·yoon *million*
milimetar ⓜ mee·lee·me·tar *millimetre*
mineralna voda ⓕ mee·ne·ral·na vaw·da
mineral water
ministar predsjednik ⓜ mee·nee·star
pred·syed·neek *prime minister*
minuta ⓕ mee·noo·ta *minute*
mir ⓜ meer *peace*
miris ⓜ mee·rees *smell (pleasant)*
misa ⓕ mee·sa *mass (Catholic)*
(po)misliti (paw)mee·slee·tee *think*
miš ⓜ meesh *mouse*
mišić ⓜ mee·sheech *muscle*
mišljenje ⓝ meesh·lye·nye *opinion*
mito ⓝ mee·taw *bribe*
mjehur ⓜ mye·hoor *bladder*
mjesec ⓜ mye·sets *month* • *moon*
mjesečnica ⓕ mye·sech·nee·tsa
menstruation
mjesni mye·snee *local*
mjesto ⓝ mye·staw *place*
— **kontrole** kawn·traw·le *checkpoint*
— **rođenja** raw·je·nya *place of birth*
— **za kampiranje** za kam·pee·ra·nye
camp site
mlad mlad *young*
mlijeko ⓝ mlee·ye·kaw *milk*
mljeveno meso ⓝ mlye·ve·naw me·saw
mince
mnogi mnaw·gee *many*
mobilni telefon ⓜ maw·beel·nee
te·le·fawn *mobile phone*
moći imp maw·chee *can (be able)*
moćnica ⓕ mawch·nee·tsa *shrine*
moda ⓕ maw·da *fashion*
modem ⓜ maw·dem *modem*
modrica ⓕ maw·dree·tsa *bruise*
moguć maw·gooch *possible*

moj ⓜ moy *my*
moja ① moy·a *my*
moje ⓝ moy·e *my*
mokar maw·kar *wet*
(po)moliti se (paw·)maw·lee·tee (se) *worship*
molitva ① maw·leet·va *prayer*
molitvenik ⓜ maw·leet·ve·neek *prayer book*
momčad ① mawm·chad *team*
mononukleoza ①
    maw·naw·nook·le·aw·za *glandular fever*
more ⓝ maw·re *sea*
most ⓜ mawst *bridge*
motel ⓜ maw·tel *motel*
motocikl ⓜ maw·taw·tsee·kl *motorbike*
motor ⓜ maw·tawr *engine*
motorni čamac ⓜ maw·tawr·nee cha·mats *motorboat*
možda mawzh·da *maybe*
moždani udar ⓜ mawzh·da·nee oo·dar *stroke (health)*
mračan mra·chan *dark*
mrav ⓜ mrav *ant*
mraz ⓜ mraz *frost*
mreža ① mre·zha *net*
    — za komarce za kaw·mar·tse *mosquito net*
mrkva ① mrk·va *carrot*
mrtav mr·tav *dead*
mučnina ① mooch·nee·na *nausea*
    — od vožnje awd vawzh·nye *travel sickness*
muesli ⓜ pl moo·zlee *muesli*
musliman/muslimanka ⓜ/①
    moo·slee·man/moo·slee·man·ka *Muslim*
muškarac ⓜ moosh·ka·rats *man (male person)*
muzej ⓜ moo·zey *museum*
muzičar ⓜ moo·zee·char *musician*
muž ⓜ moozh *husband*

N

na na *at • in • on • per (day)*
    — vrijeme vree·ye·me *on time*
nabrojan ⓜ na·broy·an *itemised*
nacionalni park ⓜ na·tsee·aw·nal·nee park *national park*
nacionalnost ① na·tsee·aw·nal·nawst *nationality*
način ⓜ na·cheen *way (manner)*

naći/nalaziti na·chee/na·la·zee·tee *find*
nad nad *to*
nadimak ⓜ na·dee·mak *nickname*
nafta ① naf·ta *oil (petrol)*
najam automobila ⓜ na·am a·oo·taw·maw·bee·la *car hire*
najbliži nai·blee·zhee *nearest*
najbolji nai·baw·lyee *best*
najmanji nai·ma·nyee *smallest*
najveći nai·ve·chee *biggest*
nakit ⓜ na·keet *jewellery*
namirnice ① pl na·meer·nee·tse *groceries*
namještaj ⓜ na·mye·shtai *furniture*
naočale ① pl na·aw·cha·le *glasses (spectacles)*
    — za skijanje za skee·ya·nye *goggles (skiing)*
    — za sunce (za soon·tse) *sunglasses*
naplata za usluge ① na·pla·ta za oo·sloo·ge *service charge*
(na)praviti (na·)pra·vee·tee *make (bring about)*
naprijed na·pree·yed *ahead*
naranča ① na·ran·cha *orange (fruit)*
narančast na·ran·chast *orange (colour)*
narediti/naređivati na·re·dee·tee/ na·re·jee·va·tee *order (demand)*
naručiti/naručivati na·roo·chee·tee/ na·roo·chee·va·tee *order (request)*
nastavnik ⓜ na·stav·neek *lecturer*
nastup ⓜ na·stoop *gig*
nasuprot na·soo·prawt *opposite*
naš ⓜ nash *our*
naša ① nash·a *our*
naše ⓝ nash·e *our*
naturoterapije ①
    na·too·raw·te·ra·pee·ye *naturopathy*
naušnice ① pl na·oosh·nee·tse *earrings*
navigacija ① na·vee·ga·tsee·ya *navigation*
navijač ⓜ na·vee·yach *supporter (sport, etc)*
nazvati/nazivati naz·va·tee/na·zee·va·tee *ring (of phone)*
ne ne *no • not*
nebo ⓝ ne·baw *sky*
nedavno ne·dav·naw *recently*
nedjelja ① ne·dye·lya *Sunday*
nedostajati imp ne·daw·stai·a·tee *miss (feel absence of)*
nedostatak ⓜ ne·daw·sta·tak *shortage*
negativan ne·ga·tee·van *negative*

nekoliko ne·kaw·leek·aw *few • several*
nektarinka ① nek·ta·reen·ka *nectarine*
nemoguć ne·maw·gooch *impossible*
neobičan ne·aw·bee·chan *strange • unusual*
neoženjen ne·aw·zhen·yen *single (man)*
nepotpuno pečen ne·pawt·poo·naw pe·chen *rare (meat)*
nepravedan ne·pra·ve·dan *unfair*
nepromočiv ne·praw·maw·cheev *waterproof*
nepušački ⓜ ne·poo·shach·kee *nonsmoking*
nesiguran ne·see·goo·ran *unsafe*
nešto nesh·taw *something*
netko net·kaw *someone*
neudata ① ne·oo·da·ta *single (woman)*
neudoban ne·oo·daw·ban *uncomfortable*
nevezan ne·vez·an *free (not bound)*
nevin ⓜ ne·veen *innocent*
nezaposlen ne·za·paw·slen *unemployed*
nezavisnost ① ne·za·vee·snawst *independence*
nezgoda ① nez·gaw·da *accident*
nijem nee·yem *mute*
nikada nee·ka·da *never*
nikakav nee·ka·kav *none*
ništa neesh·ta *no • nothing*
niti nee·tee *neither*
nizak nee·zak *low • short (height)*
nizbrdo neez·br·daw *downhill*
Nizozemska ① nee·zaw·zem·ska *Netherlands*
noć ① nawch *night*
noćni klub ⓜ nawch·nee kloob *nightclub*
noga ① naw·ga *leg*
nogomet ⓜ naw·gaw·met *football (soccer)*
Norveška ① nawr·vesh·ka *Norway*
nos ⓜ naws *nose*
nositi imp naw·see·tee *carry • wear*
nov nawv *new*
novac ⓜ naw·vats *money*
novčana globa ① nawv·cha·na glaw·ba *fine (penalty)*
novčanica ① nawv·cha·nee·tsa *banknote*
novčarka ① nawv·char·ka *purse*
novčići ⓜ pl nawv·chee·chee *coins*
Novi Zeland ⓜ naw·vee ze·land *New Zealand*
novinar(ka) ⓜ/① naw·vee·nar(·ka) *journalist*
novine ① pl naw·vee·ne *newspaper*

novogodišnji dan ⓜ naw·vaw·gaw·deesh·nyee dan *New Year's Day*
nož ⓜ nawzh *knife*
nožni prst ⓜ nawzh·nee prst *toe*
nuklearna energija ① noo·kle·ar·na e·ner·gee·ya *nuclear energy*
nuklearna testiranja ⓜ pl noo·kle·ar·na te·stee·ra·nya *nuclear testing*
nuklearni otpad ⓜ noo·kle·ar·nee awt·pad *nuclear waste*

Nj

njegov ⓜ nye·gawv *his*
njegova ① nye·gaw·va *his*
njegovo ⓜ nye·gaw·vaw *his*
njen ⓜ nyen *his*
njena ① nye·na *his*
njeno ⓜ nye·naw *his*
Njemačka ① nye·mach·ka *Germany*
njihov ⓜ nyee·hawv *their*
njihova ① nyee·haw·va *their*
njihovo ⓜ nyee·haw·vaw *their*

O

o oo *about • on*
oba ⓜ&ⓝ aw·ba *both*
obala ① aw·ba·la *coast*
obaren aw·ba·ren *boiled*
obećati/obećavati aw·be·cha·tee/ aw·be·cha·va·tee *promise*
običaj ⓜ aw·bee·chai *custom*
običan ⓜ aw·bee·chan *ordinary*
obična pošta ① aw·beech·na pawsh·ta *surface mail (land)*
obična voda ① aw·beech·na vaw·da *still water • tap water*
obitelj ① aw·bee·tel' *family*
obje ① aw·bye *both*
oblačan aw·bla·chan *cloudy*
oblak ⓜ aw·blak *cloud*
oblik ⓜ aw·bleek *shape*
obližnji aw·bleezh·nyee *nearby*
obrano mlijeko ⓝ aw·bra·naw mlee·p·kaw *skim milk*
obrazovanje ⓝ aw·bra·zaw·va·nye *education*
obrtnik ⓜ aw·brt·neek *tradesperson*
ocat ⓜ aw·tsat *vinegar*
ocean ⓜ aw·tse·an *ocean*

oči ① pl *aw*·chee *eyes*

od awd *from* • *since (May etc)* • *with*

odbiti/odbijati awd·*bee*·tee/
awd·*bee*·ya·tee *refuse*

odbojka ① awd·*boy*·ka *volleyball (sport)*
— **na pjesku** na *pye*·skoo
beach volleyball

odgovor ⓜ awd·*gaw*·vawr *answer*

odjeća ① awd·*ye*·cha *clothing*

odlazak ⓜ awd·*la*·zak *departure*

odličan awd·*lee*·chan *excellent*

odložena prtljaga ① awd·*law*·zhe·na
prt·*lya*·ga *left luggage*

odlučiti/odlučivati awd·*loo*·chee·tee/
awd·loo·*chee*·va·tee *decide*

odmoriti/odmarati se awd·*maw*·ree·tee/
awd·*ma*·ra·tee se *rest*

odnos ⓜ awd·*naws* *relationship (not family)*

odnosi s javnošću ⓜ pl awd·*naw*·see s
yav·nawsh·choo *public relations*

odrasla osoba ① aw·*dra*·sla aw·*saw*·ba
adult

odredište ① aw·*dre*·deesh·te *destination*

odrezak ⓜ aw·*dre*·zak *fillet* • *steak*

odsjesti/odsjedati awd·*sye*·stee/
awd·*sye*·da·tee *stay (at a hotel)*

odvojen awd·*voy*·en *separate*

oglas ⓜ aw·*glas* *advertisement*

ogledalo ① aw·*gle*·da·law *mirror*

ograda ① aw·*gra*·da *fence*

ogrlica ① aw·*gr*·lee·tsa *necklace*

ogroman aw·*graw*·man *huge*

ogrtač ⓜ aw·*gr*·tach *cape (cloak)*

oklada ① aw·*kla*·da *bet*

oko ① aw·*kaw* *eye*

oko aw·*kaw* *about*

okrenuti/okretati aw·*kre*·noo·tee/
aw·*kre*·ta·tee *turn*

okrug ⓜ aw·*kroog* *county*

okrugao aw·*kroo*·ga·aw *round*

Olimpijske igre ① pl aw·*leem*·peey·ske
ee·gre *Olympic Games*

olovka ① aw·*lawv*·ka *pencil*

oltar ⓜ awl·*tar* *altar*

oluja ① aw·*loo*·ya *storm*

omekšivač (za kosu) ⓜ
aw·*mek*·*shee*·vach (za *kaw*·soo)
conditioner (hair)

omlet ⓜ aw·*mlet* *omelette*

omotnica ① aw·*mawt*·nee·tsa *envelope*

on ⓜ awn *he*

ona ①&ⓜ aw·*na* *she* • *they* ⓜ

one ① aw·*nee* *they* ①

onesposobljen aw·ne·*spaw*·sawb·lyen
disabled

oni ⓜ aw·*nee* *they* ⓜ

ono aw·*naw* *it* • *that (one)*

opasan aw·*pa*·san *dangerous*

opatica ① aw·*pa*·tee·tsa *nun*

opeklina ① aw·pe·*klee*·na *burn*

opekline od sunca ① pl aw·pe·*klee*·ne
awd *soon*·tsa *sunburn*

opera ① aw·*pe*·ra *opera*

operacija ① aw·pe·*ra*·tsee·ya *operation*

operator ⓜ aw·pe·*ra*·tawr *operator*

operna dvorana ① aw·*per*·na dvaw·*ra*·na
opera house

opet aw·*pet* *again*

(o)prati (aw·)*pra*·tee *wash (something)*

(o)prati se (aw·)*pra*·tee se *wash (oneself)*

oprema ① aw·*pre*·ma *equipment*

Oprez! aw·*prez* *Careful!*

oprostiti/opraštati aw·*praw*·stee·tee/
aw·*prash*·ta·tee *forgive*

opruga ① aw·*proo*·ga *spring (coil)*

optičar ⓜ awp·*tee*·char *optometrist*

opustiti/opuštati se aw·*poo*·stee·tee/
aw·*poosh*·ta·tee se *relax*

orah ⓜ aw·*rah* *nut*

orgazam ⓜ awr·*ga*·zam *orgasm*

originalan aw·ree·gee·*na*·lan *original*

orkestar ⓜ awr·*ke*·star *orchestra*

ormar ⓜ awr·*mar* *cupboard*
— **za odjeću** za aw·*dye*·choo *wardrobe*

osiguranje ① aw·see·goo·*ra*·nye
insurance

osim aw·*seem* *but*

osip ⓜ aw·*seep* *rash*
— **od pelena** awd pe·*le*·na *nappy rash*
— **u struku** aw·*seep* oo *stroo*·koo
shingles (illness)

osjećaj ⓜ aw·*sye*·chai *feeling*

osjećaji ⓜ pl aw·*sye*·chai·ee *feelings*

osoba ① aw·*saw*·ba *person*

osobna iskaznica ① aw·*sawb*·na
ee·*skaz*·nee·tsa *identification card (ID)*

ospice ① pl aw·*spee*·tse *measles*

ostati/ostajati aw·*sta*·tee/aw·*sta*·ya·tee
stay (in one place)

ostaviti/ostavljati aw·sta·*vee*·tee/
aw·*stav*·lya·tee *quit*

suh aw·*seem* *dry*

ošamućen aw·*sha*·moo·chen *dizzy*

oštrige ① pl *awsh*·tree·ge *oyster*

otac ⓜ aw·*tats* *father*

oteklina ① aw·te·klee·na *swelling*
otići/odlaziti aw·tee·chee/aw·dla·zee·tee *depart (leave)*
otirač ⑩ aw·tee·rach *mat*
otkako awt·ka·kaw *from • since (May etc)*
otok ⑩ aw·tawk *island*
otrovan aw·traw·van *poisonous*
otvarač awt·va·rach *opener*
  — za boce za baw·tse *bottle opener*
  — za limenke za lee·men·ke *can opener*
otvoren awt·vaw·ren *open*
otvoriti/otvarati awt·vaw·ree·tee/awt·va·ra·tee *open*
ova ① aw·va *this*
ovaj ⑩ aw·vai *this*
ovca ① awv·tsa *sheep*
ovdje awv·dye *here*
ovisnost ① aw·vee·snawst *addiction*
  — o drogama aw draw·ga·ma *drug addiction*
ovo ⑩ aw·vaw *it • this (one)*
ozbiljan aw·zbee·lyan *serious*
ozonski omotač ⑩ aw·zawn·skee aw·maw·tach *ozone layer*
ožujak ⑩ aw·zhoo·yak *March*

P

pad ⑩ pad *fall*
padavica ① pa·da·vee·tsa *epilepsy*
paket ⑩ pa·ket *package • parcel*
Pakistan ⑩ pa·kee·stan *Pakistan*
palača ① pa·la·cha *palace*
pamuk ⑩ pa·mook *cotton*
pansion ⑩ pan·see·awn *boarding house*
PAPA test ⑩ pa·pa test *pap smear*
papar ⑩ pa·par *pepper*
papir ⑩ pa·peer *paper*
papirnati rupčići ⑩ pl pa·peer·na·tee roop·chee·chee *tissues*
paprika ① pa·pree·ka *bell pepper • capsicum*
par ⑩ par *pair (couple)*
paraplegičar ⑩ pa·ra·ple·gee·char *paraplegic*
parfem ⑩ par·fem *perfume*
park ⑩ park *park*
parkiralište ① par·kee·ra·leesh·te *car park*
parkirati imp par·kee·ra·tee *park (a car)*
pas ⑩ pas *dog*
  — vodič vaw·deech *guide dog*

pasta za zube ① pa·sta za zoo·be *toothpaste*
patka ① pa·tka *duck*
patlidžan ⑩ pa·tlee·jan *aubergine • eggplant*
pauk ⑩ pa·ook *spider*
pčela ① pche·la *bee*
pećnica ① pech·nee·tsa *oven • stove*
pedala ① pe·da·la *pedal*
pegla ① pe·gla *iron (for clothes)*
pekara ① pe·ka·ra *bakery*
pelene ① pl pe·le·ne *diaper • nappy*
pelud ⑩ pe·lood *pollen*
peludna groznica ① pe·lood·na grawz·nee·tsa *hay fever*
penis ⑩ pe·nees *penis*
peniša ① pe·nee·sha *lighter*
pepeljara ① pe·pe·lya·ra *ashtray*
peron ⑩ pe·rawn *platform*
petak ⑩ pe·tak *Friday*
peticija ① pe·tee·tsee·ya *petition*
piće ⑩ pee·che *drink*
pijan pee·yan *drunk*
pijesak ⑩ pee·ye·sak *sand*
piknik ⑩ peek·neek *picnic*
piletina ① pee·le·tee·na *chicken (as food)*
pinceta ① peen·tse·ta *tweezers*
pisac ⑩ pee·sats *writer*
pisač ⑩ pee·sach *printer (computer)*
(na)pisati (na·)pee·sa·tee *write*
pismo ⑩ pee·smaw *letter (mail)*
pita ① pee·ta *pie*
pitanje ⑩ pee·ta·nye *question*
(u)pitati (oo·)pee·ta·tee *ask (a question)*
(po)piti (paw·)pee·tee *drink*
pivnica ① peev·nee·tsa *beer hall*
pivo ⑩ pee·vaw *beer*
pjena za brijanje ① pye·na za bree·ya·nye *shaving cream*
pjenušavo vino ⑩ pye·noo·sha·vaw vee·naw *sparkling wine*
pjesma ① pye·sma *song*
(pro)pješačiti (praw·)pye·sha·chee·tee *hike*
pješačenje ⑩ pye·sha·che·nye *hiking*
pješački put ⑩ pye·shach·kee poot *hiking route*
pješak ⑩ pye·shak *pedestrian*
pjevač/pjevačica ⑩/① pye·vach/ pye·va·chee·tsa *singer*
(za)pjevati (za·)pye·va·tee *sing*
plaća ① pla·cha *salary • wage*
plahta ① pla·hta *sheet (bed)*

plan grada ⓜ plan *gra*·da map (of town)

plan puta ⓜ plan *poo*·ta itinerary

planeta ⓕ pla·*ne*·ta planet

planina ⓕ pla·*nee*·na mountain

plastičan *pla*·stee·chan plastic

(u)platiti (oo·)*pla*·tee·tee pay

plato ⓜ pla·*taw* plateau

plav paw blue

plaža ⓕ *pla*·zha beach

plesanje ⓝ *ple*·sa·nye dancing

(za)plesati (za·)*ple*·sa·tee dance

pletenasti ukras ⓜ *ple*·te·na·stee oo·kras plaited ornamentation

plima i oseka ⓕ *plee*·ma ee *aw*·se·ka tide

plin ⓜ pleen gas (for cooking)

plinski uložak ⓜ *pleen*·skee oo·law·zhak gas cartridge

plivanje ⓝ *plee*·va·nye swimming (sport)

(za)plivati (za·)*plee*·va·tee swim

(o)pljačkati (aw·)*plyach*·ka·tee rob

pločnik ⓜ *plawch*·neek footpath

plosnat *plaw*·snat flat

pluća ⓝ pl *ploo*·cha lung

po paw after · per

pobačaj ⓜ *paw*·ba·chai abortion · miscarriage

pobijediti/pobjeđivati paw·bee·*ye*·dee·tee/paw·bye·*jee*·va·tee win

pobjednik ⓜ *paw*·byed·neek winner

pobožan *paw*·baw·zhan religious (person)

početak ⓜ paw·*che*·tak start
— **radnog vremena** *rad*·nawg *vre*·me·na opening hours

pod pawd floor (ground)

podatci ⓝ pl paw·*dat*·tsee details

podijeliti perf paw·dee·*ye*·lee·tee share (with)

podne ⓝ *pawd*·ne midday

područni paw·*drooch*·nee regional

podzemna željeznica ⓕ *pawd*·zem·na zhe·lye·znee·tsa subway · underground railway

poezija ⓕ paw·e·*zee*·ya poetry

pogoditi/pogađati paw·*gaw*·dee·tee/paw·*ga*·ja·tee guess

pogreb ⓜ *paw*·greb funeral

pogreška ⓕ *paw*·gresh·ka mistake

pokazati/pokazivati paw·*ka*·za·tee/paw·ka·*zee*·va·tee point · show

poklon ⓜ *paw*·klawn present (gift)

pokretne stepenice ⓕ pl *paw*·kret·ne ste·*pe*·nee·tse escalator

pokušati/pokušavati paw·koo·sha·tee/paw·koo·*sha*·va·tee try (attempt)

pokvaren paw·*kva*·ren broken down · corrupt · faulty · spoiled

polica ⓕ paw·*lee*·tsa shelf

policajac ⓜ paw·lee·*tsai*·ats police officer

policija ⓕ paw·*lee*·tsee·ya police

policijska stanica ⓕ paw·*lee*·tseey·ska sta·nee·tsa police station

političar ⓜ paw·*lee*·tee·char politician

politika ⓕ paw·*lee*·tee·ka politics

poljodjelac ⓜ paw·lyaw·*dye*·lats farmer

poljodjelstvo ⓝ paw·lyaw·*dyel*·stvaw agriculture

poljubac ⓜ paw·*lyoo*·bats kiss

polovina ⓕ paw·law·*vee*·na half

polovni paw·*lawv*·nee second-hand

pomoć ⓕ *paw*·mawch help

pomoći/pomagati paw·*maw*·chee/paw·*ma*·ga·tee help

ponedjeljak ⓜ paw·ne·*dye*·lyak Monday

ponekad paw·ne·kad sometimes

poništiti/poništavati paw·*nee*·shtee·tee/paw·nee·*shta*·va·tee cancel

ponoć ⓕ *paw*·nawch midnight

popeti/penjati se paw·*pe*·tee/*pe*·nya·tee se climb

poplava ⓕ paw·*pla*·va flood

popraviti/popravljati paw·*pra*·vee·tee/paw·prav·*lya*·tee repair

popularan paw·poo·la·ran popular

popunjen paw·poo·nyen booked out

popust ⓜ *paw*·poost discount

pored paw·red beside · next to

poredak ⓜ paw·*re*·dak order

poremećaj srca ⓜ paw·re·me·chai sr·tsa heart condition

porez ⓜ *paw*·rez tax
— **na dohodak** na *daw*·haw·dak income tax
— **na promet** na *praw*·met sales tax
— **na zračni prijevoz** na *zrach*·nee pree·*ye*·vawz airport tax

poriluk ⓜ *paw*·ree·look leek

poruka ⓕ *paw*·roo·ka message

posao ⓜ *paw*·sa·aw job

poseban ⓜ *paw*·se·ban special

poširan paw·*shee*·ran poached

posjetiti/posjećivati paw·*sye*·tee·tee/paw·sye·*chee*·va·tee visit

poslano expres poštom paw·sla·naw eks·pres pawsh·tawm by express mail

poslastice ⓕ pl *paw*·sla·stee·tse dessert

poslije *paw·slee·ye after*

(ovo) poslijepodne ⓝ *(aw·vaw) paw·slee·ye·pawd·ne (this) afternoon*

poslodavac ⓜ *paw·slaw·da·vats employer*

poslovna osoba ⓕ *paw·slawv·na aw·saw·ba business person*

pospan *paw·span (to be) sleepy*

posramljen *paw·sram·lyen embarrassed*

post ⓜ *pawst Lent*

posteljina ⓕ *paw·ste·lyee·na bed linen*

poster ⓜ *paw·ster poster*

postići/postizati *paw·stee·chee/ paw·stee·za·tee score*

postotak ⓜ *paw·staw·tak per cent*

posuda ⓕ *paw·soo·da dish (plate) • pot (ceramics)*

posuditi/posuđivati *paw·soo·dee·tee/ paw·soo·jee·va·tee borrow*

pošta ⓕ *pawsh·ta mail (letters) • postal system*

poštanska marka ⓕ *pawsh·tan·ska mar·ka stamp (mail)*

poštanski broj ⓜ *pawsh·tan·skee broy postcode*

poštanski sandučić ⓜ *pawsh·tan·skee san·doo·cheech mailbox*

poštanski ured ⓜ *pawsh·tan·skee oo·red post office*

poštarina ⓕ *pawsh·ta·ree·na postage*

potkošulja ⓕ *pawt·kaw·shoo·lya singlet*

potomak ⓜ *paw·taw·mak descendant*

potpis ⓜ *pawt·pees signature*

potpuno paralizirana osoba ⓕ *pawt·poo·naw pa·ra·lee·zee·ra·na aw·saw·ba quadriplegic*

potreban *paw·tre·ban necessary*

potres ⓜ *paw·tres earthquake*

— **mozga** *maw·zga concussion*

potvrda vlasništva automobila ⓕ *paw·tvr·da vlas·neesh·tva a·oo·taw·maw·bee·la car owner's title*

potvrditi/potvrđivati *pawt·vr·dee·tee/ pawt·vr·jee·va·tee confirm (a booking) • validate*

povijesni *paw·vee·ye·snee historical*

povijest ⓕ *paw·vee·yest history*

povrat novca ⓜ *pavv·rat nawv·tsa refund*

povratan *paw·vra·tan return (ticket)*

povrće ⓝ *paw·vr·che vegetable*

povreda ⓕ *paw·vre·da injury*

povremeni posao ⓜ *paw·vre·me·nee paw·sa·aw casual work*

povrijeđen ⓜ *paw·vree·ye·jen injured*

pozadina ⓕ *paw·za·dee·na back (position)*

pozitivan *paw·zee·tee·van positive*

poziv na račun nazvane osobe ⓜ *paw·zeev na ra·choon naz·va·ne aw·saw·be collect call • reverse charge call*

pozvati/pozivati *pawz·va·tee/ paw·zee·va·tee invite*

požar ⓜ *paw·zhar fire*

prah ⓜ *prah powder*

pranje rublja ⓝ *pra·nye roob·lya laundry (clothes)*

praonica ⓕ *pra·aw·nee·tsa laundry (place)*

pratiti imp *pra·tee·tee follow*

pravilo ⓝ *pra·vee·law rule*

pravnik ⓜ *prav·neek lawyer*

pravo ⓝ *pra·vaw law (study, professsion)*

prazan *pra·zan empty • vacant*

praznici ⓜ pl *praz·nee·tsee holidays • vacation*

praznovjerje ⓝ *praz·naw·vyer·ye superstition*

pred *pred in front of*

predgrađe ⓝ *pred·gra·je suburb*

predmenstrualna napetost ⓕ *pred·men·stroo·al·na na·pe·tawst premenstrual tension*

prednje svjetlo ⓝ *pred·nye svyet·law headlights*

predsjednik ⓜ *pred·syed·neek president*

predstava ⓕ *pred·sta·va play (theatre) • show*

pregled ⓜ *pre·gled review (article)*

prehlada ⓕ *pre·hla·da cold*

prekid ⓜ *pre·keed intermission*

prekjučer ⓜ *prek·yoo·cher day before yesterday*

preko *pre·kaw across*

— **noći** *naw·chee overnight*

prekomjerna cijena ⓕ *pre·kawm·yer·na tsee·ye·na rip-off*

prekomorska pošta ⓕ *pre·kaw·mawr·ska pawsh·ta surface mail (sea)*

prekosutra ⓝ *pre·kaw·soo·tra day after tomorrow*

prekršaj ⓜ *pre·kr·shai foul*

prema *pre·ma to • towards (direction)*

prenoćište za mladež ⓝ *pre·naw·cheesh·te za mla·dezh youth hostel*

prenosivi računar ⑩ pre·naw·see·vee ra·choo·nar *laptop*

preporučenom poštom pre·paw·roo·che·nawm pawsh·tawm *registered mail (by)*

preporučiti/preporučivati pre·paw·roo·chee·tee/ pre·paw·roo·chee·va·tee *recommend*

preporuka ① pre·paw·rooka *reference*

prepun pre·poon *crowded*

prethodni pred·hawd·nee *last (previous)*

pretinac za odlaganje prtljagc ⑩ pre·tee·nats za awd·la·ga·nye prt·lya·ge *luggage lockers*

pretpostaviti/pretpostavljati pret·paw·sta·vee·tee/ pret·paw·stav·lya·tee *prefer*

prevelika doza ① pre·ve·leeka daw·za *overdose*

prevesti/prevoditi pre·ve·stee/ pre·vaw·dee·tee *translate*

prezervativ ⑩ pre·zer·va·teev *condom*

prezime ⑩ pre·zee·me *surname*

pri pree *at • on*

pribor za jelo ⑩ pree·bawr za ye·law *cutlery*

pribor za prvu pomoć ⑩ pree·bawr za pr·voo paw·mawch *first-aid kit*

priča ① pree·cha *story*

pričest ① pree·chest *communion*

prigovor ⑩ pree·gaw·vawr *complaint*

prijatelj/prijateljica ⑩/① pree·ya·tel'/ pree·ya·te·lyee·tsa *friend*

prijazan pree·ya·zan *kind (nice)*

prije pree·ye *ago • before*

prijemni šalter ⑩ pree·yem·nee shal·ter *check-in (airport)*

prijevoz ⑩ pree·ye·vawz *transport*

primjer ⑩ pree·myer *example*

primorje ⑩ pree·mawr·ye *seaside*

pripremiti/pripremati pree·pre·mee·tee/ pree·pre·ma·tee *prepare*

priredba ① pree·red·ba *performance*

priroda ① pree·raw·da *nature*

prirodna okolina ① pree·rawd·na aw·kaw·lee·na *environment*

pristaša ⑩ pree·sta·sha *supporter (politics)*

pritisak ⑩ pree·tee·sak *pressure*

privatan pree·va·tan *private*

privatni smještaj za najam ⑩ pree·vat·nee smyesh·tai za nai·am *guesthouse*

privlačan pree·vla·chan *sexy*

priznanje ⑩ pree·zna·nye *confession (admission)*

priznati/priznavati pree·zna·tee/ pree·zna·va·tee *admit (confess)*

prizor ⑩ pree·zawr *view*

prljav pr·lyav *dirty*

probati/probavati praw·ba·tee/ praw·ba·va·tee *try*

probavne smetnje ① pl praw·bav·ne smet·nye *indigestion*

prodati/prodavati praw·da·tee/ praw·da·va·tee *sell*

prodavač droga ⑩ praw·da·vach draw·ga *drug dealer*

prodavač duhana ⑩ praw·da·vach doo·ha·na *tobacconist*

prodavaonica ① praw·da·va·aw·nee·tsa *shop*

— **alkohola** al·kaw·haw·la *bottle shop • liquor store*

— **bicikala** bee·tsee·ka·la *bike shop*

— **cipela** tsee·pela *shoe shop*

— **električne robe** e·lek·treech·ne raw·be *electrical store*

— **foto-aparata** faw·taw·a·pa·ra·ta *camera shop*

— **igračaka** ee·gra·cha·ka *toy shop*

— **metalne i tehničke robe** me·tal·ne ee teh·neech·ke raw·be *hardware store*

— **muzike** moo·zee·ke *music shop*

— **novina i časopisa** naw·vee·na ee cha·saw·pee·sa *newsagency*

— **odjeće** aw·dye·che *clothing store*

— **opreme za kampiranje** aw·pre·me za kam·pee·ra·nye *camping store*

— **polovne robe** paw·lawv·ne raw·be *second-hand shop*

— **ribe** ree·be *fish shop*

— **sa produženim radnim vremenom** sa praw·doo·zhe·neem rad·neem vre·me·nawm *convenience store*

— **sira** see·ra *cheese shop*

— **sportske robe** spawrt·ske raw·be *sports shop*

— **suvenira** soo·ve·nee·ra *souvenir shop*

— **uredskog materijala** oo·reds·kawg ma·te·ree·ya·la *stationer's (shop)*

produženje ⑩ praw·doo·zhe·nye *extension (visa)*

program ⑩ praw·gram *program*

proizvesti/proizvoditi praw·eez·ve·stee/ praw·eez·vaw·dee·tee *produce*

projektor ⓜ *proy-ek-tawr projector*
prokulica ⓕ *praw-koo-lee-tsa Brussels sprout*
prolaz između sjedišta ⓜ *praw-laz eez-me-joo sye-deesh-ta aisle (plane etc)*
proljeće ⓝ *praw-lye-che spring (season)*
proljev ⓜ *praw-lyev diarrhoea*
promet ⓜ *praw-met traffic*
promjena ⓕ *praw-mye-na change*
prosinac ⓜ *praw-see-nats December*
prosjak ⓜ *praw-syak beggar*
proslava ⓕ *praw-sla-va celebration*
prostitutka ⓕ *praw-stee-toot-ka prostitute*
prostor *praw-stawr space*
prosvjed ⓜ *praws-vyed protest*
prosvjedovati imp *praw-svye-daw-va-tee protest*
prošli *prawsh-lee last (week)*
prošlost ⓕ *prawsh-lawst past*
provesti/provoditi se *praw-ve-stee/ praw-vaw-dee-tee se enjoy (oneself)*
provjeriti/provjeravati *praw-vye-ree-tee/ praw-vye-ra-va-tee check*
provod ⓜ *praw-vawd party (night out)*
prozor ⓜ *praw-zawr window*
prsa ⓕ *pr-sa breast (body) · chest (body)*
prsluk za spasavanje ⓜ *pr-slook za spa-sa-va-nye life jacket*
prst ⓜ *prst finger*
prsten ⓜ *pr-sten ring (on finger)*
prtljaga ⓕ *prt-lya-ga luggage*
prvenstvo ⓝ *pr-vens-tvaw championships*
prvi *pr-vee first*
— razred ⓜ *ra-zred business class · first class*
prženi *pr-zhe-nee fried*
(is)pržiti (ees-)*pr-zhee-tee fry*
ptica ⓕ *ptee-tsa bird*
puder za bebe ⓜ *poo-der za be-be baby powder*
pumpa ⓕ *poom-pa pump*
pun *poon full*
punac ⓜ *poo-nats father-in-law (of husband)*
punica ⓕ *poo-nee-tsa mother-in-law (of husband)*
punim radnim vremenom *poo-neem rad-neem vre-me-nawm full-time*
(na)puniti (na-)*poo-nee-tee fill*
puno ⓝ *poo-naw (a) lot*
puran ⓜ *poo-ran turkey*

pustinja ⓕ *poo-stee-nya desert*
(is)pušiti (ees-)*poo-shee-tee smoke*
puška ⓕ *poosh-ka gun*
put ⓜ *poot route · track · trail*
(u)pucati (oo-)*poo-tsa-tee shoot*
putna agencija ⓕ *poot-na a-gen-tsee-ya travel agency*
putna karta ⓕ *poot-na kar-ta road map*
putnički čekovi ⓜ pl *poot-neech-kee che-kaw-vee travellers cheque*
putnik ⓜ *poot-neek passenger*
putovanje ⓝ *poo-taw-va-nye journey*
(pro)putovati (praw-)*poo-taw-va-tee travel*
putovnica ⓕ *poo-tawv-nee-tsa passport*
puž ⓜ *poozh snail*

R

račun ⓜ *ra-choon account (bank) · bill (account) · check · receipt*
računalo ⓝ *ra-choo-na-law computer*
rad ⓜ *rad work*
— za barom *za ba-rawm bar work*
radijator ⓜ *ra-dee-ya-tawr radiator*
radio ⓜ *ra-dee-aw radio*
radionica ⓕ *ra-dee-aw-nee-tsa workshop*
raditi imp *ra-dee-tee work*
radna dozvola ⓕ *rad-na dawz-vaw-la work permit*
radnik ⓜ *rad-neek labourer*
— u tvornici *oo tvawr-nee-tsee factory worker*
radno iskustvo ⓝ *rad-naw ee-skoos-tvaw work experience*
ragbi ⓜ *rag-bee rugby*
rajčica ⓕ *rai-chee-tsa tomato*
rak ⓜ *rak cancer*
rakija ⓕ *ra-kee-ya brandy*
rame ⓝ *ra-me shoulder*
rani *ra-nee early*
raniti/ranjavati *ra-nee-tee/ra-nya-va-tee hurt (physically)*
raskošan *ra-skaw-shan luxury*
rasna netrpeljivost ⓕ *ra-sna ne-tr-pe-lyee-vawst racism*
rasprodaja ⓕ *ra-spraw-dai-a sale*
(po)rasti (paw-)*ra-stee grow*
rat ⓜ *rat war*
ravan *ra-van straight (not crooked)*
ravnopravnost ⓕ *rav-naw-prav-nawst equality*

razbijen ra-*zbee*-yen *broken*

razlika u vremenu ① *raz*-lee-ka oo vre-me-noo *time difference*

razlog ① *raz*-lawg *reason*

razmažen raz-*ma*-zhen *spoiled*

razmijeniti/razmjenjivati raz-mee-*ye*-nee-tee/raz-mye-*nyee*-va-tee *exchange*

razmjena ① *raz*-mye-na *exchange*

razuman ra-*zoo*-man *sensible*

razumjeti/razumijevati ra-*zoo*-mye-tee/ra-*zoo*-mee-ye-va-tee *understand*

razveden raz-*ve*-den *divorced (of man)*

razvedena raz-*ve*-de-na *divorced (of woman)*

realan re-a-lan *realistic*

rebro ① *re*-braw *rib*

recept za lijekove ① *re*-tsept za lee-ye-*kaw*-ve *prescription*

reciklirati perf re-tsee-*klee*-ra-tee *recycle*

reći perf *re*-chee *tell*

red ① red *queue*

redovnik ① *re*-*dawv*-neek *monk*

refleksologija ① *re*-flek-saw-*law*-gee-ya *reflexology*

registarska tablica ① *re*-gee-*star*-ska *ta*-blee-tsa *numberplate*

registracija re-gee-*stra*-tsee-ya *car registration*

rejv parti ① reyv *par*-tee *rave*

reket ① *re*-ket *racquet*

relikvija ① *re*-*leek*-vee-ya *relic*

rep ① rep *tail*

republika ① re-*poo*-blee-ka *republic*

restoran ① re-*staw*-ran *restaurant*

rezanci ① pl re-*zan*-tsee *noodles*

(na)rezati (na-)re-za-tee *cut*

rezervacija ① re-zer-*va*-tsee-ya *reservation (booking)*

rezervirati perf re-zer-*vee*-ra-tee *book (make a booking)*

rezime ① re-zee-*me* *résumé*

riba ① *ree*-ba *fish*

ribar ① *ree*-bar *fisherman*

ribarsko selo ① *ree*-bar-skaw *se*-law *fishing village*

ribolov ① *ree*-baw-lawv *fishing*

riječ ① *ree*-yech *word*

rijedak ree-ye-dak *rare (uncommon)*

rijeka ① *ree*-ye-ka *river*

ritam ① *ree*-tam *rhythm*

riva ① *ree*-va *waterfront*

rizik ① *ree*-zeek *risk*

riža ① *ree*-zha *rice*

rječnik ① ryech-neek *dictionary*

robna kuća ① *rawb*-na koo-cha *department store*

rock grupa ① rawk *groo*-pa *rock group*

rock ① rawk *rock (music)*

roditelji ① pl *raw*-dee-te-lyee *parents*

rođendan ① *raw*-jen-dan *birthday*

romantičan raw-*man*-tee-chan *romantic*

ronilačka oprema ① raw-*nee*-lach-ka *aw*-pre-ma *diving equipment*

ronjenje ① *raw*-nye-nye *diving (underwater)*
— **s disalicom** s *dee*-sa-lee-tsawm *snorkelling*
— **sa bocama** sa *baw*-tsa-ma *scuba diving*

rolšulanje ① raw-*shoo*-la-nye *rollerblading*

rolšulati se imp raw-*shoo*-la-tee se *skate*

rotkva ① *rawt*-kva *radish*

rt ① rt *cape • promontory*

rubeola ① roo-be-*aw*-la *rubella*

ručak ① *roo*-chak *lunch • meal*

ručna svjetiljka ① *rooch*-na svye-*teel*-ka *flashlight • torch*

ručna torbica ① *rooch*-na *tawr*-bee-tsa *handbag*

ručni radovi ① pl *rooch*-nee ra-*daw*-vee *handicrafts*

ručni zglob ① *rooch*-nee zglawb *wrist*

ručnik ① *rooch*-neek *towel • wash cloth*
— **za lice** za *lee*-tse *face cloth*

ručno izrađen *rooch*-naw eez-ra-jen *handmade*

rujan ① *roo*-yan *September*

ruka ① *roo*-ka *arm • hand*

rukavica/e ① sg/① pl roo-*ka*-vee-tsa/e *glove(s)*

rukomet ① *roo*-kaw-met *handball*

ruksak ① *rook*-sak *backpack*

rum ① room *rum*

rupčić ① *roop*-cheech *handkerchief*

ruševine ① pl *roo*-she-vee-ne *ruins*

ruž za usne ① roozh za *oo*-sne *lipstick*

ružičast *roo*-zhee-chast *pink*

S

sa sa *with*

sabor ① *sa*-bawr *parliament*

SAD ① pl es a de *USA*

sada *sa*-da *now*

S

sadašnjost ① *sa*-dash-nyawst *present (time)*
salama ① sa-*la*-ma *salami*
salata ① sa-*la*-ta *salad*
saldo ⑩ *sal*-daw *balance (account)*
salveta ① sal-*ve*-ta *serviette*
sam ⑩ sat *alone*
samo sa-maw *only*
samoposluga ① sa-maw-*paw*-sloo-ga *self-service*
samostalno zaposlen sa-maw-stal-naw za-paw-slen *self-employed*
samostan ⑩ sa-maw-stan *convent • monastery*
san ⑩ san *dream*
sandala ① san-*da*-la *sandal*
sanjkanje ⑩ san'-ka-nye *tobogganing*
sapun ⑩ sa-poon *soap*
sardina ① sar-*dee*-na *sardine*
sastanak ⑩ sa-sta-nak *appointment*
sastojak ⑩ sa-stoy-ak *ingredient*
sašiti/šivati sa-shee-tee/*shee*-va-tee *sew*
sat ⑩ sat *clock • hour • watch*
sauna ① sa-oo-na *sauna*
savjet ⑩ sa-vyet *advice*
savršen sa-vr-shen *perfect*
sebičan ⑩ se-bee-chan *selfish*
sedlo ⑩ sed-law *saddle*
seks ⑩ seks *sex*
sekunda ① se-*koon*-da *second (clock)*
selo ⑩ se-law *village*
semafor ⑩ se-ma-fawr *scoreboard • traffic light*
senf ⑩ senf *mustard*
seosko područje ⑩ se-aw-skaw paw-drooch-ye *countryside*
sestra ① se-stra *sister*
sezona ① se-*zaw*-na *season (for activities)*
shiatsu ⑩ shee-*a*-tsoo *shiatsu*
sići/silaziti sa see-chee/see-la-zee-tee sa *get off (a train, etc)*
sićušan ⑩ see-choo-shan *tiny*
SIDA ① see-da *AIDS*
sigornosni pojas ⑩ see-goor-naw-snee poy-as *seatbelt*
sef ⑩ sef *safe*
siguran see-goo-ran *safe*
— seks seks *safe sex*
siječanj ⑩ se-ye-chan' *January*
silovanje ⑩ se-law-va-nye *rape*
silovati perf see-*law*-va-tee *rape*
sin ⑩ seen *son*
sinagoga ① see-na-*gaw*-ga *synagogue*

Singapur ⑩ seen-ga-poor *Singapore*
sintetičan ⑩ seen-*te*-tee-chan *synthetic*
sir ⑩ seer *cheese*
siromašan see-*raw*-ma-shan *poor*
siromaštvo ⑩ see-raw-*mash*-tvaw *poverty*
sirov ⑩ see-rawv *raw*
sirup za kašalj ⑩ see-roop za ka-shal' *cough medicine*
sitan see-tan *fine (delicate)*
siv ⑩ seev *gray • grey*
sjedalo za dijete ⑩ sye-da-law za dee-ye-te *child seat*
sjedište ⑩ sye-deesh-te *seat (place)*
sjekira za razbijanje leda ① sye-kee-ra za raz-*bee*-ya-nye le-da *ice axe*
sjena ① sye-na *shadow*
sjesti/sjedati sye-stee/sye-da-tee *sit*
sjever ⑩ sye-ver *north*
skalp ⑩ skalp *scalp*
skijanje ⑩ skee-ya-nye *skiing*
— na vodi na vaw-dee *water-skiing*
skijati imp skee-ya-tee *ski*
skočiti/skakati skaw-chee-tee/ska-ka-tee *jump*
skoro skaw-raw *almost*
skulptura ① skoolp-*too*-ra *sculpture*
skup ⑩ skoop *rally*
skup skoop *expensive*
slab slab *weak*
sladak sla-dak *sweet*
sladoled ⑩ sla-daw-led *ice cream*
sladoledarna ① sla-daw-le-*dar*-na *ice-cream parlour*
slanina ① sla-nee-na *bacon*
slanutak ⑩ sla-*noo*-tak *chickpea*
slastičarnica ① sla-stee-*char*-nee-tsa *cake shop*
(po)slati (paw-)sla-tee *send*
slavan sla-van *famous*
slavina ① sla-vee-na *faucet • tap*
sleđ ⑩ slej *herring*
sličan slee-chan *similar*
slijedeći slee-ye-de-chee *next (month)*
slijep slee-yep *blind*
slijepo crijevo ⑩ slee-ye-paw tsree-ye-vaw *appendix (body)*
slika ① slee-ka *painting (a work)*
slikar ⑩ slee-kar *painter*
slikarstvo ⑩ slee-*kars*-tvaw *painting (the art)*
slikati perf slee-ka-tee *photograph*
slobodan slaw-baw-dan *free (available)*

slobodno mjesto ⓝ *slaw·bawd·naw mye·staw* **vacancy**

Slovačka ⓕ *slaw·vach·ka* **Slovakia**

Slovenija ⓕ *slaw·ve·nee·ya* **Slovenia**

složiti/slagati se *slaw·zhee·tee/sla·ga·tee se* **agree**

(po)slušati *(paw·)sloo·sha·tee* **listen (to)**

slušni aparat ⓜ *sloosh·nee a·pa·rat* **hearing aid**

službenik/službenica ⓜ/ⓕ *sloozh·be·neek/sloozh·be·nee·tsa* **office worker**

službeno putovanje ⓝ *sloozh·be·naw poo·taw·va·nye* **business trip**

smeće ⓝ *sme·che* **garbage**

smeđ *smej* **brown**

(na)smijati se *(na·)smee·ya·tee se* **laugh**

(na)smiješiti se *(na·)smee·ye·shee·tee se* **smile**

smjer ⓜ *smyer* **direction**

smješan *smye·shan* **funny**

smještaj ⓜ *smye·shtai* **accommodation**

smjeti imp *smye·tee* **can (have permission)**

smokva ⓕ *smaw·kva* **fig**

smrad ⓜ *smrad* **smell (unpleasant)**

snaga ⓕ *sna·ga* **power**

snijeg ⓜ *snee·yeg* **snow**

snimak ⓜ *snee·mak* **recording**

snimiti/snimati *snee·mee·tee/snee·ma·tee* **record (music etc)**

soba ⓕ *saw·ba* **room**

soba za pranje rublja ⓕ *saw·ba za pra·nye roob·lya* **laundry (room)**

socijalistički *saw·tsee·ya·lee·steech·kee* **socialist**

socijalna skrb ⓕ *saw·tsee·yal·na skrb* **social welfare**

soja ⓕ *soy·a* **soy sauce**

sojino mlijeko ⓝ *soy·ee·naw mlee·ye·kaw* **soy milk**

sok ⓜ *sawk* **juice**
— **od naranče** *awd na·ran·che* **orange juice**

sol ⓕ *sawl* **salt**

soli za rehidrataciju ⓕ *saw·lee za re·hee·dra·ta·tse·yoo* **rehydration salts**

spavaća kola ⓕ *spa·va·cha kaw·la* **sleeping berth**

spavaća soba ⓕ *spa·va·cha saw·ba* **bedroom**

spavaći kupe ⓜ *spa·va·chee koo·pe* **sleeping car**

(od)spavati *(awd·)spa·va·tee* **sleep**

spilja ⓕ *spee·lya* **cave**

spirala ⓕ *spee·ra·la* **IUD**

spoj ⓜ *spoy* **date (appointment)**

spolna bolesta ⓕ *spawl·na baw·les·ta* **venereal disease**

spolna diskriminacija ⓕ *spawl·na dee·skree·mee·na·tsee·ya* **sexism**

spomenik ⓜ *spaw·me·neek* **monument**

spor *spawr* **slow**

sporo *spaw·raw* **slowly**

sport ⓜ *spawrt* **sport**

sportaš/sportašica ⓜ/ⓕ *spa·wr·tash/spawr·ta·shee·tsa* **sportsperson**

spreman *spre·man* **ready**

spriječiti/sprječavati *spree·ye·chee·tee/spree·ye·cha·va·tee* **stop (prevent)**

Srbija ⓕ *sr·bee·ya* **Serbia**

srčani udar ⓜ *sr·cha·nee oo·dar* **heart attack**

srce ⓝ *sr·tse* **heart**

srebro ⓝ *sre·braw* **silver**

sreća ⓕ *sre·cha* **luck**

srednja škola ⓕ *sred·nya shkaw·la* **high school**

sredstva za sprječavanje neželjene trudnoće ⓝ pl *sreds·tva za sprye·cha·va·nye ne·zhe·lye·ne trood·naw·che* **contraceptives**

sresti/sretati *sre·stee/sre·ta·tee* **meet (run into)**

sretan *sre·tan* **happy • lucky**

srijeda ⓕ *sree·ye·da* **Wednesday**

srodstvo ⓝ *srawd·stvaw* **relationship (family)**

srpanj ⓜ *sr·pan'* **July**

stablo ⓝ *sta·blaw* **tree**

stadion ⓜ *sta·dee·awn* **stadium**

stajati imp *stai·a·tee* **cost**

staklenka ⓕ *sta·klen·ka* **jar**

staklo ⓝ *sta·klo* **glass (material)**

stan ⓜ *stan* **apartment**

stanica ⓕ *sta·nee·tsa* **station • stop (bus etc)**

Stanite/Stani! pol/inf *sta·nee·te/sta·nee Stop!*

stanovati imp *sta·na... ·tee ... (somewhere)*

star *star* **old**

staviti/stavljati *sta·vee·tee/stav·...ya·tee put*

staza ⓕ *sta·za* **path • track (sport)**

stepenica ⓕ *ste·pe·nee·tsa* **step**

stepenište ⓝ ste·pe·neesh·te *stairway*
stići/stizati stee·chee/stee·za·tee *arrive*
stidljiv steed·lyeev *shy*
stijena ⓕ stee·ye·na *rock*
stil ⓜ steel *style*
stjenica ⓕ stye·nee·tsa *bug (insect)*
sto staw *hundred*
stol ⓜ stawl *table*
stolica za sklapanje ⓕ staw·lee·tsa za *skla·pa·nye chair*
stolni tenis ⓜ stawl·nee te·nees *table tennis*
stolnjak ⓜ stawl·nyak *tablecloth*
stopalo ⓝ staw·pa·law *foot*
stopirati imp staw·pee·ra·tee *hitchhike*
strana ⓕ stra·na *side*
stranac ⓜ stra·nats *stranger*
strani stra·nee *foreign*
stranica ⓕ stra·nee·tsa *page*
stranka ⓕ stran·ka *client* · **party** *(politics)*
strašan stra·shan *terrible*
stražnji strazh·nyee *rear (seat etc)*
stražnjica ⓕ strazh·nyee·tsa *bottom (body)*
strm strm *steep*
stroj ⓜ stroy *machine*
 — za pranje rublja za pra·nye roob·lya *washing machine*
stručnjak ⓜ strooch·nyak *specialist*
struja ⓕ stroo·ya *current (electricity)* · *stream*
struna ⓕ stroo·na *string*
studeni ⓜ stoo·de·nee *November*
student ⓜ stoo·dent *student*
stupnjevi ⓜ pl stoop·nye·vee *degrees (temperature)*
subota ⓕ soo·baw·ta *Saturday*
sud ⓜ sood *court (legal)*
sudac ⓜ soo·dats *judge* · **referee**
sudar ⓜ soo·dar *crash*
suknja ⓕ sook·nya *skirt*
sunčan soon·chan *sunny*
sunčanica ⓕ soon·cha·nee·tsa *sunstroke*
sunce ⓝ soon·tse *sun*
suncobran ⓜ soon·tsaw·bra·n *umbrella*
supermarket ⓜ soo·per·mar·ket *supermarket*
sušen soo·she·nee *dried*
(o)sušiti (aw)soo·shee·tee *dry*
sutra soo·tra *tomorrow*
 — popodne paw·pawd·ne *tomorrow afternoon*
 — ujutro oo·yoo·traw *tomorrow morning*
 — uvečer oo·ve·cher *tomorrow evening*

suvenir ⓜ soo·ve·neer *souvenir*
suviše soo·vee·she *too (expensive etc)*
suvremen soo·vre·men *modern*
svadbena torta ⓕ svad·be·na tawr·ta *wedding cake*
svadbeni dar ⓜ svad·be·nee dar *wedding present*
(po)svađati se (paw·)sva·ja·tee se *argue*
svaki ⓔ sva·kee *each* · *every*
svatko svat·kaw *everyone*
sve sve *all* · *everything*
svećenik ⓜ sve·che·neek *priest*
svekar sve·kar *father-in-law (of wife)*
svekrva ⓕ sve·kr·va *mother-in-law (of wife)*
svemir ⓜ sve·meer *universe*
svetac/svetica ⓜ/ⓕ sve·tats/sve·tee·tsa *saint*
sveučilište ⓝ sve·oo·chee·leesh·te *university*
svi svee *all* · *everything*
svibanj ⓜ svee·ban' *May*
svijeća ⓕ svee·ye·cha *candle*
svijet ⓜ svee·yet *world*
svila ⓕ svee·la *silk*
svinja ⓕ svee·nya *pig*
svinjetina ⓕ svee·nye·tee·na *pork*
svinjska kobasica ⓕ sveen'·ska kaw·ba·see·tsa *pork sausage*
(od)svirati (awd·)svee·ra·tee *play (instrument)*
svjedodžba ⓕ svye·dawj·ba *certificate*
svjetao svye·ta·aw *light (of colour)*
svjetiljka ⓕ svye·teel'·ka *light (lamp)* · *flashlight* · *torch*
svjetlomjer ⓜ svyet·law·myer *light meter*
svjetlost ⓕ svyet·lawst *light (illumination)*
svjetski kup ⓜ svyet·skee koop *World Cup*
svjež svyezh *fresh*
svrbež ⓜ svr·bezh *itch*
svrha ⓕ svr·ha *point (logic)*

Š

šah ⓜ shah *chess*
šahovska ploča ⓕ sha·hawv·ska plaw·cha *chess board*
šal ⓜ shal *scarf*
šala ⓕ sha·la *joke*
šalica ⓕ sha·lee·tsa *cup*

šalter m *shal*·ter *ticket office*
— **za podizanje prtljage**
za *paw*-dee-za-nye prt-*lya*-ge
baggage claim
šampanjac sham-*pa*-nyats *champagne*
šampon m sham-*pawn shampoo*
šank m shank *counter (at bar)*
šansa f *shan*-sa *chance*
šator m *sha*-tawr *tent*
šatorski kolčić m *sha*-tawr-skee
kawl-cheech *tent peg*
šarmantan shar-*man*-tan *charming*
šećer m *she*-cher *sugar*
šef kuhinje shef koo-hee-nye *chef*
šešir m *she*-sheer *hat*
šibice f pl *shee*-bee-tse *matches*
(for lighting)
širok shee-*rawk wide*
šišanje n *shee*-sha-nye *haircut*
škamp m shkamp *prawn*
škare f pl *shka*-re *scissors*
škarice za nokte f pl *shka*-ree-tse za
nawk-te *nail clippers*
škola f *shkaw*-la *school*
Škotska f *shkawt*-ska *Scotland*
šlic m shleets *zip • zipper*
šljiva f *shlyee*-va *plum*
šminka f *shmeen*-ka *make-up*
šmrkav nos m *shmr*-kav naws *runny nose*
Španjolska f *shpa*-nyawl-ska *Spain*
šparoga f *shpa*-raw-ga *asparagus*
špinat m *shpee*-nat *spinach*
štakor m *shta*-kawr *rat*
štapići za jelo m pl shta-*pee*-chee za
ye-law *chopsticks*
štrajk m shtraik *strike*
štrcaljka f *shtr*-tsal'-ka *syringe*
šuma f *shoo*-ma *forest*
šunka f *shoon*-ka *ham*
šutnuti/šutirati *shoot*-noo-tee/
shoo-*tee*-ra-tee *kick*
Švedska f *shved*-ska *Sweden*
Švicarska f *shvee*-tsar-ska *Switzerland*

T

tableta f ta-*ble*-ta *pill*
— **protiv bolova** *praw*-teev *baw*-law-va
painkiller
— **za spavanje** za *spa*-va-nye *sleeping pills*
tajnik/tajnica m/f *tai*-neek/*tai*-nee-tsa
secretary

također ta-*kaw*-jer *also*
taksi m *tak*-see *taxi*
— **na vodi** na *vaw*-dee *water taxi*
— **stanica** f *sta*-nee-tsa *taxi stand*
taman *ta*-man *dark (of colour)*
tamo *ta*-maw *there*
tampon m *tam*-pawn *tampon*
tanak *ta*-nak *thin*
tanjur m *ta*-nyoor *plate*
tastatura f ta-sta-*too*-ra *keyboard
(computer)*
tata f *ta*-ta *dad*
tava f *ta*-va *frying pan • pan*
tečaj razmjene m *te*-chai *raz*-mye-ne
exchange rate
tečaj stranih valuta m *te*-chai *stra*-neeh
va-*loo*-ta *currency exchange*
tegovi m pl *te*-gaw-vee *weights*
tehnika f *teh*-nee-ka *technique*
tekućina za kontakt leće f
te-*koo*-chee-na za *kawn*-takt *le*-che
contact-lens solution
telefaks m *te-le*-faks *fax machine*
telefon m *te-le*-fawn *telephone*
telefonirati imp te-le-faw-*nee*-ra-tee
telephone
telefonska centrala f te-*le*-fawn-ska
tsen-*tra*-la *telephone centre*
telefonska govornica f te-*le*-fawn-ska
gaw-vawr-nee-tsa *phone box*
telefonska kartica f te-*le*-fawn-ska
kar-tee-tsa *phonecard*
telefonski imenik m te-*le*-fawn-skee
ee-me-neek *phone book*
telegram m *te*-le-gram *telegram*
teleskop m *te*-le-skawp *telescope*
teletina f *te*-le-tee-na *veal*
televizija f te-le-*vee*-zee-ya *television
(general)*
televizor m te-le-*vee*-zawr *television set*
temperatura f tem-pe-ra-*too*-ra
temperature (weather)
tenis m *te*-nees *tennis*
tenisko igralište n *te*-nee-skaw
ee-gra-*leesh*-te *tennis court*
tepih m *te*-peeh *rug*
teren za golf m *te*-ren za gawlf *golf course*
teretana f te-re-*ta*-na *gym (place)*
termofor m *ter*-maw-fawr *water bottle (hot)*
tesar m *te*-sar *carpenter*
test m test *test*
— **na trudnoću** na trood-*naw*-choo
pregnancy test kit

tetka ① *tet*·ka aunt
težak te·*zhak* difficult • heavy
težina ① te·*zhee*·na weight
ti tee you inf
tih teeh quiet
tijelo ① *tee*·ye·law body
tijesan tee·*ye*·san tight
tipičan *tee*·pee·chan typical
titlovi pl *teet*·law·vee subtitles
(ovaj) tjedan ⑩ (*aw*·vai) *tye*·dan (this) week
tjelovježba ① *tye*·law·vyezh·ba workout
tjestenina ① tye·ste·*nee*·na pasta
tkanina ① *tka*·nee·na fabric
tko tkaw who
tlak krvi ⑩ tlak *kr*·vee blood pressure
to ⑩ taw it
toaletni papir ⑩ taw·a·*let*·ne pa·*peer* toilet paper
točno *tawch*·naw exactly
toksični otpad ⑩ *tawk*·seech·nee *awt*·pad toxic waste
ton ⑩ tawn volume
topao *taw*·pa·aw warm
topla voda ① *taw*·pla *vaw*·da hot water
toplice ① pl *taw*·plee·tse spa
toranj ⑩ *taw*·ran' tower
torba ① *tawr*·ba bag
tost ⑩ tawst toast
toster ⑩ *taw*·ster toaster
trajekt ⑩ *trai*·ekt ferry
tramvaj ⑩ *tram*·vai tram
tranzitna čekaonica ① *tran*·zeet·na che·ka·*aw*·nee·tsa transit lounge
traperice ① pl *tra*·pe·ree·tse jeans
trava ① *tra*·va grass (lawn) • pot (dope)
travanj ⑩ *tra*·van' April
(po)tražiti (paw·)*tra*·zhee·tee look for
(za)tražiti (za·)*tra*·zhee·tee ask for (something)
trčanje ① *tr*·cha·nye running
(po)trčati (paw·)*tr*·cha·tee run
(za)trebati (za·)*tre*·ba·tee need
treći *tre*·chee third
trener ⑩ *tre*·ner coach (sports)
trešnja ① *tresh*·nya cherry
trg ⑩ trg square (town)
trgovac ⑩ *tr*·gaw·vats trader
— **drogama** *draw*·ga·ma drug dealer
— **povrćem** *paw*·vr·chem greengrocer
— **ribom** *ree*·bawm fishmonger
trgovački centar ⑩ *tr*·gaw·vach·kee *tsen*·tar shopping centre

trgovina ① *tr*·gaw·vee·na trade
— **drogama** ① *draw*·ga·ma drug trafficking
trišlja ① *treesh*·lya pistachio
trkaći bicikl ⑩ *tr*·ka·chee bee·*tsee*·kl racing bike
trkalište ① *tr*·ka·leesh·te racetrack
trudna ① *trood*·na pregnant
trudnička jutarnja mučnina ① *trood*·neech·ka yoo·*tar*·nya mooch·*nee*·na morning sickness
tržnica ① *trzh*·nee·tsa market
tucet ⑩ *too*·tset dozen
tuča ① *too*·cha fight (fisticuffs)
tumač ⑩ *too*·mach interpreter
tumor ⑩ *too*·mawr tumour
tuna ① *too*·na tuna (fish)
tunjevina ① too·nye·*vee*·na tuna (as food)
turist ⑩ *too*·reest tourist
turistička agencija ① too·*ree*·steech·ka a·*gen*·tsee·ya tourist office
tuš ⑩ toosh shower (bathroom)
tužan *too*·zhan sad
tvoj *tvoy* your
tvoja ① *tvoy*·a your
tvoje ① *tvoy*·e your
tvornica ① *tvawr*·nee·tsa factory
tvrd tvrd hard (not soft)
tvrdo kuhan *tvr*·daw koo·han hard-boiled
tvrdoglav tvr·*daw*·glav stubborn

U

u oo aboard (train, bus) • at • in • on • to
— **inozemstvu** ee·*naw*·zemst·voo abroad
— **vezi** *ve*·zee about • to do with
ubiti/ubijati oo·bee·tee/oo·*bee*·ya·tee murder
ubod ⑩ oo·*bawd* bite (insect)
ubojstvo ① oo·*boys*·tvaw murder
ubrizgati/ubrizgavati oo·breez·ga·tee/ oo·breez·ga·va·tee inject
učitelj ⑩ oo·chee·*tel'* teacher
(na)učiti (na·)oo·chee·tee learn
ući/ulaziti oo·chee/oo·la·zee·tee enter
udaljen oo·*da*·lyen remote
udati/udavati se oo·da·tee/oo·*da*·va·tee se marry
udvarati se imp oo·*dva*·ra·tee se chat up
uganuće ⑩ oo·ga·*noo*·che sprain

ugao ⓜ oo·ga·aw *corner*
ugodan oo·gaw·dan *comfortable*
ugovor ⓜ oo·gaw·vawr *contract*
ugriz ⓜ oo·greez *bite (dog)*
ugrožene vrste ⓕ pl oo·*graw*·zhe·ne *vr*·ste *endangered species*
uhititi perf oo·hee·tee·tee *arrest*
uho ⓝ oo·haw *ear*
uključen ook·lyoo·chen *included*
ukraden oo·*kra*·den *stolen*
ukrcan na oo·kr·tsan na *aboard (boat, plane)*
ukrcati/ukrcavati se oo·kr·tsa·tee / oo·kr·*tsa*·va·tee se *board (a plane, ship etc)*
ukusan oo·koo·san *tasty*
ulaz ⓜ oo·laz *entry*
ulaznica (cijena) ⓕ oo·laz·nee·tsa (tsee·*ye*·na) *admission (price)*
ulica ⓕ oo·lee·tsa *street*
ulična tržnica ⓕ oo·leech·na *trzh*·nee·tsa *street market*
ulični zabavljač ⓜ oo·leech·nee za·*bav*·lyach *busker*
ulje ⓝ oo·lye *oil*
ultrazvuk ⓜ ool·tra·zvook *ultrasound*
umak ⓜ oo·mak *sauce*
umirovljen oo·*mee*·rawv·lyen *retired*
umirovljenik ⓜ oo·mee·rawv·*lye*·neek *pensioner*
umjetnički obrti ⓜ pl oo·myet·neech·kee *aw*·br·tee *crafts (handicrafts)*
umjetnik/umjetnica ⓜ/ⓕ oo·myet·neek / oo·myet·nee·tsa *artist*
umjetnost ⓕ oo·*myet*·nawst *art*
umoran oo·maw·ran *tired*
umrijeti/umirati oo·mree·ye·tee / oo·mee·ra·tee *die*
uniforma ⓕ oo·nee·fawr·ma *uniform*
unovčiti/unovčavati oo·*nawv*·chee·tee / oo·nawv·*cha*·va·tee *cash (a cheque)*
unuk/unuka ⓜ/ⓕ oo·nook / oo·noo·ka *grandchild*
unutra oo·*noo*·tra *inside*
unutrašnji oo·noo·trash·nyee *indoor*
upala ⓕ oo·pa·la *inflammation*
upaljač ⓜ oo·pa·lyach *cigarette lighter*
uplata ⓕ oo·pla·ta *payment (by someone)*
Upomoć! oo·paw·mawch *Help!*
upoznati/upoznavati oo·*pawz*·na·tee / oo·pawz·*na*·va·tee *meet (for first time)*
upozoriti/upozoravati oo·paw·*zaw*·ree·tee / oo·paw·zaw·*ra*·va·tee *warn*

uprava ⓕ oo·pra·va *administration*
ured ⓜ oo·red *office*
— **za izgubljene stvari** za eez·goob·lye·ne stva·ree *lost property office*
— **za odlaganje prtljage** za *awd*·la·ga·nye prt·*lya*·ge *left luggage (office)*
urednik ⓜ oo·red·neek *editor*
urod ⓜ oo·rawd *crop*
uska ulica ⓕ oo·ska oo·lee·tsa *alley*
uskoro oo·skaw·raw *soon*
uskrs oos·krs *Easter*
usluga ⓕ oo·sloo·ga *service*
usne ⓕ pl oo·sne *lips*
uspinjača ⓕ oo·spee·nya·cha *cable car*
usta ⓕ oo·sta *mouth*
ustajao oo·stai·a·aw *stale*
uši ⓕ pl oo·shee *lice*
utakmica ⓕ oo·tak·mee·tsa *match (sports)*
utikač ⓜ oo·tee·kach *plug (electricity)*
utorak ⓜ oo·taw·rak *Tuesday*
utrka ⓕ oo·tr·ka *race (sport)*
uvala ⓕ oo·va·la *bay*
uvijek oo·vee·yek *always*
uvjetna karta ⓕ oo·vyet·noo *kar*·ta *stand-by ticket*
uz ooz *beside*
uzbrdo ooz·br·daw *uphill (to go)*
uzeti/uzimati oo·ze·tee / oo·zee·ma·tee *take*
uznemiravanje ⓝ ooz·ne·mee·*ra*·va·nye *harassment*
uzrast ⓜ ooz·rast *age (person)*
užasan oo·zha·san *awful*
uže ⓝ oo·zhe *rope*
uživati imp oo·*zhee*·va·tee *(have) fun*
užurban oo·zhoor·ban *in a hurry*

V

vadičep ⓜ va·dee·chep *corkscrew*
(iz)vagati (eez)va·ga·tee *weigh*
vagina ⓕ va·*gee*·na *vagina*
val ⓜ val *wave*
vani va·nee *outside*
važan va·zhan *important*
večer ⓕ ve·cher *evening*
večera ⓕ ve·che·ra *dinner*
večeras ve·che·ras *tonight*
već vech *already*

veći *ve*-chee *bigger*

vedar *ve*-dar *fine (weather)*

vegetarijanac ⓜ *ve*-ge-ta-ree-ya-nats *vegetarian*

veleposlanik ⓜ ve-le-paw-*sla*-neek *ambassador*

veličina ⓕ ve-lee-chee-na *size (general)*

velik *ve*-leek *big*

veliki tjedan ⓜ *ve*-lee-kee *tye*-dan *Holy Week*

veljača ⓕ *ve*-lya-cha *February*

vena ⓕ *ve*-na *vein*

Venecija ⓕ *ve*-ne-tsee-ya *Venice*

venecijanski ve-ne-*tsee*-yan-skee *Venetian*

ventilator ⓜ ven-tee-*la*-tawr *fan (machine)*

veslanje ⓝ *ve*-sla-nye *rowing*

veza ⓕ *ve*-za *connection*

vi vee *you* pol sg & pl

video kazeta ⓕ *vee*-de-aw ka-*ze*-ta *video tape*

video rekorder ⓜ *vee*-de-aw re-*kawr*-der *video recorder*

vidik ⓜ *vee*-deek *lookout*

vidjeti/vidati vee-dye-tee/vee-ja-tee *see*

vijesti ⓕ pl vee-*ye*-stee *news*

vikend ⓜ *vee*-kend *weekend*

viknuti/vikati veek-noo-tee/*vee*-ka-tee *shout*

viljuška ⓕ vee-*lyoosh*-ka *fork*

vino ⓝ *vee*-naw *wine*

vinograd ⓜ *vee*-naw-grad *vineyard*

vinova loza ⓕ *vee*-naw-va *law*-za *vine*

virus ⓜ *vee*-roos *virus*

visina ⓕ vee-*see*-na *altitude*

viski ⓜ *vee*-skee *whisky*

visok vee-*sawk* *high • tall*

visoka stolica za bebe ⓕ vee-*saw*-ka staw-lee-tsa za *be*-be *highchair*

višak prtljage ⓜ *vee*-shak prt-*lya*-ge *excess (baggage)*

više *vee*-she *more*

vitamini ⓜ pl vee-ta-*mee*-nee *vitamins*

viza ⓕ *vee*-za *visa*

vječanje ⓝ *vye*-cha-nye *conference (small)*

vjenčan *vyen*-chan *married (of man)*

vjenčana *vyen*-cha-na *married (of woman)*

vjenčanje ⓝ vyen-*cha*-nye *wedding*

vjera ⓕ *vye*-ra *religion*

vjeren *vye*-ren *engaged (marriage)*

vjerenica ⓕ vye-re-nee-tsa *fiancée*

vjerenik ⓜ *vye*-re-neek *fiancé*

vjerenje ⓝ *vye*-re-nye *engagement*

(po)vjerovati (paw-)vye-raw-va-tee *trust*

vjerski *vyer*-skee *religious (concerning religion)*

vjetar ⓜ *vye*-tar *wind*

vjetrobran ⓜ *vye*-traw-bran *windscreen*

vlada ⓕ *vla*-da *government*

vlak ⓜ vlak *train*

vlasnik ⓜ *vla*-sneek *owner*

voče ⓕ *vaw*-che *fruit*

voda ⓕ *vaw*-da *water*

vodene kozice ⓕ pl vaw-*de*-ne *kaw*-zee-tse *chickenpox*

vodič ⓜ *vaw*-deech *guide (person) • guidebook*

vodka ⓕ *vawd*-ka *vodka*

vodopad ⓜ *vaw*-daw-pad *waterfall*

vojna obveza ⓕ *voy*-na *awb*-ve-za *military service*

vojnik ⓜ *voy*-neek *soldier*

vojska ⓕ *voy*-ska *military*

volan bicikla ⓜ *vaw*-lan bee-*tsee*-kla *handlebars*

voljeti imp *vaw*-lye-tee *like (a person) • love*

vozačka dozvola ⓕ *vaw*-zach-ka *dawz*-vaw-la *driving licence*

voziti imp *vaw*-zee-tee *drive*

   — bicikl imp bee-*tsee*-kl *cycle*

vozni red ⓜ *vawz*-nee red *timetable*

vožnja ⓕ *vawzh*-nya *ride (trip)*

   — biciklom bee-*tsee*-klawm *cycling*

   — na skateboardu na *skeyt*-bawr-doo *skateboarding*

vrač ⓜ vrach *fortune-teller*

vrata ⓕ *vra*-ta *door*

vratar ⓜ *vra*-tar *goalkeeper*

vratiti/vraćati se vra-tee-tee/vra-cha-tee se *return (come back)*

vreća za spavanje ⓕ *vre*-cha za spa-va-nye *sleeping bag*

vremenski uvjeti ⓜ pl vre-men-skee oo-vye-tee *weather*

vrh ⓜ vrh *summit*

vrhnje ⓝ *vrh*-nye *cream (food)*

vrijednost ⓕ vree-*yed*-nawst *value (price)*

vrijeme ⓝ vree-*ye*-me *time*

vrlo *vr*-law *very*

vrsta ⓕ *vr*-sta *type*

vrt ⓜ vrt *garden*

vrtić za djecu ⓜ vr·teech za dye·tsoo
kindergarten
vrtlar ⓜ vrt·lar gardener
vrtlarstvo ⓝ vrt·lars·tvaw gardening
vruć vrooch hot
vručina ⓕ vroo·chee·na heat
(po)vući (paw·)voo·chee pull
vuna ⓕ voo·na wool

Z

za za to · with
zabavan za·ba·van fun
zaboraviti/zaboravljati
za·baw·ra·vee·tee/za·baw·rav·lya·tee
forget
zabrinut ⓜ za·bree·noot worried
zagađenje ⓝ za·ga·je·nye pollution
zaglavljen za·glav·lyen blocked
zagrijan za·gree·yan heated
zahod ⓜ za·hawd toilet
zahvalan za·hva·lan grateful
zahvaliti/zahvaljivati za·hva·lee·tee/
za·hva·lyee·va·tee thank
zajedno zai·ed·naw together
zakašnjenje ⓝ za·kash·nye·nye delay
zaključan za·klyoo·chan locked
zaključati/zaključavati zak·lyoo·cha·tee/
zak·lyoo·cha·va·tee lock
zakon ⓜ za·kawn law
zakonit za·kaw·neet legal
zakonodavstvo ⓝ za·kaw·naw·davs·tvaw
legislation
zalazak sunca ⓜ za·la·zak soon·tsa sunset
zaleđen za·le·jen frozen
zalihe hrane ⓕ pl za·lee·he hra·ne
food supplies
zamijeniti/zamjenjivati
za·mee·ye·nee·tee/
za·mee·ye·nyee·va·tee change (money)
zamrznuti/zamrzavati za·mr·znoo·tee/
za·mr·za·va·tee freeze
zanimljiv za·neem·lyeev interesting
zapad ⓜ za·pad west
započeti/započinjati za·paw·che·tee/
za·paw·chee·nya·tee start
zaposlenik/zaposlenica ⓜ/ⓕ
za·paw·sle·neek/za·paw·sle·nee·tsa
employee
zaraditi/zarađivati za·ra·dee·tee/
za·ra·jee·va·tee earn
zaraza ⓕ za·ra·za infection

zastava ⓕ za·sta·va flag
zaštićen zash·tee·chen protected (species)
(za)štititi (za·)shtee·tee·tee protect
zašto zash·taw why
zato za·taw because
zatvor ⓜ zat·vawr gaol · jail
zatvoren zat·vaw·ren closed
zatvorenik ⓜ zat·vaw·re·neek prisoner
zatvorenje ⓝ zat·vaw·re·nye constipation
zatvoriti/zatvarati zat·vaw·ree·tee/
zat·va·ra·tee close (shut)
zaušnjaci ⓜ pl za·oosh·nya·tsce mumps
zaustaviti/zaustavljati za·oo·sta·vee·tee/
za·oo·stav·lya·tee stop (cease)
zauvijek za·oo·vee·yek forever
zauzet za·oo·zet busy · engaged (phone)
zavoj ⓜ za·voy bandage
završiti/završavati za·vr·shee·tee/
za·vr·sha·va·tee finish
zbirka fraza ⓕ zbeer·ka fra·za phrasebook
zbog zbawg about
Zbogom. zbaw·gawm Goodbye.
zdjela ⓕ zdye·la bowl
zdravlje ⓝ zdrav·lye health
Zdravo. zdra·vaw Hello. (not answering
telephone)
zec ⓜ zets rabbit
zelen ze·len green
zelena salata ⓕ ze·le·na sa·la·ta lettuce
zemlja zem·lya country · Earth · land · soil
zgodan zgaw·dan handsome
zgrada ⓕ zgra·da building
zid ⓜ zeed wall (outer)
zima ⓕ zee·ma winter
zimski kaput ⓜ zeem·skee ka·poot
overcoat
zlato ⓝ zla·taw gold
zmija ⓕ zmee·ya snake
znak ⓜ znak sign
znanost ⓕ zna·nawst science
znanstvenik ⓜ znanst·ve·neek scientist
(sa)znati (sa·)zna·tee know
zob ⓕ zawb oats
zodijak ⓜ zaw·dee·yak zodiac
zoološki vrt ⓜ zaw·lawsh·kee vrt zoo
zora ⓕ zaw·ra dawn
zračna luka ⓕ zrach·na loo·ka airport
zračna pošta ⓕ zrach·na pawsh·ta airmail
zračnica ⓕ zrach·nee·tsa tube (tyre)
zrak ⓜ zrak air
zrakoplov ⓜ zra·kaw·plawv airplane
zrakoplovna tvrtka ⓕ zra·kaw·plawv·na
tvr·tka airline

zrakoplovna ulaznica ① *zra·kaw·plawv·na oo·laz·nee·tsa* boarding pass
zub ⓜ zoob tooth
zubar ⓜ zoo·bar dentist
zubi ⓜ pl zoo·bee teeth
zubobolja ① zoo·baw·baw·lya toothache
(po)zvati (paw·)zva·tee call
zvjezda ① zvyez·da star
(sa četiri) zvjezdice ① pl (sa che·tee·ree) zvye·zdee·tse (four·)star

Ž

žal ⓜ zhal beach
(po)žaliti se (paw·)zha·lee·tee se complain
žarulja ① zha·roo·lya light bulb
žbica ① zhbee·tsa spoke
žedan zhe·dan (to be) thirsty

(po)željeti (paw·)zhe·lye·tee like • want • wish
željeznička stanica ① zhe·lyez·nee·chka sta·nee·tsa railway station
želudac ⓜ zhe·loo·dats stomach
žemička ① zhe·meech·ka roll (bread)
žena ① zhe·na wife • woman
ženski zhen·skee female
žica ① zhee·tsa wire
žičara ① zhe·cha·ra chairlift (skiing)
Židovski zhe·dawv·skee Jewish
žitarica ① zhee·ta·ree·tsa cereal
život ⓜ zhe·vawt life
životinja ① zhee·vaw·tee·nya animal
žlica ① zhlee·tsa spoon
žličica ① zhlee·chee·tsa teaspoon
žmigavac ⓜ zhmee·ga·vats indicator (car)
žohar ⓜ zhaw·har cockroach
žulj ⓜ zhool' blister
žut ⓜ zhoot yellow
žvakača guma ① zhva·ka·cha goo·ma chewing gum

KEY PATTERNS

When's (the next day trip)?	*Kada je (idući dnevni izlet)?*	*ka*·da ye (*ee*·doo·chee dnev·nee *eez*·let)
Where's (a market)?	*Gdje je (tržnica)?*	gdye ye (*tr*·zhnee·tsa)
Where do I (buy a ticket)?	*Gdje mogu (kupiti kartu)?*	gdye *maw*·goo (koo·pee·tee *kar*·too)
How much (is it)?	*Koliko (stoji)?*	kaw·*lee*·kaw (*stoy*·ee)
Do you have (any others)?	*Imate li bilo (kakve druge)?*	ee·ma·te lee *bee*·law (*kak*·ve *droo*·ge)
Is there (a blanket)?	*Imate li (deku)?*	ee·ma·te lee (*de*·koo)
I'd like (that dish).	*Želim (ono jelo).*	zhe·leem (*aw*·naw ye·law)
I'd like to (hire a car).	*Želio/ Željela bih (iznajmiti automobil).* m/f	zhe·lee·aw/ zhe·lye·la beeh (eez·*nai*·mee·tee a·oo·taw·*maw*·beel)
Can I (take a photograph of you)?	*Mogu li ja (slikati vas)?*	*maw*·goo lee ya (*slee*·ka·tee vas)
Could you please (help)?	*Molim vas, možete li (mi pomoći)?*	*maw*·leem vas *maw*·zhe·te lee (mee *paw* maw-chee)
Do I have to (pay)?	*Trebam li (platiti)?*	*tre*·bam lee (*pla*·tee·tee)